CADOGAN
island guides

THE SOUTH CARIBBEAN

Introduction and Guide to the Guide	vii
The Caribbean at a Glance	ix
Travel	1
Practical A–Z	11
A Sailing Guide	35
Topics	43
Barbados	53
Grenada	85
St Vincent and the Grenadines	115
St Lucia	149
Martinique	173
Dominica	207
Guadeloupe	231
Index	267

Cadogan Books plc
London House, Parkgate Road, London SW11 4NQ

Distributed in the USA by
The Globe Pequot Press
6 Business Park Road, PO Box 833, Old Saybrook, Connecticut 06475-0833

Copyright © James Henderson 1994
Illustrations © Charles Shearer 1994

Book and cover design by Animage
Cover illustrations by Sue Dray
Maps © Cadogan Guides, drawn by Thames Cartographic Ltd

Series Editors: Rachel Fielding and Vicki Ingle
Editing: Linda McQueen
Proofreading: Linda McQueen
Indexing: Isobel McLean
Production: Rupert Wheeler Book Production Services
Mac Help: Jacqueline Lewin

ISBN 0-947754-77-6

A catalogue record for this book is available from the British Library
US Library of Congress Cataloging-in-Publication-Data available

All rights reserved. No part of this publication may be reproduced, stored in a retrieval system, or transmitted, in any form or by any means, electronic or mechanical, including photocopying and recording, or by any information storage and retrieval system except as may be expressly permitted by the UK 1988 Copyright Design & Patents Act and the USA 1976 Copyright Act or in writing from the publisher. Requests for permission should be addressed to Cadogan Books Ltd, London House, Parkgate Road, London SW11 4NQ.

The author and publishers have made every effort to ensure the accuracy of the information in this book at the time of going to press. However, they cannot accept any responsibility for any loss, injury or inconvenience resulting from the use of information contained in this guide.

Printed and bound in Great Britain by Redwood Books Ltd, Trowbridge, Wiltshire on Jordan Opaque supplied by McNaughton Publishing Papers Ltd.

About the Author

For the past six years, James Henderson has studied the Caribbean from a top-floor flat in London, from the window of tiny island-hopping planes and through scuba-diving masks. He travels there as much as possible, braving flash tropical downpours and droughts, *coups d'état*, 'jerk', drunken bus drivers and posses of mad Californians; dodging safari buses of cruise-ship passengers and the attentions of over-zealous aloe masseuses, jumbies and machete-flourishing coconut salesmen. Half English and half Scots, he has lived in the UK, USA, Cyprus and the Arabian Gulf, and has wandered Europe, Pakistan and Afghanistan.

He has lingered longest in the Caribbean, still watching for the Green Flash and writing features for the *Financial Times*.

Acknowledgements

For the third time, my thanks go to all West Indians, native and adoptive, who make travelling in the islands such fun; for all the lifts (cars, bikes, boats and planes), beers, beds for the night; to all the voluble taxi-drivers, limers and tourism officials who responded so kindly to hours of questions, and then replied to urgent and demanding faxes. I'd like to thank, in particular: Marsilyn Browne in Barbados; the whole team in Grenada, Edwin Frank, Natalie Evans and Llewelyn Simon; Vidal Brown on Young Island; in St Lucia Maria Monplaisir; in Dominica, Steve Johnson (despite the best efforts of the world's postal services); and in Martinique, Robert Conrad and in Guadeloupe Guy-Claude Germain.

Back in London, thanks go to all tourist board members and others who sat through a further bombardment of questions and to those who took the trouble to write with Caribbean tales of joy (and sometimes woe).

Please help us to keep this guide up to date

Keeping a guide to the Caribbean up to date is a daunting task—you need to start again as soon as you've reached the end. We need your thoughts to create as complete a picture as possible for each update. If you feel that you have some ideas for the guide, send them in; be as opinionated as you like. Writers of the best letters each year are awarded a complimentary guide of their choice from the series.

Contents

Introduction	vii	The Southeastern Caribbean	
Guide to the Guide	ix	at a Glance	x

Travel 1–10

Getting There	2	Specialist Caribbean Tour	
By Air	2	Operators	5
By Boat	4	Getting Around	8
Entry Requirements and		By Air	8
Customs	5	By Boat	10

Practical A–Z 11–34

Beaches	12	Money	24
Bookshops	12	Packing	25
Calendar of Events	12	Photography	25
Children	15	Post Offices	26
Climate	15	Shopping	26
Electricity	16	Sports	26
Food and Drink	17	Telephones	30
Health	20	Time Zones	30
Insurance	22	Tourist Information	31
Language	22	Where to Stay	31
Living and Working in		Women	34
the Caribbean	23		
Maps and Publications	23		

A Sailing Guide 35–42

Sailing in the Eastern		Life on Board	39
Caribbean	36	Sailing A–Z	40
Planning Your Trip	36		
Arrival	38		

Topics 43–52

Caribbean Indians	44	'The Muse of Wise Men'	49
Columbus	45	Music	50
The English-speaking Caribbean and its Culture	46	The Volcanic Origins of the Islands	51
French Caribbean Culture	47		

Barbados 53–84

Getting There and Around	60	The Sugar Heartland	72
Bridgetown	67	Suburbs and South Coast	74
The West Coast	69	Where to Stay	76
Scotland and St Lucy	70	Eating Out	79

Grenada 85–114

Getting There and Around	93	Where to Stay	105
St George's	98	Eating Out	107
The West Coast	101	Carriacou and Petit Martinique	109
The South Coast	102		
Over the Grand Etang to the East Coast	103		

St Vincent and the Grenadines 115–148

St Vincent	116	Mayreau	144
The Grenadines	134	Tobago Cays	145
Bequia	137	Union Island	146
Mustique	141	Palm Island	148
Canouan	143	Petit St Vincent	148

St Lucia 149–172

Getting There and Around	154	South to Soufrière	162
Castries	159	Where to Stay	166
North from Castries	161	Eating Out	169

Martinique 173–206

Getting There and Around	179
Fort de France	186
South of Fort de France	188
N2—The Caribbean Coast	191
St Pierre	192
St Pierre to the Atlantic Coast	194
N3—the Pitons du Carbet	196
N1—Fort de France to the Atlantic Coast	196
Where to Stay	198
Eating Out	201

Dominica 207–230

Getting There and Around	215
Roseau	218
South and North from Roseau	221
The Transinsular Road	224
Carib Territory	225
Where to Stay	226
Eating Out	229

Guadeloupe 231–266

Getting There and Around	236
Grande-Terre	243
Basse-Terre	246
Where to Stay	251
Eating Out	255
La Désirade	260
Marie Galante	261
The Saints	263

Index 267–276

Maps

Eastern Caribbean	front cover
Barbados	55
Grenada	87
St Vincent	117
The Grenadines	135
St Lucia	151
Martinique	175
Dominica	209
Guadeloupe	233

Introduction

Every Caribbean island-hopper has a charmed isle. An island may grow on you gradually and make you feel at home, or it might enchant you in seconds as you set foot on a rickety landing stage and wander ashore. Either way, there will be a feeling of ease and contentment, an inexplicable liaison, like finding a long-lost love, as though it was always meant to be.

A visit to the islands throws everything into a new focus. While winter closes in in the northern hemisphere, the Caribbean is a land of perpetual summer where the sunlight perks you up with the fresh warmth of July and the unfamiliar splashes of tropical colour. New smells and tastes tease you in a land of unaccustomed fertility. Steadily you will cast off the numbing cloak of winter and begin to feel revitalized.

But the Caribbean is more than an unseasonal shock to the senses. There is a carefree abandon about the islands. You'll soon be wondering what the fuss is all about at home and thinking of schemes to delay your return. For most people a trip to the Caribbean is the fulfilment of a dream, but it can be addictive. Some are so taken by it that it becomes an annual pilgrimage, a sort of crusade against winter.

The islands of the southeastern Caribbean are neatly representative of the whole area and a visit will give you a good exposure to Caribbean island life. They are all of a similar, manageable size, no more than fifty miles long by about fifteen or twenty. And they are mostly similar in appearance. With the exception of Barbados and the eastern half of Guadeloupe (which are coral-based) they are tall, volcanic islands that soar to four or five thousand feet, their steep slopes mantled with rainforest. Certainly they are very beautiful. And, despite their similarities, each has its own distinctive feel.

The major islands have a population of between 75,000 (Dominica) and 385,000 (Martinique). Barbados and the French islands are quite developed and crowded. But then there are groups of very small land masses too, where just a few hours' sail will take you from pretty postcard islets to slumberstruck cays, where you will see tropical island life at its most relaxed and undeveloped. The Grenadines and the small islands off Guadeloupe offer some of the best areas to explore in the whole Caribbean.

There is cultural variety in the islands too. The main colonial influences are Britain and France; but the strongest legacy of all is African. However these influences have not remained static in their new tropical setting. They have continued to develop and have created unique creole styles: of music, like the béguine and the mazurka, and lately zouk in the French islands, and string bands and most recently calypso in the former British islands; of architecture, in the pretty wooden houses with their tin roofs and wrap-around balconies; of language (French *créole*, which you will hear in some of the British islands too, and the lilting English *patois*, a slightly different version in each of the islands). And then there is the general Caribbean style of life, which appears easy-going and at times laid back to the point of ridicule.

The variety makes island-hopping a worthwhile option. The area is easy to travel around; there are plenty of little island-hopping planes, also ferries and hydrofoils, and of course there is the option of sailing, which allows you to take in the best of the islands at your own leisurely pace (*see* p. 35).

Some places, particularly Barbados and St Lucia, and the French islands of Martinique and Guadeloupe, have opted for package tourism in quite a big way and so what was an exclusive area now has a full range of hotels on offer (with some excellent deals, if you are prepared to be flexible and to shop around a bit). But there are still many places to be found off the beaten track, in some of the most dramatic settings in the Caribbean.

Guide to the Guide and a Little Geography

The islands of the southeastern Caribbean stand like a line of Titans up to their waists in sea, raging green volcanic peaks rooted in a submarine mountain range that runs from Grenada in the south to Guadeloupe. They stand at the fault line of the Atlantic Ocean and the Caribbean Sea (*see* **Topics**, pp.51–2). Barbados is the odd man out: it is a coral cap that lies isolated out in the Atlantic, a hundred miles to the east of the other islands. Geologically the islands make up the southern half of the Lesser Antilles (less Trinidad and Tobago).

The area has a variety of names: 'Caribbean' comes from the indigenous tribe of American Indians, the Caribs, who inhabited the Lesser Antilles (*see* **Topics**, p.44) until the arrival of the Europeans; the origin of the term 'West Indies' lies with Columbus himself, who found the islands while trying to find a route via the west to India; and the 'Antilles' derive from Antillia, supposedly a corruption of 'Atlantis', the lost continent that was presumed to lie beyond the Azores.

The islands of the southeastern Caribbean are all Independent nations (formerly colonies of Britain) or overseas *départements* of France. This guide book approaches them in geographical order, starting with Barbados and then tracking north from Grenada, along the island-chain, to Guadeloupe and its offshore islands of the Saints, Marie Galante and La Désirade (Saint Martin and St Barthélémy, both also *communes* of Guadeloupe, are treated in the Cadogan Guide to the Northeastern Caribbean).

Each island is divided up according to the same format, with an introduction to set the scene and to bring out the island's unique characteristics. This is followed by a history of the island, 'Topics' of interest that are unique to the island and a section on island flora and fauna. Next come the practical details: 'Getting There', from the UK and Europe and the USA and other Caribbean islands, with details of services by boat where they exist; 'Getting Around' the island, by bus, taxi and rental car, with prices and contact numbers; some 'Tourist Information'—where to get information before you travel and once you are on-island—and 'Money'.

Next come the all-important sections on beach-bound Caribbean life: a round-up of the best beaches (for activities and seclusion) and beach bars and sports (including advice on snorkelling, scuba-diving, windsurfing and other watersports, and deep-sea fishing). For sailors there are recommendations of favourite anchorages and the liveliest marinas. Where applicable, land-based sports are mentioned too, including tennis, horse-riding and golf.

Next is the gazetteer, with descriptions of island sights, including the capital city and places to visit around the island; this is concluded with a list of festivals and events worth attending if you are on the island at the right time. Then there is more practical information, with a listing of recommended hotels (in all price brackets), a selection of the best restaurants and the best bars and clubs to visit. Finally there are details of places to go shopping and a selection of further reading.

The Southeastern Caribbean at a Glance

Here is a thumbnail sketch of the islands, including recent changes.

Barbados

Barbados is the gentleman of Caribbean tourism and is winter home to a crowd of English sophisticates; it has some of the Caribbean's best-known and smartest hotels along the west coast. The south coast offers a lower-key atmosphere with riotous nightlife. Barbados boasts excellent beaches, a delightful climate, and many good restaurants and bars. It is easily accessible and caters well for all tastes. The Bajans are among the most charming people in the West Indies.

Carriacou

A classic, small island of easy Caribbean life in the Grenadines, Carriacou has superb beaches and some hip bars. A great sailing stopover.

Dominica

Least developed and poorest of the Windwards, Dominica has a natural charm. It has supreme natural life above and below the waterline—a rainforest with over 100 species of birds, whale-watching in season and excellent scuba diving. There are just a few golden-sand beaches, and tourism is extremely undeveloped and low-key.

Grenada

Grenada has volcanic peaks and rainforests, fruit and spice plantations and easy-going islanders. It is less developed and less well known than St Lucia and has good beaches in the south of the island. It is easy to reach, with some good small hotels; a full range from luxury to budget. *See also* **Carriacou.**

The Grenadines

Strung between St Vincent and Grenada, the Grenadines boast fantastic sea, beaches and sailing; a good mix of attractive tourist islands—including island-enclaves of super-luxury—and accessible West Indian life. Island-hopping is possible. **Canouan** has fine anchorages and hidden coves; **Mayreau** is secluded with beaches on all sides; the **Tobago Cays** are uninhabited islets in paradise. **Union Island** is the local transit point. *See also* **Bequia, Carriacou, Mustique, Palm Island, Petit St Vincent** and **Young Island.**

Guadeloupe

Guadeloupe is a highly developed French island, with a large tourist industry, particularly on the south coast of Grande-Terre in the east (for the white sand beaches). Less crowded, Basse-Terre has golden beaches in the north west, and rainforest for walking. The charming offshore islands, **Marie Galante** and **La Désirade,** are very low-key; **Terre de Haut** in **The Saints** is pretty and well developed.

Martinique

Martinique is also highly developed. Martiniquans are chic and their restaurants excellent—in town and in the resorts. The beaches are best in the south, where most of the tourism is concentrated. Elsewhere there are forests and French creole life to explore.

The Southeastern Caribbean at a Glance

Mustique

Mustique is well known as an exclusive holiday domain for the rich and famous. It is just a series of luxurious, privately owned villas, with one hotel, one beach bar and an airstrip.

Palm Island

An island-resort in the southern Grenadines, reached by boat, Palm Island is comprised of just a few villas, a beach and an easy life.

Petit St Vincent

An island-resort in the southern Grenadines, reached by boat or by helicopter, Petit St Vincent has just a few villas, where you communicate by flag and call room service to your beach-hammock.

St Lucia

The most developed and best known of the volcanic Windwards, St Lucia has some very smart and comfortable hotels along its good beaches. It is lively in the main centres, but has some lovely hideaway places to stay among the coves of the leeward coastline.

St Vincent

St Vincent is an unspoilt, quite poor, English-speaking Windward Island; it has grand natural fertility and just a few comfortable, family-run hotels. It is a good starting point for a tour of the Grenadines.

Young Island

Young Island is a tiny, forested blip just a couple of hundred yards off St Vincent's southern coast. It has just one charming West Indian hotel.

Getting There	2
By Air	2
By Boat	4
Entry Requirements and Customs	5
Specialist Caribbean Tour Operators	5
Getting Around	8
By Air	8
By Boat	10

Travel

humming bird & nest

Getting There

By Air

From the UK

The eastern Caribbean is quite well served from the UK, both by scheduled and charter flights. The transatlantic flight takes around 8 hours and so with the time change (chasing the sun around the earth) you usually arrive in good time to catch onward flights to almost all the Caribbean islands or just to settle down and watch the sunset. Peak fares are charged in the weeks around Christmas, and between July and September. This is slightly curious because it does not coincide with the Caribbean's own high season (the winter in the northern hemisphere), which runs from about mid-January to mid-April.

British Airways has the widest range of services to the eastern Caribbean from the UK, with direct flights to Antigua, Barbados, Grenada and St Lucia. Concorde flies to Barbados during the winter season, nearly cutting the journey time in half. All BA flights except Concorde depart from Gatwick (*see* individual island sections for regularity of service, reservations ✆ 071 759 5511).

BWIA, the airline of Trinidad and Tobago, also has a number of flights, departing London Heathrow for Port of Spain in Trinidad (occasionally Tobago *en route*), Barbados and Antigua, with easy onward connections to the other eastern Caribbean islands and Guyana. BWIA reservations in the UK: ✆ 071 839 9333.

Generally speaking, scheduled flights from the UK to the Caribbean are expensive. Peak season fares (a scheduled economy return) cost between £800 and £900 and in the low season they drop to between £700 and £800. Prices do not vary that much between the airlines and they vary little according to your destination, although Port of Spain in Trinidad is marginally more expensive than the others. These fares require 21 days' advance booking, and there are penalties for changing reservations. There are slightly more expensive fares available if you want a bit more flexibility. The trip on Concorde will set you back a cool £4500.

Lower fares (than the official published rates above) are almost always on offer, subject to availability, on the scheduled airlines and these can be booked through travel agents. The charter airlines (Caledonian, Air UK and Airtours) also offer seats on a flight-only basis and these are perhaps your best bet for a cheap ticket, but there are very tight restrictions. Contact the Caribbean travel agents mentioned below. With luck, you can find a return fare to the Caribbean for as little as £300.

UK travel agents specializing in flights to the Caribbean, on scheduled and charter airlines, include **Transatlantic Wings**, 70 Pembroke Rd, London W8 6NX (✆ 071 602 4021), **Caribbean Gold**, 7 Albion Court, Albion Place, London W6 0QT

(✆ 081 741 8491), **Caribbean Travel**, 367 Portobello Road, London W10 5SG (✆ 081 969 6230), **New Look Travel**, 111 High St, London NW10 4TR (✆ 081 965 9657), **Newmont Travel**, 85 Balls Pond Road, London N1 4BL (✆ 071 254 6546) and **Stoke Newington Travel**, 168 Stoke Newington Road, London N16 7UY (✆ 071 254 0136). There are two flights clubs in the UK. You join for a minimal fee and then are sent information about fares at considerable reductions (subject to the usual availability). BWIA's **Sunjet Reunion Club** can be contacted at 48 Leicester Square, London WC2H 7LT (✆ 071 930 1335), and the **Reunion Club** run by tour operator Caribbean Connection can be reached at 93 Newman Street, London W1P 3LE (✆ 071 344 0101).

From Europe

Lufthansa fly from Frankfurt to Antigua and Sint Maarten (weekly); **BWIA** to Antigua, Barbados and Trinidad from Frankfurt in Germany (reservations ✆ 069 628 025) and Zurich in Switzerland (reservations ✆ 1 312 7373); **Air France** from Paris to Martinique, Guadeloupe and Sint Maarten. Scheduled fares are expensive. There are also European charter operators which offer discounted fares.

From the USA

American Airlines have the most extensive service from the States to the eastern Caribbean. They fly to all the major islands, usually in time to catch onward flights. Many services originate in New York (JFK) or Miami (there are often two flights a day), or touch them *en route*. American Airlines also have a hub in the Caribbean island of Puerto Rico, from where their subsidiary American Eagle has onward flights to the British Virgin Islands, Anguilla, Sint Maarten, St Kitts and St Lucia (Vigie airport near Castries). **Continental Airlines** fly from Newark, New Jersey to Kingston (Jamaica), Port of Spain (Trinidad), Antigua and the Virgin Islands.

Fares from the USA vary little from one carrier to another. The seasons are strictly observed: mid-December to mid-April is high season, late June to mid-September is the summer peak, and the rest of the year is low season. Sample scheduled mid-week round-trip fares from Miami to Jamaica are $250 and to Antigua $400, from New York to Jamaica $350 and to Antigua $450 in low season. From the Midwest add around $100, from the West Coast $200. These fares require advance booking and there is usually a minimum stay of a week; supplements are payable for weekend travel and cancellations. Charter flights are also available through travel agents and this may mean as much as a third off the scheduled price. Check the newspapers and your travel agent.

From Canada

Air Canada flies direct, usually out of Toronto but occasionally Montreal, to a number of destinations in the eastern Caribbean, including Antigua, Guadeloupe,

St Lucia and Barbados. Another alternative is to connect with American or Caribbean carriers in New York or Miami. **BWIA** also fly from Toronto in Canada to Port of Spain in Trinidad, stopping over in Antigua and Barbados. Once again, there are plenty of charter flights from Canada servicing the vacation packages. Further details on flights to and between the islands are listed under the 'Getting There' sections for each island.

By Boat

Cruise liner is a popular way of travelling around the Caribbean, and it enables you to visit as many as four or five different islands in a week, without the hassle of delayed flights or even packing your suitcase. Most depart from Miami or Fort Lauderdale and a few are based in San Juan, Puerto Rico. They sail all year round.

Cruise-ship companies include **Celebrity Cruises,** with three liners (UK ✆ 071 412 0290, fax 412 0908, USA toll free ✆ 800 437 3111), **Cunard** (UK ✆ 071 839 1414, fax 839 1837, USA toll free ✆ 800 221 4770), **Kloster Cruise Lines** (UK ✆ 071 493 6041, fax 081 748 4542, USA toll free ✆ 800 327 3090), which has six liners, and **Princess Cruises** (UK ✆ 071 831 1881, USA toll free ✆ 800 421 0880).

The possibilities of independent travel to the Caribbean by sea are more limited and may not be convenient because of the time involved. If you are prepared to pay the fairly steep rates you can travel on the **Geest Line** that sails out of Southampton Docks; contact The Windward Terminal, Herbert Walker Avenue, Southampton SO1 0XP (✆ 0703 334415, fax 334416). The price is about £2900 per person for the full 23-day round-trip, and between £1800 and £2100 for a one-way passage, depending on your island. It no longer seems possible to work a passage out to the islands, even swabbing the decks, unless you have a merchant marine card.

A large number of yachts make the Atlantic crossing to the Caribbean towards the end of the year (after spending the summer in the Mediterranean), arriving in time for the winter sailing season. You might be able to pick up a yacht on the south coast of Britain, in the south of France, in Gibraltar, or even in the Canaries any time from September (just after the hurricane season). Try the yacht club noticeboards and yachting magazines. The **Cruising Association**, CA House, 1 Northey Street, Lime House Basin, London E14 8BT (✆ 071 537 2828), has a crewing service, connecting skippers and crew in a monthly newsletter (£18 to have your name on the list). You negotiate from there with the skipper.

Experience is not necessarily required. Most yachts will charge you just enough to cover food or nothing at all, but there are one or two sharks around who have been making outrageous charges for what can be quite a hard three-week sail. If you are worried about the crossing, catamarans are more comfortable. The return journey across the Atlantic generally takes place at the end of April, fairly soon after Antigua Race week, and the ports of Antigua are the best places to look if you wish to make the eastward crossing.

In the same way, the American yachting community migrates down to the Caribbean over the winter. Once again, try yacht club noticeboards, the yachting magazines and the ports on the eastern seaboard.

Entry Requirements and Customs

As a British citizen you do not need a visa to any of the Commonwealth Caribbean countries or the French Antilles. Americans and Canadians travelling as tourists do not need a visa to enter any Caribbean country. Citizens of other countries do not usually need a visa, except sometimes to Puerto Rico and the US Virgin Islands (same regulations as USA). In most of the Caribbean islands, a proof of identity is enough, though a passport is the best document for Europeans. Business visitors should consult the Embassy before departure.

The Caribbean may be known for being laid back. Their immigration authorities, however, are most definitely not so. Invariably they will demand to see an onward ticket and they will hold your passport until you produce one. Some islands may require proof of funds. On the immigration form you will also be asked to give a local address: this is almost a formality as they rarely check up, but it eases entry to put something down. Addresses of hotels and guest houses are at the end of each separate island chapter.

It is worth remembering to keep some change for when you leave, because most countries levy a **departure tax**, usually payable in US dollars, but sometimes demanded in local currency (listed in the separate island sections).

Drugs not issued on prescription are illegal in the Caribbean and people do occasionally end up inside for possession of user quantities. Customs officials operate a strict policy against them and they search bags going in and out of the countries. While on an island you will probably be approached by 'oregano salesman' with an offer of marijuana (weed, ganja etc.) and occasionally cocaine. You will not be popular if you are caught. Alcohol and tobacco allowances vary from island to island.

Specialist Caribbean Tour Operators

Most holidays to the Caribbean are sold as scheduled or charter packages, and with these you can get anything from a two-week, two-destination package at two different luxury resorts at opposite ends of the Caribbean Sea, through the proliferation of wedding and honeymoon packages (complete with nuptial underwear if you want), to the charter holidays that take advantage of the low season rates and give you a return flight and two weeks' accommodation for less than the price of a normal scheduled return air fare. Because of the discounts they can get by block-booking airline seats and hotel rooms, tour operators can put together a package more cheaply than an independent traveller. A well-informed travel agent can sift through the multiplicity of packages and find the best one for you. Many of the tour companies include obligatory **insurance** in their packages, but travel agents will always sell you a policy. Check your existing policies—it is worth insuring against medical problems, cancelled flights and lost luggage.

Tour Operators in the UK

The biggest Caribbean tour operator in the UK, and one of the most flexible when it comes to tailor-making a holiday is **Caribbean Connection**, Concorde House, Forest Street, Chester CH1 1QR (℗ 0244 341131, fax 0244 310255), which offers a wide-ranging selection of hotels and villas in many of the Caribbean islands. **Elegant Resorts**, 24 Nicholas Street, Chester CH1 2ER (℗ 0244 329671, fax 0244 341084) also offer top-of-the-range packages and have knowledgeable staff; as do **Thomas Cook Holidays**, PO Box 36, Thorpe Wood, Peterborough, Cambridgeshire PE3 6SB (℗ 0733 332255, fax 0733 505784). Smaller operators include the friendly **Caribtours** at 161 Fulham Road, London SW3 6SN (℗ 071 581 3517, fax 071 225 2491) who will give a personalized service; **Harlequin Worldwide Travel** at 2 North Road, South Ockendon, Essex RM15 6QJ (℗ 0708 852780, fax 0708 854952), who tailor-make to off-beat hotels in lesser-known island destinations as well as the big Caribbean hotels; and **Silk Cut Faraway Holidays**, Meon House, Petersfield, Hants GU32 3JN (℗ 0730 265211, fax 0730 260263), a smaller operator which offers tailor-made trips to smaller hotels around the islands. They also have a villa programme through their sister company, **Meon Villas**. **Palmer and Parker Holidays**, The Beacon, Penn, Buckinghamshire HP10 8ND (℗ 0494 81411, fax 0494 814184) work exclusively to villas in Barbados, Jamaica and St Lucia.

If your main desire is to get to the West Indies for as little money as possible, you can travel with one of the charter package companies and the best prices are in summer. Some of the cheapest are offered by **Airtours** at Wavell House, Holcombe Road, Helmshore, Rossendale, Lancs BB4 4NB (℗ 0706 260000). **Thomson Holidays**, Greater London House, Hampstead Road, London NW1 7SD (reservations: London ℗ 081 200 8733; Birmingham ℗ 021 632 6282; Manchester ℗ 061 236 3828) reach most of the major Caribbean islands, departing from Heathrow, Gatwick and Manchester.

special-interest holidays

Honeymoon packages (with wedding included if you want) get ever more popular and most of the tour operators above will arrange one for you. Some tour operators are offering twin-destination holidays, perhaps with a week in another Caribbean island or in Florida. If you have specific requirements, most would be happy to tailor-make a holiday for you, though it may cost a fair bit. If you wish to spend less, the specialist Caribbean travel agent **Transatlantic Wings**, 70 Pembroke Road, London W8 6NX (℡ 071 602 4021, fax 071 603 6101), offer transatlantic flights and bookings in a number of smaller and more off-beat Caribbean hotels. The **Caribbean Centre** (℡ 081 940 3399) will also book hotels for you (with some considerably discounted rates), either for a full two-week period or for a couple of days before you set off travelling.

Holidays with a specialist interest are less easily arranged through the regular tour operators, but there are some smaller operators in contact with outfits in the Caribbean itself. You can arrange **scuba diving** through the **Barefoot Traveller** (℡ 081 741 4319) in the islands of St Vincent and Dominica. **DB Jazz Tours** (℡ 0386 852194, fax 0386 852763), 4 Cotswold Court, Broadway, Worcestershire WR12 7AA, arranges some music tours to the Caribbean, including one to the St Lucia Jazz Festival held each year in May, and a jazz cruise in October. When the England **cricket** team tours the West Indies there are a number of companies offering tours, often with former players as guides. Contact the tourist boards of the islands you wish to visit. **International Chapters** (℡ 071 722 9560), 102 St John's Wood Terrace, London NW8 6PL, have luxury villas throughout the Caribbean, all with pool and usually staffed.

Some operators visit only certain islands: **VFB Holidays** 'Faraway France' arrange trips to the French Caribbean. **BVI Holidays** (℡ 0279 656111, fax 0279 506616) specialize in the BVI and **Kestours** (℡ 081 658 7316, fax 081 402 9517) have a range of packages to Barbados.

Tour Operators in the USA

Many Caribbean hotels have a booking agent in the United States or a dedicated reservation number, so you may choose to arrange your bookings direct and fix your own transport. Tour operators working out of the USA include **Caribbean Concepts**, 575 Underhill Boulevard, Syosset, NY 11791 (℡ 516 496 9800, fax 516 496 9880, toll free ℡ 800 423 4433), a small operator catering to the upper end of the market, who will arrange flights, car hire and hotel accommodation; **Alken Tours** (℡ 718 856 7711, fax 718 282 1152); **French Caribbean International**, 5662 Calle Real, Suite 333, Santa Barbara, CA 93117–2317 (℡/fax 805 967 9850, US and Canada ℡ 800 373 6246), specialists in the French Caribbean islands; and **Fling Vacations**, 999 Postal Road, Allentown PA 18103 (℡ 215 266 6110, fax 266 0280, toll free ℡ 800 523 9624). Big Caribbean operators include **American Express Vacations** (toll free ℡ 800 241 1700), **GoGo Tours**, with offices all over the country (head office 201 934 3500 or toll free in

New York City (✆ 800 526 0405) and **Travel Impressions** (toll free ✆ 800 284 0044). Most tour companies will arrange a **honeymoon** for you in the Caribbean.

special-interest holidays

Caligo Ventures at 156 Bedford Road, Armonk NY 10504 (✆ 914 273 6333, fax 914 273 6370) arrange birding trips and natural history tours of Trinidad centred on the Asa Wright Nature Centre.

Getting Around

Island-hopping is one of the pleasures of a holiday in the eastern Caribbean. There is a grand variety of islands within a relatively short distance of one another, and they are visible one from the next for the 500 miles from Grenada in the south to Anguilla in the north), 20 minutes' flying can get you from a French overseas *département* to independent islands that have a strong British heritage, from busy, developed countries to tiny, comatose blips with just a few shacks and palm trees.

Most of the big Caribbean tour operators will arrange an island-hopping itinerary for you, with flights between hotels. If you wish to travel more independently (and less expensively) you can take off on your own with one of the island-hopper tickets issued by the local Caribbean airlines (*see* below). The specialist Caribbean travel agent **Transatlantic Wings** (✆ 602 4021, address above) is the most knowledgeable agent in the UK and they will make suggestions and book itineraries for you. If you do not want to arrange an actual island-hopping itinerary, it is perfectly possible to make short day or weekend tours (some by sailboat, others by plane) of the islands near to the one on which you are staying. Barbados, St Lucia and Martinique have many trips to the Grenadines.

By Air

Most island-hopping nowadays is by **aeroplane** (often Twin Otters or Islanders and increasingly DASH 8s). Some of these planes, which carry about twenty passengers, do look a bit like coffins with wings on and when they take off they have so much lift that it feels almost alarming, but they are very safe and reliable. The pilot will stand at the beginning of the runway and run the engines hard until the control panel becomes a blur and the plane thrums like an outsize tuning fork. Then he lets off the brakes and puts the props in drive. Flight can be a bit of a novelty (some people actually pay for rides like this at funfairs). Planes this size tend to bounce off clouds—there are vertical streams of air within them which will leave your stomach a hundred feet above you in a matter of a second or so. If you do find a penetrable cloud, you might find it coming through the overhead blowers. In calmer moments the views of the islands and the sea from 3000ft are fantastic.

Island-hoppers are affectionately known as the islands' bus service. They tend to run along the island-chain and will simply miss out a destination if nobody wants to get on or off. The main centres for travel around the eastern Caribbean are San Juan in Puerto Rico, Sint Maarten, Antigua and islands down to Trinidad. Generally, island-hopping by plane is a good and reliable way of travelling. A couple of words of warning, however. Booking can be a little haphazard. Planes are sometimes oversold, and those booked in advance may well leave half empty. Travelling standby often works. And it is worth reconfirming obsessively. If you miss one flight you may find that the whole of the rest of the itinerary is cancelled. A dose of judicious anger in the airline office sometimes helps you get what you want. Most airlines are usually quite amenable when it comes to excess luggage, except when the plane is full.

The biggest carrier in the eastern Caribbean is **LIAT** (officially this is Leeward Islands Air Transport, but it is also known as 'Leave Island Any Time', 'Likeable Interested Attentive Tolerant', 'Lost in Air Transit' or 'Luggage in Another Town'). Many LIAT flights originate in Antigua and they fly as far south (usually at least two a day) as Barbados and Port of Spain, Trinidad, and to Puerto Rico in the north (with some flights to Santiago in the Dominican Republic). There is also a link from St Lucia to Caracas. LIAT has three hopper tickets which are ideal for people travelling around the Caribbean. The *Super Caribbean Explorer* ticket allows you unlimited stops in one direction (though you are permitted to return to a destination to make a connection) for a period of a month, with return to point of start, price US$367. The *Caribbean Explorer* lasts for a 21-day period and allows three stops (none repeated except for connections), with return to point of origin, price US$199. The *Eastern Caribbean Airpass* allows stops in between three and six LIAT destinations over a 21-day period, each leg being charged at US$60. There are some restrictions. Super Explorer tickets may be bought in the Caribbean, but the other two must be bought before departure from your country of residence, in conjunction with a ticket to the Caribbean (any carrier will do, despite what some airlines assure you).

BWIA (pronounced Beewee), the Trinidad and Tobago airline, has the *Intra-Caribbean Airpass* which allows you one stop at any BWIA destination in the Caribbean; connections are allowed (maximum stay 24 hours) over a 30-day period, with return to the original point of departure, price US$356. This is particularly interesting because it includes Jamaica, which is not covered by LIAT. Other BWIA destinations are Antigua, Barbados, Grenada, Guyana, Trinidad and Tobago.

Many islands have their own individual airline. **Air Martinique** (local ℂ 596 51 11 11, fax 596 63 61 75) flies south from Martinique to Barbados and to St Lucia, St Vincent and several Grenadine islands. **Air Guadeloupe** (℃ 590 82 47 00) radiates north and south from Guadeloupe, flying south to Dominica and north to Antigua and Sint Maarten.

There are plenty of smaller airlines, usually linking a smaller island to the nearby hub for international flights. **Mustique Airways** (UK ✆ 0453 835801, fax 0453 835525, local ✆ 809 458 4380, fax 456 4586) connects Barbados and the Grenadines. Many airlines link the British Virgin Islands to the US Virgin Islands and to San Juan. For details, *see* the separate island sections. The last option is to **charter** a small plane, which can work out at a good price if there are enough people. All Caribbean airports have a charter company (five-seaters, nine-seaters and sometimes helicopters) on call.

The Caribbean also has some pretty hairy airstrips. Some are very short—you will know about this just after landing when the whole plane shudders because the pilot applies reverse thrust. Others are hairy because there is an obstacle course on approach to landing. Two airstrips worth being aware of, and then watching other planes approach once you are safely on the ground, are Terre de Haut in the Saints, where there are a couple of peaks on the approach path, and Union Island in the Grenadines, now less heartstopping as they've extended the runway, but sporting none the less beacause you nearly clip the treetops as you bank right steeply coming in over Clifton.

By Boat

Until thirty years ago all the islands of the Caribbean were linked by elegant old sloops and schooners once or twice a week. These have mostly gone now, but it is still sometimes possible to hitch a ride on the **freighters** which bring provisions and manufactured goods into the islands. Go to the dock and ask around and they might sign you on as 'crew'. There is a regular service out of Barbados to Trinidad, St Vincent and South America. If you are making the ride between Grenada and Trinidad, you can usually get a lift on the magnificent sloops that tie up in St George's harbour, Grenada. Boats from the Grenadines go as far north as Sint Maarten, though they won't necessarily stop at other islands *en route*.

Ferries connect all the Virgin Islands: Grenada, the Grenadines and St Vincent; the French islands of Martinique and Guadeloupe (via Dominica) and on to St Lucia; the islands off Guadeloupe. Another possibility is to travel by hitching a ride on a **yacht**, which you can catch at the main centres (BVI, USVI, Antigua, Martinique, St Lucia and some of the Grenadines). If you go down to the marina and ask around, you may come up with something: the crews are often happy to take along the occasional passenger who is prepared to help out.

For details of **car hire**, **public transport**, **taxis**, etc., *see* the 'Getting Around' sections located at the beginning of each island chapter of this guide.

Beaches	12
Bookshops	12
Calendar of Events	12
Children	15
Climate	15
Electricity	16
Food and Drink	17
Health	20
Insurance	22
Language	22
Living and Working in the Caribbean	23

Practical A–Z

Maps and Publications	23
Money	24
Packing	25
Photography	25
Post Offices	26
Shopping	26
Sports	26
Telephones	30
Time Zones	30
Tourist Information	31
Where to Stay	31
Women	34

Beaches

If the 20th century's ultimate quest is the finest sun-drenched, palm-fringed curve of satin-soft, ankle-deep sand, washed by warm waves, and set in gin-clear shadows and an aquamarine sea, all of course with a perfect sunset view, then the Caribbean offers happy hunting grounds. In the south-eastern Caribbean the best sand is to be found in the lower-lying islands such as Barbados, Grande Terre on Guadeloupe and the smaller coral-clad islands that lie in shallows in the Grenadines, but you will also find some magnificent, palm-backed, often secluded coves tucked between the vast headlands of the volcanic islands (where the beaches will often be of dark volcanic sand). Steep-sided Dominica has few beaches and most of those are of dark sand.

All the islands are big enough to have a large and active beach where you can arrange most watersports, but there will also be a few secluded retreats where you can expect to be alone (*see* the individual island chapters). Swimming is safe in most places, but you are warned not to swim alone, particularly not on an unprotected Atlantic shore. For more information, *see* the 'Beaches' paragraphs in the individual island chapters.

Bookshops

In the UK, the following London shops have a wide selection of travel books with special sections for the Caribbean:

Daunt's bookshop at 83 Marylebone High Street, London W1M 4DE (© 071 224 2295)—they will send you a reading list of their material.

The **Travel Bookshop**, 13 Blenheim Crescent, London W11 2EE (© 071 229 5260).

Stanfords at 12–14 Longacre, London WC2E 9LP (© 071 836 1321). This is also a specialist map shop.

In the USA, try:

British Travel Books, 40 West 57th St, New York, NY 10019 (© 212 765 0898).

Rand McNally Map Travel, 444 North Michigan Avenue, Chicago, IL 60611.

The Complete Traveller, 4038 Westheimer, Houston, TX 77027.

Traveller's Bookstore, 22 W 52nd St, New York, NY 10019 (© 212 664 0995).

Travel Logs, 222 West 83rd Street, New York, NY 10024 (© 212 799 8761).

Travel Merchandise, 1425 K St NW, Washington, DC 20005 (© 202 371 6656).

Calendar of Events

The biggest festivals in the Caribbean are the various **Carnivals**, usually pre-Lenten (Dimanche, Lundi and Mardi Gras and in some islands *Mercredi des Cendres* or Ash Wednesday), but sometimes held at the end of the sugar harvest (Cropover in

Barbados). The summer months are a particularly popular time of year for festivities (the West Indians think the weather is better then) and so there are many official celebrations and general blow-outs in the British islands (around Emancipation Day, 1 August) and religious festivals in the Catholic islands (e.g. the *fiestas patronales* of Martinique and Guadeloupe). Many islands have slightly more formal events commemorating Independence days and National Memorials, even military parades in some islands. As you would expect in the Caribbean there are many other less formal get-togethers, centred around music—calypso, steel pan, merengue, reggae and most recently jazz (*see* below)—and around sports, some tennis and golf competitions sponsored by big international companies; and other events centred around the sea, with local and open sailing regattas and fishing competitions. Finally, there are some island cultural events, from story-telling in St Lucia and Dominica to gastronomic blowouts in the French islands.

Whatever the official reason for the celebration, almost all Caribbean festivals are also an excuse for an organized party and so they invariably involve a **jump-up** (more Caribbean dancing) which will spontaneously appear in the streets or in a field or on the beach. It is often a bit like an oversized picnic, with cook-ins going on on the sidelines, where a half oil-barrel is turned on its side to make a brazier. Here chicken and fish are barbecued and then sprinkled with hot pepper sauce and soldier crabs are roasted in their shells.

The summer months are the best if you want to see the West Indians at play and there are a number of festivals in June, July and August. Things also get booked up then. Generally speaking you will have no problem joining in the festivities in any Caribbean event: you will find that the islanders make you welcome.

January

The end of Christmas is celebrated on 6 January with gastronomic flair in Martinique as **La Fête des Rois**. Grenada holds a fishing tournament and a sailing regatta and there are windsurfing competitions in Barbados. Most of the pre-Lenten **Carnivals** are just warming up, with weekend fêtes and the early stages of calypso and carnival king and queen competitions.

February

Grenada holds its **Independence Day** celebrations on 7 February, with jump-ups, followed by St Lucia on 22 February. The Holetown Festival in Barbados commemorates the first settlement of the island in 1627.

Most Caribbean **Carnivals** culminate in February, in a three-day jump-up, with calypso and steel band competitions and masked parades in the streets on Shrove Tuesday (Mardi Gras) or Ash Wednesday: Carriacou, Dominica, Guadeloupe, Martinique and St Lucia.

April

There are also celebrations for **Easter**, including a **Fish Festival** in Oistins Town on Barbados. Easter sees kite-flying all over the Caribbean; more formal events include a Food Festival in Martinique, and a three-day Easter Opera Season in Barbados. Many of the **sailing** competitions get under way, including the Spring Regatta in Bequia in the Grenadines.

May

Abolition Day is remembered with picnics and fêtes in the French islands on 27 May. St Lucia holds a Jazz Festival for three days.

June

Vincie Mas takes place towards the end of the month in St Vincent and the Grenadines.

July

Martinique has a **Cultural Week** with performances of classical art. Late in the month a number of islands get their carnivals moving, including Barbados (**Cropover**), so that they culminate in the first few days of August. Dominica's **Domfesta** stages Caribbean cultural activities in July or August.

August

Most of the former British islands have festivities on 1 August, the date of emancipation, which in Jamaica also coincides with the **Independence Day** celebrations on the first Monday in August. The extraordinary and colourful **Fête des Cuisinières** takes place on 11 August, St Laurent's day (the patron saint of cooks) in Guadeloupe, with parades of dishes and blow-outs. Grenada stages **Carnival**, in which the masqueraders drag the carnival floats over the hills of St George's. There are plenty of regattas with the **yoles rondes** sailing races in Martinique, the **Carriacou** regatta, and races at **Canouan** in the Grenadines. St Lucia's **Rose Festival**, held on 30 August, has a mock court, ball and music.

October

St Lawrence in Barbados holds a music festival, and in St Lucia the festival of the Marguerite is held on 17 October, also **Jounen Kweyol** on 28 October, a day of creole festivities.

November

Dominica celebrates **Independence** on 3 November and Barbados on 30 November.

December

St Lucia celebrates its **National Day** is on 13 December. The **ARC** Rally arrives in the island about the same time after an Atlantic crossing. There are jazz and guitar festivals in alternate years in Martinique. All Caribbean islands celebrate Christmas; **Nine Mornings** in St Vincent sees a week of celebrations in the run up to it; and of course the New Year itself is yet another good excuse for a jump-up. In Grenada, you may come across **Parang**, a special style of Christmas singing.

Children

Despite its reputation as a honeymooners' and couples' destination, travelling with children in the Caribbean is perfectly possible and you will find that in most islands the locals are indulgent and friendly towards them. Just a few hotels at the top of the range have a policy of not accepting any children below a certain age (usually 12); others have built special playgrounds for them (notably Malliouhana in Anguilla and the Sandy Lane Hotel in Barbados) and provide nannies so that you can sun yourself in peace. The majority of hotels will accept children, though they will have only limited facilities for them. Children are sometimes allowed to stay free in the same room as their parents and baby-sitters are usually on call in any hotel. If you have a large family it might be easiest to opt for a two- or three-room flat in an apartment complex. Many of these will have hotel-like facilities including watersports concessions and a restaurant. If you are happy to look after yourself, then you might take a villa. Children are accepted happily in restaurants, and with the tendency towards American food you can always find a burger and chips to keep them quiet. However, the Caribbean islands have few museums or daytime activities designed with children in mind.

Climate

Colonists once knew the Bahamas as the 'isles of perpetual June' because of their fair and clement weather. Generally speaking the climate over the whole Caribbean area is impeccable. As islands their temperature is kept constant by the sea and so the climate is far gentler than that in the continent that surrounds them. The sun is hot, of course, but particularly in winter the edge is taken off the heat by a breeze. For most of the year, air-conditioning is not really necessary. The temperature varies just a few degrees across the year and across the geographical area, from Barbados to Guadeloupe. In the larger islands it will occasionally reach 100°F. Temperatures drop at night; in summer there is no need to cover up, but you might need a thin jersey on a winter evening, particularly at high altitudes.

There are just two main seasons in the Caribbean: wet, in which tropical showers pass by, offload thousands of gallons of water in seconds, and then the sun comes out to dry it all up again; and the dry season, in which it still rains but less frequently or heavily. The wet seasons are in May or June and October or November. A tropical shower will drench you (with warm rain) in a matter of seconds.

Of more concern are cold fronts which spin off the continental weather system up north, putting a blanket of cloud over the islands for three or four days at a time. They have been a bit more frequent in recent years.

Average winter and summer temperatures, °C (°F)

	Barbados	**Grenada**	**Guadeloupe**
Winter	29 (84)	27 (80)	25 (76)
Summer	30 (87)	29 (84)	29 (84)

hurricanes

Hurricanes are the severest natural disaster in an area of otherwise benign weather. The worst ones in the last few years were Hurricane Gilbert in 1988, which laid waste Jamaica and the Cayman Islands, and Hurricane Hugo in 1989, the worst hurricane this century, which carved a swathe through Guadeloupe and then flattened Montserrat and St Croix. Turning anti-clockwise in the northern hemisphere, hurricanes rise near the coast of Africa. Fed by warm winds over the water, they get a couple of thousand miles' run-up before they slice their way through the islands, blowing with winds up to 200mph and at the same time delivering a massive deluge of rain, which causes yet more destruction. They uproot telegraph poles, blow tin roofs around and disturb the sea as much as 200ft below the surface (causing damage to the corals). After a hurricane, an island looks like a grey moonscape, with every leaf stripped off the trees in what is normally an overwhelmingly green area.

If you hear that a hurricane is on the way, find the strongest concrete bunker possible and shelter in it with everybody else. If all goes quiet at the height of the storm, then you are in the eye (the very centre of the hurricane): batten down the hatches because it will start again in a few minutes. If you are in a sailing boat, the best place to head for is a mangrove swamp. The most likely month for hurricanes is September. The traditional rhyme runs:

> *June too soon, July stand by,*
> *September remember, October all over.*

Electricity

In most Caribbean islands the electrical supply is 110 or 120 volts at 60 cycles, and so American electrical appliances need no adaptor (British and French visitors will need to take one). The French islands work to 220 volts and the Dutch islands at 110. The British islands are mixed; those that have developed recently tend to be on the American standard (BVI and Anguilla), but some of the British Caribbean islands have a 230 or 240 volt supply at 50 cycles per second. Even then, some hotels work on the American system, so it may be worth checking before you go. If hotel rooms are not fitted with electrical appliances, ask at the front desk, where they may well keep some stashed away.

Food and Drink

When visiting the Caribbean on his trip to write *The Traveller's Tree*, Patrick Leigh Fermor decided that: 'Hotel cooking in the island is so appalling that a stretcher may profitably be ordered at the same time as dinner'. Admittedly this was in the late forties, but Caribbean food, particularly hotel food, is generally pretty unadventurous, and has a universal lacklustre 'international style'. The former British colonial influence may have something to do with it, and recently the overwhelming number of US visitors, because a quick trip to the French Antilles will tell a different story. On the restaurant circuit things have improved recently and you will find at least a couple of good and often adventurous restaurants in every island now. Some chefs and restaurateurs have taken the best of West Indian ingredients and traditions and applied continental techniques to produce a sophisticated and satisfying Caribbean cuisine. Also a number of famous chefs have made their way down to the Caribbean. You can expect to pay as much or more for this as you would at home.

Dress codes for dinner have almost entirely died out in the Caribbean and only a couple of hotel dining rooms will request that you wear even a jacket or a tie. Service is often a problem, though. Even in quite smart restaurants and hotel dining rooms it can be haphazard. Wine is available in the smartest restaurants, but it does not take well to the heat and few restaurants have cooled cellars.

A week's worth of curry goat or stew fish might be more than any newcomer could take, but it is worth getting out in search of West Indian food. It is distinctive, cheaper, and the restaurants are often more fun. It is also worth seeking out the beach bars, where you will have barbecued local fish and vegetables.

Gastronomes should really head for the French islands, where there is a strong tradition of creole cookery with luxurious sauces, served with meticulous attention to detail both in the preparation and in the service. Like their metropolitan counterparts, the French Antilleans treat their food with a little more ceremony than other West Indians. The tastes of India have come through strongest in Trinidad and the French islands, but curry goat and *roti* (an envelope of dough with a meat or vegetable filling) have reached everywhere now.

Caribbean food is traditionally quite spicy and West Indians can be quite liberal with chilli pepper in their cook-ups. Beware of bottles marked *Hot Pepper*. Fish is abundant, and often delicious, as are seafoods such as lobster and crab and an island favourite, conch. Other foods that have become popular are made of ingredients that were originally hardship foods, often fed to the slaves. The Jamaican national dish is **ackee and saltfish**; now that there is refrigeration and food is no longer salted in order to preserve it, salted cod is expensive and difficult to get hold of. **Rice 'n' peas** (or peas 'n' rice depending on which island you are in) is another standard meal in the cheaper restaurants in the British islands and is particularly good when served with coconut milk. **Callaloo** is a traditional West Indian soup made from spinach and **oil-dung** is a pot of vegetables cooked in coconut oil.

West Indian dishes are usually served with traditional vegetables, many also brought to the Caribbean as slave food from elsewhere in the tropical world. Try **breadfruit**, fried **plantain** (like a banana) and **cassava** (originally an Arawak food) and the delicious **christophene**. The Caribbean is of course famous for its **fruits**—mango, banana, pineapple, watermelon, soursop and papaya among others—which taste especially good in the ice-creams. Lesser-known fruits seen around the islands include **guava**, a pip-filled mush of sweetness with a hard skin, often used in jams; the distinctively shaped **carambola** or star apple (it looks like a five-pointed star in cross section), which has a crisp, juicy flesh usually yellow in colour; the **golden apple**, a small round and slightly golden-coloured fruit which looks not dissimilar to a pomegranate and has an aromatic flavour; and the **guinep**, a hard green lump just smaller than a golf-ball; inside there is a large pip covered in sweet white flesh not unlike a lychee. Yet more exotic varieties include **tamarind**, an extremely bitter taste extracted from a pod like a brown, knobbly broad bean; and **jackfruit**, foot-long fleshy lumps of fruit covered in hooks. You can even eat **sea grape** found along the beach, best once they have turned purple, although these are something of an acquired taste. Finally, if you see someone selling **cocoa pods** at the roadside, stop and get one. Inside there is a white flesh, a delicious sweet and tart silky stickiness which you suck off the cocoa beans.

It is not usually necessary to make a **reservation** in Caribbean restaurants, except at the most popular in the high season. Some restauarants will close out of season. Under the 'Eating Out' sections in this book, restaurants are divided into three **price categories:** *expensive, moderate* and *cheap*. As some islands are generally more expensive than others, the pricing of these categories will vary a little according to the island. Lobster, shrimp and imported steak tend to be about 30% more expensive than other dishes and so they are not included within the different pricing categories.

Cocktails

The Caribbean is famous for cocktails and many of them were invented here, making the best use of the exotic fruits. The **Piña Colada** (pineapple and coconut cream and rum) supposedly originated in Puerto

Rico and the **Daiquiri** (crushed ice, rum and fruit syrup whisked up like a sorbet) in Havana. The **Cuba Libre**, mixed after the Cuban Revolution in 1959, is made of rum with lemon and cola, and Hemingway's **Mojito** is made with white rum, fresh mint and Angostura bitters. The **Planter's Punch**, traditionally drunk all over the Caribbean, is made from rum and water with a twist of lime and sugar, topped with ground nutmeg. Unfortunately many barmen will use over-liberal dashes of bright red, sweet Grenadine syrup. Almost every bar has a speciality.

Rum and Red Stripe

Rum is the Caribbean 'national' drink—fifty years ago bars kept their bottles of rum on the counter free of charge and it was the water you had to pay for. Distilled from sugar molasses, rum is produced all over the islands and, though it often tastes like rocket fuel, it gives the West Indians their energy for dancing, so it cannot be all bad. The most popular local variety of rum and the quickest to produce is 'white rum', which is drunk in the rum bars and at local dances. Gold rums are a little mellower; their colour comes from caramel which is introduced as they age in wooden barrels; some are blended. In the French islands rums are treated much as brandies and they are laid down to mature for years. There are even vintages (*see* **Martinique** and **Guadeloupe**). Look out for **Mountgay** in Barbados, and the varieties of **Trois Rivières**, **Rhum Bally** and **Rhum St James** in Martinique. Finally, some rums are flavoured with tropical fruits, either by the producer during the ageing process or by individual restaurants, who then serve them as a digestif.

Far more so than wine, the West Indians prefer a cool beer to combat the heat and nowadays almost every island brews its own, often under licence from the major international drinks companies. Some of the best known are **Red Stripe** from Jamaica, **Banks** from Barbados and **Carib** from Trinidad. There are two new beers from Antigua (**Wadadli**) and St Lucia (**Piton, La Bière Sent Lisi**). Perhaps the best of all the Caribbean beers is produced in the Dominican Republic, a light lager called **Presidente**. Heineken and American beers are almost universally available.

Soft Drinks

Life in the Caribbean sun is hot work, and so, besides the bottled drinks available in the shops, the West Indians have an array of drinks on sale in the street. *Snow cones* and *Sky juice* are made with crushed ice (scraped off a huge block), water and a dash of fruit concentrate and put into a bag or cup. You swill it around with a straw and the effect is something like a cold Ribena. You have to be careful not to drink the water and the concentrate too quickly otherwise you are just left with a mound of ice crystals. In some islands you get weird and wonderful toppings with condensed milk and crushed peanuts.

Tropical fruits make excellent non-alcoholic drinks: fruit punches are often good if you are not ready for the evening's alcoholic intake. A particularly good drink, which originates in Trinidad, is a **Bentley**, lemon and lime with a dash of bitters. If in doubt, lime juice is an excellent choice for a soft drink, though not all places have fresh limes in stock all the time. Other popular West Indian drinks are sorrel, the red Christmas drink not unlike Ribena, ginger beer, and mauby juice, a disgusting bitter concoction made of tree bark. The usual international soft drinks, Coke, Fanta, Sprite etc., are sold all over the Caribbean, and some more Caribbean ones like **Ting**.

Box juice seller

Another option is coconuts, which are often sold in the street. Do not be alarmed when the vendor pulls out a 2ft machete, because he will deftly top the coconut with a few strokes, leaving just a small hole through which you can drink. Get an older nut if you can, because the milk will be fuller and sweeter. Once you have drunk the milk, hand it back to the vendor, who will split it for you so that you can eat the delicious coconut slime that lines the inside (it eventually turns into the white coconut flesh). You will also be offered sugar-cane juice, either as a liquid, or in the sticks themselves, which you bite off and chew to a pulp (very sweet).

Health

In the 18th century if you were caught in a cholera epidemic you could have looked forward to a tonic of diluted sulphuric acid and tincture of cardamom or ammoniated tincture of opium as treatment. There are references to 'this fatal climate' on gravestones and memorials throughout the Caribbean. Today, however, the Caribbean is basically a very healthy place and unless you are unlucky there is no reason that you should experience health problems.

You should check that your polio and typhoid inoculations are up to date and you may wish to have yourself immunized or take precautions against the following diseases. **Hepatitis** occurs rarely: you can have an injection giving some cover against Hepatitis A, which is caught mainly from water and food. There has been some incidence of **cholera** in South America over the last few years and there have recently been warnings in Trinidad. If you are travelling to the less developed islands and wish to take sterile needles (and possibly plasma), make sure they are packed up to look official otherwise customs might begin to wonder.

There is quite a high incidence of venereal diseases around the Caribbean, including **HIV**, which some reckon started in Haiti (there is little evidence that this is true, though it is prevalent there). The risks from casual sex are clear.

Warnings

Sunburn can ruin your holiday and so it is worth taking it easy for the first few days. You are recommended to keep to short stints of about 15–20 minutes in the hottest part of the day (11am–3pm). Take high-protection-factor sun-cream. Sun-hats are easily found. Be particularly careful if you go snorkelling, because the combination of the sun and the cooling water is lethal. Take sunglasses. Traditional West Indian methods of soothing sunburn include the application of juice of **aloe**, a fleshy cactus-like plant, which is used a lot in cosmetics anyway. Break a leaf and squeeze out the soothing juice. After-sunburn treatments include calamine lotion. And if you will be spending most of your time in and out of the water, you might take some talcum powder for your feet.

There are very few poisonous things in the Caribbean, but you may come across the **manchineel tree** growing on the beach. These are tall, bushy trees with a fruit like a small apple, known by Columbus's men as the apple of death (*manzana* means apple in Spanish). Do not eat them! Steer clear of the tree itself because the sap is poisonous. You should not even shelter under them in the rain because the sap will blister your skin. A **palm tree** may seem the ideal place to shade yourself in the height of the sun. Beware! People have been killed by falling coconuts.

Mosquitoes are a plague, though many tourist areas are treated to get rid of them. They can cause dengue fever (in the Greater Antilles) and malaria (in Hispaniola only). Burn mosquito coils, and off the beaten track you might take a mosquito net. There are many repellents, including Autan, Jungle Formula and *OFF!*

Less potentially harmful, but equally irritating, are the tiny invisible **sand-flies** which plague certain beaches after rain and towards the end of the afternoon. In 1631, Sir Henry Colt wrote: 'First you have such abundance of small knatts by ye sea shore towards ye sun goinge down yt bite so as no rest cann be had without fyers under your Hamaccas'. For a barely visible insect, they pack a big bite. There are one or two poisonous centipedes and only certain islands have poisonous snakes (or snakes at all for that matter).

Swimming holds very few dangers in the Caribbean, though among the reefs and rocks you should look out for fire coral and particularly for spiny sea urchins (little black balls with spines up to 6 inches long radiating in all directions). If you stand on one, the spines break off, and give you a very unpleasant and possibly infectious injury. Sharks are occasionally spotted in Caribbean waters by divers, but have hardly ever been known to attack humans.

Health

Water

The **water** in most islands in the eastern Caribbean is drinkable from the tap, but to make sure, particularly in the larger islands, you might want to drink the water served by the hotel to begin with. There is a shortage of water in many of the smaller islands (Barbados and the Grenadines), and so, even in expensive hotels, you may find that nothing comes out when you turn on the tap. You are always asked to conserve water where possible. In the larger islands there is so much water that they actually sell it to the drier islands to the north.

Insurance

You don't have to believe everything you might hear about theft and illness in the Caribbean, but you can't afford to ignore it either. Good travel insurance is essential. Take great care when choosing your policy and always read the small print. A good travel insurance should always give full cover for your possessions and your health. In case of illness, it should provide for all medical costs, hospital benefits, permanent disabilities and the flight home. In case of loss or theft, it should recompense you for lost luggage, money and valuables, also for travel delay and personal liability. Most important, it should provide you with a 24-hour contact number in the event of medical emergencies. Should anything be stolen, a copy of the police report should be asked for and retained. It will be required by your insurance company when making a claim.

If your bank or insurance company hasn't an adequate travel insurance scheme (they usually have), then try the comprehensive schemes offered by **Trailfinders** (✆ 071 938 3939) or **Jardine's** (✆ 061 228 3742), or the 'Centurion Assistance' policy offered by **American Express** (✆ 0444 239900). Tour operators often include insurance in the cost of a luxury tour, but this is not always adequate.

Language

English is spoken in the tourist industry in most Caribbean countries, partly because many of the islands have a former colonial connection with Britain and partly because of the large number of American visitors. Most islands also have a local *patois*, an everyday language based on the original official colonial language, but these are often incomprehensible to the foreign visitor.

English is the official language of all the British Commonwealth Caribbean countries—Barbados, Trinidad and Tobago, the Windward Islands (Grenada, St Vincent and the Grenadines, St Lucia, Dominica), the Leeward Islands (Antigua, Montserrat, St Kitts and Nevis and Anguilla), the British and United States Virgin Islands, Jamaica, the Caymans, the Turks and Caicos and the Bahamas.

French is the official language of the French Antilles, Martinique, Guadeloupe, St Martin and St Barts, but English is widely spoken in the hotels.

Living and Working in the Caribbean

Like sailing around the world, setting up in the Caribbean is a lifetime's dream for some. Beware! Things are not necessarily what they seem during a short visit. Battling with bureaucracy and local prejudices is a perennial problem (small island communities are notoriously inward-looking and once you scratch the surface of the West Indies you will find things are no different there) and island inertia can get people down too (West Indian plumbers may not be on call quite as you are used to elsewhere). There is a heartless expression which says that people arrive with a container full of belongings and (after a year's frustration) leave with a suitcase. Perhaps it is best to rent for six months or a year to learn the ropes and see if you like the way of life before you put money in.

Having said that, many people do adapt to the West Indies and certain islands encourage investment. Buying rights vary from island to island, but most require that if you buy a plot of land you must build within a certain period, and often that you employ a local person. Details are available from the individual High Commissions and embassies.

Working in the Caribbean is also not as easy as it might seem because most islands impose strict quotas of foreign workers on businesses, ensuring that the work remains for the locals. Casual work is almost impossible to find. If you are lucky, you might find some work in the bars in islands where there is a large expatriate community or in islands with a large sailing contingent, where crews are sometimes needed. EC members can work (officially at least) in the French islands, but the British have no special rights in their former colonies.

Maps and Publications

There are just a few general Caribbean maps and they are available from any good bookstore or map store. Really detailed maps of individual islands are not generally available (either on island or in the UK). You might find them at a map specialist, but they are not really needed when on island unless you are going walking in remote areas. In most places it is enough to get a photocopied map at the tourist offices (or you can tear one out of the many tourism magazines—*see* 'Tourist Information', p.31).

Most islands have their own newspaper; these tend to be dailies in the larger islands (islands such as Jamaica and Trinidad will have a broadsheet and some tabloids) and perhaps two or three times weekly in the smaller ones. Many American papers and magazines are on sale (usually a day or so late), but not so many papers make it over from Europe. There are just a couple of pan-Caribbean papers, including *Caribbean Week*. The BWIA inflight magazine *Caribbean Beat* covers Caribbean-wide affairs and is a good read.

Money

Generally speaking the Caribbean is not cheap. Flights are quite expensive, and if you stay on the tourist circuit you will find yourself paying prices not unlike those in Europe or the USA. If you get off the tourist track and stay in local West Indian guest houses in town and eat local food, you will pay considerably less in most islands. All the same, do not expect to stay anywhere for much less than US$20.

A few Caribbean countries have their own currency, but many of the smaller islands share a denomination, often according to the past colonial set-up. The US dollar, however, is the currency in universal demand around the area and so many countries have pegged their currency to it. At the moment the greenback is permitted to circulate more or less freely in all the islands and so there is not much of a black market.

Prices in the tourist industry throughout the Caribbean are also quoted in or fixed to US dollars and it is even possible in places to spend a couple of weeks working exclusively in that currency (in tourist hotels and their watersports concessions, restaurants and shops). However, if you go off the beaten track, it is a good idea to have local notes and change. It is also sensible to take small denominations.

Hustling is fairly widespread in the Caribbean. All visitors are presumed to have a few dollars that they would not mind releasing (they could afford the airfare after all) and some islands have a band of opportunists who will try to persuade you to do so in return for a variety of services, anything from an errand to collect a box full of different fruits from the local market to drugs, or just as a gift. You are vulnerable particularly in the first 48 hours or until you have a bit of colour. It varies from island to island, but in some islands you can expect to be accosted if you go to the downtown area and on any public beach. A firm and polite no to whatever is offered is the easiest way to guarantee your peace.

Official Currencies

You will need to check the exchange rates before you travel, as those not listed as fixed can alter on the exchange:

Barbados—Barbados dollar, fixed to US dollar (US$1 = BDS$1.98), US currency also accepted.

Windward Islands (the former British islands of Grenada, St Vincent and the Grenadines, St Lucia, Dominica)—the Eastern Caribbean dollar, fixed to US dollar (US$1 = EC$2.65), US currency also accepted.

French Caribbean (French Antilles—Martinique, Guadeloupe, also St Martin, St Barthélémy)—French franc, (US$1 = Fr5.5 approx), US dollar also accepted in tourist areas.

Exchange

The banks give the best rate of exchange. At hotels you will usually receive a lower rate. The exchanges in most islands will accept hard currency **traveller's cheques**—sterling, French franc, Deutschmark and Canadian dollar, though the most popular is the US dollar, especially if you are going to a country where the dollar is an acceptable alternative currency. You will also get a better exchange rate. Some banks are beginning to charge for the exchange of traveller's cheques, however. Take some small denomination cheques and remember to record the number so you can be refunded if you lose them. Generally, banking is quite sophisticated in most islands, but service is often slow. **Credit cards** are widely accepted for anything connected with the tourist industry—in hotels, restaurants and tourist shops. If you need to, you can draw cash on a credit card at the bank—there are AMEX and VISA representatives on all the islands. **Personal cheques** are rarely accepted. Service charges are usually 10%, unless otherwise indicated.

Packing

With such pleasant weather and such an informal air in the Caribbean, you can take a minimalist approach to packing. There are just a couple of restaurants and hotel dining rooms in the whole area which require even a jacket and a tie for men (though most do like trousers and a shirt with a collar). Daytime wear is a skirt or shorts and a light shirt, evening wear about the same, perhaps a longer skirt or trousers. Jeans are too warm in the summer months, so you might consider taking cotton trousers. Also pack a sunhat, sunglasses, suncream and a swimsuit (though they can be bought on arrival).

Photography

You will find that many West Indians either dive for cover or start remonstrating violently at the very sight of a camera. Some will talk about you stealing their soul and others about the money you will have to pay. If you see a good shot and go for it, you can usually talk your way out of trouble, but if you stop and chat first then most people will allow you to photograph them.

In the middle of the day, the brightness of the Caribbean sun bleaches all colour out of the landscape except the strongest tropical shades, but as the afternoon draws in you will find a stunning depth of colour in the reds, golds and greens. The plants of the Caribbean are bright and colourful and particularly good after rain.

Film is very expensive in the islands and the heat can be a problem too (you might put it in the hotel fridge). The officials will swear that no damage will be done by the X-ray machines at the airports, and this is usually true, but you may prefer that it goes through in an X-ray proof bag, or is searched by hand.

Post Offices

Post can take anything from 2 days to 3 months to get from the Caribbean to Europe or North America. Don't depend on it. You probably have no need to go anywhere near a post office anyway because hotels usually have postcards and stamps and once you have written them they are happy to post them for you. Opening hours vary from island to island.

Shopping

Shopping is one of the Caribbean's biggest industries, but hardly any of the things that are sold here originate in the area. There are objects of cultural value to be found, particularly in the larger islands, but most of it is shipped in to satisfy the collector passions of long-distance shoppers (some of whom take the same cruise year after year to take advantage of preferential customs allowances). On the shelves of all the air-conditioned boutiques and the newer shopping malls that have begun to infest the area you can find jewels and precious stones, perfumes, photographic equipment, clothes, Cuban cigars, etc.

The islands follow roughly speaking the historical patterns of their nation, with the French the leaders in perfumes and designer clothes and the Dutch, always great traders, with well-priced photographic equipment from the Far East. The lure is, of course, the reduced prices (in comparison to the mainland) and every shop announces itself as 'duty-free' or 'in-bond'.

There is quite an active art scene now in many of the islands: galleries exhibiting work by local and expatriate artists are mentioned in the text.

Sports

Diving

The Caribbean and the Bahamas have some superb corals and fish, the best in the Western hemisphere. The variety is stunning; from the world's third-largest barrier reef just a few miles off the coast of Andros in the Bahamas, warm and cool water springs under the sea off the volcanic islands.

The reefs are incredibly colourful. You will see yellow and pink tube sponges and purple trumpet sponges, sea feathers and seafans (gorgonians) that stand against the current alongside a forest of staghorn, elkhorn and black coral and the more exotic species like the domes of startlingly white brain coral, star corals and yellow pencil coral. Near the surface the corals are multicoloured and tightly bunched as they compete for space; as you descend, the yellows and the reds and whites fade, leaving the purples and blues of the larger corals that catch the last of the sunlight at depth (until you shine a light and see them in their full glory).

Many islands have laws to protect their reefs and their fish (there are hardly any places left in the Caribbean where you are allowed to use spearguns). In certain islands you are asked not to buy coral jewellery because it will probably have been taken illegally from the reef. One of the few dangerous things on the reef are fire corals, which will give you a nasty sting if you touch one. Do not annoy Moray eels and watch out for sea urchins.

Other underwater life includes a stunning array of crustaceans and of course tropical fish. On the bottom you will find beautifully camouflaged crabs that stare at you goggle-eyed, starfish, lobsters, sea anemones and pretty pink and white featherduster worms. Around them swim angelfish, squirrelfish, surgeonfish, striped sergeant majors, grunts and soldierfish. Above them little shoals of wrasses and blue tang shimmy in the bubbles. If you get too close, puffer fish blow themselves up like a spiky football, smiling uncomfortably. And beware the poisonous stonefish. If you hear of lobsters migrating (as many as a hundred following one another in a line across the sea bed), then make sure to go out and look.

At night a whole new seascape opens up as some corals close up for the night and others open up in an array of different colours. While some fish tuck themselves into a crevice in the reef to sleep (eyes kept open or in a sort of sleeping-bag of mucus so that they cannot be detected by their scent), starfish, lobsters and sea urchins scuttle around the seabed on the hunt for food. If you stop breathing for a moment, you will hear the midnight parrotfish crunching on the coral polyps, spitting out the broken-down fragments of reef that eventually turn into sand.

In the southeastern Caribbean the best diving is in Dominica, followed by the Grenadine Islands. All the islands have facilities for scuba dives. Most dive-shops in the Caribbean are affiliated to PADI (many also to NAUI) and they will expect you to present a certificate of competence if you wish to go out on to the reefs straight away, but all islands except the smallest have lessons available in the resorts if you are a novice. An open-water qualifying course (which allows you to dive in a pair with another qualified open-water diver) takes about a week, but with a resort course you can usually get underwater in a morning. You will have a session in the swimming-pool before you are allowed to dive with an instructor in the open sea. The **snorkelling** is also good off many of the islands and most hotels have equipment for their guests and on hire to non-residents. Beware, if you go snorkelling on a sunny day soon after you arrive, because the water and the sun make a fearsome

Sports

combination on unprotected skin (wear a shirt, perhaps). In most places you can arrange glass-bottom boat tours and snorkelling trips. For those who would like to see the deeper corals, but who do not dive, there is a submarine in Barbados.

Fishing

A sport that is traditionally renowned in the Gulf Stream (between Key West and Havana, and between Florida and the Bahamas), but which is now possible in all islands is **deep-sea** or **big game fishing**. Docked at the yachting marina, the deep-sea boats are huge, gleaming cruisers, slightly top-heavy because of their tall spotting towers, usually equipped with tackle and bait and 'fighting chair'. Beer in hand, you trawl the line behind the boat, waiting for a bite and then watch the beast surface and fight as you cruise along, giving line and steadily hauling it in.

The magnificent creatures that you are out to kill are fish such as the blue marlin, which inhabits the deepest waters and can weigh anything up to 1100lb and measure 10ft in length. Giant or bluefin tuna can weigh up to 1000lb. Wahoo, around 100lb, is a racer and a fighter and the white marlin can weigh up to 150lb. Perhaps the most beautiful of them all is the sailfish, with a huge spiny fan on its back, which will jump clean out of the water and 'tail' (literally stand upright on its tail) in its attempts to get free. Smaller fish include blackfin and allison tuna, bonito, dorado and barracuda. The best known areas are the ports off the Gulf Stream, on Bimini, and around Havana (though things are quieter there now), but you can easily charter a boat from most islands. The most famous fishing story is *The Old Man and The Sea* by Ernest Hemingway, set in a small fishing village east of Havana. There is another excellent description in Hemingway's *Islands in the Stream*.

Sailing

For practical information and advice *see* **A Sailing Guide**, p.35.

Windsurfing

Because of the warmth and the constant winds off the Atlantic Ocean, the Caribbean offers superb windsurfing, particularly when the winds are at their highest in the early months of the year. The sport is well developed—a number of championship competitions have been held in the Caribbean—and you can hire a board on any island. Instruction is usually available. The best places to go are the southern tip of Barbados, and the Atlantic coasts of Martinique and Guadeloupe (*see* separate island sections).

Miscellaneous Watersports

On the smaller islands there is usually at least one beach where you will find all the **watersports**: anything from a windsurfer and a few minutes on waterskis to a parasail flight, a trip on a pedalo or a high-speed trip around the bay on an inflated sausage (it'll keep the kids quiet anyway). Glass-bottom boat tours are usually available and in most hotels you are able to hire small sailboats such as hobie cats and sunfish. Jetskis (standing up) and wetbikes (sitting) have made their mark in the West Indies and are available for hire at most major centres (though some islands have banned them recently) and a recent arrival are kayaks, which are good for reaching remoter snorkelling areas around a rocky coastline. Hotels set on their own beach will invariably have a selection of watersports, though not usually as complete as above. Prices vary considerably across the Caribbean. Most things can be booked through the hotels or their beach concessionaires. Rum cruises and sunset tours aboard a resurrected galleon complete with boozatorium and lots of walking the plank are available on the larger and more touristed islands.

The mountainous islands of the Caribbean literally create rain as the water-filled Atlantic winds race over them. They have rivers worthy of continents and all over the islands you will find waterfalls and rockpools that make for excellent **river bathing**. There is a problem in some islands including St Lucia with bilharzia (in lakes and slow-flowing rivers) so you are not advised to swim there, but the other Windwards are clear. In some islands you can also take a **canoe** trip on the larger rivers.

Other Sports

Sports based on land include **tennis**, which is well served all over the Caribbean. There are courts in many of the hotels and in island clubs. There are occasional pro-am competitions. If there is no court at your hotel, arrange with another through the front desk, or simply wander in and ask. Hotels generally charge a small fee and they usually have racquets and balls for hire. **Riding** is also offered on the majority of the islands and this is a good way to see the rainforest and the sugar flats if you think that your calves might not be up to the hike.

On the larger islands and those with a developed tourist industry there are **golf** courses open to visitors on payment of a green fee (except in some hotels where it is included in the package). If you decide to play, be flexible because the courses will often give priority to hotel guests. Most courses have equipment for hire.

There is good **walking** in the Caribbean islands, which are cut and crossed with traditional trails originally used by the likes of the *porteuses* (*see* **Martinique,** p.194) and the farmers of today. The rainforest is fascinating to walk in because the growth is so incredibly lush. Many of the eastern Caribbean islands have an active volcano in whose crater you can climb—or you could make the walk to the boiling lake in Dominica's Valley of Desolation.

The heat will be most bearable between dawn, usually at around 6am, and 10am, before the sun gets too high and then between 4pm and dusk. However, the higher you go, the cooler it gets, and the temperature in the forest is not bad anyway. It gets dark quickly in the Caribbean, so be careful to be back by 6pm otherwise you may find yourself stranded, at the mercy of such fearsome spirits of the Caribbean night as the *Soucouyant* and *La Diablesse*. It often rains, of course, so take a waterproof coat and high up in the hills you will need a jersey underneath because the winds can make it cold. Big heavy boots are not necessary. Gym-shoes or sneakers are usually enough, unless you are headed into very steep and slippery country, when you should have some ankle support—perhaps a pair of light tropical boots. There are tour companies on all the larger islands who will transport you to and from your hotel and provide a guide.

Telephones

Communications in the Caribbean are quite good. Many hotel rooms are fitted with direct dial phones as standard, though in both the less developed and the larger countries getting through can be a bit haphazard. Public phones are not that dependable, but there are usually booths at the marinas and in the towns. Calls seem to cost a quarter in almost every Caribbean currency and many islands have a system of phonecards. The former British islands and remaining British Crown colonies have an extensive network run mainly by Cable and Wireless (with the advantage that a cardphone bought in an EC$ country can be used all the way along the chain between Grenada and the BVI). There are no coin phones on the French islands, where you will need a *télécarte*, which is also valid on all other French islands. If you are having trouble placing a call you can always wander into the nearest hotel, where they will help you out for a fee.

Time Zones

Apart from Club Med enclaves (which have their own time schedule for some reason), the whole of the eastern Caribbean (Barbados up to the Virgin Islands) and Puerto Rico and the Dominican Republic are 4 hours behind GMT.

'Caribbean Time' is an expression you will hear all over the islands and it refers to the West Indians' elastic and entirely unpredictable schedules. Businesses can be punctual, but in restaurants and shops they will have little sympathy with a slave to the second hand. The Jamaicans say 'soon come', which means any time from now to tomorrow.

Tourist Information

There is usually a tourist information office at the airport, which will be happy to help out with accommodation, directions and pertinent local advice and gossip. You will also find an information office in main towns and on larger islands there will be tourist offices in the major tourist spots. For those who want more detail there is usually an information department in the Department of Tourism. If you cannot find a tourist office, do not be reticent about asking information or directions of a West Indian because they will almost always go out of their way to help. All the Caribbean islands publish some sort of tourism magazine to help with orientation when you arrive on island. These usually include lists of accommodation, restaurants and shops (listed even-handedly without selection or recommendation) and some feature articles. Tourist boards often put out leaflets about 'sights' of local interest and if you do visit a local museum there is usually printed material on sale.

Local Tourist Information Offices

Barbados: Harbour Rd, West Bridgetown, ℂ 427 2623, fax 426 4060.

Grenada: St George's Harbour, ℂ 440 2001, fax 440 6637.

St Vincent: Financial Complex, Bay St, Kingstown, ℂ 457 1502, fax 456 2610.

St Lucia: Point Seraphine Shopping Complex, Castries, PO Box 221, ℂ 452 4094, fax 453 1121.

Martinique: 26 rue Ernest Deproge, BP 520, 97206 Fort de France Cedex, ℂ 596 63 79 60, fax 73 66 93.

Dominica: Box 73, Roseau, Dominica, ℂ 448 2351, fax 448 5840; also the kiosk at Old Market Place on the waterfront.

Guadeloupe: Office Départementale, 5 square de la Banque, 97110 **Pointe-à-Pitre**, ℂ 590 82 09 30, fax 83 89 22.

Maison du Port, just off place de la Victoire, **Basse-Terre**, ℂ 81 24 83.

Avenue de l'Europe, **St François**, ℂ 88 48 74.

Where to Stay

The West Indies have some of the finest and most luxurious hotels in the world. You can stay at island resorts, on endless beaches which are deserted at dawn, in 18th-century plantation splendour, and in high-pastel luxury in the newest resorts. Many of the islands offer top-notch hotels, but try the Grenadines for isolated island settings, Barbados for grand and long-established hotels set in magnificent gardens, and St Lucia for some elegant retreats in magnificent, dramatic settings.

It is easy to imagine that you have arrived in some remote corner of paradise when you reach the Caribbean, but these hotels are businesses and operate under quite difficult circumstances. To get an idea of what goes on behind the scenes, make sure to read Herman Wouk's *Don't Stop the Carnival!* It is thirty years old, but still killingly accurate. It is hard to look a hotelier straight in the eye after reading it.

The ultimate Caribbean setting, perhaps a private beachfront cabin with a personal hammock hanging between two palm trees, can be found all over the area, but there are many other styles of Caribbean hotel. The most recent Caribbean hotels tend to be large, humming palaces with blocks of rooms decorated in a symphony of bright pastel colours. But you will find a grand variety of hotels in the islands.

Choosing Where to Stay

You are quite likely to select your holiday for the hotel, perhaps because of its reputation, or because of a deal on offer through the tour operator. It is worth asking around. Hotels are selected for this book on grounds of value (within their price category), but also for other reasons such as setting, service, friendliness and general management. Many of the big names in Caribbean hotels are included, but smaller, more off-beat places are included too. Hotels and guest houses are listed in the following six categories:

luxury	—	US$500 and above for a double per night
very expensive	—	US$300–500
expensive	—	US$150–300
moderate	—	US$75–150
cheap	—	US$30–75
very cheap	—	under US$30

In almost every Caribbean island the hotels will add an obligatory government tax (usually between 3% and 7%) and a service charge, usually 10%.

Note: All prices quoted in this book are for a double room in the peak winter season unless otherwise stated.

Plans and Seasons

MAP means Modified American Plan (with breakfast and dinner included in the price) and **EP** means European Plan (no meals). You may also come across **CP**, Continental Plan, with room and breakfast, and **FAP**, or Full American Plan, with a room and all meals. See also **all-inclusive**. The Caribbean high season is mid-December or January until mid-April and prices will be highest then. 'Off-season' travel will bring reductions of as much as 30% in some cases, making some of the idyllic places suddenly affordable. One serious problem with the Caribbean is that holidays invariably seem to revolve around the couple and so single travellers will often find themselves paying the same as a couple for a room. You can try bargaining, but it is unlikely to do any good.

All-inclusive Hotels

The all-inclusive hotel plan has become increasingly popular in recent years and has spread to most Caribbean islands now. As the name implies, the rate is all-inclusive, and once you have paid the initial bill you do not have to pull out your wallet again. It is easier to budget, but it may discourage you from leaving the hotel and exploring, or going out to try the restaurants for dinner. There is now quite a wide variety of standards and prices within the all-inclusives and some have gone upmarket, offering champagne and *à la carte* dining instead of the traditional buffet-style meals. Jamaica, Antigua and St Lucia have the most all-inclusive hotels and the Sandals chain has many resorts throughout the Caribbean; there are also all-inclusives that specialize in looking after children. Originally the concept was a Caribbean version of Club Med, with a permanently ongoing diet of sports and entertainment for those who wanted it. This has altered in some cases recently, with some hotels offering a straight all-inclusive plan (all meals and drinks paid for) and less of the activities. It is worth checking what facilities are included.

There is still a holiday-camp atmosphere about some all-inclusives, however, and their names often give a good indication of their theme—for example, Hedonism II or Couples (with the symbol of a pair of lions humping). These high-pressure fun factories seem to encourage riotous behaviour—with as much alcohol as you can drink, dancing on the tables, mirrors on the bedroom ceiling and crash courses in marriage. They are well worth a look, at least for a couple of days, after which you might suddenly feel like immersing yourself in a book.

Inns

Dotted sporadically around the Caribbean are some magnificent old gingerbread-style homes, often former plantation houses, that have been converted into inns, ideal for the independent traveller with a bit of cash. Usually they will offer a more personal style than the bigger hotels.

Villas, Apartments and Condominiums

In addition to the many hotels there are also **villas** all over the islands, most of them relatively modern and well equipped. You can cater for yourself, or arrange for a cook. Contact them through the individual island villa rentals organizations or the tourist boards. The Caribbean now copes reasonably well with self-catering or efficiency holidays and so there are a large number of **apartments** on all the islands, some built in one building like a hotel, others scattered in landscaped grounds. Finally, **condominiums** are also springing up in many islands, answering to those who wish to invest in their vacation.

Where to Stay

Guest Houses

These are the cheapest option and they are more fun, cheaper, and have far more character than bottom-of-the-range tourist hotels. They are usually presided over by an ample and generous mother figure (something of a West Indian institution, she has not changed much for about two hundred years, *see* **Barbados**, 'Where to Stay') and staying in them can be a good way to be introduced to local West Indian life in just a few days. In some you may notice a remarkable turnover of guests as these guest houses often rent rooms out by the hour as well as by the night.

In the major yachting centres you can sometimes persuade the yachties to give you a berth on the charter boats while they are in dock. Simply go down to the marina and ask around and you may come up with something.

Camping

Rules vary throughout the islands and although it is generally not encouraged, particularly on the beaches, there are camp sites on the larger islands (the French Antilles are quite well organized for camping). As a general rule, permission should be obtained from the police before camping, but you will probably get away with it.

Women

West Indian men are quite macho by nature, so visiting women can expect a fair amount of public attention—matador poses in the Latin islands, or in the British islands the *soots* (soups, tss!), a sort of sharp hiss between the teeth. Advances of this sort are usually laughed off or ignored by local women and visitors can do the same; they are often quite public and loud, but they are not usually persistent and are verbal rather than physical. There is quite a big thing going between local lads and visiting women in the Caribbean. West Indians are quite forthright about sex anyway. Male staff in some surprisingly smart hotels will make a pass at a single woman, or one whose man happens to be absent.

West Indian women are quite modest when it comes to showing their bodies in public. It is almost unknown except in the French islands for a West Indian to go topless on the beach (though they do often go naked when washing in rivers, so be careful when out walking). They expect foreigners to observe the same rules. They also expect women to wear more than a swimsuit when out and about or in town, so you might take a cotton wrap.

Sailing in the Eastern Caribbean	36
Planning Your Trip	36
Arrival	38
Life on Board	39
Sailing A–Z	40
Anchorages in the Islands	40
Immigration and Customs	41
Marinas and Chandleries	41

A Sailing Guide

Provisioning and Rubbish	41
Security	42
Telephones	42
Winds and Weather	42

Sailing in the Eastern Caribbean

With its many islands so close to one another, the eastern Caribbean has endless cruising grounds, some of the best in the world. Over the 500-mile length of the Lesser Antilles there are perhaps a hundred or so islands and cays, some highly developed, with busy marinas and strings of waterfront restaurants, others no more than isolated sand-spits with a just a few palm trees and a rickety shack of a bar.

At moments, as you cruise under full sail, you can be completely surrounded by islands, crouched on the horizon like animals ready to pounce. As you carve through the water, dolphins dance at your prow, and at night, in certain places, you will leave a trail of phosphorescence in your wake. You can coast the massive volcanic Windwards where headlands and inlets gradually glide by, until you find your cove and anchorage for the night, then buy your supper from local fishermen, or you can head for an isolated bay, drop anchor and listen for the noise of a party from a nearby beach bar.

For many, sailing off into the sunset is a lifetime's dream. It restores a sense of independence and self-reliance lost in the hectic business of modern life. For some it is escapism in its finest form: your most important decisions revolve around what to have for dinner and when to up-anchor and move on to another harbour. But the Caribbean is not only for the world's seaborne gypsies. Caribbean sailing is relatively easy and forgiving, particularly if you have cut your teeth in the cold northern hemisphere. Caribbean winds are fairly constant, gentle and reliable (there is the great advantage that the trade winds blow perpendicular to the chain of islands) and you can usually expect to put up a full configuration of sails without the yacht becoming unmanageable. A fully provisioned yacht can be waiting on your arrival and you can sail as much or as little as you want. You don't even have to put up a sail if you don't want to (just switch on the motor).

With dependable sun and warmth and a magnificently beautiful setting, an island-hopping trip on a yacht can offer the best of the Caribbean to many travellers. Fly-in visitors who stay on land will rhapsodize about their time in the islands, but as far as sailors are concerned they simply have no idea what the Caribbean is about.

Planning Your Trip

There is a huge variety of yachts on offer in the Caribbean: sailing yachts can vary from compact fibreglass 30-footers for two, through to custom-built wooden craft contructed to a classic design. And then there are motor cruisers, gleaming white with four-storey superstructures, golf-ball radar navigation and onboard Renoirs and clay-pigeon traps.

A Sailing Guide

With regard to hire, essentially there are two options: bare-boats and crewed yachts. If you take a **bare-boat** then you basically look after yourself, though the charter company will help with briefing and provisioning in advance, and often will support you in case of emergencies. **Crewed yachts** come with a skipper at least, often a cook as well, and you will be looked after during the trip. If you so require, you can be waited on by a whole retinue of flunkies all apparelled in neatly pressed white uniforms.

Bare-boats

As a general rule, bare-boats can be booked direct through the established companies (*see* below) and some of these have offices in the metropolitan countries. If not, you can go through a broker (*see* below). Some companies will allow you to take a yacht from one island and leave it at the next.

Worldwide Charter Companies with Caribbean Fleets

The Moorings: in the UK, 188 Northdown Road, Cliftonville, Kent CT9 2QN (✆ 0843 227140, fax 0843 228784); **in the USA**, 19345 US 19 North, Suite 402, Clearwater, Florida 34624-3193 (✆ 800 535 72 89, fax 813 530 97 47); **in France**, 20 rue des Pyramides, 75001 Paris (✆ 42 61 66 77, fax 42 97 43 58); **in Germany**, Kaiser Ludwig Strasse 17, D-82027 Gruenwald (✆ 89 64 15 90, fax 89 64 15 917).

Sunsail: in the UK, The Port House, Port Solent, Portsmouth, Hampshire PO6 4TH (✆ 0705 210345, fax 0705 219827); **in the USA**, 115 E. Broward Blvd, Fort Lauderdale FL33301 (✆ 305 524 7553, fax 305 524 6312; **in France**, 3, rue de Paradis, 75010 Paris (✆ 44 79 01 10, fax 42 46 39 90).

Crewed Yachts

For crewed yachts a system has developed in which you contact a broker in your own country; they in turn contact a management company in the islands which has a number of yachts on their books and will make the arrangements at that end. In this case, it is usually up to you to arrange your own flights and transfers, though of course the crew will look after everything once you have arrived at the yacht. If you are taking a skippered yacht it is worth making sure that you have a suitable crew (there are husband-and-wife teams who would prefer a family to a crowd of rowdy lads on a stag-week). Of course the skipper of a crewed yacht is usually happy to pick you up and drop you wherever you wish.

Brokers in the UK

Yacht Connections, The Hames, Church Road, South Ascot, Berks SL5 9DP (✆ 0344 24987, fax 0344 26849).

Tenrag, Bramling House, Bramling, New Canterbury, Kent CT3 1NB (℡ 0227 721874, fax 0227 721617).

Camper and Nicholsons, 25 Brixton Street, London W1X 7DB (℡ 071 491 2950, fax 071 629 2068). A company that specialises in a large selection of luxurious yachts for those who would prefer a motor vessel (gin palace).

Brokers in the USA

Yacht Connections, PO Box 3160, Coos Bay, Oregon 97420 (℡ 503 888 4482, fax 503 888 5582), toll free 800 238 6912.

Interpack, 1050 Anchorage Lane, San Diego, California 92106, (℡ 619 222 0327, fax 619 222 0326).

Whitney Yacht Charters, 4065 Crockers Lake Blvd, 2722 Sarasota, Florida 34238, (℡ 813 927 0108, fax 813 9227819, toll free 800 223 1426).

Camper and Nicholsons, 450 Royal Palm Way, Palm Beach, Florida 33480 (℡ 407 655 2121, fax 407 655 2202).

Some of the big Caribbean tour operators (who usually offer hotel-based holidays) will arrange a week aboard and a week ashore packages. *See* the listing in **Travel**, p.5). There are also a number of hotels around the Caribbean with a yacht on call which you can take in exchange for nights ashore. Finally you might also consider a holiday on one of the Caribbean's many tall ships—classic-style four-masted sailing yachts done up in 20th-century comfort. They work like cruise ships except that they take 50–150 passengers and so are more personal (you can even operate the computerized sails). Contact **Windstar Cruises** (℡ 071 628 7711) and the **Windjammer Company** (℡ 0272 272273).

Arrival

If you are chartering a bare-boat, the charter company will brief you on the area. This will include a recommended itinerary (according to whether you are looking for isolation or a lively, bar-hopping trip); the best places to stay overnight; good spots for swimming and snorkelling; recommended bars and restaurants; and the best bets for an isolated beach. You can arrange to have your yacht provisioned (packed with food and drink) in advance of your arrival.

You will also be asked to prove that you can sail. At least one person within the group should be an experienced sailor who understands navigation. This is particularly important in the Windward Islands, where the sailing is more complex and the distances between anchorages greater.

Life on board a yacht can be quite intimate. If you don't know your fellow travellers well already, by the end of a week on board together you certainly will. It is worth choosing the other members of the charter with a certain care. Perhaps those with a certain easy-going tolerance and general self-reliance are the best bet.

Life on Board

Of course yachts are very compact. It seems admirable somehow that all the requisites for cooking and washing-up can fit into an average galley a tiny fraction of the size of a normal kitchen, all carefully designed so that they work just as well when the yacht is bounding along at a tilt of 45 degrees.

Usually the hatchway leads straight down into the saloon or main cabin and galley (kitchen), and this is the main living area. Because of the Caribbean heat and the American influence, there tend to be huge coolers (fridges) on even the smallest yachts. Many yachts will have a small library and some have videos (there are video stores on most islands). Cabins tend to be small. They can also be quite hot (though most are fitted with fans, and are designed to benefit from any breeze). A good alternative is to sleep up on deck (though you might easily be woken by a rainshower in the cool of the early morning). Bathrooms are also tiny, and fresh water becomes a precious commodity; the water for washing and drinking has to be piped aboard, so yachtsmen are usually manic about not wasting it.

Most on-board life takes place on deck. The cockpit is ideally suited for general sitting about, or waiting until the sun goes over the yardarm (if you know which bit that is). There is usually a sunshade and a fold-away table so that you can eat there. Otherwise, there is deck space where you can sunbathe and generally lounge around. A word of warning: with little shelter and strong tropical sun reflected off the sea, and the many white surfaces, you can be seriously burned in a short time. When you feel like cooling off, just slither over the side. Most yachts have snorkelling gear and some of the larger yachts also carry a windsurfer.

The VHF radio is a novel addition to life on a sailing holiday. As well being useful for emergencies, it can be used for co-ordinating beach picnics and chatting to friends. You may even find yourself using it to order dinner in advance at the local beach restaurant: 'Marina Cay, this is Amberjack; that'll be two lobsters in lime butter, a creole shrimp and a kingfish, please; eight o'clock OK? Over.' 'Marina Cay, copy that, dinner at eight, over and out.' Frequencies vary from island to island, but there is usually an open channel (often VHF 16 or 68) on which people make contact. Then they switch to a different channel to have their conversation. Taxi-drivers and shopkeepers will also listen out on these frequencies. Another novelty for those who generally live in a house is the yacht's dinghy, usually an inflatable with an outboard motor attached, used to take you to the nearby snorkelling spot or beach or out to dinner in the evening.

Life on Board

Days tend to start quite slowly. Yachts begin to scatter from the night's anchorage in the late morning (if passengers can bear the idea of any activity in the heat), making their way to a lunchtime stop on a beach or at a snorkelling area. Many don't move at all until the late afternoon, heading off to a new anchorage by dusk. (Beware, though: in the busier areas in high season you will find that the more popular anchorages fill up quite early in the day.) However, if you are sailing into a difficult anchorage it is a good idea to have the sun overhead as it will enable you to read the reefs more easily.

Evenings can be lively, and in the Virgin Islands particularly you will find that you come across the same crowd as you move from anchorage to anchorage. There is a certain feeling of camaraderie among yacht-borne travellers and many of the bars are run by sailors, who are usually sympathetic to visitors. If there is a good crowd then it can get very active and noisy. In some bars jam sessions will materialise spontaneously as the night's drinkers pick up any instrument lying around and start to play. However, if you are not feeling up to making whoopee you can always stay on board, where you will be left alone. A yacht is a person's castle.

Sailing A–Z

Anchorages in the Islands

There is a good variety of sailing in the eastern Caribbean. As a very general rule it is easiest in the Virgin Islands and becomes more demanding as you head further south through the Leeward Islands down to the Windwards, where the distances between the island are greater and you are more exposed. The northerly islands are also more developed: there are more restaurants, marinas and general facilities like chandleries and boatyards in the Virgin Islands and in Sint Maarten and Antigua than in the Windward Islands. The French islands are highly developed.

The **Virgin Islands** serve their sailors well. Anchorages are close together, usually not more than a couple of hours' sailing from each other, and there are few reefs (except around Anegada, where many companies ask you not to go). And in many of the anchorages there are beach bars, which provide nightly entertainment as you move from bar to bar; there is even a sort of circuit in high season. Though the Virgin Islands can become quite crowded in winter, there are still plenty of isolated anchorages where you can expect to be alone.

Sint Maarten/Saint Martin is also a very popular centre. It is the hub of the Leeward Islands and acts as a convenient stopover for yachts travelling further south. There are plenty of marinas and restaurants, and excellent repair facilities. From here it is easy to make short trips to Anguilla and St Barts.

Antigua is another centre, with excellent all-round sailing, secluded anchorages off the beaches and the island of the northeast, as well as a lively shoreside life, particularly around Race Week in April. The great gathering point is English Harbour in the southeast.

Guadeloupe has excellent variety in its combination of volcanic and the coral-based land, and also because of its offshore islands Marie Galante and the Saints. Both Guadeloupe and **Martinique** are similarly developed, with good facilities and excellent provisioning.

Further south, **St Lucia** has a steadily growing reputation for sailing, particularly as a starting point for the Grenadines.

The **Grenadines** are another classic sailing centre. The many islands are close to one another and have excellent beaches and coves. They have a slightly raw, more West Indian quality about them than the Virgin Islands, with more accessible local life as well as pretty tourist spots.

Immigration and Customs

You are required to clear with immigration on arrival, and sometimes again on departure from each island (or country in certain cases like the Virgin Islands and the Grenadines). It may not be vital to complete the formalities first thing, but check with official publications or with other sailors. Outside office hours you may have to pay an overtime fee for registration; you can also usually expect to pay a departure tax when you leave. In some islands a cruising fee is charged.

Ports of entry are mentioned in the separate island chapters. Customs procedures are less formal, and are usually located along with immigration.

Marinas and Chandleries

Facilities vary considerably across the islands and they are generally more comprehensive in the islands mentioned above as sailing 'centres'. The smallest islands may not have a marina, but there is usually a place where you can get the most important sailing requisites like fuel, water and ice. Most marinas have a laundry, postal facilities and showers; where there is no marina, there is usually a hotel which will help out. Some smaller islands may have a chandlery, but don't count on it. When it comes to technical work on your yacht, you will be dependent on the main centres: Antigua, Guadeloupe, Martinique, St Lucia, St Thomas in the USVI, Tortola in the BVI, and Sint Maarten/St Martin.

Provisioning and Rubbish

In all the major centres there is a supermarket within walking distance of the dock, usually strategically positioned to catch sailors. They will also have ice for sale. In less developed islands you will have to go to the local supermarket or to the market, though you can get water at most docks. There are usually video stores on shore too, and some marinas have cable TV on-line. It is worth asking around because fishermen may well be happy to sell you fish they have caught. In some of the islands (mostly the Windwards) you will be approached by lads who will offer to fetch food from the market and to act as general fixer for you. If you decide to use them, it is best to choose just one and stick with him.

Rubbish should be bagged and sealed and then dropped at a marina. Biodegradeable items can be thrown overboard, but never any plastic items; these have caused problems with the fishlife around the islands.

Security

This is generally not a problem, but it is sensible to take the few simple precautions. Lock your yacht if you leave it alone and go ashore. Also lock your dinghy to the dock and the outboard motor to the dinghy. You can usually arrange for someone to watch over it for you.

Telephones

There will often be a telephone in the marina. Details of telephones are given in the 'Tourist Information' sections of the separate island chapters.

Winds and Weather

The **trade winds** (*Alizés* in French and *Passaatwinden* in Dutch) are well known with land-based Caribbean travellers for taking the edge off the tropical heat, but for sailors they provide the perfect means to make their way around the islands. They are equatorial winds, northeasterlies and easterlies, and they blow fairly reliably across the year at between 10 and 25 knots. They vary in strength a little, at their strongest over the winter and gentler in August and September, and in direction: in winter they are northeasterly, but with the tilting of the earth they verge towards southeasterlies over the summer. Sometimes the winds are a little fluky around dusk, when there are offshore breezes as the islands cool down.

The weather in the islands is also pretty benign, though over the winter the occasional swell will be set off by the weather systems in the north, making the sea uncomfortable in certain anchorages. Westerly winds are very unusual.

The other major consideration is the hurricane season (July to September). There is usually ample warning over the radio as well as on the grapevine. You are advised to head for a 'hurricane hole', as the most protected harbours have become known, or an area of mangroves.

Caribbean Indians	44
Columbus	45
The English-speaking Caribbean and its Culture	46
French Caribbean Culture	47
'The Muse of Wise Men'	49
Music	50
The Volcanic Origins of the Islands	51

Topics

Caribbean Indians

Virtually no indigenous Caribbean Indians survive today, but when the Europeans first arrived in the New World there were two principal races of Amerindians living in the islands. In the north were the tribes of the Arawaks, spread over the Greater Antilles and the Bahamas, and to the south the islands of the eastern Caribbean were inhabited by the Carib Indians, who had worked their way up along the chain of the Lesser Antilles from South America as far as the Leeward Islands.

The Amerindians are thought to have made their way over from Asia to the American continent about 40,000 years ago, fanning out into different areas to become Inuit, the North American Indians and the settled tribes of South America. A few hundred years BC, the Arawaks (from South America's coastal area) started to island-hop along the Lesser Antilles, settling the Windwards and the Leewards, and eventually the Greater Antilles. The Arawaks were to live in peace for a thousand years or so, until the Caribs, a belligerent tribe who originated in the Amazon jungle, started to follow them up the chain and force them out. When Columbus arrived, the Caribs had got as far as the northernmost of the Lesser Antilles and were just starting to make raids on Puerto Rico. If the Spaniards had not arrived and set about killing the Arawaks, the Caribs would probably have done so.

History has been pretty mean to the Caribs (the European powers had to justify their act of genocide), but these people were hardly philanthropic towards their fellow Indians or the Europeans. They were widely accused of being cannibals (for which there is in fact not really much evidence: the eating was probably more ceremonial than for nourishment). Their love for alcohol, however, was so great that they would have no qualms about killing the crew of a ship which might have brandy aboard. And they were a fearsome enemy—in their *piragua* canoes, which could hold as many as a hundred men, they could paddle as fast as a sailing ship.

The Caribs never harmed women, merely taking them to live with them, but for men they reserved a special ceremony—the barbecue. They would prepare the unfortunate captive by slitting his legs and back, stuffing the cuts with pimentoes and herbs before despatching him with a club and putting him on the spit. There was even reckoned to be a pecking order of tastiness among the Europeans. The French were regarded as the most delicate and tasty, followed by the English and Dutch, but Spaniards were so stringy as to be almost inedible (a rumour presumably put about by the Spaniards themselves). On land the men were expert hunters and excellent shots with bows and arrows. They astonished early visitors by the speed with which they fired arrow after arrow in succession. They would capture parrots by burning hot pepper beneath them until they suffocated and they could entrance an iguana out of its hole by whistling monotonously. Fish were shot or poisoned with dogwood bark and collected when they floated to the surface.

The Carib features were similar to those of other South American Indians and they were stocky. They painted their skin bright red and adorned themselves with parrot feathers and necklaces strung with the teeth of their victims. But their pride was their long blue-black hair which was oiled by the women after breakfast. While men fished and hunted, the women worked around the *carbet*, a round palm-thatch house and living area. They tended crops such as yucca (cassava) and sweet potato. Many of the women were Arawak captives and so they spoke a different language among themselves. The Caribs had a hazy conception of good and evil spirits in the world but were uninterested in religious matters. Missionaries gave up in the end—the Caribs got baptized just for the presents that they would receive.

Columbus

Columbus is famous as the discoverer of America. One Caribbean calypso singer objected that this view was Eurocentric arrogance, as American Indians clearly beat him to it by about 40,000 years. However, his voyages were to have an importance that changed the world. Certainly he gave the West Indies their name. He was sailing for the Indies via the west, trying to reopen the spice trade with the East recently cut off by the Arabs. Discovery of new lands was secondary.

Cristoforo Colombo (or Cristobal Colon in Spanish) was born in the 1450s in Genoa, son of a weaver, but he chose his career as a sailor while still a young man. Columbus was largely self-taught. He was obviously intelligent and forceful, but he was domineering in authority and this was his downfall; he was also inflexible and jumped to illogical geographical conclusions, deciding at one stage that the world was pear-shaped. All the same, he was a bold and accomplished explorer and a fine navigator. He was persuasive and even charismatic in court, impressing Queen Isabella so much that she helped him despite the advice of her courtiers.

If he was a visionary—and he stuck to his plan for years before he was granted the opportunity to carry it out—his dreams also tipped into self-delusion. He considered himself chosen by God to bring Christianity to the New World, and he was paranoid about others encroaching on what he considered his domain. He insisted on huge public honour as reward for his service to the Crown of Spain: he was granted the titles of 'Admiral of the Ocean Sea' and 'Viceroy of India'. But he fulfilled the dreams of the age. The world was outgrowing its Mediterranean confines and Columbus was a master mariner who was acquainted with all available maps. Slowly the plan evolved. He would try to reach the east by sailing west.

On 3 August 1492 Columbus set off from Palos, touching the Canaries and then navigating due west. He expected to come to Japan or China after about 2500 miles (about where America is). They sailed with the wind behind for over a month, through the Sargasso Sea, into the unknown. But steadily the crew became more rebellious (fearing they might not get home). On 12 October 1492, they sighted land, one of the Bahamian islands. Columbus called the island San Salvador in honour of the Saviour, but clearly he had not found Japan, so after a few days he set off in search of it. He touched Cuba and then his flagship was wrecked off Hispaniola and he was forced to leave about forty men behind when he sailed for Spain, where he announced that he had reached Asia. A second expedition was sent the same year, with 1500 settlers to colonize the island of Hispaniola. Administrative problems began almost at once and were compounded when Columbus left his brother Diego in charge during his exploration of Cuba and Jamaica.

Columbus led a third voyage in 1498, arriving in Trinidad, narrowly missing the continent of South America. From here he sailed to Hispaniola by dead reckoning, no mean feat. He found the colony in disarray and was forced to treat with the rebels. Eventually his viceregal authority was revoked and he was shipped back to Spain in chains. He was treated kindly by Ferdinand and Isabella and permitted to return to the New World on a fourth journey in 1502, on the express understanding that he was not to set foot on Hispaniola. In some ways his last trip was the most successful; however he was shipwrecked on the coast of Jamaica and had to wait a year before he was rescued and made it back to Spain.

Columbus died in Spain in 1506, faintly ridiculed because of all his problems in the Indies, his eccentric behaviour and his excessive claims against the Crown. Though his experience as a seaman had probably told him otherwise, he maintained to his death that he had arrived in the Far East.

The English-speaking Caribbean and its Culture

At times it seems hard to agree when a person says the former British Caribbean islands are just like England. The islands are lush and green, but the growth is distinctly tropical. Most of the islanders are clearly of African descent. But then you hear a clock chime, or a strain of West Country English that could only come from Bristol; there are teams of cricketers dressed in whites; the St John Ambulancemen, in their traditional uniform, stand slightly to one side at public events. There are even Barbadian women who wear socks in the tropical heat.

Three hundred years of association with Britain has left many British institutions and some deeply rooted ideals. The Westminster political model is used throughout the former British islands—the islands are divided into parishes—and the education and examination system is adopted from the British with O levels (now CXC) and A levels. Barbados was known as Little England for a while. People have even been known to queue there. Barbados and the Windwards all use English as their official language (even though the majority of people in St Lucia and Dominica use French *patois* as their daily tongue). When spoken, Windward Islands and

Barbados English is not that difficult to understand, though some raw versions of it are used in the bars; the most curious aspect, though, is the range of accents you hear within it. Barbados English really does sound as though it comes from the West Country (from where many of the early settlers came); there are places in Trinidad where you will hear strains of Welsh, and in the northern islands, in Anguilla, Saba and of course in Montserrat, you will hear distinct echoes of Irish.

But, as with all the Caribbean islands, things are never quite as they seem; the British influences have creolized into something new. The language, though recognisably English, has a wonderful West Indian lilt. And the islands have changed considerably over the last thirty years as they have taken their independence (when the time came, the British were happy to let the islands go and all the former colonies in the southeastern Caribbean became independent nations). The old British reserve and stuffiness has all but gone and the influence of the United States has grown ever stronger. Today's heroes are basketball players, not just cricketers.

The former British islands of the eastern Caribbean have a fairly typical history in that they were developed as sugar factories in the 18th century and then fell into a gradual decline in the 19th. As the plantations fell into disuse the islanders mostly became subsistence farmers, selling excess produce at market for other essentials, and for all the modernization with supermarkets, traditional markets are still a vibrant and important part of life.

In general terms the former British islands are still quite poor and undeveloped, depending mainly on bananas for export exchange and other small-scale agricultural industries such as nutmeg in Grenada; economically, small island life is not easy. The largest earner is tourism, which contributes vital foreign currency. There is a constant need for foreign exchange and a need to buy in almost everything regarded as requisite for a modern life—essentials like medicines and some foods, and desirable luxuries like white goods and cars.

Whereas the older generation has lived a tough farmer's existence attached to the land, the young people today are unwilling to follow this pattern. Many prefer to take their chances in town, and on an island like St Lucia, a large proportion of the population lives in the capital, Castries. However, the Windward Islanders—town and country folk—are generally welcoming and friendly and you will find that people say good morning and chat when they get on a bus. If you ever want to talk, you simply stop anyone you come across in the street.

French Caribbean Culture

French colonization was a more thorough-going affair than that of the British. Where British planters mostly hoped to 'return' to England with a fortune (many were West Indian born and bred, but still thought of England as home), the French installed themselves in the islands and made their lives there.

The familiar verve of the French is ever-present in the French Caribbean islands. Chic customers glide by shops filled with Christian Lacroix and Yves St Laurent, and lovers linger over a meal under coloured awnings while citizens play *boules* in the dusty town squares. In Fort de France, the capital of Martinique, there is even a Parisian haste, a *je m'en foutisme* untypical of the Caribbean. The illusion of being in France is only spiked by the bristle of palm trees and the variety of skin tones.

But for those who know France it is the departures from French culture, not these similarities, which are most fascinating: the steep rainforested slopes and the flatlands blanketed with sugar-cane or bananas, where the islanders walk at a relaxed and graceful pace; the rivers where the *blanchisseuses* have laid out washing on the rocks; the markets that are mercantile mayhem. Like all the Caribbean islands, the French Caribbean islands have developed their own unique creole culture. The air pulses to the sound of the relentless French Caribbean rhythm, zouk (as it did in times past to the famous rhythms, the béguine and the mazurka).

It is often said how beautiful the people of Martinique and Guadeloupe are. Though the French islands always had a slightly higher proportion of whites, the old settlers were clearly also less prudish about taking an African mistress and so the mix of racial strains is more thorough. It has created some striking faces; a hundred years ago the creole beauties of Martinique were renowned all over the Caribbean. These 'doudous' (from *douce chérie*) presented themselves with characteristic Gallic flair, bedecked in reams of brightly coloured cotton and yards of lace petticoat, with a foulard thrown over one shoulder. (You can still see the chequered madras material in the islands.) But the focal point of the outfit was the hat. This too was fashioned of bright silk material, often yellow and checked, and there was supposedly a code in its design—*tête à un bout* (one point): my heart is for the taking; *tête à deux bouts*: my heart is taken; *tête à trois bouts*: my heart is spoken for, but you can try your luck.

The official language of the islands is French, the language of the people is *créole*, that curious mix of French and African which has crystallized into a new language. Each of the Caribbean islands which has seen a French presence has a version of its own. You will hear it spoken in Dominica, St Lucia and occasionally Grenada, which the French have owned at one time or other, and even as far away as Trinidad, taken there by French Royalists fleeing the *patriotes* in revolutionary times. The eastern Caribbean *créoles* and the *kweyol* of the Haitians, once also French subjects, are not, however, mutually comprehensible.

Some of the leading figures of the French black consciousness and literary movement of the 1930s, the Négritude, were from Martinique. Etienne Lero and Aimé

Césaire, together with Léopold Senghor of Senegal, re-examined the position of the black man, formerly the slave, and his relation to the white man, the colonial master. Aimé Césaire became famous with his *Cahier d'un retour au pays natal* in 1939 and a later play *La Tragédie du roi Christophe*. He has only recently retired from Martiniquan politics after nearly fifty years as mayor of Fort de France.

More recent French Caribbean authors (most of whom write in French) worth looking out for include, from Martinique, Edouard Glissant, recent winner of the Prix Goncourt with *Texaco*, Aimé Césaire, Patrick Chamoiseau (*Solibo Magnifique*, which is set in Fort de France), Joseph Zobel (*Rue Cases-Nègres*), Rafaël Confiant (*Eau de café*, winner of the 1991 Prix Novembre), Boukman and Xavier Orville. Guadeloupean writers include Maryse Condé, whose finest book is probably *La Vie scélérate*, Simone Schwarz-Bart (known for her *Un Plat de porc aux bananes vertes* and *Ti Jean l'Horizon*), Max Jeanne and Daniel Maximin.

Politically, France has taken a radically different approach to the Caribbean from Britain. Instead of encouraging a gradual move to independence, France has embraced her islands, taking them into the *république* and giving them the status of overseas *départements*, equal to that of Savoie or Lot-et-Garonne. Martinique and Guadeloupe are *régions* in their own right, with the extra powers and responsibilities brought by decentralization in 1985. They are administered by a *préfet* appointed by the French government. Their people vote in French elections and they each send three deputies and two senators to the National Assembly in Paris. Milk costs the same as it does in the *métropole*, as continental France is called, and so does a car. There is National Service. Rumour has it that they even fly in croissants. In standard of living alone, the contrast with neighbouring islands is striking, and it could never be maintained without direct support from Paris.

There are some who envy the other islands their autonomy—independence movements have expressed themselves in graffiti campaigns and have occasionally erupted into violence, with bomb attacks—but most French Antilleans appreciate the benefits and would not change their situation, except to gain the maximum self-government while under the French umbrella.

'The Muse of Wise Men'

A familiar sight in the Windward Islands is the messy swathes of banana trees covering the whole valley floor, their leaves tousled and arched in irregular directions. Look closely and you may see them lashed together for support with a network of string, their dark green fruits, or 'hands', protected by blue plastic bags.

The banana is native to China and Malaya and had made its way to the Canary Islands by 1510. Its botanical name is *musa sapientum*, or 'the muse of wise men', and according to Indian legend sages would sit under the huge leaves for shade and savour the fruit. They had lost their popularity with Caribbean colonists by the start of the 19th century, when they were regarded as suspect because of their colour and shape: they were thought 'to excite urine and to provoke venery'. However, the banana became popular again and it has been an important export crop in the Windwards since the 1950s. The packing stations are everywhere and you will see farmers carrying the fruit downhill in time for the weekly visit of the Geest ships that make the 3-week round-trip from Europe. Boxes of Windward Islands bananas are a common sight in British markets.

There are many varieties of banana, the most widely known in Europe being the cavendish and the gros michel, both of which are large and yellow when ripe. Less known is the smaller, sweeter canary banana or rock fig (considered *l'amie de la poitrine* by Père Labat), which is about 4 inches long. But the sweetest of them all is the secret fig, which grows no longer than about 2 inches. There are unsweet varieties such as plantain, delicious when fried, and other starchy vegetables, the green fig and the fatter bluggo. Names vary from island to island.

In fact bananas do not grow on trees at all, but on a stem of unripe leaves packed closely like a cigar. As each new leaf forces its way up, it stands erect like a bright green scroll and gently unfurls, bending gracefully as it is superseded by another. When a plant bears fruit, it throws out a long trunk with a purple heart at the tip, which opens to reveal little black teeth in rows. These teeth are the end of the fruit, which swell until the bunches appear like so many fingers sticking up. A trunk produces one 'bunch' of bananas, which may have as many as ten 'hands' or 'finger rolls'. Each plant produces fruit only once, after which it dies and another shoot takes its place. The blue plastic bags protect the maturing bananas from the scratches of lizard claws, insects and birds. The 'Banana Boat Song', with its 'Day Oh!' chorus made famous in the fifties by Harry Belafonte, was originally sung by banana packers as they loaded the United Fruit Company ships in Jamaica.

> *'Come, Mr Tallyman, come tally me banana,*
> *Daylight come and me waan go home.'*

Music

People joke that the West Indians change the roll of their gait as they walk along the street, switching rhythm to each successive stereo system that they pass. Music has been central to Caribbean life since slave days when it was a principal form of recreation, and you will hear it everywhere, all day. At Carnival they dance for days.

There are almost as many beats as there are islands in the Caribbean and they go on changing and developing over time. The roots are audible in many cases—you will see marching bands dressed in their red tunics playing 'O, when the Saints' **reggae**-style, Indian flourishes appear in Trinidadian **calypso**, the Latin beat is so clear in Cuban and Puerto Rican **salsa** and the vocals of rap appear in calypso and Jamaican **dancehall**. But in all the Caribbean sounds the rhythm is relentlessly fast and the beat is as solid as the African drums from which it is derived.

The West Indians will use anything to make music. At carnival the crowds shuffle along to the sound of a couple of drums, a car wheel-rim, a cheese-grater and a cowbell. Even garden forks have been tuned up in Curaçao. But the best example of them all is the steel drum in Trinidad, which was invented in the yards of Port of Spain after the last war. Discarded biscuit tins and oil-drums were bashed out and then tuned up and an orchestra was created.

As you travel around the islands, you will see speakers set up in the street just for the hell of it. Cars practically bulge with the beat and they can often be heard before they can be seen coming along the road. If you are invited to a *fête*, go, because they are a wild side of West Indian life.

The rhythms of one island often spread to another. The main popular rhythms and their countries of origin are as follows:

Soca (soul-calypso)—Trinidad, where calypso itself started. Barbados and other islands nearby also produce their own calypsonians, some of them very good.

Zouk—Martinique and Guadeloupe, with a bustling double beat.

Salsa—two different sorts, one each from Cuba and Puerto Rico, the latter influenced by the 'Neo-Riceñans' (Puerto Ricans in New York).

Merengue—the Dominican Republic, also a strongly Latin sound. Another local rhythm, *bachata*, has recently been revived and become popular.

Compas—Haiti, a bit rougher, but not dissimilar to the zouk of the French Antilles, also echoes of West Africa.

Any of the Caribbean **carnivals** is worth attending if you happen to be on the island. You can often join in by asking around (usually for a small fee to cover the cost of the costume). It is worth crossing half the world to get to the **Trinidad Carnival**, which takes place at the beginning of Lent. Many Trinidadians do.

The Volcanic Origins of the Islands

The Lesser Antilles are made up of two distinct types of land. The islands are the partly submerged peaks of two mountain ranges which run more or less north to south; their lines are easily visible on the map. The islands of the inner chain, which runs from Grenada in the south to Saba in the north, are vast, in many cases active, volcanoes. They soar from the water to thousands of feet and they are immensely lush, covered in rainforest. The outer islands, which are lower and therefore less fertile, touch the volcanic chain at Guadeloupe and run north through Barbuda, St Barts, St Martin and Anguilla.

The volcanic islands have sprouted at the fault line of the Caribbean and Atlantic tectonic plates. As the Atlantic crust gradually forces its way under the Caribbean plate, lava escapes from the magma beneath and explodes through the volcanoes. Though the eruptions have calmed down somewhat over the last few million years, the main soufrières do blow about once a century and cause earthquakes that reverberate along the whole chain of the Lesser Antilles. On one day in 1867, weird happenings on Grenada in the far south, where the harbour water swelled and contracted as though the underworld were breathing, were echoed by seismic activity as far north as the Virgin Island of St Thomas.

Strictly speaking, the outer chain of islands is volcanic in origin as well. These volcanoes were active about a hundred million years ago (the inner chain is only about 15 million years old), when the rift between the tectonic plates was further east. Now the outer islands stand on a shelf under which the Atlantic plate has moved. Over the millions of years their old volcanic peaks have subsided and been repeatedly submerged in the sea and then exposed by the Ice Ages. As the water rose and receded around them they became encrusted with generations of coral growth, and this left them with a coral limestone cap.

Each one of the Windwards has its soufrière, a sulphurous volcanic vent, and if you go exploring you will be greeted by its smell ('*soufrière*' means sulphur, so it smells like a stink-bomb). The St Vincent volcano and those on nearby Martinique and Guadeloupe are the most violent, tending to blast out volumes of lava and superheated gases that collapse mountains and destroy anything in their path, as well as belching plumes of gas and a showers of pumice stones. On the other islands, including the northerly islands in the chain, things are a little less extreme. Here there are fumaroles which constantly vent, letting off pressure which might otherwise build up and cause an explosion. In the Grenadines there is an underwater volcano (Kick 'em Jenny), now quite close to the surface, whose activity has been spotted by pilots and yachtsmen passing over the area. Elsewhere, the release of gases underwater makes for interesting dive-sites.

An American seer has predicted that the 1990s are to be an active time for the Windward Islands. According to her, one island will appear during the decade—presumably Kick 'em Jenny—but, more worryingly, she has also predicted that another island will disappear.

History	56
Getting There and Around	60
Tourist Information	62
Beaches and Sports	63
Bridgetown	67
The West Coast	69
Scotland and St Lucy in the North	70
The Sugar Heartland	72
Suburbs and the South Coast	74
Where to Stay	76
Eating Out	79

Barbados

villa Nova

Barbados stands alone, out in the Atlantic, about 100 miles beyond the rest of the eastern Caribbean, a coral island with some of the finest golden sand beaches anywhere and perhaps the most agreeable climate in the West Indies. The island is long established as a winter getaway and has had a trusty following of wealthy visitors over the last fifty years.

'The whole place has an appearance of cleanliness, gentility and wealth which one does not find in any other island.' So thought Père Labat, a Dominican monk and roving gastronome who visited Barbados at the height of its prosperity in 1700. The spirit of his opinion still stands. Education, literacy and health care, the social services in general, are the best in the English-speaking Caribbean (with the present exception of the Cayman Islands) and the poor are better off in Barbados than in most of the neighbouring islands. Barbados commands a position of influence out of proportion to its size within the Caribbean. This is the source of the renowned Bajan (native Barbadian) self-esteem, and quite a bit of mockery from other islanders. Altogether, the national motto 'Pride and Industry' is quite appropriate for the Bajans.

Just 21 miles by 14, Barbados is occasionally dismissed as small, crowded and flat, but away from the built-up areas the cane-covered hinterland rises gently to 1000ft heights at Hackleton's cliff above the Atlantic. The island is quite populous, however; its 250,000 inhabitants make it the most densely inhabited in the area. Most Bajans live along the sheltered west coast of the island and in the massive extended suburb of the south coast that runs to the capital, Bridgetown. Just a few villages are tucked away inland. The Barbadians are over 90 per cent of African descent, but there are small communities of white Bajans (a visible and influential business community) and the 'poor whites', descendants of indentured servants who have scraped a living from the land for centuries. There are not that many Bajans of mixed race, and if the island has a problem it is the residue of a rigid system of colour prejudice.

Barbados's British heritage, which is stronger than in any other Caribbean island, once led the island to be called 'Little England' and even 'Bimshire'. The British influence is hardly strong now, but the 300-year connection has left a delightful and often old-fashioned charm in the manners, the buildings and even the language (you can

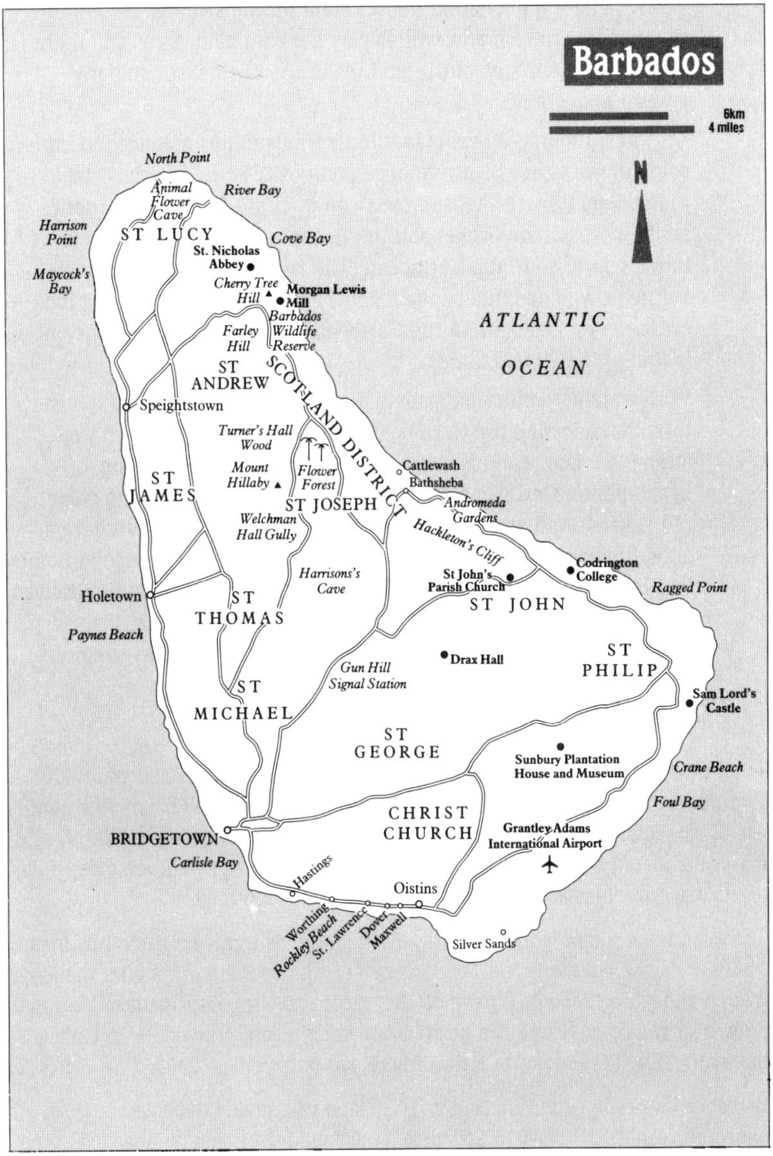
Barbados
6km
4 miles
N
North Point
Animal Flower Cave
River Bay
Harrison Point
ST LUCY
Cove Bay
St. Nicholas Abbey
Maycock's Bay
Cherry Tree Hill
Morgan Lewis Mill
Barbados Wildlife Reserve
Farley Hill
ATLANTIC OCEAN
ST ANDREW
SCOTLAND DISTRICT
Speightstown
Turner's Hall Wood
Mount Hillaby
Flower Forest
Cattlewash
Bathsheba
ST JAMES
ST JOSEPH
Andromeda Gardens
Welchman Hall Gully
Hackleton's Cliff
Codrington College
St John's Parish Church
Harrisons's Cave
Ragged Point
Holetown
ST THOMAS
ST JOHN
Paynes Beach
Drax Hall
ST PHILIP
Gun Hill Signal Station
ST MICHAEL
Sam Lord's Castle
ST GEORGE
Sunbury Plantation House and Museum
Crane Beach
Foul Bay
CHRIST CHURCH
Grantley Adams International Airport
BRIDGETOWN
Carlisle Bay
Hastings
Oistins
Worthing
Rockley Beach
St. Lawrence
Dover
Maxwell
Silver Sands

hear distinct traces of a West Country accent in Bajan speech). Classically beautiful plantation houses stand in the swathes of sugar-cane; cricketers in whites play beneath palm trees and there is even an isolated area of rugged hills in the northeast familiarly known as Scotland.

At times, though, it seems that Little England has managed to inherit some of the worst British foibles: pomposity and cliquish social attitudes. Functionaries will address you in clipped and hushed tones about a dress code (jacket and tie) in some clubs, which comes as a bit of a surprise in the Caribbean. The island's colonial legacy is fading now (since Independence in 1966) as it thrusts on and modernizes. As elsewhere in the Caribbean, the strongest influence now is that of the United States.

With a stable political climate and charming islanders used to visitors, Barbados is a top Caribbean destination. Guests return year after year. The island is fairly crowded, so if you are looking for beach-bound Caribbean seclusion this is hardly the place to come, but it has a well-organized tourist industry and it is easy to have a good holiday here. The famous west coast of Barbados, second home to a crowd of international sophisticates (people measure themselves by whether they arrived on Concorde or by First Class in the season), has given it the nickname 'the millionaires' playground'.

History

The history of Barbados is bound inextricably with that of England and with the fortunes of West Indian sugar. In an area where islands changed hands with almost every war, colonial Barbados had three hundred years of uninterrupted British rule. It was the first in the Caribbean to exploit sugar successfully, and even today many of the roads are lined each side with curtains of tall green cane.

The island was supposedly named by Portuguese visitors who passed by in the 1580s. They called the island *los Barbudos* or 'the bearded ones' after the long, matted and straggly shoots thrown off the upper branches of the banyan trees that grew near the coast. There had been native Amerindian settlements on Barbados, but by the time the Europeans arrived there was none left.

Barbados was claimed for England in 1625, and was settled two years later, in an expedition sent by Sir William Courteen. They found the island uninhabited except by some wild boars (left by early visitors as food for shipwrecked mariners). After wrangling and intrigue in the court of King Charles I, with the Earls of Pembroke and Carlisle in dispute over rights of colonization (and after a parallel armed battle on the island itself between the Windward and the Leeward men), the settlement flourished, assisted by a family of forty Arawaks from Guyana who demonstrated how to cultivate tropical plants.

The colony exploded, and within thirty years Barbados was overcrowded. Fortune-hunters flooded in; indentured servants put themselves in servitude for years with a promise of land at the end of their term. Refugees came from the Civil War in England; others were deported by the notorious Judge Jeffreys for their part in the Monmouth Rebellion and sold into slavery. To be Barbadosed was a recognized punishment in 17th-century England.

In an early piece of industrial espionage, the Dutch brought sugar-cane to Barbados from Brazil. They taught the Barbadians how yield could be increased by *ratooning*, in which the cane was planted not sticking out of the ground but laid flat and buried; and they introduced boiling techniques. At first the crop was used only for producing rum, but it soon became clear how profitable sugar was for export to Europe. By the 1650s the whole of Barbados was planted with cane, even to the exclusion of growing provisions—cultivating sugar was so profitable that the Barbadians were happy to pay the price of imported food. 'Good merchantable muscovado sugar' was used as currency for barter, even for the Governor's salary. Willoughby Fort in Bridgetown was constructed as a defence against pirates in 1656 at a price of 80,000 pounds of sugar.

Whistler, a soldier, visited Barbados during the 1650s and described the population like this:

> *The island is inhabited with all sortes, with English, French, Dutch, Scotes, Irish, Spaniards, they being Jues, with ingones [Indians] and Miserabell Negors borne to perpetual slavery thay and theyer seed...This Iland is the dunghill whar our England dost cast forth its rubidg. Rodgs [rogues] and Hors and such like peopel are those that are generally broght heare.*

The whores and rogues were sent out to provide manpower for the cultivation of sugar. Many of them moved on, leaving the 'Miserabell Negors', the African slaves who were already being brought over in their thousands from the west coast of Africa and whose descendants make up the majority of the Bajan population today.

The empire-builders were so successful with their sugar that Barbados came to be called 'the brightest jewel in the English Crown' at the end of the 17th century. The monopoly did not last, despite Barbadian efforts to protect their markets, as other islands started to cultivate the crop. Expensive equipment forced out the smallholders and the plantations became fewer, larger and more profitable. Their fortunes waxed and waned with war and peace in the 18th century, as Britain, France and Spain vied for supremacy in the Americas. Fortunes were handsomely augmented by the usual Caribbean trade of smuggling, avoiding port taxes. Père Labat wrote that the captain of his barque worked hard unloading during the day, but far harder at night.

Barbados's unconquered history was due mainly to its position out in the Atlantic. Ships had to beat upwind towards it and could be seen from miles off, and it was formidably protected by a string of forts down the west coast. The island was the headquarters of the British forces in the Caribbean for many years.

But it was not only from outside that the island was threatened. The plantation slaves plotted rebellion from the beginning and they were ruthlessly treated when found out. The most famous revolt was **Bussa's Rebellion**, in 1816, caused by thoughts of freedom at the time of the abolition of the slave trade in 1807. It was initiated by torching the canefields and was put down with the loss of nearly three hundred lives. Many more rebel slaves were deported to Honduras.

In 1838 the slaves were finally freed (after a four-year 'apprenticeship' period in which they were paid minimally, but had to remain on their plantations) and the industry faltered. Many of the freed slaves emigrated because there was no land for them other than on the plantations. As sugar beet was developed in Europe, the sugar industry nearly collapsed, but after fifty years in the doldrums West Indian sugar was given preferential treatment and it was profitable again by 1910. Sugar and the rum produced from it is still very important to Barbados. The national coat of arms shows a fist grasping two canes, and the Bridgetown coat of arms has three rum puncheons. The 20th century brought further pressure for political change and the growth of trades unions. Eventually universal franchise came in 1951. After the failure of Federation in 1962, Barbados took Independence on 30 November 1966, remaining within the British Commonwealth.

Life has changed radically since Independence and the influence of the United States has clearly replaced that of Britain. There is still a small sugar (and rum) industry as well as a manufacturing sector which produces garments, stainless steel and paper products. Off-shore finance services are expanding and there is some data processing, but by far the biggest earner is tourism. Recent years have been hard on the Barbados economy and the Bajans have felt the recession badly. Public employees were laid off and the island narrowly avoided a devaluation of its currency. Today Barbados is led by Prime Minister Erskine Sandiford of the Democratic Labour Party (re-elected with a majority of eight in early 1991). The next elections are due in 1996.

Cricket and the Constitution

The two most hallowed institutions to be adopted during 300 years' association with Britain are cricket and Parliament. Barbados is the home of players like Sir Frank Worrell (the first black captain of the West Indies team), Sir Gary Sobers and more recently Joel Garner, Gordon Greenidge and current player Desmond Haynes. The island provides many international players and, despite its small size, it has won the regional championship more timesthan all the other islands combined. If a Test Match is being played while you are visiting, be sure to go along (you will find that most of Barbados life stops for it anyway).

Founded in 1637, the Barbados Assembly is the third-oldest parliamentary body in the British Commonwealth, after Bermuda and Westminster itself. The destruction of its official building, the State House, in a fire in 1668 meant that the Legislative Assembly spent 60 years conducting its business in taverns. The late 19th century was a time of political crisis in the West Indies because Britain was keen to impose direct rule from London, thus bypassing the islands' assemblies. Barbados was the only Caribbean colony to keep its legislative powers intact.

Barbados has a bicameral parliamentary system, with elections held every five years to the 28-seat House of Assembly. The 21 senate members are appointed by the Governor General (currently Dame Nita Barrow) on the advice of senior politicians. The newly restored parliamentary buildings in Bridgetown can be visited.

Flora and Fauna

When the Europeans first arrived in 1627, Barbados was entirely forested, but the trees were stripped within twenty years as cultivation went ahead. Turner's Hall Wood in the north of the island is the only place where the original forest remains.

There are few wild animals, though you will come across green monkeys (more brown with green patches), which were brought over from Africa three hundred years ago. Other animals can be seen in the Barbados Wildlife Reserve in the north of the island. Birdlife is more varied. In the remote northern areas you can see three hummingbirds—the Antillean crested hummingbird, the purple-throated carib and the green-throated carib, as well as colourful tanagers and kingbirds. In the inland swamps you can see sandpipers, terns and warblers, and along the coast you will see solitary pelicans digesting their meal on an isolated rock.

One pleasure in Barbados is the gardens, all impeccable, festooned with plants that flower all year round, palms and flowering trees, like the flamboyant that explodes into scarlet in the summer and the poinsettia, or 'Christmas tree', whose leaves turn scarlet in the month of December.

✆ (809)– **Getting There**

Barbados is geographically distinct from the other islands in the eastern Caribbean, but it is well served by air. As well as regular connections from Europe and North America there are easy links to islands nearby and Guyana and Venezuela. On your departure, you may wish to ease your passage through the airport (via the VIP lounge) with **Airport Executive Service** (✆ 426 9869). All air tickets sold in Barbados are supplemented with a 20% government tax. Departure tax Bds$25. During the winter, British Airways runs a weekly direct flight on Concorde; a snip at £4500. The journey time is better than halved at 3½ hours. They also offer subsonic services on most days from Gatwick. BWIA (✆ 426 2111) has two or three direct flights each week from Heathrow. There are numerous charter services on which you can buy seat-only tickets through UK travel agents. BWIA also fly from Frankfurt and Zurich in **Europe**.

By Air from the USA: The best gateways on the American mainland are Miami and New York, from where there are a couple of scheduled flights each day, on American Airlines or BWIA. Connections are also possible through San Juan on Puerto Rico. Other US cities with scheduled flights include Boston and Philadelphia, from where there is a daily scheduled service on America Airlines.

By Air from other Caribbean Islands: LIAT has the best services, flying to all the major islands between Trinidad and Antigua, and on to the Virgin Islands and San Juan. Mustique Airways fly to the Grenadines and **Air Martinique** to the French island of Martinique. There are regular scheduled hopper flights linking Barbados to nearby islands, though they are not cheap. Flights are also available to Georgetown, Guyana and Pavamaribo in Surinam through BWIA and Surinam Air.

By Boat: There are occasional connections to other islands. Eric Hassell & Co. (✆ 436 6102) have a fortnightly sailing to St Lucia and Dominica on which passengers are welcome. Other ships do make the crossing; ask around at the shallow draft dock. Windward Lines heads for Trinidad via St Lucia. Departure tax is Bds$6.

Getting Around

Barbados has quite a good **bus** system, emanating mainly from Bridgetown and reaching most areas of the island. It is a fun way to get around and gives a good exposure to Bajan life. People say good morning when they board the bus and, if you are sitting, someone may well hand you a package to hold for them. Many buses have stereo systems playing the latest soca and Jamaican dub, though this was officially banned not so long ago—schoolchildren liked them so much that they were playing truant and spending their lunch-money on a ride.

The main public bus terminal (for services south and east) is in Fairchild Street, just across Charles Duncan O'Neal Bridge from Trafalgar Square. If you are travelling north, then you leave from the Lower Green Station on Lower Broad Street. The public system, which runs to a vague schedule (West Indian time), is supplemented by private buses, and minibuses known as Z-vans (these are most likely to have the on-board discotheque). Private buses leave from next to the public terminals. Out on the roads it is best to stand at a bus stop, marked by 8ft red and white lollipops, if you want to stop a bus. The Z-vans have a bad image with the Bajans because they will happily stop in the middle of the road and hold up all the traffic in order to pick up a passenger. All fares are Bds$1.50.

As a good tourist, you are really expected to travel by **taxi**. Make sure to fix the price beforehand, though, because taxis are not metered in Barbados. Sample prices are: **airport** to Bridgetown Bds$30, or Speightstown Bds$48; and from **Bridgetown** to St Lawrence Gap Bds$16, Holetown Bds$22, Speightstown Bds$30 and Bathsheba Bds$40. A taxi driver would be only too pleased to give a tour of the island, for around Bds$40 per hour.

Island **bus tours**, a day trip to the hills of Scotland for instance and the views of the east coast, can be arranged through the **L. E. Williams Tour Co.** (✆ 427 1043) for about US$50 with lunch. They will pick you up at your hotel. For a cheaper option, contact the **Barbados Transport Co-op** (✆ 428 6565), who will offer any number of tours to suit you. If you wish to go sight-seeing by helicopter, that too can be arranged. Contact **Bajan Helicopters** (✆ 431 0669) for a tour which follows the coastline and cuts across the dramatic centre of the island.

A good way to explore the countryside is by **hire car**, or by the trusted favourite, a mini-moke. If you do set off, make sure to have a good road map because it is easy to get lost in Barbados's endless fields of sugar-cane.

Getting Around 61

In the winter season there is often a waiting list for vehicles (up to three days), so consider arranging a car when you book your holiday. Firms give better deals for a three-day hire. Expect to leave a hefty deposit with the hire company unless you present a credit card. Car hire here is expensive; rates start at US$50 per day for a mini-moke, plus taxes and CDW, and are marginally more for a large car. There are cheaper options, but you are advised to check the fine print very carefully. Reliable companies include **Payless Car Rentals** (✆ 432 5387) on the west coast, **Dear's Garage** in Bridgetown (✆ 429 9277) and Hastings (✆ 427 7853), **Courtesy Rent-a-Car**, head office near Bridgetown (✆ 431 4160) and at the airport (✆ 420 7153) and **Sunny Isle Motors** in Worthing (✆ 435 7979).

To drive in Barbados (on the left as a rule) you need a special visitor's driving licence, which can be purchased at the airport on arrival on presentation of a valid driving licence, or at any police station, cost Bds$10.

Tourist Information

Barbados Tourism Authority Offices Abroad

UK: 263 Tottenham Court Road, London W1P 9AA (✆ 071 636 9448, fax 071 637 1496).

USA: 800 Second Avenue, New York, NY 10017 (✆ 212 986 6516, fax 212 573 9850) or 3440 Wilshire Boulevard, Suite 1215, Los Angeles, CA 90010 (✆ 213 380 2198, toll free ✆ 800 221 9831).

Canada: 615 Réné Levèque Boulevard, Suite 460, Montreal, Quebec H3B 1P5 (✆ 514 861 0085, fax 514 861 7917) and 561 Yonge Street, 31800 North York, Ontario M2N GL19 (✆ 416 512 6569, fax 416 512 6581, toll free ✆ 800 268 9122).

Germany: Rathenau Platz 1A, 6000 Frankfurt Am Main 1 (✆ 069 280 982/3).

Sweden: Barbados Board of Tourism, c/o Hotel Investors (Sweden) Ltd, Nybrogatan 87, 5–114–41, Stockholm (✆ 468 662 8584, fax 468 662 8775).

France: Caraïbes, 102 Avenue des Champs Elysées, 75008 Paris (✆ 42 62 62 62, fax 40 74 07 01).

On the Island

You can get tourist information and assistance with hotels at the main **tourist offices** in Harbour Road, west Bridgetown (✆ 427 2623, fax 426 4080), at the airport (✆ 428 0937) and at the Deep Water Harbour, where the cruise ships dock (✆ 426 1716).

If you need further assistance on current events and tips about where to find shopping bargains, there is a plethora of magazines and leaflets, including *Ins and Outs of Barbados, Time Out in Barbados* and broadsheets like the *Visitor* and the *Sunseeker*.

The two main Barbadian **newspapers** are the *Advocate* and the *Nation*, which give good coverage of local and international news and list forthcoming events. The *Investigator* will plug you in to the most scurrilous of the island gossip.

In a medical **emergency**, contact the Queen Elizabeth Hospital, on Martindales Road in the north of Bridgetown (✆ 436 6450) or dial **115**.

The **IDD code** for Barbados is **809**, followed by a seven-digit island number. On-island, dial all seven digits.

Useful addresses: British High Commission, Lower Collymore Rock, St Michael (✆ 436 6694); US Consul General (✆ 431 0025); the Canadian High Commission, Bishop Court, Hill Pine Road (✆ 429 3550).

Money

The Barbados currency is the **Barbados dollar**. Like many others in the Caribbean, this is fixed to the US dollar (rate US$ = Bds$1.98) which gives an easy approximate exchange rate of one Bds$ to US50c. It is worth carrying Barbados dollars because they are used in most transactions on the island. You will also get slightly better value even after the exchange. US dollars will be accepted, but make sure to establish which currency you are dealing in. Credit cards are widely accepted by the hotels and restaurants and in tourist areas generally. **Banking** hours are 9–3, with an additional 3–5.30 on Fridays only, but you can change money any time at the hotels (usually for a marginally less favourable rate).

Beaches

The beaches of Barbados are excellent and they offer something for every taste, from the fine golden sand and calm water of the protected west coast, round the southern point where the water is a little livelier and the sand becomes coral-pink, to the windswept walking beaches of the east coast, where the sea is positively rough and huge breakers bring in the full force of the Atlantic. The west coast is the home to wetbikes and waterskiers and the sports get more adventurous with rougher water and the wind round the coastline—windsurfing is best in the south and surfing on the east coast. For an out-of-the-way beach go to the southeast, where coves are cut into the cliffs, or to the north, beyond hotel country. There are fewer hucksters on the main beaches now, but you will probably be offered the traditional array of services, including hair-braiding, tropical shirts and African carvings. They can be very persistent (and quite persuasive) when they get going. Barbadian modesty prevents nude and even topless bathing.

On the more or less continual stretch of west coast beach, north of Bridgetown, the most popular areas are at **Brighton Beach** (busy at weekends), **Paradise Beach, Treasure Beach, Payne's Bay, Folkstone** (also popular with the locals at the weekends), **Mullins Bay** and **Heywood's Beach** just north of Speightstown. The whole stretch is redolent with the aroma of bodies gently sizzling in coconut oil, but it never gets too crowded. It is an excellent place to walk and if you are feeling more active you can arrange a waterskiing trip (*about Bds$40 for 15 minutes*), try parasailing, or take out a small sailing boat. Negotiate with one of the concessionaires and hotel watersports shops based on the beaches. Be careful of the tall and bushy manchineel trees all along the coast. Their fruit was called the apple of death by Columbus, because it causes a nasty rash and swelling. Beyond the hotel strip you will find relative seclusion at **Six Men's Bay**, where Bajans build fishing boats, or at **Maycock's Bay**.

On the south coast, your local stretch of sand is likely to be **Accra, Rockley** or **Worthing Beach**. The beaches at St Lawrence Gap have a similar feel. At competition time **Silver Sands Beach**, just short of the airport, is one of the liveliest beaches on the island as it attracts a crowd of the Barbados body beautiful and a winter influx of nut-brown poseurs and straw-haired surf bums. Beyond the airport things get a bit more secluded and there are some charming pink-sand strands cut into the cliffs. Some are near hotels where you can get lunch; elsewhere you will need to take a picnic. Try **Foul Bay**, named because of its reputation as an anchorage rather than its setting, **Harrismith Beach** or **Crane Beach**, just beneath the surreal hotel of the same name. **Bottom Bay** is also charming and cut off.

On the Atlantic side the surf comes pounding in and swimming is often dangerous, but the coast is spectacular to view, from **Ragged Point** in the southeast through Bathsheba and Cattlewash to **Gay's Cove** and **River Bay** in St Lucy parish to the north, where the Bajans come for an outing at the weekend.

Beach Bars

The **Bamboo Beach Bar** is a popular spot just south of Holetown, a shady retreat from the sun on a boarded veranda above the waves of Payne's Bay. It is lively in the early evening as a crowd of white Bajans catch a beer and a chat on the way home. **Mullins Beach Bar** has a very pretty setting with a white gingerbread terrace facing the sunset. It has monkey murals and lively music daytime and evening, and is very popular and quite expensive, cocktails at Bds$10. Within walking distance of Central Bridgetown heading south is the **Boatyard** at the head of Carlisle Bay, a rustic and low-key spot, a shed under a sea almond tree. The **Sugar Reef** restaurant is quite expensive, but a pretty spot at the corner of Accra Beach, and in Worthing on the south coast you will find a mixed crowd of Bajans and visitors at the **Carib Beach Bar**: snacks by day and also often lively at night. There is a bar on **Silver Sands Beach**, which is at its most active when the windsurfers are on-island in the winter.

Sailing

So far upwind and isolated from the rest of the eastern Caribbean, Barbados is not a popular call for yachts, though some do put in after an Atlantic crossing. **Customs and immigration** are in the Deep Water Harbour just out of Bridgetown to the northwest. The main **anchorage** in Barbados is Carlisle Bay, the broad bight to the south of the Careenage and central Bridgetown. It is usually calm night and day and you can anchor anywhere; the Boatyard Bar at the northern end has a dock and offers ice, water and fuel. **Provisioning** is in town. The Royal Barbados Yacht Club at the southern end of the bay permits entry to members of certain **yacht clubs** at home. A popular day's sail while in Barbados is along the west coast of the island.

There are no major charter yacht companies based in Barbados. There is no marina on the island, but most services can be tracked down in the Carlisle Bay area.

Watersports

Windsurfing is best on the south coast—experienced windsurfers should head for the southerly point, around Silver Sands, where the 1991 World Championships were hosted and where **Mistral** keeps an outfit over the winter months (when the trade winds are at their highest). It is particularly good for waves, so if you want to put down a 360, a tabletop or a cheese roll, or watch them at it, or simply watch the crowds, this is the place to come. Another popular place for windsurfing is the **Benston Windsurfing Club Hotel** on Maxwell Beach (also Mistral), which offers equipment hire and instruction. **Surfing** is sometimes possible on the south coast but it is most popular on the east coast, at Bathsheba or Duppies, or at Crab Hill in the far north.

If you would like to go on an organized **day sail**, snorkelling and cruising up the west coast, there are plenty of options available (with hotel transfers and a meal usually included). Try the catamaran *Irish Mist* (✆ 436 9201) and sailing yachts

Secret Love (℡ 437 7490) and *Limbo Lady* (℡ 435 8206). An afternoon of rum-soaked piracy and profligacy can be had aboard the **Jolly Roger**, with lots of shiver me timbers and walking the plank to loud music—*for Bds$105*. For a more stately ride in an old riverboat, try the **Bajan Queen** (reservations for both, ℡ 436 6424). Deep-sea fishing charters after swordfish or marlin can be arranged through the boats on the Careenage, among them *Blue Jay* (℡ 422 2098).

Barbados is surrounded by reefs and **scuba diving** can be arrranged through the hotels and dive shops both on the protected west coast and on the south coast. *Average prices are Bds$80 for a one-tank dive.* Companies offering equipment and qualified instruction are **Willie's Water Sports** (℡ 432 5980) with two operations on the west coast and **Shades of Blue** (℡ 422 3215) near Holetown. On the south coast there is a PADI five-star dive centre in St Lawrence Gap, **Explore Sub Barbados** (℡ 435 6542), and you might also try **Sandy Beach Water Sports** in Worthing (℡ 435 8000).

Snorkelling equipment can be hired from any of the diving shops and most hotels. Good places to **snorkel** on the reefs are the **Folkstone National Marine Park**, near Holetown on the west coast, where the reefs are protected, and also off the Heywoods resort near Speightstown. Trips in a glass-bottomed boat on the west coast can be organized through most watersports shops. And for a view of deeper Barbados corals without getting wet, contact **Atlantis Submarine** (℡ 436 8929); reserve a couple of days in advance in season.

Other Sports

There are five **golf** courses. The best known is the 18-hole championship course at **Sandy Lane** (℡ 432 1145), *with green fees around US$85.*

Many of the hotels have **tennis** courts where you can play, usually for a fee of *about US$6 per hour.* There are even **squash** courts in Barbados. Contact the Barbados Squash Club (℡ 427 7913) or Rockley Resort in Christ Church (℡ 435 7880).

Walkers can find satisfying hikes in the hilly district of Scotland and along the rugged east coast. If you prefer to go alone, maps are easily available in town. If you would prefer to explore Barbados on **horseback** or fancy a canter along the beach at dawn, contact the Brighton Stables (℡ 425 9381) in St Michael, or Beau Geste Stables (℡ 429 0139) for a ride through the canefields to Francia Plantation. A ride out in the northern hills of the island can be arranged through Tony's Riding School (℡ 422 1549).

Spectator sports include the **horse-racing** on alternate Saturdays in the seasons at the Garrison Savannah south of Bridgetown and even **polo** (Barbados Polo Club, ℡ 432 1802) on the west coast. But **cricket** is the Barbadian national sport, and you will come across weekend matches all over the island and less formal games being played by children in the backstreets of the towns. Details of forthcoming League matches and international Tests, held in the Kensington Oval north of Bridgetown, can be found in the newspapers.

There is an active National Trust in Barbados (© 426 2421). They organize a walk to a different site of natural and historical interest each Sunday, starting 6am and 3pm and lasting about 3 hours (*details in the local newspapers or © above, adm free but donations welcomed*). They have introduced a programme of 'Open Houses' once a week which enable you to visit Barbadian houses not normally open to the public—locations published in advance in a leaflet. Their *Heritage Passport* allows you to visit about fifteen of the best known 'sights' of Barbados on one ticket, purchased in advance, *Bds$70*.

Bridgetown

Set on the broad sweep of Carlisle Bay on the southwest coast of Barbados, Bridgetown is a thriving Caribbean capital with a population of over 100,000. Grand old colonial structures jostle with purposeful glass-fronted and modern pastel offices, while hucksters fill the streets, touting their wares from trays.

The heart of the city is the old harbour at the **Careenage**, an inlet surrounded by warehouses which takes its name from the process of *careening*, in which a weight would be tied to a boat's mast to upturn it, revealing the hull to be cleaned and painted. The lighters that once loaded the ships at anchor in the bay from here are now gone because Barbados has a deep-water harbour, but the jetties of the Careenage still have some café life and local fishing craft and pleasure boats at dock. It is all quite picturesque now, but about 300 years ago it was an offence worthy of prosecution to disturb the waters of the Careenage because the smell was so bad.

Presiding over the scene from Trafalgar Square on the northern shore of the Careenage is a statue of **Lord Nelson** in full uniform, erected in 1813 following his death at the Battle of Trafalgar. Nelson had been based in the West Indies for several years, and the Barbadians were grateful to him as the 'preserver of the West Indies'. The Barbadian tribute to him preceded the statue in London by 27 years. Traditionally he faces any danger that threatens Barbados and so in the past he has always faced the sea. In a recent redevelopment, however, he was inexplicably turned around. In the present economic difficulties, Bajan wags claim that he now faces the twin threats of the Government buildings and the Central Bank.

Trafalgar Square was originally known as **the Green** in English fashion and was once home to the pillory and the ducking stool (quite some punishment, evidently, with the foul waters of the Careenage). On the north side of the square are the **Public Buildings**, home of the Barbados Parliament, which were recently cleaned up to reveal bright Barbadian coral rock. Opened in 1874, the two long rounded Italian renaissance-style buildings have been adapted to the tropics with green-louvred shutters and red tin shades. In the **House of Assembly** there is a stained glass window commemorating the monarchs of England, from James I to Victoria, including a portrait of Cromwell, interesting in itself because of Barbados's royalist sympathies during the Civil War.

Two minutes' walk east of Trafalgar Square is **St Michael's Cathedral**, rebuilt with money raised in a lottery in 1789 after the early wooden structure was destroyed in the hurricane of 1780. It became a cathedral when William Hart Coleridge arrived in 1825 as the first Bishop of Barbados. Among the sculpted memorials and tablets is a font that dates from 1680 and is decorated with a Greek palindrome: NIΦON ANOMH MAMH MONA NOΦIN, meaning: *Wash the sin, not just the skin.*

On Magazine Lane, leading up to the functional buildings of the Law Courts and the Public Library, presented to Barbados by Andrew Carnegie in 1906, is the recently restored 19th-century **Synagogue**. It occupies the site of the original 17th-century building constructed by Jews who had escaped from Brazil and obtained permission to settle in Barbados on hearing that Cromwell had granted freedom of worship. Just inside the graveyard can be seen the bemusing headstone commemorating a certain Benjamin Massiah, no doubt a local celebrity, who 'performed the office of circumciser with great Applause and Dexterity'.

Now behind Nelson is **Broad Street**, Bridgetown's main thoroughfare and business street, where elaborate colonial edifices that might belong in an English south coastal town are interspersed with modern shopping centres and banks. Parallel to Broad Street is Swan Street, a popular local market, and on the other side is the seafront road, which leads to the deepwater harbour and cruise ship terminal. On the road is the **Rasta Mall**, with rastaman stalls painted in red, gold and green with anything from the speeches of Haile Selassie to herbal medicines on sale, and **Pelican Village**, an artisans' mall selling paintings, wickerwork and clothes.

Headed south from the centre of town, **Bay Street** skirts Carlisle Bay, where yachts lie at anchor off the beach and the esplanade. A hundred years ago this area was a poor quarter renowned for smuggling and so the government bought it out and built the esplanade. Bay Street itself is still a tatty area of old wooden buildings and poky bars that by night is Bridgetown's red light district, but there are also some very elaborate townhouses with gingerbread pointings as intricate as lace.

The Barbadian flag was first raised in place of the Union Jack on the **Garrison Savannah**, a 50-acre park surrounded by trees a couple of miles from central Bridgetown. It takes its name from its original use as a military training ground and barracks, in varying states of repair, still surround the Savannah—today's military, the Barbados Defence Force, occupies the 18th-century St Anne's Fort across the road on the south side. The original Guard House, with its green-domed clock tower, is occupied by the **Savannah Club**. Nowadays, as well as the parades, the Savannah hosts sports such as racing, rugby and cricket.

In the handsome setting of the former garrison jail is the **Barbados Museum** (© 427 0201), *open Mon–Sat 9–5, Sun 2–6, adm*, which gives an enlightening view of Barbadian history from its start as a coral-encrusted shelf, inhabited by various Amerindian tribes, to the archetypal sugar island and on to *Bimshire* and Independence. There are some particularly good displays in the Aall maps and prints gallery, and some peep-in views of old-time Barbados. Naturally there is an exhibit of a prisoner's cell. The temporary exhibition gallery has revolving exhibits of local artists and there is a hands-on children's gallery.

The West Coast—North to Scotland and St Lucy

Highway 1 leads out of Bridgetown to the north, along the west coast of the island, to Speightstown, Barbados's second town. Winter home to transient millionaires, the west coast is all hotels and expensive villas muscling in for frontage on the 10-mile strip of extremely fine beaches. Interspersed you will find local clapboard houses, rum-shops, restaurants and the best sunset beach bars. Until the Second World War, people would avoid this area and make the journey by boat. It was considered unhealthy because of the coastal swamps and the road was awful. But since the fifties people have flocked here from all over the world. Barbados's most exclusive hotels are situated here. In tourist jargon it is referred to as the Gold Coast, recently updated to the Platinum Coast.

Heading north out of Bridgetown you can join the Spring Garden Highway, where the Parade of Bands is held at Cropover, and where you will find the Kensington Oval, the island's main stadium and home of the cricket internationals. There are two chances to see the story of Barbados rum explained here. At the **West India Rum Refinery**, (© 435 6900), *open Wed, adm Bds$55*, you can take the Cockspur 'Where the Rum Comes From' tour, with a look at the production process, lunch and a rum-tasting session. A shorter tour can be made at the **Mount Gay Visitor's Centre** nearby, (© 425 9066), *open Mon–Fri 9–4, Sat 10–1, adm*. There is a video explaining production, a visit to the warehouses where the rum is aged in barrels and a tasting on the veranda. The Spring Garden Highway joins

Highway 1 at the Cave Hill Campuses, one of three that make up the **University of the West Indies**. The other two are in Jamaica and Trinidad.

Following the west coast road, which winds over the small headlands and occasionally touches the seafront, you come to **Holetown**, 7 miles north of the capital, where the first European settlers made their home. It is apparently called so because the sailors who put in here were reminded of 'the Hole' on the River Thames. It was here that Captain John Powell claimed the island for England. His sign, 'James K. of E. and of this island', was placed in 1625 on a fustic tree, and has now disappeared, but the event is recalled by a memorial in the town. Originally the town was called Jamestown, the name given to the Parish and the Holetown church, **St James's**, the oldest on the island. The church has recently been restored, revealing the bright coral rock.

Speightstown (pronounced rather like 'spikestong') is about 12 miles north of the capital. Very early on the town was a thriving port, used to land goods for the northern part of Barbados, before good roads were built. The town was known as Little Bristol because it had links with Bristol, then England's second-largest port. Its name even derives from a Bristol man, William Speight, a member of the Barbados Parliament in 1639.

If you follow Highway 2, which leads inland from Bridgetown, you come to **Harrison's Cave**, (© 438 6640), *open 9–4, adm expensive*, a series of underground rivers and limestone caverns hung with stalactite shark teeth that drip on to glutinous stalagmites, due to join up in a couple of million years. It is all a bit overplayed, with hard hats, strict guides and yet another handicraft shop, but the 500,000-year-old caverns are genuinely a stimulating sight.

Welchman Hall Gulley, (© 438 6671), *open 9–5, adm*, a couple of miles farther along Highway 2, is a cleft in Barbados's limestone cap that drips with tropical greenery, a canopy that nearly blocks out the sun and drops lianas down on to the array of shrubs and trees. On the short walk through the gulley you might think that you have descended to the depths of the island, but when you come out into the open you are presented with a fantastic view over northern Barbados and the Atlantic. The gulley and the caves were used by runaways and escapers of all sorts.

Scotland and St Lucy in the North

The imposed sophistication of the west coast evaporates with the last hotel just north of Speightstown, giving way to fishing villages in the bays and the simple attractive parish of **St Lucy**. The land is covered in sugar-cane, sweeping plains that descend from the mountainous **Scotland District** in the centre of the island. It was to Scotland that the Catholics, 'Barbadosed' by Cromwell, were sent to keep them out of the way. Some of their descendants are still there, in the communities of 'poor whites' as they are known.

At the most northerly point of the island is **Animal Flower Cave**, *adm*, a series of caverns thrashed out by the force of the waves. There are blow-holes and you might see an 'animal flower', a flower-like sea anemone which snaps back into its tube when disturbed. You can get a drink in the nearby Pirate's Tavern.

Inland from Speightstown you come to the rugged and mountainous **Scotland District**, where crags tower above sparsely grassed moorland. Escaped slaves would come to lie up in the hope of casting off for St Vincent, 100 miles directly downwind, and visible on the clearest days from Mount Hillaby. The area also found favour with the planters, who built some of the finest plantation houses here. The roads are rough in the remoter areas of Scotland District, but it is worth making the effort to go there just for the views.

One of the finest views is from **Cherry Tree Hill**, from where one can look north to St Lucy and south over the island as far as **Hackleton's Cliff** in the parish of St Joseph. Just beneath Cherry Tree Hill is a cool avenue of casuarina and mahogany trees where the Bajans come to take their picnics. There is another fine view of Scotland from **Farley Hill**, *gardens open until dusk, adm*, where there is the shell of a 19th-century mansion that was renowned as the smartest in Barbados in the late 1880s, when lavish receptions were held here. It is a little sad because it was gutted by fire in the sixties, but the gardens, with their magnificent royal palms and other labelled trees and plants, are peaceful and pleasant.

Newly opened **Grenade Hall Forest and Signal Station**, *adm*, is another link in the communication chain that once covered the whole of Barbados by semaphore. The original building, which has superb views, has been restored, and to it has been added a forest trail with signs to illustrate the complexities of the eco-system.

A couple of miles away is **St Nicholas Abbey** (© 422 8725), *open Mon–Fri, 10–3:30. Do not miss the film shown twice-daily (11am and 2pm) of Barbados in the 1930s, which includes footage of the Bridgetown Careenage, loading rum puncheons, mauby ladies pouring drinks from a barrel on their head and shots of Barbados's windmills; adm.*. One of the two oldest mansions on the island, it is among only three Jacobean houses surviving in the whole of the Americas (along with Drax Hall, also in Barbados, and Bacon's Castle in Virginia, USA). Built around 1650 by a Colonel Berringer, it is not really an abbey but a fine stone building with curved gables (a reminder of Dutch influence in the early days of settlement). One oddity is that the house has fireplaces, as though the inhabitants feared cold nights in the hills of Scotland. It was a working plantation up to the forties.

Old prints of Barbados show the island dotted with windmills and at one time about five hundred were employed in crushing cane. Among the ruins there is only one that survives intact, the **Morgan Lewis Mill,** *open Mon–Sat, 9–5, adm*, in the hills of St Andrew's Parish. Its original crushing gear is on view.

St Andrew's Parish is the least populous in Barbados and boasts the highest point on the island, **Mount Hillaby**, 1160ft above sea level. It also has Barbados's only untouched forestland, **Turner's Hall Wood**, on a ridge leading from Mount Hillaby, the last remnant of the forest that once covered the whole of the island. The wood has a variety of trees including the sandbox, the buttressed locust tree, which has a pod with foul-smelling but reasonably tasty flesh, and the jack-in-a-box tree that takes its name from its seed which stands erect in a pod. You might also see a grey kingbird or a carib grackle.

The Sugar Heartland—Bridgetown to the Atlantic Coast

Highways 3 and **4** leave Bridgetown to the northeast and pass into Barbados's sugar-cane heartland, where they disappear between curtains of the 12ft grass-like crop. The roads are a maze linking small villages of colourful clapboard houses, *chattel houses* to the Bajans, and some of the island's finest plantation houses. The land rises steadily from west to east, culminating in a cliff that gives sweeping views of the windward coast, where the Bajans like to escape from Bridgetown.

The first landmark on Highway 4 out of Bridgetown is the award-winning **Banks Brewery**. (© 429 2113), *visits Tues, Thurs.* **Francia Plantation House**, (© 429 0474), *open Mon–Fri, 10–4, , adm*, set in open tropical gardens with a panoramic view of the west coast, is a Bajan family home with echoes of Brazil in some architectural features and in the imported hardwood. There are West Indian prints and maps as well as a three-way seat for a pair of lovers (the third seat is for the girl's chaperon) and a dripstone, which provided clean and filtered water.

Gun Hill Signal Station, *open Mon–Fri, 9–5, adm*,.is one of a string of semaphore stations that could link the whole of Barbados within minutes. Set up in 1818, it was used by the military to warn of impending trouble from the sea, by using flags by day and coloured lanterns at night, and also to pass the message quickly of uprisings among the slaves or even advise that a ship had arrived in port with merchandise. The communication tower at Gun Hill has been restored and provides a fine view of the island, as well as a map of the other stations in the network and some military memorabilia. Gun Hill was also used for convalescence for troops suffering from malaria and yellow fever. They tended to recover because the climate was fresher away from the sea and there were no mosquitos at this height. On approach to the signal station you will see an odd-looking white lion, sculpted by a Colonel Wilkinson during his convalescence (hardly a masterpiece).

Villa Nova (© 433 1524), *adm*, is a strikingly beautiful Bajan Great House swallowed in a profusion of tropical greenery. The coral-stone house is surrounded by a gallery to allow breezes through the open rooms while excluding the rain. On view is Chippendale furniture and the desk of former owner and British Prime Minister Sir Anthony Eden. In the garden is a cannonball tree and an African tulip tree with flowers like hanging trumpets.

There is an extremely fine view from **St John's Parish Church**, which stands on the cliff 800ft above the Atlantic coast. The original church was constructed at a cost of 100,000 pounds of sugar in 1667 and was rebuilt in 1836 after the 1831 hurricane. St John's also has a strange history concerning its early vestryman Ferdinando Paleologus, who came to Barbados as a refugee after fighting on the side of the Royalists in the Civil War. His ancestors had been the Christian Emperors of Constantinople until they were driven out by the Turks in the 15th century. His remains were discovered in the destruction of the 1831 hurricane, head pointing west according to the Greek custom, and they were moved and reinterred in a vault with Greek columns.

To the southeast, on a shelf in the descending cliff, is **Codrington College**, (✆ 433 1274), a magnificent coral-stone seminary with an arched portico and views down to Consett Bay. Approached through an avenue of mighty cabbage palms, living columns up to 100ft in height, it is set in a garden of tropical plants with a lake. It was built in the early 18th century with money from a bequest from Christopher Codrington, a Governor-General of the Leeward Islands whose grandfather was one of the earliest settlers of Barbados. A story is attached to two of the cabbage palms in the avenue, planted in 1879 by Prince Albert and Prince George who were on a visit to the island. One palm flourished, but the other did not. When the news came that Prince Albert had died, the local Bajans showed no surprise and said, 'We knew he die soon. His cabbage die!'. It is still a working theological college, but the grounds are accessible and there is a nature trail.

Hackleton's Cliff runs parallel to the coastline and commands another of Barbados's fine panoramas with views both north and south along the windward coastline from about 1000ft above the sea. Just inside the parish of St Joseph is a former signal station, the **Cotton Tower**, a link in the semaphore chain from Gun Hill. It stands above a gully, the Devil's Bowling Alley, and has cracking views over Scotland to the north.

The windward coast of Barbados is lined with reefs sometimes up to 3 miles offshore, making it impossible for all but the smallest ships to put in here. But the reefs have little effect on the Atlantic breakers that barrel in and crash on the poised rocks on the coastline, eroding it at the rate of 1ft a year. A typical windward coast settlement is **Bathsheba**, a slightly ragged fishing village dotted with houses and windblown palm trees, set on a bay popular with surfers. It is still possible to see the fishing boats making their way out to sea through the reefs.

Andromeda Gardens, *open daily, adm*, above the village are full to bursting with tropical plants from all over the world, ranging from tiny orchids to the tree that gave Barbados its name, the banyan, or bearded fig tree. Started in 1954 and recently bought by the Barbados National Trust, there are paths through a valley alive with the smells and colours of a tropical explosion (the plants are labelled). You will see the native *frangipani*, with bright red and yellow petals, orchids that look like five-winged purple and white butterflies and *Ravenala madagascariensis*, the traveller's tree, which has a fan of broad leaves similar to a banana tree.

The east coast road leads north into the parish of St Andrew, following the track of the old railway to its terminus at Belleplaine, where the Bajans would come on their picnics earlier this century. Inland there is another garden, the **Flower Forest**, *open 9–5, adm*, with paths through more tropical splendour and views of Scotland in the distance. Tropical plants include breadfruit, golden apple and mango, as well as spices and citrus.

Suburbs and the South Coast

Like the west coast, the south coast of Barbados is gilded with beaches, mounds of golden sand on which the waves clap and rush. Just behind them are apartment-blocks and hotels jostling for space in the extended suburb that contains the homes of the Bajan *bons bourgeois*. **Highway 7** runs from central Bridgetown to Oistins Town (about 5 miles), throwing off lanes that seek out the gaps and the coves. The suburbs have names like Hastings, Worthing and Dover, a reminder of home for nostalgic colonists in centuries past, but certainly less demure than their British counterparts. The hotels and restaurants of the south coast do not have the sophistication of the west, but there is a lively, relaxed atmosphere and good nightlife.

Oistins, where the sea flashes with colourful Barbadian fishing boats, is a fishing centre and Barbados's third-largest town. It comes alive each day in the late afternoon when the catch is brought in and sold. According to Ligon, a visitor in the 1650s, it was called 'Austins Bay, not in commemoration of any Saint, but of a wilde mad drunken fellow, whose lewd and extravagant carriage made him infamous in the Iland'. It was in Oistins Town in 1652, at Ye Mermaid's Inn, that the 'Magna Carta of Barbados', the articles of capitulation, were signed by the Royalists, surrendering Barbados to the Commonwealth Commissioners sent by Cromwell after a long siege.

Farther along the coast is a notorious house in Long Bay, the crenellated **Sam Lord's Castle**, *open in the day, adm*, solidly built in 1820 (it was undamaged in the 1831 hurricane but scaffolding on the walls ended up 3 miles away). It is now surrounded by a hotel complex, but it is famous for the legend that surrounds its first owner, Sam Lord, a story that becomes more embellished with each telling. Lord was a greedy man, who was suspected of murder to gain inheritance and who was found out mistreating his wife cruelly, but he is also credited with causing shipwrecks on the reefs below his house, luring ships in to land by hanging lanterns in his windows, his palm trees, the horns of his cattle, or the antlers of his deer (delete as applicable). Then, so the story goes, he would offload the booty and bring it to his castle by way of an underground passage (conspicuously absent today).

He became an extremely rich man, favoured by a series of sudden deaths, but he was busily chasing yet another inheritance when he was uncovered. He had locked up his wife before a journey to England to talk her family into giving him some of her money, but she escaped and managed to get there before him and so he was arrested. However, a case brought against him was inconclusive. He is remembered in a book by Lieutenant Colonel Drury, *The Regency Rascal*: whatever the legend that surrounds him, he was undoubtedly an extravagant rogue whose only bequests were debts, an impressive £18,000 in 1845, to go with his magnificent castle. It is suitably and lavishly decorated according to the period, with plasterwork ceilings and mahogany trimmings, Regency furnture and an extremely fine staircase. (It is often crowded because it works as the hotel lobby as well.)

Ragged Point is the most easterly place on the island, a limestone cliff thrashed by the Atlantic.

Off Highway 5, the direct route back towards Bridgetown, is the **Sunbury Plantation House and Museum** (© 423 6270), where the pleasant lawned garden is set with coaches and iron farm machinery. The house, originally constructed in the 1660s, is restored in Georgian style to the state of a plantation house at the height of the island's sugar prosperity. There is a café in the grounds.

Festivals

The highlight of the Barbadian Festival year is 'Cropover', which culminates on the first Monday in August, Kadooment Day (the crop referred to is the sugar-cane harvest). It is a major blow-out along Carnival lines, with calypso-singing competitions, steel band music and carnival 'bands' made up of hundreds of costumed players who strut through the streets to *soca* music. You can **play mas** by buying a costume and joining the masquerade, or just dance on the sidelines.

There is a **jazz** festival in January, with international players performing in three different venues across the island, and in February the **Holetown Festival** commemorates the first settlement of the island in 1627 with a week's worth of exhibitions, tattoos and general jamboree. **Easter Opera**

Season stages a round of open-air opera and Shakespeare plays, along with polo matches, and church music is performed at **Gospelfest** in May. The **St Lawrence Music Festival** stages mostly local bands in the nightclubs of St Lawrence in October and in November you can see visual arts exhibitions at **NIFCA**, the National Independence Festivities of the Creative Arts.

✆ *(809)–* *Where to Stay*

As the nerve centre of the British presence in the eastern Caribbean, Barbados has a tradition of hotels going back 200 years. The best known was the 19th-century 'Ice House', patronized because it brought the first cooled drinks to Barbados, but most were famous for a series of prodigious creole landladies who kept houses of varying states of disorder: Sabina Brade, Hannah Lewis who would complain of her lumbago and Betsy Austin, a lady of massive size and earthy language, who would become violent if her bill was questioned. For many of the tavern girls 'of erect figure and stately carriage...without shoes or stockings, in a short white jacket and thin short petticoat...a white turban on the head, neck and shoulders left bare', it was a business profitable enough to buy their freedom from slavery. But the most popular image is that of the gargantuan Rachel Pringle, an expansive matriarch, dressed in voluminous silk, of almost immovable disposition, whose caricature by the cartoonist Rowlandson can be seen all over the island.

Barbados offers one of the best ranges of hotels in the Caribbean and prices are fairly high in season . However it is possible to find a good deal in the summer months, in hotel rooms and self-catering flats. Villas are also available for hire. Contact **Bajan Services Ltd** at Seascape Cottage, Gibbs, St Peter, Barabados (✆ 809 422 2618, fax 422 5366), with options between one and eight bedrooms, or in Britain **Palmer and Parker** (✆ 0494 815411), or **Exclusive Villas** (✆ 081 947 7300, fax 947 9712) who cover many two- to six-bedroom, staffed villas on the west coast.

The smart set go to the Platinum Coast, which runs north along the west coast from Bridgetown to just beyond Speightstown. Some of the finest hotels in the Caribbean are here, set in gardens of tropical splendour and giving on to the gentle bays with golden strands, a fine place to see the Green Flash at sunset. The busy south coast is more active, and with one or two exceptions the hotels are less luxurious. Bear in mind that all accommodation bills in Barbados will be supplemented with a 5% government tax and, in almost all cases, a 10% service charge as well.

very expensive–luxury

The **Sandy Lane Hotel** in St James (℗ 432 1311, fax 432 2954, booking agents Forte and Leading Hotels of the World) has long been one of the Caribbean's best-known and most luxurious hotels. Limousine service will whisk you from the airport to this classical, coral-stone enclave of sumptuousness with north and south wings either side of an amphitheatrical courtyard and set on 300 yards of delightful beachfront on Payne's Bay. Soft shades of pink and white run throughout the resort in the coral stone and pickled oak fittings. All imaginable concessions to luxury—24-hour room service, watersports, children's centre—right down to the chilled towels at the pool and the fitness centre. A large and busy hotel with 120 rooms. The **Royal Pavilion** (℗ 422 5555, fax 422 3940, UK reservations ℗ 081 366 5477), farther north in St James, has a similar feel of manicured luxury, again with a certain formality (no children in winter). There is a charming dining room set on a veranda right above the waves and all 72 elegant rooms look on to the ocean from deep balconies, luxury. Guests have the use of the facilities at **Glitter Bay**, the larger and less formal sister-hotel next door.

A number of the west coast hotels have villas rather than formal rooms in a block style. A charming small resort is **Cobbler's Cove** (℗ 422 2291, fax 422 1460, UK reservations ℗ 081 367 5175), on the coast just south of Speightstown. There are 39 very elegant beachfront and garden suites, each decorated with wicker, rattan and Barbadian clay tiles, and with a balcony or terrace. Above the central drawing room, which lends the hotel a very comfortable air, is the Camelot Suite, almost a legend in luxury. Cobbler's Cove is one of the Caribbean's few *Relais et Châteaux* (character, courtesy, calm, charm and not least, particularly in the Caribbean, cuisine). MAP in winter.

Settler's Beach in Holetown (℗ 422 3052, fax 422 1937, UK reservations ℗ 0453 835801) is another very private and secluded beachside retreat, where there are just 22 large and personally decorated two-room town-houses and cottages staggered around a pretty garden. Dining room and full kitchens, with house-keeper service, but restaurant for when you are so inclined. Children accepted; luxury for two, very expensive for four. Guests return year after year to the **Coral Reef Club** (℗ 422 2372, fax 422 1776, UK reservations ℗ 0800 282124, USA reservations ℗ 800 223 1108) nearby, a family-run hotel with the stately grace of old-time Barbados. The 69 individually decorated rooms are set in coral-rock cottages scattered around luxuriant gardens of casuarina and mahogany trees. MAP.

Slightly more casual, wrapped in bougainvillea, are the suites of the **Sandpiper Inn** nearby (© 422 2251, fax as Coral Reef).

moderate–expensive

There are a number of less lavish options if you particularly want to stay on Barbados's famous west coast. At **Smuggler's Cove** (© 432 1741, fax 432 1749), moderate, there are comfortable studios and one-bedroom apartments in a block above the pool, right on Payne's Bay, with kitchenettes (but also a restaurant), pool and watersports. If you are happy to cater for yourself, you can also try **The Beachcomber** (© 432 0489, fax 432 2824), where there are studios and two-bedroom apartments with full kitchens, each with large balconies above the beach. On the south coast you can find reasonable prices for studios and apartments in the St Lawrence Gap area at **Bresmay Apartment Hotel** (© 428 6131, fax 428 7722) and across the road at the **Monteray Apartment Hotel** (© 4218 9125, fax 428 7722), both moderate.

Farther afield, on the southeast coast of St Philip, the **Crane Beach Hotel** (© 423 6220, fax 423 5342) has a thoroughly dramatic setting on the clifftops. A surreal shade of turquoise runs as a leitmotif through the hotel, from the absurdly rich colour of the sea to the clifftop pool with its classical columns and balustrades. The 18 very comfortable rooms and suites (four set in a miniature castle) are expensive. Another haven of old-time Barbadian grace and comfort, yet further afield, can be found at Cattlewash on the east coast, at the **Kingsley Club** (© 433 9422, fax 433 9226). Earlier this century, well-to-do Bajans would escape the turmoil of Bridgetown to this traditional timber-frame villa. Now it is an ideal writer's retreat and professional's rest-cure, as you can tell by the faded copies of *Architectural Digest* and *Forbes Magazine*. Eight double rooms, moderate. And there is a similar old-time grandeur at the **Ocean View Hotel** in Hastings (© 427 7821, fax 427 7826) which has presided over its fine view since 1901. Antique furniture, four-poster beds and creaking floorboards, with a charming waterfront restaurant.

cheap

One of the best areas to stay in Barbados is the southern tip of the island around Silver Sands. It has an easy feel and is popular with windsurfers and independent travellers. There is public transport into town. **Peace and Quiet**, Inch Marlow, Christ Church (© 428 5682, fax 428 2467) has 22 suites in stark white stucco and shingle-tile buildings in a windy seafront setting of palms and casuarinas. Very relaxed and peaceful and impeccable value; good restaurant and beach nearby, cheap to moderate. The windsurfers themselves tend to gather at the **Silver Rock Hotel** (✆ 428 2866, fax 420 6982), where comfortable studios and apartments are moderately priced; it has a bar and restaurant. Windsurfers also gravitate around the **Benston Windsurfing Club Hotel** in Maxwell (✆ 428 9095, fax 435 6621). Simple rooms and restaurant, but good balconies.

very cheap

There is a clutch of small **guest houses** just off the beach in Worthing, the cheapest on the island. Try **Shells Guest House** (✆ 435 7253) and **Crystal Waters** (✆ 435 7514), both with a restaurant, or **Rydal Waters Guest House** (✆ 435 7433). Some rooms with shared bathrooms.

✆ *(809)–* *Eating Out*

Bajan food

As in many of the Caribbean islands, some Bajan traditional dishes have a slave heritage. Thus **cou-cou**, a dish made from cornmeal and okra, is served with salt fish, once a hardship food. In Barbados '**peas 'n' rice**' is a staple, often flavoured with coconut. Besides the traditional **pepperpot stew**, a four-day boil-up, there is also plenty of seafood, including crab and **sea-egg**, the roe of the white sea-urchin, which is supposely an aphrodisiac.

The best-loved fish in Barbados is the **flying fish**, which you may well see if you go out sailing. It is a winged fish that flits and glides over the waves, sometimes for distances up to 100 yards. As well as being a national symbol, it is also something of a national dish, and you can see the daily catch brought in to the Careenage in the late afternoon, in season between December and June.

Bajan drink

The chiefe fudling they make in the iland is Rumbullion, alias Kill Divill and this is made of suggar canes distilled, a hot hellish and terrible liquor.

Barbados produces some of the finest **rum** in the world. Distilled from molasses, the thick liquid left over from the sugar-boiling process, many rums are left to mature in oak, taking on a darker colour. Mountgay is the best known: try their special 5-year-old. Others are Cockspur Old Gold and VSOR. Local white rums include ESAF, jokingly called 'Erskine Sandiford And Friends' in a reference to the current Prime Minister and 'Every Sunday Afternoon

Free'. There are hundreds of 'rum shops' on the island, mostly small clapboard shacks, where you will find the Barbadians 'liming', passing the time of day. If you would like to see the distillation process, there are tours available of two distilleries near Bridgetown (*see* p.69).

The restaurants in Barbados serve superb fruit punches, fresh fruit and juices crushed with ice, and free from the usual sticky grenadine syrup that elsewhere obliterates the taste. More traditional drinks include **mauby juice**, a bitter drink made by boiling bark and spices—100 years ago 'mauby ladies' would ply the streets of Bridgetown with urns on their heads, offering drinks to quench a midday thirst. Its 20th-century equivalent is a **snow-cone** in a plastic cup. You will also find delicious home-brewed **ginger beer**, boiled up from grated root ginger, and **sorrel**, a sweet concoction made from the red flowers of the sorrel plant, known as the Christmas drink all over the Caribbean. The Bajan beer is the award-winning **Banks** brew.

Restaurants

Barbados has some good restaurants, known both for fine food and for charming locations: terraces on the waterfront just above the waves and the garden settings of Bajan galleries, verandas threatened by explosive tropical flora. Many of the hotels also have fine kitchens and it you are staying at one of the Elegant Resorts of Barbados you may try the others out. You can even dine out in old-time plantation splendour at **Sunbury** (© 423 6270) and **Villa Nova** (© 433 1524). No restaurants require a dinner jacket any more, though there may be a dress-code of trousers and a sleeved shirt. There is an encrustation of pizza huts and steak houses, but you can of course also eat fast-food Bajan style, taking away rice 'n' peas in a polystyrene box.

Eating out in Barbados is not cheap and an already hefty restaurant bill will be supplemented by a 10% service charge and a 5% government tax. Credit cards are widely accepted. You are advised to reserve a table in winter.

expensive

Only the quiet clink of cutlery will rise above the murmur of the night air at **Bagatelle Great House** (© 421 6767), where you dine in the coral stone rooms of one of the oldest plantation houses in Barbados. French cuisine with a twist of the Caribbean in the spices or ingredients; try Dijon steak *flambéd* in local sugar-cane brandy or Bajan catch Baxter's Road style (in tin foil, *see* below). Finish off with chocolate Amaretto. They have recently opened a supper club, **Mr Charles**, with 1920s cabaret and cigarette girls. **La Cage aux Folles** (✆ 424 2424), *closed Tues*, has great grace and style, in a spruce Bajan house with louvres, chandeliers and a polished wooden floor. There are dishes from across the world, including Hunanese duck, but from closer to home comes local catch *amandine* with slivered almonds.

There is extremely fine waterfront dining at **La Maison** (✆ 432 1556) on the St James coast, with French service in a Bajan gallery looking onto a lit garden framed with casuarina pines. The menu is French with Caribbean overtones—lobster in olive oil and sesame seeds and a sherry sauce. **Carambola** (✆ 432 0832), *closed Sun, main dish from Bds$50*, has another charming waterfront setting, with tables strung out on a cliffside 10ft above the calm waters of St James, under white awnings and umbrellas. The menu is French and Thai—filet of dolphin in Dijon mustard, *nuea yam nam tok* (waterfall beef). **The Mews** (✆ 432 1122) has a very pretty setting in a small town-house in Holetown. You dine in the garden under the trellises or in the many small rooms upstairs. There is a long fish menu—*paupiette* of snapper and crab or *tournedos tarragon*, followed by honey and hazelnut mousse.

Two slightly less expensive but equally good restaurants on the south coast are: in St Lawrence Gap, **Josef's** (✆ 435 6541), where you dine on a veranda with classical columns in a pink and white coral-rock house; the menu is international—dolphin *meunière* and even a Swedish dish, Skagen toast, chopped shrimp with mayonnaise and dill; and **Ile de France** in Hastings (✆ 435 6869), *closed Mon*, a French restaurant in style and service on a veranda with statuettes. *Ballotine de canard au sirop d'érable vinaigré* is followed by a superb *Marquise Monique au chocolat.*

moderate

Just south of Bridgetown in Aquatic Gap, **Brown Sugar** (✆ 426 7684) is set in an extended veranda festooned with hanging vines and mini-rock-pools, with a Caribbean-inspired menu—pepper chicken, Jamaican jerk and kingfish *en papillote*. The best waterfront setting on the south coast is at **Pisces** (✆ 435 6564), a white wicker dining room wrapped in greenery just above the calm waters of St Lawrence Gap. As the name suggests they have a long fish menu, including snapper caribe, stuffed with shrimp, tomato and herbs, with occasional exotic offerings like chub and sennet, or surf and turf. Not far off, **Secrets** also has a waterfront setting. Bagshot chicken, marinated in wine and soy sauce or 'tourist trap', dolphin steamed in a banana leaf.

It is well worth taking a trip to Holetown on the west coast to visit **Ragamuffin** (© 432 1295). The setting is a brightly painted Caribbean clapboard house and its name gives a good idea of the slightly raucous atmosphere. A lively bar, but good Caribbean fare too: jerk chicken *escaloped*, or blackened 'doll-fin' followed by rum and orange cake. At **The Fathoms** (© 432 2568) you dine above the waves on Payne's Bay. Start with octopus, or sea-egg (an aphrodisiac, they say) and move on to other creatures of the deep, such as caramelized parrot-fish with a mild chili sauce. A few of the hotels offer a buffet Sunday lunch. One of the best known is at the **Atlantis Hotel** in Bathsheba (© 423 1526) above the dramatic east coast of the island.

cheap

There are any number of small eat-in/take-aways around Barbados, particularly along the south coast, where you can get a meal for a few dollars. A recent appearance is **Jerk It**, a Jamaican jerk theme take-away. In the day you can grab a local meal of a 'cutter' (a hefty sandwich) or a box of rice 'n' peas from a 'Lunch Box' (a wagon) or the ever-popular *chefettes*. Finally, **Baxter's Road**, on the northern road out of Bridgetown, is an excellent place to get a night-time snack. The street is lined with hole-in-the-wall bars and golfing umbrellas, under which expansive Bajan ladies fry up on charcoal braziers. They start at about midnight and carry on until 5 or 6 am.

Bars and Nightlife

A French priest who came to Barbados in the 1650s claimed that there were 100 taverns for a population of 2000. The ratio of 1 for every 20 people may have gone down a bit since the 17th century, when even the Barbados Assembly used to meet in the pub, but evenings in Barbados can be very lively. Generally speaking the best areas are Bridgetown and the south coast, particularly around St Lawrence Gap. Bajan entertainment for Bajans tends to be in rum shops, usually local wooden houses with their shutters pinned open. It is worth stopping at one. Try **Muster's** in town, **John Moore's**, the Little Man's Club, on the west coast, where you can catch a game of dominoes, or **Buffy's Bar** if you're in the Silver Sands area.

If you want something more chichi, Barbados even has a small collection of wine bars, where the Bajan *bons bourgeois* congregate over a glass of Chablis with garlic bread and grilled goat's cheese; try **Nico's** in Holetown or the **39 Steps** in Hastings.

The trick with **nightlife** in Barbados is to bar-hop with the Bajans. Each different club has its night. In town are two quite local clubs: **Frontline**, popular at *weekends*, and the **Warehouse**, *Mon, Thurs and Sat,* with a large black and white dancefloor and international music. **Harbour Lights** on Carlisle Bay is a very lively club; the best nights are *Wed and Fri.* In St James is the **Coach House**, which has live music on *Thursdays.*

St Lawrence Gap is the most popular area for bars and clubs, and the day's lightly grilled flesh comes in for a night-time roasting here. You can start the evening in the bars, at **Boomers**, or at **Limer's Bar**, where there is nightly *karaoke* if that's your thing. From here you can spill straight into the clubs: **After Dark** is air-conditioned with five bars, one of them 75ft long. It offers live music, sports on the television and mixed Caribbean and international sounds. Dress code: 'No men with braided hair, no tracksuit, tank tops, no torn jeans, no bare feet, no men in short pants'. It's busiest on *Fri and Sat.*

Next door the **Ship Inn** is also popular, with live music and a sound system. The big night is *Tuesday*, when visitors and young Bajans dance or pulsate, depending on how much room there is. Dress code: 'Please dress nicely'. A recent addition is the **Reggae Lounge**, an open-air club strong on reggae as well as local calypso. If you are feeling peckish, head off to Baxter's Road. There are some excellent bands in Barbados and they play live in the many clubs: 'Spice' is one to look out for. Clubs usually charge an entry fee.

For raw and wholesome Bajan entertainment, you might go to a weekend dance or **Bram**—*details in the paper (location, admission price and a picture of the host)*—boozing and bit of wining and grinding to the latest soca and Jamaican dub.

For those who prefer a more formal setting, there are shows depicting Barbadian life and history. The best is probably *1627 and All That*...which celebrates Bajan history from the beginning and takes place *twice a week, Thurs and Sun,* in the Barbados Museum. For US$42 you have a tour of the museum, dinner, and see the show (© 435 6900). The Plantation Restaurant in the old boiling house of the Balls Estate in St Lawrence stages a couple of shows, the *Plantation Tropical Spectacular* (*Sat*) and *Barbados by Night* (*Wed, Fri*) with fire-eating and flaming limbo, adm Bds$85 for drinks and dinner (reservations ✆ 428 5048). Yet more formal entertainment, classical concerts and plays, are usually held in the **Frank Collymore Hall** in Bridgetown.

Shopping

The opening hours of most shops on Barbados are weekdays 8–6, Saturdays 8–noon. For Bajan or Bajan-designed products, try the **Best of Barbados**, with branches throughout the island, or **Fairfield Greathouse Pottery**, set in an old boiling house in St Michael.

Further Reading

By Barbadian authors: *In the Castle of my Skin*, by George Lamming, is about a black Barbadian boy growing up; *Christopher*, by Geoffrey Drayton, narrates the stifling life of a white Barbadian boy. Edward Braithwaite's collections of poetry include *Rights of Passage*. Good beach material is Thomas Hoover's *Caribbee*, set in the time when Barbados had a tavern for every twenty inhabitants. A recent publication set in modern times in a mythical hotel on the west coast of Barbados is *Platinum Coast*, a steamy tale of international people with unfeasibly large bank accounts. There are many well-written histories of the island and plenty of lifestyle books. The **bookshops** are stocked with books on the Caribbean and most magazines. Try the Cloister Bookstore on the Wharf or Cave Shepherd on Broad Street.

History	88
Getting There and Around	93
Tourist Information	94
Beaches and Sports	95

Grenada

St George's	98
The West Coast	101
The South Coast	102
Over the Grand Etang to the East Coast	103
Where to Stay	105
Eating Out	107
Carriacou and Petit Martinique	109

Grenada and its Grenadines are strung out over 50 miles or so in the far south of the Caribbean, at the foot of the Windward Islands chain, about 90 miles from Trinidad and the South American coast. The island of Grenada itself is typical of the Windwards in its tropical beauty, with towering mountains mantled in explosive rainforest, and coastal inlets and bays furred with palms and white sand beaches.

To its north Grenada (pronounced 'gre-nay-der') is linked to the island of St Vincent by the Grenadines, a 60-mile string of coral islands and cays, towering peaks that soar out of the water and sandbars that barely make it to the surface. Two of the inhabited Grenadines, Carriacou and Petit Martinique, belong to Grenada, and altogether the three islands make up a population of about 95,000. Grenada's capital, St George's, is the prettiest harbour town in the whole Caribbean. It is set in a massive volcanic bowl, and its slopes are lined with red-tiled roofs that descend to the edge of the bay, where cruise ships, yachts and old-fashioned schooners sit in dock, dwarfing the daily activity on the waterfront.

Measuring just 12 miles by 21, Grenada calls itself the Spice Island of the Caribbean because its fertile soil produces spices for markets all over the world. In the valleys of the mountainous interior you will see the fruit and spice plantations and the cocoa walks, where orange immortelle trees stand aflame above the cocoa trees early in the year. Nutmeg, from which come the spices nutmeg and mace, is the island's most famous spice.

Grenada is quiet and easy-going in true Caribbean style, but not so long ago, in October 1983, it was thrust into the international news because of its revolution and the subsequent invasion that put the might of the United States on to a tiny Caribbean island. The customary Caribbean quiet did not take long to return and now the island sees a steady stream of tourists.

Grenada is building steadily and, although it is less developed than St Lucia, it has a broad range of hotels and a pleasant feel about it at the moment. It is also well positioned for exploring the Grenadines, by yacht, by ferry and by island-hopping plane, where you will find another charming style of easy Caribbean island life.

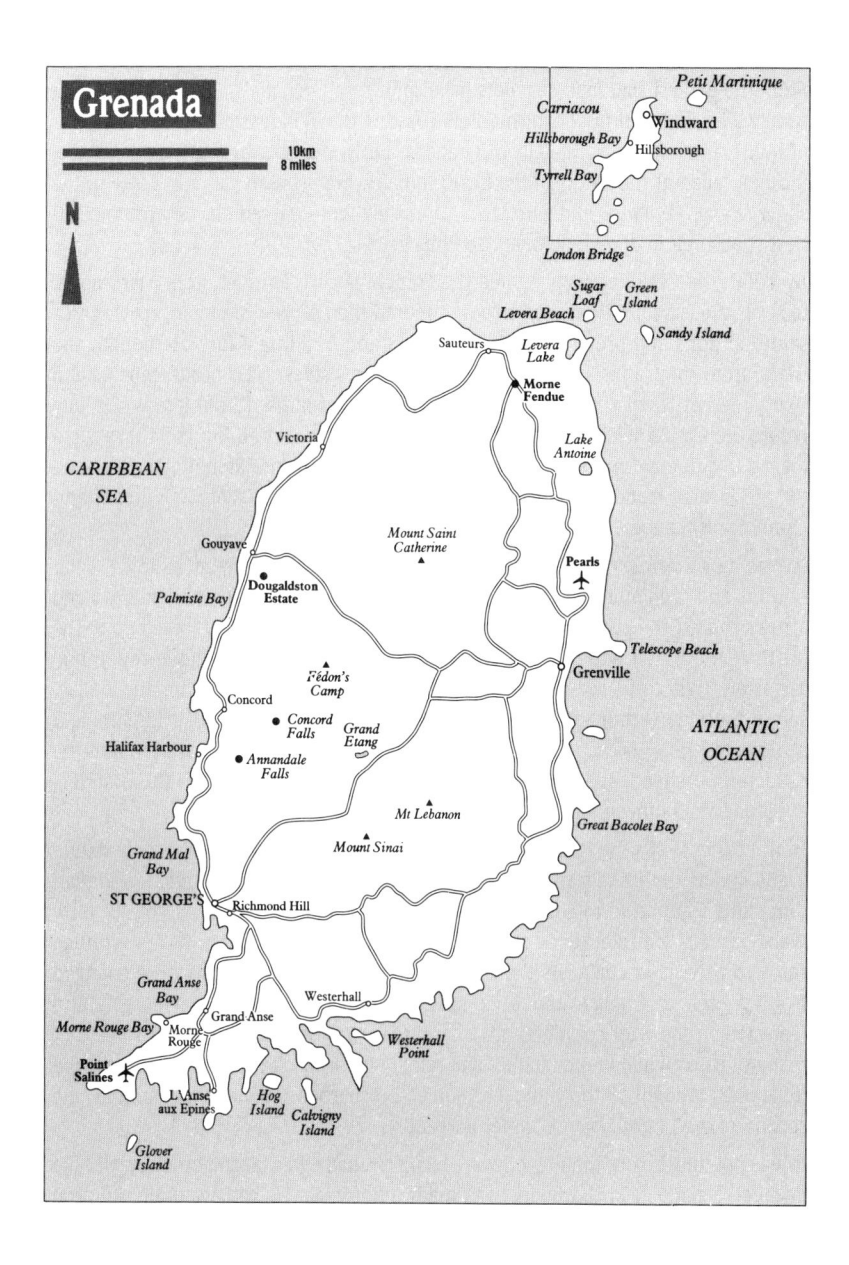

Grenada

10km
8 miles

History

From the earliest sightings travellers have spoken of Grenada's physical beauty and fertility. To 16th-century Spanish sailors coasting the Windwards it was a reminder of home, the hills above the city of Granada. Early attempts to settle Camerhogne, though, failed at the hands of the Carib Indians. Englishmen came in 1609 in the ships *Diana, Penelope* and *Endeavour*, but they were chased off, as were the settlers sponsored by the Frenchman De Poincy.

By 1650, the Caribs actually invited the Frenchman Du Parquet, from Martinique, to settle the island. He came with 'two hundred men of good stamina', arriving to a salute of guns and promptly erecting a cross and building a fort. He bought the island from the Caribs for 'cloth, axes, bill-hooks, knives, glass beads, mirrors and two large bottles of *eau-de-vie* (brandy) for the chief himself', but it was not long before the Caribs decided the deal was not a good one after all. By 1654 they were locked in a duel with the French for possession of the island. Reinforcements came for the French from Martinique by ship and for the Caribs from St Vincent and Dominica by canoe.

It was an extremely brutal time. The Caribs roamed the island killing French hunters and then attacked the French settlement. But, armed only with bows and arrows against the guns of the French, the Caribs were eventually forced up to the north of the island where, rather than be captured and killed, they threw themselves off a cliff to their deaths. A new owner of the island, the Comte du Cerillac, sent a brutal governor who so abused his power that the islanders tried him and sentenced him to be hanged. At this he pleaded noble birth, which gave him the right to be beheaded. There was no executioner on Grenada, but the islanders eventually had him shot.

In the early 1700s the island became an important French colony, as a plantation island and as a refitting station on the route from Martinique, the French headquarters in the Caribbean, to South America. But in the endless rounds of 18th-century wars Grenada was blockaded and captured again and again as the navies whittled through the island chain. As the island changed hands, the names were changed from French to English and back again; Fort Royal became St George's and Gouyave on the west coast became Charlotte Town. Some of the names stuck, but many of the original French names still remain in Grenada even today. Despite the difficulties brought by the wars, it remained prosperous and was thought of as 'the second of the English Islands' (after Barbados).

It was not long before the French were back. Grenada was taken almost by mistake because an attack on Barbados was made impossible by bad weather. Admiral d'Estaing entered St George's harbour and the Irish troops of his ally Count Arthur

Dillon attacked by land. The island surrendered. Hard on his heels came the British Admiral, Foulweather Jack Byron, but even though some of his ships made it into the harbour, he could not draw the 'mere gasconade of a vapouring Frenchman' into battle and so the French won Grenada again. The British Governor and the island's colours were shipped off to France. The latter were strung up above the High Altar in Notre Dame and the former was eventually returned to Britain.

When the British were back in control, the British Grenadians were vengeful over their treatment at French hands. They confiscated church lands and made the French Grenadians submit to the 'Test', an oath demanding a rejection of Transubstantiation, impossible for a Catholic. Many chose to emigrate to Trinidad, where the Spaniards were crying out for settlers. Much of Trinidad's French heritage dates from these Grenadian refugees. But on the island itself the grievances increased, fired by the harsher treatment of the slaves under the British and by the French Revolution, which was being spread from Guadeloupe by Victor Hugues (*see* p.234). Eventually it erupted into open rebellion in 1795.

Fédon's Rebellion

The revolt was led by Julien Fédon, a mulatto planter. From Guadeloupe the revolutionaries brought back 'arms and ammunition, caps of liberty, national cockades and a flag on which was inscribed in large characters, *Liberté, Egalité ou la Mort*.' The rebels overran the whole island, killing prisoners along with suspected collaborators. Their first strike was on the east coast, at La Baye, near modern Grenville, where British settlers were taken from their beds and shot, and at Charlotte Town, where the Governor himself, Sir Ninian Home, was captured trying to return to St George's. He was one of 51 hostages taken to the rebel mountain stronghold, eventually to be slaughtered on Fédon's personal instructions as the rebels came under threat from the advancing British troops.

St George's never fell to the rebels but it took a year before reinforcements under Sir Ralph Abercromby defeated the guerrillas. Their leaders were captured and executed immediately or exiled to Honduras, but Fédon himself was never taken. Some think he drowned in an attempt to escape to Trinidad, but others think that he made it to Cuba. His estate at Belvidere, from where he ran the insurrection, is just below one of Grenada's mountain peaks, now known as Fédon's Camp. By the end of the conflict, Grenada was in ruins.

When the slaves were freed in 1838 they took over small plots of Grenada's fertile land. Unlike the other Windwards, Grenada remained reasonably prosperous during the decline of the 19th century. Agriculture was the economic mainstay; bananas and cocoa were grown, among lesser-known spices such as cinnamon, bay leaf, allspice and ginger.

With the failure of the Federation, when attempts to unite all the British Caribbean islands into one country foundered in 1962, and after a later failure to unite with Trinidad and Tobago, Grenada became an Associated State of Britain in 1967. They were not long in deciding on Independence and Grenada became an independent nation within the British Commonwealth on 7 February 1974.

Grenada's first leader was Eric Gairy, a volatile and charismatic man whose political heritage was in the oil-fields of the Caribbean island of Aruba. Elected as early as 1951, he was fondly thought of by many Grenadians as the champion of workers' rights against the colonial government. After Independence his leadership became steadily more corrupt, wasteful and bullying, and he used a secret army called the Mongoose Gang to impose his will unofficially.

In the early seventies the New Jewel Movement was formed. Initially clandestine, to avoid harassment from the overbearing government, this socialist movement steadily gained ground, allying itself with the disillusioned opposition to Gairy, including the influential and traditionally conservative business class.

Revolution and Invasion

On 13 March 1979, with Gairy out of the country, 38 armed members of the NJM stormed the army barracks at True Blue on the south coast of the island and in a bloodless coup the NJM was in power. With popular support, they began a social experiment unprecedented in the Commonwealth Caribbean. Considerable strides forward were made in health care and in education, with general economic growth over the next four years. However, the repressive nature of the People's Revolutionary Government's programmes gradually became clearer: the press was stifled, political detainees were held untried and then, when Grenada forged closer ties with Cuba and the Eastern bloc, the Grenadian Revolution began to excite international disapproval.

Under this pressure from outside and facing straitened economic circumstances on the island, the PRG foundered in a split from within. The leader, Maurice Bishop, was placed under house arrest by the other members of the Central Committee, but eventually his supporters brought him to St George's, where they congregated at Fort George. Bernard Coard and others of the opposing faction of the PRG sent down troops who fired on the crowd to disperse it, killing about sixty people, then shooting Bishop and five of his close associates inside the fort. The whole island was placed under a 24-hour curfew for four days until the US 82nd Airborne Division arrived on 25 October 1983.

Massive aid and assistance came in the first couple of years and President Reagan himself made a visit in February 1986, but it has tailed off now that Grenada has acquiesced. Many Grenadians do think of the invasion as the 'rescue mission' and are grateful to Reagan for sending troops. Others will never forgive the USA for what seemed to them an unwarranted show of force against a small country by a big power in whose backyard Grenada happened to be. There is still considerable support for Maurice Bishop, if not for his deputies.

Grenada remains within the British Commonwealth and has two Houses of Parliament, a 13-member Senate and a 15-member House of Representatives elected for five-year terms. The Prime Minister is Nicholas Braithwaite of the National Democratic Congress. Eric Gairy remains an active figure in island politics even today. He may well stand again in the next elections, due in April 1995.

The Spice Island of the Caribbean

Grenada was known as the Isle of Spice—the source of the island's prosperity at the turn of the century. Spices are still a profitable business even though Grenada's one-third share of the world market in nutmeg is now gone and market prices are at a low ebb. You are bound to be offered spices for sale in the streets while you are in Grenada. Otherwise, two good places to visit are the **Minor Spices Society** next to the Market in St George's and **Arawak Islands Ltd**, which is set in a pretty creole house in Belmont just out of town.

Nutmeg is the island's principal spice, and was once so important to the island that it is commemorated on the colourful Grenadian flag. In the past nutmeg has been used as a charm to ward off illness and today it is used locally in remedies against colds as well as in Vicks Vapour Rub. In the Second World War, oil of nutmeg was in demand for aircraft engine oil because it does not freeze at high altitudes. Nutmeg was introduced into Grenada in 1843, supposedly at a party, where it was added as a mystery ingredient to the top of the regular planter's punch—the party was no doubt a success, but, more importantly, Grenadians have never drunk a rum punch without nutmeg since. The tree (botanical name *Myristica fragrans*) is evergreen and grows up to 60ft in height. Its fruit looks like a yellow apricot and the Grenadians will tell you that no part of it goes to waste. When it ripens, the flesh splits open, revealing a brown nut covered with a red wax netting, and it drops to the ground. The fruit must be collected at once to prevent it from rotting and then the parts are separated. The outer flesh goes into making jams or preserves and the nutmeg kernels are graded by throwing them in water. Those that float are used in pharmaceuticals, but the good ones sink and are processed to make the spice. Finally, the red netting is used for a second spice, mace. It is not commonly known that the two spices come from the same

Cocoa beans drying in mobile boucans

plant. A London bureaucrat caused hilarity among the estate workers when he sent notice that the international market price of nutmeg was on the decrease and that of mace increasing and so cultivators would be advised to hold on the first and to step up production of the latter. The two biggest nutmeg factories are in Gouyave and Grenville and they are worth a visit.

Another tree seen all over the island is the **cocoa** tree, *theobroma* or 'Food of the Gods', with hand-sized purple pods sprouting indiscriminately from trunk and branches. They grow in cocoa walks, as the valley plantations were called, alternate male and female trees up to 30ft high, which go on producing for up to a hundred years, usually in the shade of the much larger immortelle tree, famed for its orange blooms. The pods are collected and broken open to reveal a (delicious) white sticky-sweet gel and up to thirty cocoa beans. The beans are fermented, piled into a wooden sweating box with a little water and turned regularly, until the white pulp degrades. Next the brown beans are laid out on to huge trays, or 'boucans', where they are dried in the sun, again constantly being turned, or 'danced', by the workers, who shuffle through them in lines. At this stage they begin to smell of bitter unsweetened cocoa. From here they are exported, as Grenada has no large processing plant. For local consumption, some beans will be processed and the oily product rolled into sticks, which can be grated into boiling water to make cocoa for breakfast.

Other spices cultivated in Grenada are **cinnamon** bark, bundles of which can be bought in the markets rolled up in pink ribbon, **cloves** and **pimento** or **allspice**, so-called because it tastes like cinnamon, clove and nutmeg all at once. **Ginger**, **bay leaves** and **vanilla** are also grown. Many are used in confectionery and the flavouring of food or as a preservative. Apart from local use for their alternative medicinal properties (bay rum and lemon grass are used to quell fevers, and corilie for hypertension; oil of ginger is said to reduce pain), many are exported for use in the pharmaceutical industry.

Flora and Fauna

Like the other Windward Islands, much of the interior of Grenada is too wild and remote to be inhabited and so there are large tracts of rainforest that are untouched, but which you can explore by a series of trails (many start out from the Grand Etang in the National Park, where no building is allowed anyway). You will see huge gommier and mahogany trees, grappled by creeping vines and lianas that threaten to throttle the path, and if you go higher, beyond the montane forest into the elfin woodland, there are stunted trees and ferns. Living in the forest are a few animals, including mona monkeys, opossum, a species of nine-banded armadillo and many birds, including tanagers and the odd hawk.

There are a number of mangrove areas in Grenada, including Levera in the northeast and La Sagesse estuary in the southeast (a national park area), which have an entirely different bird life. Here you may see coots and flycatchers and the more traditional seabirds such as pelicans and boobies. The national flower of Grenada is the bougainvillea, which you will see at hotels all over the island.

✆ (809)– ***Getting There***

Grenada has reasonable international air links, from both Europe and North America, arriving at Point Salines airport in the southwestern tip of the island. The airport has certainly opened the island up for visitors, whatever its military applications might have been. If there is no direct flight, it is nearly always possible to make a connection the same day, via Barbados, Trinidad or St Lucia. A departure tax of EC$25 and a security charge of EC$10 are payable by all adults who stay more than 24 hours; children aged 5–11 years pay half as much; under 5s are exempt.

By Air from the UK: One direct flight a week on British Airways (✆ 440 2796) from Gatwick. BWIA (✆ 440 3818) fly via Barbados and in the winter months there are charter flights. In **Europe**, Frankfurt and Zurich are linked to Grenada via Barbados, Paris via Martinique.

By Air from the USA: American Airlines (✆ 444 2222) flies daily via Puerto Rico and BWIA has daily direct flights from Miami.

By Air from other Caribbean Islands: LIAT (✆ 440 4297) connects Grenada with Barbados, Tobago, St Vincent and several of the Grenadines, including Carriacou and Union Island. BWIA flies between Grenada and Trinidad. Airlines of Carriacou (✆ 444 3549, fax 444 2898) hop through the Grenadines. Aerotuy fly twice weekly from Margarita off the Venezuelan coast. Charter planes are available through Helenair (✆ 444 4101).

By Boat: There are many ferry services each week (not quite one a day) between Grenada and Carriacou; the journey time is 3 hours. The schedule is fairly flexible and depends on which boats are running. Check at the Carenage in St George's or the Tourist Board. The one-way fare is EC$25, EC$50 return. From Windward in Carriacou you can take a boat to Petit Martinique *Mon, Wed, Fri*. There are occasional boats to Trinidad which may allow you to travel as a paying passenger.

Getting Around

Buses run all the main roads in Grenada and can be flagged down from the side of the road with a frantic downward-pointing finger. On board they are quite crowded and often they give you a good introduction to local music. They leave from the main Market Square on the Esplanade side of town, starting at dawn and running until about seven in the evening and infrequently into the night. After the run to church on Sundays, services are less frequent. Some prices are **St George's** to Gouyave EC$4, Grenville EC$4 and to Sauteurs EC$5. To the Grand Anse area and to the top of the L'Anse aux Epines road, the ride costs EC$1.25.

The alternative is to go by **taxi**, which is expensive but easily arranged at a hotel, in town or at the major beaches. As usual, the drivers are a mine of information and are happy to give an impromptu tour. Sample rates, set by the Grenada Board of Tourism, are: from **St George's** to Grand Anse US$7, L'Anse aux Epines US$12, to Point Salines Airport US$12, to the Grand Etang US$30 return, and to Gouyave and Dougaldston US$40 return. To hire a taxi by the hour costs US$15 and drivers are available for a day's outing. The Grenada Hotels Taxi Drivers Association can be contacted on ✆ 444 4882.

Car hire is another possibility and a good way to see the island if you are prepared to brave the vagaries of the Grenadian road and can remember to keep to the left. You will need a visitor's licence, which can be bought from the police at the fire station on the Carenage, or from the the rental companies, on presentation of a valid licence from home, for EC$30. Rental cars, from about US$40 per day, are available from **Spice Isle Rentals**, the Avis rental in St George's (✆ 440 3936), jeeps also available, **David's Car Rentals** (✆ 440 2399), **SR Car Rentals** (✆ 444 3222) and **Maitland's Motor Rentals** (✆ 444 4022), which also rents out motorbikes.

Tourist Information

In **Britain**, the Grenada Tourist Office is at 1 Collingham Gardens, London SW5 0HW (✆ 071 370 5164/5, fax 071 370 7040). In the **USA** you can contact them at 820 Second Avenue, Suite 900D, New York, NY 10017 (℅ 212 687 9554 or toll free ℅ 800 638 0852) and in **Canada** at 439 University Avenue, Suite 820, Toronto, Ontario M5G 1Y8 (℅ 416 595 1339).

In Grenada itself, the main **Board of Tourism** (℅ 440 2001, fax 440 6637) is in St George's, on the waterfront in the Carenage. There are smaller offices at the cruise ship terminal (℅ 440 2872) and at Point Salines airport (℅ 444 4140). They are helpful with accommodation and advice. Open 8–4 in St George's and 7am–9pm at the airport.

The *Grenadian Voice*, the *Informer* and the *Grenadian Today* are the island's weekly newspapers and they list local events as well as covering Caribbean news. The Grenada Board of Tourism puts out a number of complimentary publications: *Greeting*, a glossy magazine with tourist information and a list of options if you are struck with a shopping crisis; and the pocket-sized *Discover Grenada*. A monthly tourist paper, *Spicy Grenada*, covers current events and activities.

The **IDD code** for Grenada is **809**, followed by a seven-digit island number. In a **medical emergency**, contact St George's Hospital (℅ 440 2051/2/3).

Money

The Grenadian currency is the Eastern Caribbean dollar (shared with a number of other British Commonwealth Caribbean countries), which is fixed to the US dollar at a rate of about EC$2.65 = US$1. It is advisable to be sure which currency you are dealing in, as a bargain may suddenly turn out to be nearly three times better or a taxi fare considerably more expensive. **Banking hours** are Mon–Fri, 8–1, some until 2; and 3–5 Fri. **Shops** are open 8–4 weekdays, Sat morning until noon.

Beaches

Grenada has plenty of beaches—Caribbean-style strands mounded with silken white sand, and tiny secluded coves bristling with the coconut palms that are so typical of the mountainous Windward Islands. Easily the best known is **Grand Anse**, 2 miles of pristine sand where many of the island's hotels are located. There are more secluded strands beyond Grand Anse, towards the western tip of the island; for instance **Morne Rouge Bay**, sometimes known as BBC Beach after a defunct discotheque, an attractive stretch of sand in a deep bay, and two delightful coves, **Dr Groom** and **Magazine Beach**. Another popular beach area is **L'Anse aux Epines** (when spoken, it sounds something more like 'lansapeen'), to the south of Grand Anse.

Along the southern and eastern coasts, beaches can be found at **Westerhall Point**, in an attractive bay at **La Sagesse**, at **Bacolet Bay** and at **Telescope Beach** near Grenville. At the northeastern tip of the island are the two good strands which look out into the Atlantic. **Bathway Beach** is safe for swimming because it has an offshore reef, but the water at **Levera Beach** is rougher. Take a picnic to this area. On the west coast, the Grenadians like **Palmiste Bay** and **Grand Mal Bay**.

Beach Bars

There are some good seaside haunts with secluded bars where you can spend an excellent day's sunning and snorkelling. On the southwestern peninsula off the airport road there are two excellent spots set in small, high-sided coves: the **Aquarium**, on Portici beach, is set back from a quiet cove and attracts a friendly crowd, and **Dr Groom's Café** is also on a superb strip of sand. There is a quiet and charming bar and restaurant in the trees at **La Sagesse Bay**, also ideal for a day out in the isolated southeast. *Transfers, lunch and a guided walk through the local woodlands for about US$30 (© 444 6458).* If you are travelling independently there is another bar in **Petit Bacaye** nearby. On **Grand Anse** there are any number of hotel and beach bars to retreat to: **Cotbam** is pretty characterless unles the stereo system is up and running, so the smaller **Umbrella Beach House**, under the police station next door, is a preferable spot for a burger and a beer. The **Paradise Club**, set back from the beach proper, is also a good place to take time out from sizzling in coconut oil. A little further afield on BBC Beach is **Sur la Mer** restaurant, an ideal liming spot with a cracking view of the sunset through the fishnets and shutters.

Sailing

Grenada offers an excellent starting point for a sailing holiday. The island's ragged southern coastline has endless coves to explore and then from here you can run by St George's and coast north beneath Grenada's towering, rainforested mountains to the Grenadines, where the sea, sand and snorkelling are superb and there are islands with just a few palm trees and swim-up bars. There are **ports of entry** in St George's, in the Lagoon area, in L'Anse aux Epines on the south coast and in Grenville in the east.

St George's is a good harbour, though it can get hot on a still day so you may prefer to head for the south coast. The facilities for yachts are in the Lagoon at Grenada Yacht Services (© 440 2548), where you will find water and fuel and excellent **provisioning** in the nearby supermarket, also an amusing bar at Island Paradise. On the south coast, a couple of miles east of Point Salines, is an excellent harbour at L'Anse aux Epines (also known by its English equivalent of Prickly Bay). There is a small marina at Spice Island Marine Services, good for fuel and water, but also a boatyard for repairs. A chandlery, a small supermarket and a laundry are nearby. There are a couple of hotels and restaurants in the immediate area: the Boatyard is busiest on a Friday. The Moorings have a marina in the excellent and sheltered setting of Mount Hartman Bay. Of the many islands and inlets on Grenada's southern shore that make good daytime stopovers, head for Hog Island and Calvigny in Clarke's Court Bay and the protected reaches of Port Egmont. Further afield try Westerhall Bay, though you should beware of reefs in this area. Heading north of St George's there are few protected **anchorages**.

A week-long **Sailing Festival** is held out of Grenada in January each year, with competitive and less competitive yachting races around the island, starting as far away as Bequia and Trinidad. There are many other regattas during the year, of which the liveliest is probably the **Carriacou Regatta** in August.

The Moorings (℡ 444 4439), in the quiet inlet of Mt Hartmann Bay behind L'Anse aux Epines, has the biggest selection of yachts for bareboat charter. **Seabreeze Yacht Charters** (℡ 444 4924) works out of the Spice Island Marine Centre in L'Anse aux Epines. There are marinas and good repair services in both these places.

Watersports

For beachborne watersports it is best to go to Grand Anse, where you can fix up a jetski (try Worldwide Watersports), a flight under a parasail or be dragged around the bay on a bouncy banana. Contact **Skyride** (℡ 440 7375). Waterskiing, small sailing craft and windsurfers are available through the hotel concessionaires.

The companies mentioned in 'Sailing' above will also arrange a day's sail to an offshore island—usually Calivigny or Hog Island off the south coast, but you can also try *Psyche* (℡ 444 4010) or *Whistler* (℡ 440 3075). For an afternoon of fun with the cruise ship passengers or a rum-and-reggae-soaked sunset cruise you can try a *Rhum Runner* tour (℡ 440 2198). A deep-sea fishing trip, trawling the depths to the west of Grenada, can be arranged through **Tropix Professional Sport Fishing** (℡ 440 4961) and **Evans Chartering Services** (℡ 444 4422). *About US$500 a full day, $300 for half a day.* The Spice Island International Billfish Tournament is staged in January each year (℡ 440 2018).

Scuba diving is also best arranged at Grand Anse, through **Dive Grenada** at the Grenada Renaissance Hotel (℡ 444 4371, fax 444 4800) and at **Grand Anse Aquatics** (℡ 444 4129, fax 444 4808), who also rent out kayaks. Grenada is surrounded by reefs on all sides; some of the better known are Bose Reef and Whibble Reef in the southeast. You can also dive the *Bianca C*, a 600ft liner which was scuttled after a famous fire in the Carenage and is now thought to be the largest wreck sitting upright in the world. Dive the upper decks and then take a turn around the swimming pool. *Single tank dives US$45; packages and certification available in both places.* **Snorkellers** will find good shallow seascapes in L'Anse aux Epines and at Molinière north of St George's.

Other Sports

One of the pleasures of visiting Grenada lies in its natural beauty and it is well worth taking a walk through the tropical rainforests, perhaps to one of the waterfalls. **Henry's Tours** (℗ 444 5313) offer well-organized walks, reaching off-beat parts of the island, including *Fédon's Camp*, the summit from which Julien Fédon led his rebellion in the 18th century. You can also try **Arnold's Tours** (℗ 440 0531), for a variety of hiking and bus tours, and **Sunsation Tours** (℗ 444 1656). It is possible to tour Grenada on **horseback**—contact **The Horseman** (℗ 440 5368), and by mountain bike, **Ride Grenada** (℗ 444 1157).

There are **tennis courts** at many of the hotels and in the Grand Anse area. **Golfers** can play a nine-nole course near Grand Anse, at the Grenada Golf and Country Club (℗ 444 4128), green fee EC$50.

St George's

The capital of Grenada is the prettiest harbour town in the Caribbean. Stacked on an amphitheatrical hillside are lines of warehouses, homes and churches with ochre-tiled and red tin roofs that glow in the evening light against the rich tropical green of Grenada's slopes. St George's is very much a working port and many ships put into the harbour—cargo vessels, cruise ships and yachts and of course the brightly painted schooners from the Grenadines which you will see tied up on the wharves of the Carenage.

Named after King George III, the old parts of the town date from the late 18th century, when the original buildings were destroyed in fires. It is sprinkled with fine old creole houses, built of brick in soft shades of rose, yellow and beige and embellished with elaborate ironwork balconies and the occasional porch that was used to keep sedan chair passengers from getting wet in the rain.

St George's is built over the backbone of a hill and is split into two main halves: the Carenage, on the inner harbour, and the Esplanade, which fronts on to the Caribbean Sea. The two sides are linked by a network of steep cobbled streets and stepped alleys. At Carnival, when the costumed masqueraders wind through the streets of St George's, the floats have to be winched up the cobbled streets and then held back from running away down the other side.

Once, St George's Harbour was an inland lake, but now it can take ocean-going vessels. It was the crater of a volcano, from which the sides have crumbled. It is extinct, but not entirely dormant, as was shown by a curious and alarming incident in 1867, when volcanic activity was felt throughout the Caribbean. At 5 in the afternoon the level of the water in the Carenage suddenly dropped by 5ft and the Green Hole started to bubble and steam, letting off sulphurous gases. Moments later, the level of the sea rose to about 4ft above the normal, only to be sucked down and to rise again a number of times.

The statue on the waterfront at the head of the harbour, a replica of Christ of the Deep, was dedicated to the people of Grenada after their efforts to save the passengers of a cruise liner, the *Bianca C*, which burned in Grenada harbour in 1961. There are plenty of cafés and bars around the waterfront where you can catch a drink and a rest when your feet overheat. One of the best views of the town can be had from a water-taxi trip across the harbour (*price EC$1*).

The **Carenage** is the centrepiece of the town, the very attractive curved waterfront lined with old mercantile buildings which are still used by businesses today. One of the finest and oldest creole houses is the former French military barracks on Young Street, now home to the **Grenada National Museum**, *open weekdays, 9–4.30, Sat 10–1.30, small adm.* Here Arawak petroglyphs are on view, alongside Empress Josephine's marble bathtub (she spent her childhood on the nearby island of Martinique), copper kettles and a rum still from the days of sugar, and newspaper clippings of the recent political turmoil.

Forts and churches dominate the heights of St George's and many of them stand on Church Street, the ridge road that gives onto both sides of the town. Close to Fort George, which overlooks the harbour mouth, is the **Scot's Kirk**, a Presbyterian Church erected in 1831. A little farther up is the **St George's Parish Anglican Church**, rebuilt in 1825 on the site of an original 1763 French Roman Catholic Church. It contains plaques commemorating the victims of the Brigand's War, or Fédon's Rebellion, and the 51 hostages, including the Governor, Ninian Home, who were murdered by the 'execrable banditti'. Still on Church Street is **York House**, the Grenadian House of Parliament. But the best position of all is commanded by the **Roman Catholic Cathedral** (many Grenadians are still Catholic from French days), built in 1818 and remembered for its Angelus that tolled in the morning, midday and evening.

The other half of St George's is the **Esplanade** or Bay Town, which looks on to the Caribbean Sea. It was hard work getting over the ridge to the market from the Carenage and so at the end of the 19th century a tunnel was constructed, linking the two. The Sendall tunnel, named after the Governor, is over 100 yards long and still used now for heavy traffic.

The Esplanade has lines of old warehouses overlooking the sea and on the waterfront itself is the **fish market**, alive when the catch is brought in at the end of the day. The main St George's **market** is a couple of blocks inland from the Esplanade, on open ground between Granby and Hillsborough Streets. There is a typical Caribbean ironwork-covered market building, but most of the activity takes place out on the square, where golf umbrellas shelter the vendors and their produce—root vegetables and tropical fruits (and of course Grenadian spices)—from the sun and from passing rainstorms. The best day to visit is Saturday, in the morning, but it is lively on any weekday morning (it is quiet on Sundays). If you have not been waylaid already by the spice women who ply the streets of St George's, then at the back of the square on Grenville Street you can visit the **Minor Spices Society**, which smells of the cinnamon, cloves and allspice on sale here.

Close by is the **Yellow Poui Art Gallery** on Cross Street. Named after a tree, it features West Indian art, particularly impressive for its primitivist paintings, and West Indian scenes by foreign painters and sculptors. Look out for Grenadians Michael Paryag and Elinus Cato, and Carriacouans Canute Caliste and Frankie Francis.

Only two forts remain of what was once a protective ring of defences on the heights above St George's. **Fort George** dominates the harbour mouth, with a fine view of the Carenage and of the open sea, and it is now the main St George's police station. Constructed in 1706, it spent a spell more recently as Fort Rupert (named after the father of Maurice Bishop who was killed in a riot in 1974). It was here that Maurice Bishop himself and his colleagues were shot on 19 October 1983. Cannon still poke over the battlements and underground there is a warren of tunnels and caverns, supposedly leading to a series of underground passageways from one fort to the next (now blocked off). Tours are possible.

On the rising ground that forms the backdrop of St George's harbour, among the homes of prosperous Grenadians, is **Marryshow House**, a creole building that was once the home of the Grenadian political leader and architect of the West Indies Federation, T. A. Marryshow. Higher still is **Government House**, with a fine view over the harbour and town. Built in 1802, it is the residence of the Governor General. But the most spectacular view can be seen after a stiff climb up **Richmond Hill**, which commands the harbour and the coast as far as Point Salines in the southwest. Once there were four forts, started by the French after they captured the island in 1779 and completed by the British. Fort Frederick is in reasonable repair and there is a campaign to restore Fort Matthew.

There are two botanical gardens in St George's. At the foot of Richmond Hill, on the outskirts of the town, are the old **Botanical Gardens**, established in 1886. They are a little tatty now, but they are still a pleasant place to sit and rest. A better bet are the **Bay Gardens**, *open daylight hours, adm*, behind Richmond Hill, which are set in the grounds of a former sugar mill, and where you will see a huge range of Caribbean flora—vivid blooms of purple, pink and scarlet among the endless shades of green. It is well worth finding a guide to tell you about the many species on display.

The West Coast

The Grenadian coastline is a series of headlands and bays, spurs of land thrown off from the volcanic peaks and valleys carved out by rivers, where Grenada's spice plantations have grown. The road follows the coastline, all hairpins and switchbacks and overhung by cliffs, initially laid out by the French in the 18th century. The names recount the island's mixed history—Halifax Harbour, Beauséjour Bay, Happy Hill and Molinière.

From St George's the Esplanade road leads up the west coast, passing the old communal toilet on the bayfront and on to **Queen's Park**, an open ground used for cricket and football matches on the outskirts of the town. Inland from Concord, following the Black Bay River upstream among the nutmeg and cocoa plantations, are the **Concord Falls**, a series of three waterfalls lost in the forested mountains. It is possible to drive to the lowest one, but the other two must be reached on foot: the first takes 25 minutes, and the next is 1½-hour's walk. However, each fall has a pool in which you can swim after the climb. In high season you will probably not be alone, but it is a pleasant walk. It is even possible to walk up to Grand Etang (about 5 hours' climb). Back on the coast, **Black Bay** is named after its appearance, which is black volcanic rather than white coral sand.

Just outside Gouyave is the **Dougaldston Estate**, a charming old plantation of clapboard and tin-roofed buildings and dilapidated farm machinery, where cocoa and nutmeg are grown among allspice, tonka beans and coffee. In years past the estate would ring to the sound of violins as the workers 'danced' the cocoa beans to dry them evenly in the boucans, shuffling in lines and turning the cocoa beans with their feet. The boucans, vast trays that are pulled out from beneath one another to catch the sun, are on wheels so that they can be rushed back beneath the building in case of rain. In the main building, heavy with the smells of cinnamon, cloves and nutmeg, the old processes can be seen, worked by the Grenadian ladies. It is possible to buy the spices on display.

Gouyave (French for 'guava') is a little farther along the coast. Set on a promontory, the town's old creole houses are past their best now, but it is alluring in its faded prosperity. Travelling in the forties, Patrick Leigh Fermor came across a sweepstake here in which the first prize was a free funeral for the ticket holder or for any friend or relation.

The biggest building in Gouyave is the **Grenada Nutmeg Cooperative Association**—floors full of sacks, tea chests and machinery, the air redolent with the sweet-spice smell of nutmeg, (see p.91).

Set on a sweeping bay on the north coast is the village of **Sauteurs**, the island's third-largest town and the scene of one of the saddest moments in Grenada's history, when the retreating Caribs were surrounded by the French troops and reputedly threw themselves to their death in the sea rather than be killed. And so, in French, the place became known as *Le morne des Sauteurs*, Leapers' Hill.

In the northeastern point of the island is **Levera Bay**, a strip of golden sand with fine views of the offshore islands. Nearby is Levera Lake, an extinct volcanic crater like Lake Antoine to the south, and at Bedford Point are the ruins of an old fort.

The South Coast

With its pristine beaches so close to St George's, the southwestern tip of Grenada is the hotel heartland. The countryside is flatter and drier than the island interior and most of Grenada's sugar was grown here. The southern coastline is a long succession of deep bays and promontories, where many wealthy Grenadians have chosen to build their homes and where cruising yachts put in for shelter. Farther east the coast becomes remoter, but judging by the names it has a romantic history— *Morne Delice, Mamma Cannes, Perdmontemps*, and *Après tout*.

A couple of miles south of St George's, **Grand Anse** is the most popular beach on the island, with about 2 miles of blinding-white, satin-soft sand. A number of hotels front on to the beach, but usually it is not too crowded. Farther round the point are a number of small bays, pleasant and secluded, though the peace will occasionally be interrupted by planes passing overhead as they come in to Point Salines airport at the island's southwestern tip.

Just along the southern coast is another popular bay, once called Prickly Bay by the English, but now usually known by its French equivalent, *L'Anse aux Epines*. It has some fine hotels and apartments, spread out on the thin strip of sand and on the clifftops. Visible out to sea south of Grenada is Glover Island, operated as a whaling station in 1925 by the Norwegians.

Calivigny Point was the site of the main camp of the People's Revolutionary Army in the time of Maurice Bishop, and the area saw considerable military activity during the American invasion. Beyond the charming fishing village of Woburn, Fort Jeudy, now an expensive housing estate, speaks of earlier conflicts, when a fort used to guard the entrance to Egmont Harbour. A little farther on is the **Westerhall Rum Distillery**, the producer of light and dark rums, including jack-iron, an almost mystical drink in which ice sinks. You can tour the distillery.

The coast road winds through the former plantations and past secluded beaches such as **La Sagesse Bay** and **Bacolet Bay** until it reaches **Marquis**, just south of Grenville. This settlement was the first target in Fédon's rebellion, where the English inhabitants were dragged from their beds and killed.

Over the Grand Etang to the East Coast

To a Grenadian 'over the Grand Etang' means going over the mountains and through the centre of the island, on roads that wind and switchback as they climb steadily into Grenada's staggeringly lush interior of mountains dressed in ferns, grasses and elfin woodland. The best road to take from St George's goes along the St John's River, past the race course in Queen's Park, but it is possible to go via Government House and left at the roundabout. From here you climb to the oddly named Snug Corner and eventually to the Grand Etang itself. Remember to look behind as you climb for some of the island's most spectacular views, as far as Point Salines in the southwest.

Just off the road are **Annandale Falls**, a 30ft cascade (only really impressive in the rainy season) that races into a bathing pool, surrounded in tropical greenery. The valley was the scene of considerable fighting in the 1983 invasion.

At the summit of the range is the **Grand Etang** (Great Pond), another extinct volcano crater. Set in a Government Reserve, its water is cold and metallic blue (estimates of its depth vary from 14ft to fathomless). The **Grand Etang Forest Centre**, *open Mon–Sat, 8–4, adm free*, has illustrations of local flora and fauna and a description of the Caribbean's geological past: two chains of volcanic islands created by the shifting of the Atlantic and Caribbean tectonic plates. There are also short walking tours around the Grand Etang and into the mountain rainforest, with its explosions of bamboo, tree-top ferns and creeping vines. You might also see Grenada's hummingbirds, tanagers and the occasional cuckoo, as well as armadillos and opossums.

Some way off is **Morne Fédon**, also called Mt Qua Qua. Much of the fighting in the 1795 rebellion led by Fédon, who owned the estate at Belvidere just below the mountain, took place in this area. The mountain stronghold was situated on the three spurs of the peak, each named after one of their slogans, *Champ la Liberté, Champ l'Egalité* and *Champ la Mort*. It is a couple of hours' hike to get there. Also in this area are the two Mount Carmel falls, foaming cascades which drop 70ft into icy rockpools.

Descending into the windward side of Grenada the road passes among tiny villages clinging to the hillsides down to the cocoa-receiving station at Carlton, where the beans are processed and prepared for shipment. After a short walk off the road in

St Margaret's you will find the Seven Sisters Falls, worth a detour for a swim, though you should ask permission to walk over the private land. Eventually you arrive at the coast at **Grenville**, set on a large bay sheltered by reefs. It is still referred to as La Baye, as it is known in French creole. There are a few solid stone structures that speak of its former position of importance, the 'second city' to St George's. The countryside here is known as Grenada's lifeblood, the island's breadbasket, and it is dotted with plantation houses. In the town itself, the covered market and fish market are the centres of town activity. Graceful Grenadian sloops can often be seen at the waterfront, calling in on their trips between the Grenadines and Trinidad. There is also a nutmeg factory in Grenville that is worth a visit (see 'Gouyave', p.102).

North of here is the **River Antoine Rum Distillery**, which functions using old-time Caribbean machinery, its crushing gear still driven by an old waterwheel. You can sample the fearsome rum they produce. Lake Antoine is the crater of a volcano reckoned to be extinct, though underground forces are still at work just beyond here, at the mineral springs, which emit wisps of sulphurous gas from hot springs. Further on, the **Levera National Park** is best known as a picnic area by the Grenadians at the weekends. You may well see doves in the woods and oyster-catchers along the shore.

Morne Fendue

On the road to the north-coast town of Sauteurs is one of Grenada's most charming spots, Betty Mascoll's **Morne Fendue**, an old plantation house full of family memorabilia. It is an enchanting place to visit. Nutmeg shells laid out on the drive give off a heady smell of spice as you drive up. There are three rooms for rent, but it is best known for its lunch, traditional Caribbean callaloo and island specialities, taken on the veranda with fine views of the Grenadian landscape.

Festivals

Carnival in Grenada is celebrated in August rather than at the beginning of Lent, but it is still three days of dancing in the streets of St George's with carnival parades, steel bands and calypso singing. If you would like to **play mas** (i.e. buy a costume and jump up with the parades), contact the Tourist Board for the name of a band. They also have a jump-up on the anniversary of Independence Day, 7 February. It is always worth looking to see if there are any celebrations taking place in Carriacou and making your way up there. Don't miss the sailing regatta in August. **Extempo**, in which singers ad-lib on subjects given to them moments before, or spar with one another in song, is scheduled for November.

✆ (809)– *Where to Stay*

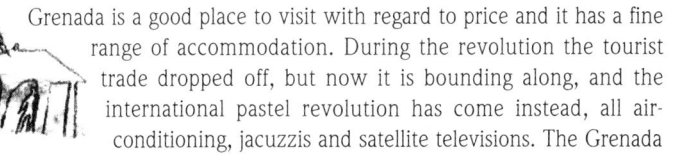

Grenada is a good place to visit with regard to price and it has a fine range of accommodation. During the revolution the tourist trade dropped off, but now it is bounding along, and the international pastel revolution has come instead, all air-conditioning, jacuzzis and satellite televisions. The Grenada Hotel Association has a free booking number in the States (✆ 800 322 1753). All hotels have to charge an 8% government tax on the bill, and most will add an extra 10% service as well.

There are few hotels outside St George's and the southwestern corner of the island, though it is possible to find cheap guest house accommodation around the island. The tourist board publications have a listing of off-beat spots. There are a number of villas for rental on the island, some of which are administered by **Grenada Realtors Limited**, PO Box 534, St George's (✆ 444 4255, fax 444 2832).

expensive

The most comfortable and elegant hotel in Grenada is the **Calabash Hotel**, PO Box 382 (✆ 444 4334, fax 444 4804, UK reservations ✆ 0778 347512, fax 0778 380815, US reservations ✆ 800 223 1108) at the head of Prickly Bay (L'Anse aux Epines). There are 28 breezy suites (some with private pools and whirlpools) set in an arc around a lawn of coconut palms and calabash trees above the pleasant beach. The dining room is open to the air, screened by creeping plants and naïve paintings. Good value, with full meal plan included (breakfast served on your balcony and afternoon tea); expensive. **Secret Harbour**, PO Box 11 (✆ 444 4548, fax 444 4819, US ✆ 800 334 2435), lives up to its name; it is a reclusive string of 20 villas overlooking Mt Hartman Bay at L'Anse aux Epines. The elegant arches of the main house are inlaid with mosaics and the roof topped with terracotta tiles, like a Spanish colonial palace above the harbour. The beach is uninspiring, but there is a pool on the heights and there is a view from your four-poster bed to the bay below, where watersports are available through the Moorings next door. No children. You can tailor-make sailing trips to the Grenadines with a stay in the hotel. **Twelve Degrees North**, PO Box 241, on L'Anse aux Epines Bay (✆ 444 4580, fax 444 4580), is another extremely fine getaway, a collection of one- and two-bedroom apartments on the clifftops with fully equipped kitchens. So named because it lies exactly 12 degrees north of the equator, it takes a maximum of 20 people, children not allowed. There is a pool and palm-thatch bar on the beach below with stunning sunset views. Very personable, no restaurant, but with maid service if you want it. The **Spice Island Inn**, PO Box 6, St George's (✆ 444 4258, fax 444 4807), has pride of place on Grand Anse beach. There are 56 suites in a variety of garden and beachfront positions, each with their own whirlpool or pool; very expensive.

Of Grenada's bigger beach hotels, which include the recently built **Rex Grenadian**, a mock-Mediterranean beach resort, and **La Source**, an all-inclusive resort with an all-over-body holiday agenda (a never-ending diet of spa treatments, light cuisine and watersports), the most preferable is probably the **Grenada Renaissance Resort**, PO Box 441 (✆ 444 4371, fax 444 4800), which is set in manicured gardens right on Grand Anse beach. A double room costs US$185 in season. A busy feel with comfortable rooms to international standards, air-conditioning, television. **Coyaba Beach Resort**, PO Box 366 (✆ 444 4129, fax 444 4808), also on the sand of Grand Anse, has a friendly feel. Rooms in blocks and a nice bamboo terrace restaurant; moderate to expensive.

moderate

The **Flamboyant Hotel**, PO Box 214 (✆ 444 4247, fax 444 1234), up the hill at the far end of Grand Anse beach, is a mixture of old-time West Indian villas (fans and wooden floors) with the more recent Caribbean (rooms in blocks). All view St George's in the distance and although all are comfortable the older rooms are preferable; 31 rooms in all. Another nice retreat in the southwest is the **True Blue Inn**, PO Box 308 (✆ 444 2000, fax 444 1247), where the three two-bedroom cottages and four apartments are festooned with bougainvillea. Comfortable and friendly with a good view from the pool and terrace restaurant. Passable beach nearby, but most guests hire cars. You get a good price in very comfortable, older-style Caribbean apartments at **L'Anse aux Epines Cottages**, PO Box 187 (✆ 444 4565, fax 444 2802). A variety of self-contained units with ceiling fans and wooden or tile floors. Low-key with no dining room or pool, but good value, right on the beach and restaurants nearby.

cheap

There are two small getaways hidden in coves in the southeast of Grenada which are well worth considering if you want island charm and isolation. **La Sagesse Nature Centre**, PO Box 44, St George's (✆/fax 444 6458) attracts easy-going travellers. Just three rooms in the small estate house and two new rooms in a wooden bungalow, fan-ventilated, with kitchenettes, and with a charming bar and restaurant in the trees giving onto a nice beach in a classic bay enclosed by headlands; cheap to moderate. Not far off is **Petit Bacaye**, PO Box 655 (✆ 443 2902, fax 443 2552), a collection of palm-thatched cottages around a small restaurant in a garden of palms and tropical flowers. Small and comfortable rooms with louvred windows, fine showers, kitchenette and porch—a very calm retreat. Daily fresh fish is landed by the fishermen who work out of the bay. In the north of the island is **Morne Fendue** ✆ 442 9330) also known as Betty Mascoll's Plantation House. The atmosphere is that of a welcoming family home on an old West Indian plantation estate. There are only three rooms, though there are always plenty of people passing by for the renowned Morne Fendue lunch. At **Roydon's Guest House** (✆ 444 4476) you can find a comfortable and simple room within a shout of Grand Anse beach. Just six rooms. You might also try **RSR Apartments** (✆ 440 3381) not far off, with full kitchens and a sitting room; both clean and cheap. And there are a couple of **very cheap** travellers' haunts in town: **Simeon's Inn** (✆ 440 2537) is on Green Street, and has bed and breakfast with an excellent view over the town from the communal balcony. Also there's **Mitchell's Guest House** on Tyrrel Street. If you are exploring the island there are simple reliable stopovers in Victoria, the **Victoria Hotel** (✆ 444 9367), and, in Grenville, the **Grenada Rainbow Inn** (✆ 442 7714) has self-contained units with a local restaurant.

✆ *(809)–* *Eating Out*

It might be that the Grenadians have retained their interest and flair for cooking from the days when the French owned the island. At any rate, the abundance of island produce makes Grenada a good place for classic West Indian fare: callaloo, breadfruit, christophene and green fig, as well as the more exotic *tatou* (armadillo) and *manicou* (opossum). There is 'international fare' on offer, often in hotels, for those who feel too far from home in the West Indies, but Grenada has plenty of charming restaurants, often taking advantage of good settings, perhaps a view over the Carenage in town or on a bay and beach of the southwest peninsula. Expect a service charge of 10% plus 8% VAT to be added to your bill.

expensive

Canboulay (✆ 444 4401) has the top position both for the cuisine and for the setting (looking over Grand Anse and St George's beyond). A strong theme of the West Indies and particularly Carnival runs through the restaurant, in the bright colours of the dining room, the carnival masks, the names of the dishes and the adventurous Caribbean cuisine. Soucouyant and Shango cocktails to start, *tamboo bamboo* (steak and shrimp kebabs in tamarind and peanut sauces), Mardi Gras shrimp (in a crab and herb crust with a rémoulade sauce). Daily changing *à la carte* and set menus (EC$70–90) and occasional exotic buffets, lunch weekdays, dinner except Sun. Not far off you will find fine West Indian cuisine at **La Belle Créole** (© 444 4316), on a breezy veranda open to the shrill night air at the Blue Horizons Hotel. Menu changes nightly; callaloo followed by lobster mousse and then creole veal roll in a white wine sauce. Set menu at EC$105. A popular Italian restaurant is **La Dolce Vita** (© 444 4301) at the Cinnamon Hill Hotel. You dine on a terrace, with white arches contrasting starkly to the black wrought-iron lamps and chandeliers. Home made pastas followed by *aragosta alla romagna* (grilled lobster in breadcrumbs). Often lively. **Coconut's beach restaurant** (© 444 4644) has a nice setting in a pretty wooden house at the head of Grand Anse Bay. You dine outside on the sand under palm thatch parasols or inside in full view of the working kitchen, which produces Caribbean and particularly French creole fare— chicken breast *à la sauce féroce* or catch of the day in lemon butter, Nantais butter or mango chutney. Simpler food during the day. Also on the waterfront, in l'Anse aux Epines, is the **Boatyard** (© 444 4662), which is set on an open veranda overlooking the yachts at anchor. It has an international menu, steak and fish, salads and burgers. Not far off, the **Red Crab** is also popular.

moderate

For a classic West Indian meal you can go to **Mamma's** (© 440 1459), on Lagoon Road heading south out of town. Sadly the inspirational Mamma has died, but her daughter has continued the tradition. The Special (the only order) brings a compendium of local dishes, from oildown (four or five vegetables boiled in coconut milk), to yam, breadfruit, turtle, booby (a local seabird) and fish broth (one of a number of local aphrodisiacs), followed by a lime or passion fruit sorbet. Specials EC$45, plus taxes, reservations essential. St George's has a number of restaurants and bars that take best advantage of a setting on the harbour (as well as snack bars for a lunchtime roti and a juice). The **Portofino** restaurant is visible by its red, white and green colouring. Pizzas and pastas, fish and other Caribbean dishes in a pleasant upstairs dining room. **Delicious Landing** serves Caribbean fare with an emphasis on fish and seafood. **Nutmeg** has a commanding view of the harbour from upstairs; simple platters followed by nutmeg ice-cream. **Rudolf's** also attracts a lively crowd, with pub-style benches and an egg-box ceiling; steaks, seafood and omelettes. Both cheap.

Bars and Nightlife

Most of the hotels and restaurants have bars, but straw-haired beach bums and medical students collect at the **Paradise Club** in Grand Anse, where the tree-sheltered bar overlooks lily-ponds and small islands. Simple meals but a young and lively crowd, particularly late on. **Island Paradise**, a West Indian yard under a mango tree on the waterfront in Lagoon, is a sometimes riotous bar, particularly popular with the yachties. There are plenty of bars in town where you can join the locals in a game of dominoes and a white rum (Clarke's Court of varying percentage proof): **007**, the floating bar on the Carenage, can get quite busy, and there is **Aboo's** nearby, **Ye Olde Farm House** opposite the Yellow Poui Gallery and **Pitch Pine** on the Esplanade waterfront.

Nightlife in Grenada is generally pretty quiet, but a number of bars and hotels have a special night and some stage entertainment during the season. **La Dolce Vita** has a bar crowd on Wednesdays and the **Boatyard** is popular on Fridays, when there is a steel band. **Le Sucrier** at the Sugar Mill south of Grand Anse can get pretty wild *Wed–Sat* and **Fantazia 2001** over in Morne Rouge can be lively at weekends.

Carriacou and Petit Martinique

Carriacou and Petit Martinique, the only two other inhabited islands in the country, lie about 15 miles north of Grenada, at the northern limits of Grenadian territory. Strictly speaking, the border with St Vincent slices the north end off the two islands, but they have not come to blows over it recently.

Among the smaller uninhabited islands are Les Tantes and the Sisters and one that even calls itself London Bridge. The underwater volcano by the name of Kick 'em Jenny, perhaps a corruption of the French *Cay qui me gêne*, is so called because the water around it is renowned for being very rough (sea-sickness pills advised if you go anywhere near it). LIAT pilots who fly over here have reported seeing movement under the water and the seismic instruments in Trinidad regularly detect it. Many reckon that it is growing slowly as it belches and that eventually another Grenadine might appear.

Getting to Carriacou is part of the fun—coasting Grenada's leeward (western) side from St George's gives spectacular views of the fertile slopes that tumble from Mt St Catherine, and then there is a horizon dotted with the Grenadines. It is possible to go by yacht or by the boats that leave from the Carenage, best of all on one of

Carriacou's own graceful schooners *about EC$25. If you are travelling on through the Grenadines, boats head for Union Island on Mon and Thurs, about midday, EC$10 plus departure tax.*

Alternatively, go by air and experience Lauriston, one of the Grenadines' gentler airstrips (no mountains to negotiate on approach), though you might be surprised to find that the island's main road runs diagonally across the middle of it. Local airlines include **Airlines of Carriacou** (✆ 443 7362) and **LIAT**, with scheduled flights down to Grenada and on to St Vincent.

Carriacou

Carriacou is gentle and quiet (just 8 miles by 5), with a population of about 6000. It is mountainous, though not high enough to have the tropical lushness of Grenada itself, but it is bordered with the white-sand beaches of the Grenadines. Tiny islets lie off its shores, nothing more than sand and a few palm trees.

The first settlers of Carriacou (from the Indian Kayryouacou) were French turtlers fishing in the abundant waters or taking the turtles on the island's fine sand beaches as they came to lay their eggs. Soon it was settled as a plantation island, growing mainly cotton, but also supporting two sugar estates that provided the island with rum.

The island is well known for its tradition of boat-building and you will still occasionally see these graceful boats being built here. And it is also known for smuggling, something of a Caribbean tradition. Shippers, legal or otherwise, are called 'traffickers' hereabouts and they take produce down to Trinidad or Barbados,

traffickers unloading

returning with tinned food, snacks and manufactured goods. Cargoes from Sint Maarten and the other duty-free islands and the odd consignment of whisky and foreign brand cigarettes do occasionally go astray in a cove *en route*. The islanders usually get a few hours' notice when the coastguard leaves St George's and so the contraband gets hidden away in the hills. The mainstay of the declared economy is agriculture, vegetables sent to market in Grenada and sheep and goats, looking confused, tied up in bags so that only their heads protrude, on their way to market in the other islands.

You will find almost every conceivable alcohol in Carriacou, but the island's special drink is jack-iron, or 'the jack', which, quite apart from being extremely strong, has the peculiar and disarming quality of making ice sink in it.

The liveliest and most spectacular moment in the Carriacouan calendar is the annual **Regatta**, held in early August, to which yachts come from all over, usually to be beaten by sailors from the next-door island of Petit Martinique. There are also celebrations on Independence Day on 7 February and at Carriacou's **Carnival** at the beginning of Lent. If you hear of a **Big Drum Dance**, or are on island during the Carriacou **parang festival** in December, it is well worth going along.

It is fascinating to see the skeletal hulls of cedar steadily take shape on the shoreline in Windward, and more recently Tyrrel Bay as the Carriacouan shipwrights create their boats. Not so many big ships are built any more, but many smaller boats are. Most of the wood comes from Carriacou, but the main keel piece is greenheart imported from Guyana. The work is done by hand, following a tradition supposedly bequeathed by a Scots ancestry. The launching ceremony is a major festivity and well worth a visit if you hear of one. The blood of a goat is sprinkled on the boat as it is blessed and then it is launched to the sound of drums, while everybody looks on dressed in their Sunday best.

Stretched along the seafront, **Hillsborough** is the only settlement that constitutes a town. The centre of activity is the jetty, which comes alive on days when the boats bring mail and provisions. The two streets contain all the island's official buildings (including immigration if you come by boat), banks and a small tourism office (✆ 443 7948). There is a museum in a restored cotton ginnery building, with a display of Carib history and even a small botanical garden, now in disrepair, where huge palms tower over the walkways.

Above the town is the great house of **Belair**, with its windmill tower, from where the view stretches both ways along the chain of the Grenadines, south to Grenada and as far as St Vincent in the north. The area was also used by the PRG as their principal army base during their tenure in the early 1980s. In L'Esterre you can visit the art shop of **Mr Canute Caliste**, whose naïve paintings are now world-famous.

Beaches

Carriacou is rimmed with fine white **beaches**, most of which will be deserted. Look normally to the west coast, or on a still day try the windward (east) coast. Beyond the airport is a fine strip called **Paradise Beach** and **L'Esterre**, where you will find **Ali's Bar** right on the sand. On the western side of the island there is a good harbour at **Tyrrel Bay** and strips of sand which make for good sunbathing and sunset viewing. There is even passable sand to be found right off Hillsborough.

The best find of all, though, is **Anse la Roche**, in the northwest. Getting there is half the fun and is something like a treasure hunt. On the track north from Bogles look for a gnarled tree leaning over the road; turn left down to a dried pond and a ruin; then down the hill at a black rock which you recognize because it usually has a conch shell perched on the top. Anse la Roche is an idyllic cove. Round the northern point is another superb beach in **Windward Bay**.

Sailing

Carriacou offers good possibilities for sailors. A stopover will cut the journey down to St George's (there are few places to put in between Carriacou and Grenada itself), but it is a good island in which to linger and explore anyway. The anchorage off **Hillsborough** is sometimes uncomfortable and so you may not want to overnight there, though there are a couple of restaurants and good bars in the town. **Sandy Island** in the bay is usually calmer, but the calmest anchorage is **Tyrrel Bay** in the southeast, where you will find places to eat and drink and a good view of the sunset. There is no marina on the island. There is a port of entry in Hillsborough.

Watersports

If you are based on land, it is fun to take a trip to one of the sandbars in Hillsborough Bay, tiny islets with just a few palms: Mabouya (from the Indian for evil spirits), Jack A Dan, whose name is a mystery, and Sandy Island, sometimes indistinguishable in the haze, which is supposedly silting away at the moment. A number of boats operate out of Hillsborough, serving day-trippers from Grenada. Ask around for spaces, or contact Snagg's Water Taxi (© 443 8293).

There are two **scuba** shops on the island, **Silver Beach Diving** (© 443 7882) and **Tanki's Watersports Paradise** (© 443 8406, fax 443 8391) in L'Esterre Bay, from where Tanki is well set to take you to Pagoda City, to the caves at Kick 'em

Jenny or to loiter among a school of barracuda. *Single tank dives US$50, novice instruction available, sunset trips and deep-sea fishing also available. An island tour can be fixed up through Carriacou Tours (✆ 443 7134), US$6 with enough takers.* A rudimentary bus service runs between Hillsborough and Tyrrel Bay.

✆ (809)– *Where to Stay and Eat*

The **Caribbee Inn** (✆ 443 7380, fax 443 8142) at Prospect towards the northern end of Carriacou is one of the Caribbean's gems. The atmosphere has the grace and charm of the old West Indies—four-poster beds, muslin nets, ceiling fans that whip the sea breezes through louvred windows, all dressed in soft shades of pink and grey. Just 10 rooms, a pool on the hilltop and Anse la Roche is nearby. Guests tend to gather in the main bar, library and dining room, where the fine kitchen serves fresh local ingredients in French and creole style; moderate to expensive, meals $30 per person day. At **Cassada Bay Resort** (✆ 443 7494, fax 443 7672), the breezy wooden cabanas are perched on the hillside and have superb views through the southern Grenadines to Grenada 15 miles away. Remote and very quiet, 16 comfortable rooms; moderate. The **Silver Beach Resort** (✆ 443 7337), on the sand in Hillsborough bay, has a faded beach club feel about it. The 18 simple air-conditioned rooms are in garden cottages and a block on the beachfront. Some watersports, some self-catering; moderate. There are comfortable rooms on L'Esterre Bay at **Tanki's Watersports** (✆ 443 8406, fax 443 8391), with private baths and a waterfront restaurant, popular with the diving crowd, cheap.

If you are happy to look after yourself, self-catering villas can be arranged through **Down Island Ltd** (✆ 443 8182). Otherwise there are a number of **very cheap** places to stay. In town is the plush **Ade's Dream House** (✆ 443 7733, fax 443 8435) a three-storey concrete giant on Main Street with 23 rooms, some self-catering. Also the **Sand Guest House** (✆ 443 7100), three rooms with kitchenettes, or **Hope's Inn** (✆ 443 7457) on the beach in L'Esterre. There is a string of guest houses across from the seashore in Tyrrel Bay: **Alexi's Luxury Apartment Hotel** (✆ 443 7179), 13 suites with kitchenettes and simple rooms with private bathrooms, or the **Constant Spring Guest House** (✆ 443 7396), very simple, three rooms and shared kitchen and bathroom.

There are quite a number of **restaurants** outside the hotels in Carriacou. A charming spot on Main Street in Hillsborough is **Callaloo** (✆ 443 8004), where there is a long list of cocktails to start, followed by callaloo soup of course and then honey ginger chicken breast or local catch in garlic butter.

It has sailing scenes painted on calabashes on the walls, lunchtime salads and sandwiches. The **Roof Gardens** or **Paradise Store** will serve you local rice 'n' peas or a roti to go. There are a couple of nice restaurants in Tyrrel Bay, where most yachts put in for the anchorage. **Poivre et Sel** serves French fare, barracuda in pepper sauce followed by crêpes suzette, or you can try **Scraper's** for a spicy barbecue chicken, or the **Twilight Bar** for chicken or fish.

There are a number of waterfront bars here too, palm-thatch lean-tos where you can sit with a rum punch and watch for the Green Flash. Every fan of the Caribbean pursues the Green Flash—one of the islands' most ephemeral moments, best sought on a palm-backed beach, rum punch in hand. The Flash occurs over the sea, only rarely, during a totally cloudless sunset, at the very moment that the last tip of the sun disappears over the horizon. It usually lasts for about half a second, and never for more than a second and a half; a green strip the width of the sun on the surface of the sea.

Finally there is one of the coolest and most unlikely bars in the islands on the waterfront in Hillsborough. The **Hillsborough Bar** looks like an English pub and disco (it was built by two lads, pub-builders by trade from Birmingham). There are barbecue dinners under the thatch on the seafront, plenty of drinking, dancing as the mood takes the customers, and an occasional film screening.

Petit Martinique

The inhabitants of this tiny island, which lies about 3 miles east of Carriacou, are also fishermen and boat-builders, reputedly even more closely involved in smuggling than their neighbours. Perhaps as a result, they are supposed to have one of the highest per capita incomes in the Caribbean. When a customs officer tried to land here once, they threw him off. Not surprisingly, they are fiercely independent. There is a small and close-knit community of about 500 islanders—the installation of telephones was apparently enough to reignite old feuds which had lain dormant for years. The atmosphere is slightly listless, the main activity being the arrival of the ferry at the main dock every other day. *There is a crossing to Petit Martinique on Mon, Wed (the doctor's visit) and Fri.* Alternatively hire a boat in Windward. Like the island of Martinique, the island's name is thought to come from the fact that it has snakes. It is said that rival colonies would introduce snakes on to other islands to make life more difficult for the settlers. You can stay at the **Sea Side View Holiday Cottages** (✆ 443 9210), just four rooms overlooking the island of Petit St Vincent and the Grenadines. Simple and low-key; cheap.

St Vincent	116
The Grenadines	134
Bequia	137
Mustique	141

St Vincent and the Grenadines

Canouan	143
Mayreau	144
Tobago Cays	145
Union Island	146
Palm Island	148
Petit St Vincent	148

St Vincent and the Grenadines offer a classic Caribbean combination: island life and isolation. Side by side stand the staggering lushness and friendly way of the Windward Islands, and the slow-time, easy life of the tiny Grenadines, thirty islands strung out over 60 miles of strikingly blue sea, each a short hop from the next. Once the heartland of Indian resistance, where Caribs would ply the waters in their war canoes, St Vincent and the Grenadines are now cruised by more peaceful craft. They has become a sailor's paradise.

St Vincent stands in the north, set in the sea like a massive cut emerald with facets of lush forested slopes stacked irregularly, rising to the central mountain range of Morne Garu. At 18 miles by 11, this fertile island is the smallest link in the Windward Islands. It is dominated by the mighty Soufrière, a distinctly active volcano, which last blew in 1979, showering the island with ash and adding yet more fertilizer to the rich land. A pencil could take root in the deep brown earth of the Mesopotamia Valley. In Kingstown are the oldest botanical gardens in the Americas, 20 acres of spectacular tropical abundance of scarlet, yellow and purple blooms.

Many of the 108,000 islanders live a simple life dependent on the land or the sea. With little industry, there is high unemployment and agriculture is still the economic mainstay. The principal exports are bananas, coconut products and arrowroot, a starch once used by the Indians as an antidote to poisoned arrows and now used in biscuits and computer paper. Fruit and vegetables are sent to nearby Barbados, where there is a greater market as much of its agricultural land is planted with sugar.

St Vincent itself is still relatively undeveloped: there are not too many tourists and as yet it is unscarred by the high-rise concrete monstrosities of mass development. Some of the Grenadines depend on tourism, though, and an hour's sail will take you from simple island life to the most expensive island luxury. In centuries past, the Grenadines would be leased out for a hundred years on West Indian charters and turned into plantations. Nowadays, developers lease them to create some of the most exclusive resorts in the world.

The tropical island idyll is perfected here, seclusion with a view over dazzling white sand to islands that fade to grey on the horizon. You can be so isolated that you communicate by flag. Two hundred years ago the message might have been 'Bear to leeward, danger, reefs'.

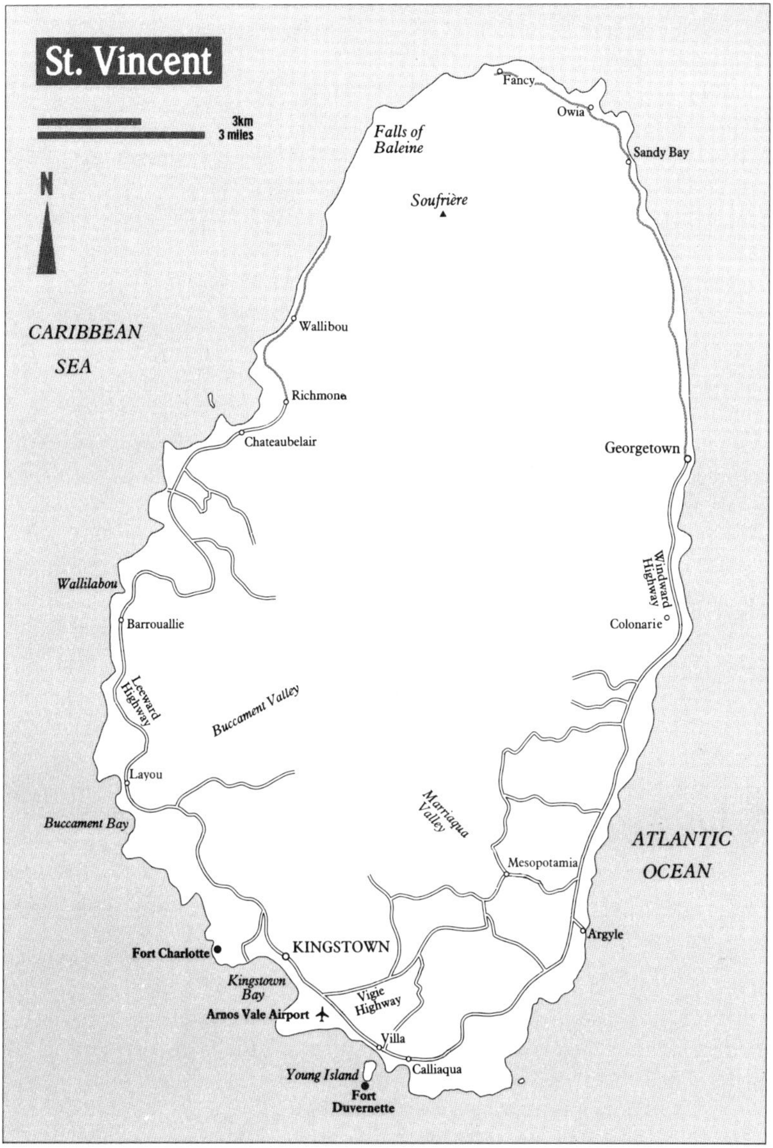
St. Vincent
3km
3 miles
N
CARIBBEAN
SEA
Falls of
Baleine
Soufrière
Fancy
Owia
Sandy Bay
Wallibou
Richmond
Chateaubelair
Georgetown
Windward
Highway
Colonarie
Wallilabou
Barrouallie
Leeward
Highway
Buccament Valley
Layou
Buccament Bay
Marriaqua
Valley
ATLANTIC
OCEAN
Mesopotamia
Argyle
Fort Charlotte
KINGSTOWN
Kingstown
Bay
Vigie
Highway
Arnos Vale Airport
Villa
Calliaqua
Young Island
Fort
Duvernette

Now, with room service just at hand to pamper you, you are more likely to string up: 'Orange juice, coffee and croissants' or 'We do not want to be disturbed'.

History

With little strategic value, inhospitable St Vincent was given a wide berth by the early European visitors. *Hairoun* was wild even among the 'Cannibal Isles'. It was a Carib stronghold, and Europeans would all too often be confronted by a shower of arrows and the barbecue spit. As the Europeans picked off the other islands in their quest for empire, St Vincent became a sanctuary for the Caribs, left as a European no-man's-land as late as 1750, a place where the Carib race could live out the last of their days.

St Vincent also became a refuge for slaves, who first arrived in 1675, when a slaveship was wrecked off Bequia. As word got out, escaping Africans made their way from the islands around, St Lucia and Grenada, to join them. From Barbados, slaves would cast off on rafts and drift a hundred miles with the wind in a desperate bid for freedom. The Africans mixed with the local Indians, the **Yellow Caribs**, to create a 'tall and stout' race known as the **Black Caribs**. This fierce new tribe took over the resistance to the European colonizers and eventually dominated the Yellow Caribs, taking their land. Faced with extinction at the hands of their cousins, the Yellow Caribs invited the French to settle St Vincent in 1719.

The French settlers brought African slaves to work plantations. Fearing for their freedom, the Black Caribs retreated to the hills, where they distinguished themselves from the newcomers with bands around their calves and upper arms and by deforming their babies' skulls in old Carib style with tightly bound slats of wood, giving them sloping foreheads.

The Black Caribs kept the colonizers at bay for another fifty years. In the Treaty of Aix-la-Chapelle in 1748, St Vincent was too hot to handle and so officially it was left neutral, with an unwritten clause that the European powers would fight over it later. By 1763 it was British. The new owners wanted the Black Carib land for their plantations and so they went in and took it in the First Carib War.

But soon afterwards the French were in control. They came in three sloops of war in 1779, unchallenged by the merchants of St Vincent, who were wide-eyed at the opportunity of trade. The soldiers were all at work on the Governor's plantation up north and the key to the battery was lost in any case, so the invaders just landed and took the place over. In moments the island had surrendered.

Four years later the British were back, and they were faced with another Black Carib uprising in the 1790s in the Second Carib War, or Brigands' War, whipped up by the revolutionary Victor Hugues in Guadeloupe. Duvallé, a violent leader, swept down the east coast, burning the plantations and killing the British planters by passing them through the crushing gear in the sugar-mills. On the west coast the overall chief, Chatoyer (also Chattawar), spared them such destruction, save for a single sideboard which he sliced with his cutlass to show his intentions. Their armies came together like pincers in the south and they fortified themselves on the hills above Kingstown.

Chatoyer was killed in combat with the Militia Colonel Alexander Leith as Dorsetshire Hill was stormed. On his body was found a silver gorget, a present from Prince William, later King William IV, who had met him on a visit to the West Indies in the ship *Pegasus*. Chatoyer had dreamed of forging an island home for the Black Caribs, but his dreams died with him.

For a year the Black Caribs held on, attacking the British from the heights and slinking back into the jungle, but eventually, in 1797, General Abercromby gained the upper hand and threatened them with surrender or extinction. He razed their settlements and destroyed their crops, and 5000 gave themselves up. They were deported to Roatan Island in the Bay of Honduras (their descendants can still be found there, a thriving community). The Caribs living in the north of the island today are descended mainly from the few Yellow Caribs to survive the wars, forced to the north coast as the settlers took their fertile land. With the cannon silenced and the colonial map fixed in the early 1800s, St Vincent ended up in British hands and became another quiet agricultural island, growing sugar, Sea Island cotton and arrowroot, of which they held a large share of the world market.

Governed as part of the colony of the Windward Islands, St Vincent and the Grenadines became an Associated State of Britain in 1969 and then took its Independence on 27 October 1979, remaining within the Commonwealth. Today the country is led by the Bequian Prime Minister James Mitchell and the New Democrats Party, elected in 1984 and returned to power in 1989 and 1994. His party holds 12 seats and the opposition is Labour MN Unity led by Vincent Beach.

Flora and Fauna

St Vincent is extraordinarily fertile and if you visit the upper valleys you will find a whole new world of explosive tropical vegetation. Close to Kingstown is the Mesopotamia (Marriaqua) Valley, where you will see all the produce growing that later makes its way to market. You will see hummingbirds and tropical mockingbirds among the heliconias and anthuriums in the Montreal Gardens at the top of the valley.

Another fertile area is Buccament Valley, inland from Layou on the west coast, where vast forests of bamboo rise to 60ft and the rainforest begins, an infestation of creeping vines and lianas that clamber over gommier and mahogany trees. There are trails in the Vermont area and it is here that you have the best chance of spotting the endangered St Vincent parrot (*Amazona guildingii*) around dawn. Unique to the island, it has a white and yellow head, a tawny brown body with blue wing-tips and a tail of green, blue and yellow. The female is more colourful than the male and usually lays two eggs. There are thought to be only about 450 to 500 of these protected birds left. Another endemic species seen in the same area is the whistling warbler.

In the north of the island is the Soufrière, where the vegetation is different again, as rainforest gives way on the heights to elfin woodland, home to the rufous-throated solitaire.

✆ *(809)–*

Getting There

There are no direct flights from outside the Caribbean to St Vincent and the Grenadines, so most visitors travel via Barbados (good connections), or via St Lucia or Grenada. There is a special transit desk at Grantley Adams airport in Barbados for passengers bound for St Vincent. Many scheduled hopper flights make their way up and down the Windward Island chain; contact LIAT (✆ 458 4841 in St Vincent) and Air Martinique (✆ 458 4528). Other smaller planes cover the Grenadines (Bequia, Mustique, Canouan, Union and Carriacou, usually two flights a day each way); contact Mustique Airways (✆ 458 4830) and Airlines of Carriacou (✆ agents LIAT, *see* above). You can charter a plane through St Vincent and the Grenadines Air (✆ 809 456 5610, fax 456 2673). There are **ports of entry** at Kingstown, Arnos Vale airport and Wallilabou bay in the northeast and in the Grenadines you can register in Bequia and Union Island. There is a departure tax of EC$20.

Getting Around

The south coast of St Vincent and the major valleys are well served with **dollar-buses**, always a lively and crowded part of Vincentian life. The buses are cheap to travel and you will get to know your passengers, and the current popular tunes, pretty well. As elsewhere in the Caribbean, many have a name on their bonnet: *Hell Raiser*, *Gundelero*, *Ragamuffin*, *Lucky Dude* and more enigmatically *Time and The Answer*. Buses leave from the new terminal on the Kingstown waterfront. Out on the road they can be waved down with a downward-pointing finger and an expectant face. To be dropped off, you must shout 'Driver! Stop!', usually to the hilarity of the other passengers. Services on the coastal roads are sporadic so leave plenty of time to get there and back, but they run to **Villa** until as late as 11pm.

Some sample fares are: **Kingstown** to Villa (Aquatic Club); EC$1.50, to Mesopotamia $2.50, to Georgetown $4, to Layou $2 and to Wallilabou $3.

Taxis are readily available, at a rate fixed by the St Vincent Government of EC$35 per hour. They can be arranged from hotels or found in the Market Square. **Kingstown** to the airport, EC$15, to Villa $20, to Fort Charlotte $10, Layou $35. From Arnos Vale airport to the Villa/Young Island area costs EC$20.

To drive a **hire car** in St Vincent you need to purchase a local driver's licence, price EC$40 (on presentation of a valid licence from home) from the Licensing Authority on Halifax Street. Cars can be hired at a daily rate of about US$40 from: **Avis** (✆ 456 5610), **Kim's Rentals Ltd** (✆ 456 1884) in Kingstown and **Sunshine Rentals** (✆ 456 5380) in Arnos Vale. Driving is on the left. Island tours can be arranged through **T's Tours** (✆ 457 1433), who offer hiking and biking as well, and **Garifuna Tours** (✆ 456 2822).

Tourist Information

In **Britain** the St Vincent and the Grenadines Tourist Office is at 10 Kensington Court, London W8 5DL (✆ 071 937 6570, fax 071 937 3611) and in the **USA** 801 Second Avenue, New York, NY 10017, (✆ 212 687 4981, fax 212 949 5946, US toll free ✆ 800 729 1726) and 6506 Cove Creek Place, Dallas TX 75240 (✆ 214 239 6451, fax 214 239 1002, toll free ✆ 800 235 3029). In **Canada** they can be contacted at: 32 Park Road, Toronto, Ontario M4W 2N4 (✆ 416 924 5796, fax 416 924 5844); and in **Germany**, Wurmberg Straße 26, D7032 Sindelfingen (✆ 70 3180 6260).

The main tourist office on the islands is in the Financial Complex on Bay Street, Kingstown (✆ 457 1502, fax 456 2610), and there is a tourist information desk at **ET Joshua airport** in Arnos Vale (✆ 458 4685). For those making connecting flights via Barbados, there is the **St Vincent and the Grenadines Desk** at the Barbados International Airport (✆ 428 0961), open from 1pm until the last flight of the day bound for St Vincent has left.

The Tourist Board puts out two magazines, the *Escape Tourist Guide*, with features and information (including ferry timings to the Grenadines) and standard prices for taxis, etc. and the smaller *Discover* magazine, also with current information.

If you have a medical **emergency**, contact the General Hospital in Kingstown (✆ 456 1185). The **IDD code** for St Vincent and the Grenadines is **809**, and this is followed by a seven-digit local number. On island, dial the full seven digits.

Money

The currency of St Vincent and the Grenadines is the Eastern Caribbean dollar (EC$2.65 = US$1), but the US dollar and traveller's cheques are widely used in tourist restaurants and hotels. Major credit cards are also accepted in the tourist centres. Be sure which currency you are dealing in, for example in taxis. For the best exchange rate, **banks** are open 8–1 or 3pm, Mon–Thur, with extended hours on Friday afternoon until 5pm. For those passing through the island on their way to the Grenadines, there is a Bureau de Change at E. T. Joshua Airport, open daily except Sun until 5pm. **Shops** are open 8–noon, 1pm–4pm, Sat 8–noon.

Beaches

Steep-sided and volcanic, St Vincent has mainly black sand beaches, except in the south where the coast slopes more gently out towards the Grenadine Islands and where the wave action on the coral reefs pushes up whiter sand. The liveliest beaches on St Vincent are in the south, thin strips of sand close to Kingstown at **Indian Bay** and **Villa**, where the Vincentians gather at weekends and holidays. There are bars to retreat to nearby after a hard day's lying about in the sun.

The east coast, with the big breakers coming in from the Atlantic, is quite rough, and so for seclusion and the afternoon sun it is best to go to the leeward coast with its sheltered bays with black sand and fishing villages. The nicest bays among them are **Peter's Hope** and **Kearton's Bay** near Barroualie; also **Buccament Bay** and **Richmond** at the limit of the Leeward Highway. Consider taking a picnic, though it is possible to buy a drink and a snack in the villages along the coast.

Beach Bars

Beachcombers is just along from Villa, a timber-frame veranda set back from the beach, where you can get a drink and a grill pizza or a lime pie. There are restaurants and bars open during the day both in **Indian Bay** and along the **Villa** strip, where you can find a drink or a light meal after roasting in the sun.

Sailing

St Vincent is really a stopover to or from the Grenadines, which offer some of the best sailing in the whole Caribbean, so many yachts bypass St Vincent altogether. Most people charter yachts out of Grenada or St Lucia, but they come from as far afield as Martinique, so you may have to stop over in St Vincent's isolated west coast. There are **customs and immigration** offices in Kingstown and Wallilabou.

The Young Island area is a protected, popular **anchorage**. There is no marina, but there are a number of places to eat and it is a short ride into town, where you will find supermarkets for provisioning and a laundry. Alternatively you can head further east to the broad and sheltered Blue Lagoon, where you can usually take on fuel and water at the **Barefoot Yacht Charters Marina**. There are a couple of anchorages on the west coast, Cumberland Bay and Wallilabou, where you can put in overnight. You will be met by boat-boys who swim out and offer their services for anything from fetching bread to taking you to a waterfall. You are advised to be careful with regard to the security of your yacht in this area.

Barefoot Yacht Charters (✆ 456 9526, fax 456 9238) offer crewed and bare boats from their base in the Blue Lagoon. The company will also offer help with limited repairs.

Watersports

St Vincent is not that developed and for equipment—snorkelling gear, windsurfers and small sailing boats—you will be dependent on the larger hotels and the dive shops listed below. There is very attractive coral within reach of snorkellers off Young Island and snorkelling tours and Grenadine Island tours are offered by **Baleine Tours** in Villa (✆ 457 4089).

Scuba diving can be arranged at **Dive St Vincent** (✆ 457 4714, fax 457 4948) in Villa and **St Vincent Dive Experience** at Blue Lagoon (✆ 456 9741, fax 457 2768). The fish life of the Grenadines is superb and there are some excellent coral reefs on the leeward shore of St Vincent, where you will find wrecks, caves and drop-offs from 60ft. An excellent option, if you are travelling down the islands, is to buy a ten-dive 'rollover' package, which can be spread between Dive St Vincent, Dive Bequia, Dive Canouan and Grenadines Dive (in Union Island).

Walking

Walking in St Vincent's fertile country is a pleasure that has been enjoyed by visitors for more than two hundred years. It is an adventurous three-hour hike up through seasonal forest, rainforest, and elfin and montane woodland to the lip of the **Soufrière**, from where there is a cracking view of the steaming crater and across the island. If a 4000ft climb seems daunting, follow instead the **Vermont Nature Trails** in the Buccament Valley off the Leeward Highway, where there is a chance of seeing the St Vincent parrot in the evergreen forest and the rainforest.

The lush mountainsides of St Vincent are cut with tumbling and racing streams, perfect for a walk through the forest and a dip. The most spectacular are the **Falls of Baleine** in the north of the island (these must be approached by sea and there are plenty of operators who will take you there), but others can be found at Trinity, up from Wallilabou and inland from here at Hermitage. On the Windward coast there is good walking around Colonaire and there are rockpools which make for good swimming in the South Rivers Valley, unless of course somebody has got there before you to do their washing or to take a bath. Guides are available through the Tourist Board or the Forestry Department.

Kingstown

The capital of St Vincent is set on the mile-wide sweep of Kingstown Bay at the southwest corner of the island. A town of about 25,000, it is surrounded by a ring of steep ridges spiked with palm trees, running from Cane Garden Point in the south to Berkshire Hill, where Fort Charlotte commands a magnificent view of the 60-mile string of the Grenadines. Downtown in quaint cobbled streets, modern glass-fronted shops stand out against the faded grandeur of old stone warehouses in the business centre near the waterfront. Vaulted walkways keep off the rain, the arches supporting the wooden upper storeys of the houses and sloping tin roofs, all strung together by a profusion of telephone wires.

On the higher ground of Kingstown Vale stand the old colonial houses, once majestic in their open tropical gardens. Now they are jostled for space as the Kingstown suburbs encroach. Overlooking the town from their perches on the heights are the modern houses of today's wealthy Vincentians, some of whom have returned to their island and built homes after working abroad for years.

Down on the waterfront Kingstown is busy; cargoes of tinned food and timber are hauled aboard and stacked under tarpaulin at the **Deep Water Pier** and the **Grenadines Wharf**, where the boats depart for the journey south to the Grenadines. Along the waterfront are the Financial Complex and the National Bank, a modern colossus towering above the town. Beyond here are the bus terminal and the new **Fish Market**, where men in stained working coats pour out boxes of sprats and slap brightly coloured snappers on the marble slabs. Close by is the main **market building**, from which the bustle spills out on to the pavements of Bay Street and Bedford Street. In the hustle, trays of sweets are thrust under your nose and the market ladies, their skirts rolled up over their knees, remonstrate with buyers, selling their fruits and vegetables from the piles on tables and blankets spread out before them.

Officialdom keeps its distance from all this activity on the other side of Halifax Street, behind the iron railings and the imposing stone façade of the **Law Courts**, where the 15-member St Vincent Parliament meets.

The Kingstown skyline of steep sloping roofs is broken by church towers. **St George's Anglican Cathedral**, which is a brightly painted Georgian church

the fish market St Vincent

with a castellated clock-tower, was built in 1820 as the Cathedral of the Anglican diocese of the Windward Islands, partly from government money from the sale of Carib lands. The stained-glass window with the red angel was supposedly commissioned by Queen Victoria for St Paul's Cathedral, in honour of her first great-grandson (later King Edward VIII), but she rejected it on the grounds that in the Bible the angels were dressed in white. It was given to Bishop Jackson by Dean Inge of St Paul's and he brought it to St Vincent. Inside, a tablet commemorates Major Alexander Leith, a hero of the Brigands' War of 1795, who killed the Carib leader Chattawar.

The most surprising architectural feature of Kingstown is the **Roman Catholic Church**, presbytery and school. Built in 1823 and enlarged in 1877 and 1891, it is a riot of styles in dark brick, a hodge-podge of Romanesque arches and Gothic pointings that would be more at home in deepest medieval Europe.

The St Vincent Botanical Gardens

On the steep slopes facing into Kingstown Valley, just off the road north to Layou, are the **Botanical Gardens**, the oldest in the Americas and one of the delights of the Caribbean, *open from the early morning until dusk, no adm, but depending on the number of people you might give a guide EC$15 for an hour's tour.* The walkways and lawns are bordered by an overwhelming abundance of tropical splendour: bushes with fluorescent flowers, trees with heavy aromas and palms that soar and sway overhead.

Founded in 1765, the gardens were run commercially in order to propagate useful species from all over the world in the Caribbean, and were connected to the Botanical Gardens at Kew in London. It was to the West Indies that Captain Bligh was heading on his fateful voyage in the *Bounty* in 1787. He was on a commission for the Society of West Indian Merchants to bring the breadfruit tree from the South Seas to St Vincent, where it could be used as food for the slaves on the plantations. Cast adrift with 18 loyal officers by his mutinous crew, he sailed 4000 miles to Timor without the loss of a life.

Six years later, this time in the ship *Providence*, he succeeded in bringing over four hundred specimens of the breadfruit tree to St Vincent intact, and offshoots of them still grow in the gardens today. Ironically, the slaves would not touch the new food when it first arrived, but nowadays the huge perennial tree, with its lustrous dark green leaves shaped like medieval flames, can be seen all over the Caribbean. The starchy fruit starts life as a small green lollipop and then turns over with the weight, swelling to the size of a cannonball and dropping to the ground with a thud. Boiled or steamed, it is a popular supplement to the 20th-century Caribbean diet.

The guides are helpful (basically you will not escape without one). In their jargon they offer an 'educational tour', one worth taking because even if their botanical knowledge is often a little shaky, they do know all the amusing plants to show off, telling stories and crushing leaves for the aroma—cinnamon, citronella, camphor and clove.

The Gardens are well worth a visit, a fascinating hour even for botanical novices. They are full of gems like the sandpaper tree, with leaves as rough as emery paper and the velcro tree, *flambago*, related to flax, to which material sticks. And there is the waterproof lotus lily, on which water rolls in beads like mercury (put them underwater and the waterproof pink leaves take on a silver sheen and then come out dry). There is the tree of life, or *lignum vitae*, whose wood is so hard that it was used to replace iron as bearings for propellor shafts, the sealing-wax or lipstick palm that seeps bright red, love-lies-bleeding and the mahogany tree, whose pods explode, releasing a shower of whirling seeds like a sycamore. At sundown, when the white-painted trunks of the palms loom in the obscurity, the flowers of the cannonball tree that open in the day fall to the ground, and the air is heavy with the aroma of jasmine.

Above the Botanical Gardens today is the house of the Governor General and in a pretty West Indian house in the grounds is the **St Vincent Museum**, *open Wed 10–12 and Sat 4–6, adm*; *also opens when there is a cruise ship in town*. It has fierce and sublime faces in stone and pottery left by the Arawaks and Carib Indians and later artefacts from the Black Carib wars of the 18th century. The chattering and squawking that rings out in the gardens comes from the blue-brown St Vincent parrot, of which a few are kept in an aviary, after recovery from illegal hunters.

Fort Charlotte

Open during office hours (roughly speaking), adm.

This lumbering giant on the Berkshire Hill promontory is worth a visit if only for the fantastic view north along the leeward coast, on to Kingstown and over the Grenadine Islands scattered to the south. It is a pleasant half-hour walk from town, mostly uphill, and on the way you must pass over **Old Woman's Point**.

> 'It received its name in the seventeenth century from a virago of Indian birth from Guadeloupe who, having 'tormented her husband to death,' married again within eight days, and repairing to St Vincent spent her honeymoon in a cottage under the point. Tiring of her second husband, she beat out his brains with a conch-shell and then, to escape justice, fled to the territory of the Caribs. There she lived until she aroused the jealousy of the wives of a powerful Carib chief. She then returned to her cottage and remained there until the English erected a battery on the spot, when she retired to the house of a Spanish priest near by. Here many jovial parties were held, and the gay spirits of Kingstown were wont to visit the house for refreshment and recreation. 'A bottle of wine or rum secured admission.' It was a tradition that the wicked old woman, who lived to a great age, was eventually carried off this earth into the unknown during a terrific hurricane which swept over the island.'

Sir Algernon Aspinall, *Pocket Guide to the West Indies*, 1907

Constructed at the turn of the 19th century and taking its name from George III's queen, Fort Charlotte was once the island's main defence, with barracks for 600 men and 34 cannon. For all this hardware and manpower, the Fort saw action only once, an argument between two men just outside the gates, in which a Private Ballasty killed Major Champion in 1824. The perpetrator was tried and hanged on the same spot.

The Fort stands 630ft above the sea, and is approached by way of a steep causeway and through an arch. Only three of the cannon remain and the barracks now house a museum of the Carib Wars. It is illustrated with a series of paintings by Lindsay Prescott, picturing important moments such as the death of the Carib Chief Chatoyer and the deportation of the Black Caribs in 1797.

The South Coast

Leaving Kingstown valley to the east, you come to the airport at Arnos Vale. From here the road (the Vigie Highway) leads inland to **Marriaqua**, often known as **Mesopotamia** after a town that is spread along the sides of this extraordinarily lush valley. The steep ground is terraced and the rivers come together at the spectacular Yambou Gorge. Kids play cricket in the road by the pastel-coloured houses perched on the hillsides among a profusion of greens: banana, breadfruit and coconut.

The ridge at **Vigie** (French for 'look out') gives spectacular views of Kingstown from above. The Carib camp was situated here in the war of 1795–6 and it was fortified with earth-filled sugar hogsheads (cone-shaped moulds through which molasses was dripped after boiling). Higher up, lost in the mountains, are the **Montreal Gardens**, with walkways through the tropical foliage, nutmegs and citrus. The gardens specialize in anthuriums, grown here commercially and seen all over the West Indies, with a heart-shaped leaf like a vividly coloured plate and a long thin protrusion. Following the coastline from E. T. Joshua airport, the Windward Highway leads past the expensive houses of St Vincent's prime residential area to **Villa Point**, a charming line of former family holiday homes built earlier this century. They are all similar in style with tall, gently sloping corrugated tin roofs and they have been converted into restaurants and small hotels, which has given the area a friendly seaside feel.

Opposite Villa, a little way out to sea, is **Young Island**, one of the Caribbean's best hotels (*see* 'Where to Stay'). Young Island takes its name from a Governor Young who brought a black charger with him to St Vincent in the 18th century. The horse was admired by a chief of the Black Caribs, whereupon the gallant Sir William Young said, 'It is yours!' The chief took him at his word and rode off on it. Some time later, the Governor was with the Carib chief again on the balcony of Government House in Calliaqua and he admired the island off the coast. Not to be outdone, the Carib, who owned the island, said at once, 'Do you like it? It is yours!' It has remained Young Island ever since.

The island is private, but visitors are allowed when the hotel is not full—you might go over in the evening for a cocktail. There is a telephone on the dock at Villa Point to call the ferry.

Fort Duvernette, behind Young Island, is an outcrop of rock that rises a sheer 200ft out of the water and is covered in dark green vegetation, marked on old maps as Young's Sugar Loaf. There are two batteries, still with ten mortars and cannon from the reigns of George II and George III, covering the southern approaches to St Vincent, though it is now favoured more for its beauty than for any strategic significance. A staircase to the heights is cut out of the rock, and is

Bird of Paradise

worth the climb for the view across to the Grenadines. *Visits can be arranged though the Young Island Hotel.*

A little farther along the coast is the quiet town of **Calliaqua**, once St Vincent's capital and the residence of the Governor in Sir William Young's day.

The Windward Highway to Georgetown

The Windward road cuts in from the south coast beyond Calliaqua and emerges on the Atlantic at Argyle. Immediately the sea is rougher, with huge ocean breakers. This fertile sloping land originally belonged to the Carib Indians but the European planters steadily ate into it. As the road twists along the coastline the skeletons of the old plantation prosperity are just visible; the buildings and aqueducts are disappearing, overwhelmed by the tropical undergrowth. New plantations, acres of bananas and coconuts, can also be seen at every turn of the road.

Inland from Argyle, a short walk off the road to Mesopotamia that passes through the Yambou Gorge, are some **rock carvings**, squiggles and ghostly faces carved by the Arawak Indians, who lived on the island until about AD 1000.

Georgetown, 22 miles and a good hour's drive from Kingstown, was once a prosperous centre, servicing the plantations of the Windward Coast. Now it is an empty town, its buildings run down. Beyond Georgetown, in the shadow of the Soufrière Volcano, the road crosses the **Rabacca Dry River**, a river course in a rainstorm and the path for lava after a volcanic explosion, and passes into the Orange Hill Estate, at 3200 acres one of the largest coconut plantations in the world. In the villages of **Sandy Bay** and **Fancy** live the descendants of the Yellow Caribs. Even though they have now mixed and have considerable African blood, their Indian heritage of lighter skin and pinched eyes is still clearly visible. There is little employment and the people live mainly on what they produce on the land.

At **Owia** on the isolated northeastern tip of the island, about an hour beyond Georgetown on the rough roads, is a large pond fed by the sea, but protected from it by a barrier of rocks, a good place to stop for a swim. There is an arrowroot factory in the town which may be visited, *adm free*.

The Soufrière Volcano

Dominating the whole of the northern end of the island is the St Vincent **Soufrière Volcano**, 3000ft high and definitely still active, blowing occasionally in a pall of smoke, thunder and flame. Farmers in St Vincent speak of extraordinary abundance following the eruptions—outsize fruits that come out of season because the ash acts as a fertilizer.

The Soufrière spat fire in 1718 and then blew properly in 1812, spewing into the air ashes and sand that floated down on the island, leaving a white covering inches thick like snow. The pall of smoke was illuminated by darting electric flashes and accompanied by violent thunder, an earthquake and a stream of lava overflowing from the boiling crater. The cloud even plunged Barbados, 100 miles away, into darkness. Then it was quiet for another ninety years until 1902 when it blew again (in tandem with the cataclysmic explosion at St Pierre on Martinique), killing 2000 people, mostly the descendants of the Caribs living on St Vincent's northern shore. On this occasion it rained stones for miles downwind, bombarding the fleeing Vincentians. The streams ran thick with ash and the noise was so terrible that people thought that the island was sinking.

It was quiet until 1971, when a minor eruption created an island of lava in the crater lake, but on Good Friday, 13 April 1979, the Soufrière blew once more; a vast cloud of ash rose 20,000ft into the sky, and explosive gases boiled over the crater lip and raced down the mountainside, destroying anything in its path.

The best places to approach it from are the Rabacca Dry River on the east coast, just north of Georgetown, and Richmond, north of Chateaubelair on the leeward coast, which is a gentler climb. It is about three hours' walk to the summit and you are advised to arrange a guide and to take a picnic.

The Leeward Highway to Chateaubelair

The Leeward Highway winds along the west coast of the island, climbing over massive ridges and promontories and dropping into deep coves, good shelters for yachtsmen, where small fishing villages of pretty clapboard houses sit on black, volcanic sand beaches. Inland the valleys are steep sided and draped in greenery.

About 3 miles from Kingstown the road passes the majestic Peniston or Buccament Valley. At the head of the valley there are nature trails that lead up into the depths of the rainforest in the hills. The road rejoins the coast at **Layou**, where there is a petroglyph, Arawak impressions scratched on a 20ft rock. It can be reached on foot by a 10-minute walk, though visitors should ask permission because it is over private land. The road then passes on to the fishing village of **Barrouallie**, and just off the road not far upriver from **Wallilabou** you will find a fall that pours into a small rockpool, ideal for a midday dip. Ask around for directions. The road continues through the town of Chateaubelair and eventually comes to an end at **Richmond** where there is an attractive bay and beach with just a few houses.

In the far north of the island are the **Falls of Baleine**. Here, the river, which rises on the Soufrière, races down through the tropical forest on the slopes of the Soufrière Volcano and drops into a rockpool in a 60ft spray of warm water. Visits are best made by boat—a great day out from Kingstown, coasting the leeward side of St Vincent, past all the fishing villages and landing on the northern tip of the island. From there it is a short walk in the river bed to the rockpool and the falls themselves where you can swim. *Expect to pay about US$40 for the day's outing, which can be arranged through one of the watersports companies on the south coast* (*see* 'Watersports', p.123).

Festivals

Carnival, or **Vincy Mas** as it is called, at the end of June or in early July, is the main event in the Vincentian calendar. A month of calypso competitions culminates in a jump-up in the streets of Kingstown, with steel bands and wild pageants of dancers all firedby rum and Hairoun, the Vincentian beer. Christmas gets anearly start with the **Nine Mornings Festival**, which runs from 15 December. Vincentians stage nightly dances and parades through the streets with carol singers and steel bands. Many of the Grenadine Islands stage **regattas**, after which there are always jump-ups.

© *(809)–* ## *Where to Stay*

St Vincent remains relatively undeveloped, untouched by international hotel corporations and their concrete plant. Most of the hotels are small (the largest has just 31 rooms) and some have the friendly atmosphere of West Indian inns, set in attractive old-fashioned houses, family homes and the old warehouses of Kingstown. Apart from the few in Kingstown, the hotels are mainly on the white sand beaches of the south coast, particularly around **Villa**, which is about 10 minutes' ride from the capital. There is never a problem finding a room in St Vincent, but you are advised to book ahead for the more exclusive retreats like Young Island and trusted faithfuls in the Grenadines. A 7% government tax will be added to all hotel bills and most hotels charge a 10% service charge on top too.

expensive–luxury

Off the south coast of St Vincent by 200 yards is **Young Island**, PO Box 211 (© 458 4826, fax 457 4567, UK reservations Unique Hotels), luxury in true Vincentian style and one of the Caribbean's loveliest hotels: 29

cottages of local stone are scattered on the slopes of the tiny island, lost in a profuse and charming tropical garden, where a salt-water pool meanders among the golden palms and ginger lilies. Each room has its own terrace and is screened, with louvred windows and ceiling fans to chop the cool sea breeze. The bright fittings are offset by dark stained wood and rattan furniture. You dine under small palm thatched huts, some looking onto the beach and across to St Vincent. There is a tennis court on the island and some watersports are laid on. You can vary nights in the hotel with nights aboard one of the resort's yachts and there are good 'Lovers' Packages' on offer in the low season, but whenever you go do not miss the hammocks on the beach, slung under a palm thatch roof, big enough for two.

Off the beaten track in style and location is **Petit Byahaut** (✆/fax 457 7008), which is hidden in a cove on the leeward coast where the emerald water is enclosed by headlands. It is accessible only by boat. Rooms are permanent tents with beds, hammocks and showers, ranged on the hillside above the bay. Plenty of peace and seclusion. All meals and watersports (except scuba) are included in the expensive daily rate (for two people).

moderate

The **Sunset Shores Beach Hotel**, PO Box 849 (✆ 458 4411, fax 457 4800) stands on the beach looking over to Young Island from the mainland. It is quite low-key and friendly, but a bit pre-fab, with the 31 comfortable rooms in blocks around the pool, and it has the facilities of a resort: air-conditioning, telephones, televisions, sunfish and windsurfers. **Browne's Beach Hotel**, PO Box 859 (✆ 457 4000, fax 457 4045) is set in a modern house on the waterfront at Villa, offering modern international standards for business travellers as well as tourists. Telephones and televisions in the rooms.

cheap

There is still a feel of old-time Villa about the **Umbrella Beach Hotel**, PO Box 530 (✆ 458 4651, fax 457 4930), which is set in one of the old wooden and tin-roofed houses. There is a nice veranda at the front and all nine fan-ventilated rooms are neat and clean and have kitchens, private bathrooms and telephones. The walls are a bit thin; impeccably priced.

For those who wish to stay in Kingstown itself, perhaps in order to catch the mail-boat early in the morning to get to the Grenadines, there is a clutch of West Indian inns among the columns and arches and the cobbled streets of the capital. The **Cobblestone Inn**, PO Box 867 (✆ 456 1937), is set around a courtyard in a fine old warehouse. Bright furnishings in the 17 air-conditioned rooms and a rooftop restaurant. The **Heron Hotel**, PO Box 226 (© 457 1631, fax 457 1189), also has an old-fashioned West Indian island charm. The 12 rooms have private bathrooms, and breakfast is served on the terrace above the inner courtyard. There is an easy feel about the **Indian Bay Beach Hotel**, PO Box 538 (© 458 4001, fax 457 4777), set on the small strip of sand at Indian Bay. The 14 rooms are air-conditioned and have kitchenettes and there is a breezy restaurant on the waterfront terrace.

very cheap

There are plenty of **guest houses**, some set on the heights above the town, in old colonial houses built there for the fine view of the town and harbour. The most attractive is the **Kingstown Park Guest House**, PO Box 41 (© 456 1532, fax 457 4174), reputedly built for the French Governor General in the 18th century, a wooden creole mansion with creaking floors and good West Indian cooking in the dining room downstairs. Best to stay in the main house. There is a homely charm about the **Bella Vista Inn** (© 457 2757), a friendly West Indian Guest House also in Kingstown Park. Breakfast and dinner available.

© (809)– *Eating Out*

Outside the hotel dining rooms and a couple of restaurants, Vincentian food is solidly West Indian. As always, restaurants also double as bars and occasionally the Villa strip can get lively at night. Some restaurants will take credit cards, but ask beforehand. There is a 7% government tax to add to all bills and most restaurants will charge 10% for service.

expensive

The **French Restaurant** (© 458 4972) is set in one of Villa's pretty houses, where you dine on the veranda, as expected on French fare. There is a long lobster menu—lobsters are picked live from the vivier in the garden and *flambéd* in cognac or *à la provençale*. *Poulet à l'hongroise* (in paprika) and fish. Some mixed reports about the service. At the **Lime 'n' Pub** (© 458 4227) close by, tables occupy a raised veranda festooned with greenery, around a central tree. International menu with seafood—devilled crab back or fillet of fish. Pizzas to take away.

moderate

The **Dolphin** next door has bench tables inside and a covered terrace outside, where you can grab a grilled fish or a plate of pasta to a musical accompaniment—international music and menu. A top spot in town, for the setting and popularity, is **Vee Jay's Rooftop Diner** (✆ 457 2845) on Upper Bay Street. Lunch and dinner, with a live band on Fridays. Good West Indian fare—chicken, fish or shrimp with veg, or international food—burgers and a chicken salad. **Basil's Bar and Restaurant** (✆ 457 2713) is set in the stone and brick surrounds of old-time Kingstown. Popular at lunch for the buffet; dinner is grilled *filet mignon* or a seafood *crêpe*. Two good local restaurants with lively bars attached, both upstairs on Grenville Street, are **Aggie's**, where you will find a variety of seafood such as whelks and conch, or souse accompanied by local fruit juices; and **Sid's Pub**, which is decorated with the cricketing memorabilia of the owner, who also serves West Indian food. On Halifax Street you can grab a roti or a sandwich at lunchtime from the **Bounty**. In Cumberland Bay on the leeward coast you can get a good local dish at **Stephen's Hideout** (✆ 458 2325).

Bars and Nightlife

Nightlife is pretty quiet in St Vincent and is centred on the hotels, which stage steel bands occasionally. Villa is a natural gathering place where you will find visitors and passing sailors ashore for a beer and a game of darts. Try the **Lime 'n' Pub**, which has a video bar and **The Aquatic Club**, which has an occasional discotheque and hosts a live band at the weekends.

In Kingstown there are any number of rumshops in which to sit and have a Hairoun or an award-winning EKU beer, both of which are brewed in St Vincent. In addition to the many excellent fresh fruit juices and St Vincent's powerful rums, you might also try a *sea-moss* (made with seaweed, milk and spices) or a *linseed* (as in linseed oil), both slightly sick-sweet drinks that are supposed to be aphrodisiacs. **Vee Jay's Rooftop Diner** is a popular haunt and **Aggie's** and **Sid's** collect an amusing crowd of locals.

The Grenadines

Scattered over the 80 miles between the volcanic peaks of St Vincent and Grenada are the Grenadines, thirty tiny islands and cays that rise dramatically out of the Caribbean Sea and many more reefs and sandbars that barely cut the surface into surf. Here you will find some superb, deserted strips of sand, glaringly white against an aquamarine sea, protected by a rim of offshore reefs, where lines of silver breakers glint in the haze.

The Grenadines

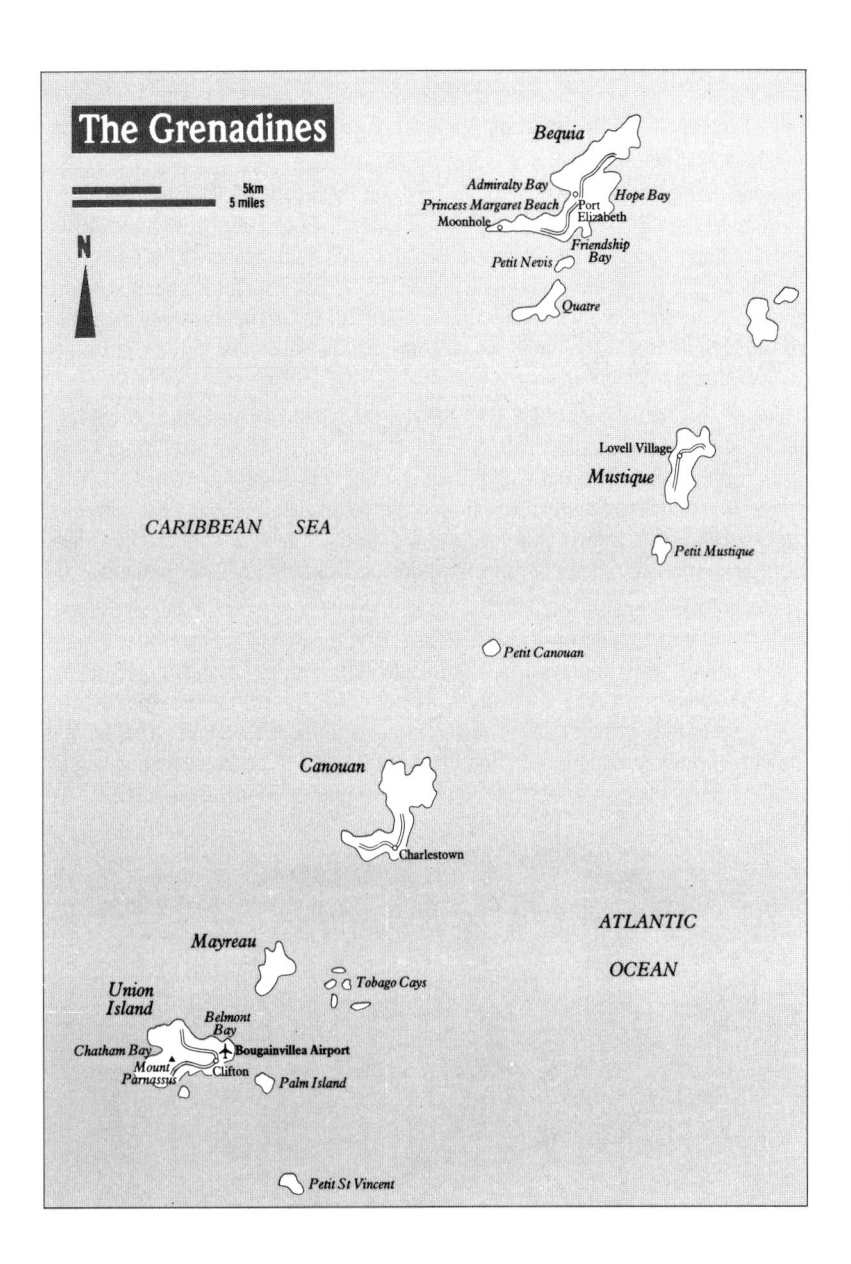

The Grenadines are some of the finest sailing grounds in the world—the white triangles of yachts ply from island to island, from the pretty waterfronts to isolated beaches and swim-up bars. An occasional clipper ship will fly by with a full rig of sails. Each one an hour's sail from the next, the Grenadine Islands are an island-hopper's paradise.

Life for the locals is a much tougher prospect. Many of the islanders are poor, earning as little as US$5 for a day's work when they can get it, with expensive imported food to buy. Unemployment is high and the inhabitants of the Grenadine islands do feel neglected occasionally, as in 1979, just after Independence, when there was an uprising on Union Island and forty of the islanders staged an armed revolt. Despite their difficulties, you can expect to be welcomed in the Grenadines with customary Caribbean charm.

There is a traditional connection with the sea; the islanders have long gone away to work on the big ships and many more who stay in the islands make their living from fishing. And on the smaller islands there is something of a 'when the boat comes in' mentality. Life revolves around the dock when the mail boat makes its twice-weekly visit, bringing the mail, as well as the weekly supply of soft drinks, beer, gas bottles and sheets of galvanized tin and sacks of cement for building.

There are some charming places to stay, many of them very expensive island resorts, just a few rooms on an isolated cove. And then there are developed islands like Mustique, with luxury villas, and Bequia, with a string of small hotels strung along the waterfront. The Grenadines are not as developed, nor as expensive, as the Virgin Islands and they have a rawer, more natural Caribbean air. Whether you are ensconced in luxurious seclusion in a private island resort or island-hopping by fishing boat and ferry, the Grenadines offer some of the best in easy island life.

Getting Around

Island-hopping by plane is the quickest and easiest way of getting around the Grenadines and the islands are well served with flights. You will also get some cracking views along the way. There are one or two slightly hairy airstrips—you can enjoy watching the next plane approach once you are safely on the ground. Canouan and Bequia often have cross-winds, there is a steep descent and sometimes a bouncy landing on Mustique, and even with Union's new strip you still nearly touch the treetops with the right wingtip. But the islands are typically low-key and you may come across nonchalant signs like:

> CAUTION—AIRCRAFT
> LOOK LEFT

Airlines with scheduled services through the islands are listed in the St Vincent section. Mayreau, the Tobago Cays, Palm Island and Petit St Vincent have no airstrip.

But the Grenadines are really about the sea and it is fun to travel by the local mail boat and the many smaller craft that make the island run. The mail boat, MV *Snapper*, makes two sailings a week each way between Kingstown and Union Island, touching Bequia (1 hour), Canouan (2 hours), Mayreau (1 hour) and on to Union Island (30 mins). It travels south on Mondays and Thursdays and north on Tuesdays and Fridays. Fares are impeccable: St Vincent to Bequia—EC$10–12, to Canouan—EC$13, to Mayreau—EC$15 and to Union Island—EC$20. Once in the Grenadines you can visit other islands on day trips, with picnic and snorkelling gear included. You might also be able to persuade a fisherman to drop you on the next island or hitch a ride on a yacht.

Bequia

Bequia (pronounced Beck-way) is one of the Caribbean's neatest and prettiest island hideaways. Largest of the St Vincent Grenadines (an amoeboid 5 miles by 2), it lies 9 miles, or an hour's sail, south of Kingstown and the sea approach to the main town of Port Elizabeth is glorious as the rocky headlands glide by on both sides, towering above you.

The island is quite developed—Port Elizabeth is full of pretty pastel boutiques and T-shirts strung up at the waterfront like washing—but it holds it well. It is a pleasure in itself to stroll along the waterfront in the Belmont area, a narrow walkway that passes between the sea and the pastel-coloured wooden villas built in the twenties and thirties which are now bars and restaurants. There is a picture-postcard perfection about Bequia and it is easy to be captivated by the island's charm.

The 5000 Bequians themselves are quiet and independent, still claiming to be a bit wary of 'Vincentians', who might almost come from a world away. There is a small community of white Bequians stuck up on the hill above Mt Pleasant; they have isolated themselves up there for years, but the younger generation have moved down now and are more visible in the community. There is a long tradition of boat-building on the island. Though no large boats have been built recently, it is possible to take a day trip on the *Friendship Rose*, an old Bequian schooner (© 458 3661).

The island is easy to get to. You fly in to Paget Farm in the southwest, *taxi fare into town, EC$30*. At least two **motor vessels** make a daily trip to Kingstown during the week, departing early in the morning and returning soon after midday and late afternoon. The mail boat MV *Snapper* stops there four times a week too. There is a small **Tourist Office** by the pier in Port Elizabeth (© 458 3286). Irregular dollar-buses, *costing EC$1.50*, ride out from Port Elizabeth down to Paget Farm.

Beaches

The best **beaches** on the island lie on the south side of Admiralty Bay. The sumptuous golden sand of **Lower Bay** is easily reached by sea-taxi, *EC$10*, or land-taxi, and the more secluded inlet of **Princess Margaret Beach** is a little walk over the headland. On the south coast is the huge half-moon of **Friendship Bay**, with the hotel bar to retreat to and its views to Petit Nevis (an island still ocasionally used by whalers from Bequia to section their catch). East-coast coves worth a visit are at **Industry Bay** (also called Crescent Bay) and **Spring Bay**. There are **beach bars** on nearly all the beaches on Bequia, pleasant spots to take time out from sizzling and snorkelling. On Lower Bay try **De Reef** and **Teresa's** and on Friendship Bay you will find a waterfront bar with chairs swinging from the ceiling to help you balance after a few rum punches. People have been known to skinny-dip at Hope Bay.

Sailing

The main **anchorage** in Bequia is the magnificent, protected Admiralty Bay, where the main town of Port Elizabeth is situated. You will be within a short dinghy ride of Bequia's best beaches and nightlife. You can anchor either side of the central ferry channel which leads straight to the jetty at the head of the bay. There is no actual marina there, but you can take on fuel and fresh water at **Bequia Marina** (✆ 458 3272) on the north shore. Nearby, Bequia Slipway has some repair facilities as well as a laundry and showers. There are supermarkets and chandleries in the town. Daytime anchorages around Bequia include Friendship Bay on the south side of the island and the small island of Petit Nevis to the south. There is a **port of entry** in Port Elizabeth.

There are some fine reefs around Bequia and the smaller islands nearby. A wall drops from 30ft to 100ft and a recent wreck lies in 50–85ft of water. The west coast of the island has been designated a national park. **Dive Bequia** (✆ 458 3504) operates out of the Plantation House Hotel and **Sunsports** (✆ 458 3527) out of the Gingerbread Complex. On the south side **Dive Paradise** (✆ 458 3563) is based at the Friendship Bay Hotel. *A one-tank dive costs about US$45.* These operators will also fix snorkelling trips and some have windsurfers and small sailing boats. **Sailing** trips, day trips to Mustique, sunset tours etc, can be arranged on the catamaran *Passion* (✆ 458 3884) and on the yacht *DéjàVu* (✆ 458 3692).

It is fun to explore Bequia, though 'sights' are limited. As you enter the harbour, Admiralty Bay (chosen by the British Navy as a port, but never occupied because of a lack of fresh water), you will see some dwellings built into the cliffside. Called **Moonhole** after a natural arch in the rock, there are some twenty private residences here, perched right above the waves. Tours can be arranged (✆ 458 3277). The residents do not take kindly to people poking around uninvited. There is a small fort on the point in Hamilton and on the more secluded Atlantic coast you may come across tropicbirds and the scissor-tailed frigatebird.

✆ *(809)–*   ***Where to Stay***

Many of Bequia's small hotels (only one has as many as 30 rooms) are set in the island's fine old buildings, restored forts or old family holiday homes. They have charm and character, lost in tropical gardens on the heights or down on the seafront in Belmont overlooking Admiralty Bay and the yachts at anchor. As the island becomes more accessible, it is worth reserving a room on Bequia, particularly in the winter season.

The Sunny Caribbee **Plantation House Hotel**, PO Box 16 (✆ 458 3425, fax 458 3612, UK ✆ 0800 373742, US ✆ 800 223 9832), is peach-coloured pastel prettiness taken to perfection. Scattered around a greathouse in a garden of palms, hibiscus and crotons, there are 20 cabins and beachfront villas decorated in old Caribbean style with clay-tile floors and louvred doors, rattan furniture and muslin bed nettings. Telephones and televisions (if you want one), pool and some sports on the small beach, some evening entertainment, but a good, quiet Caribbean retreat. Dining room Italian and Caribbean; very expensive. The small, private **Old Fort Country Inn**, PO Box 14 (© 459 3440, fax 458 3824, US reservations © 212 265 8753) stands in a restored stone house high on the hilltop in Mt Pleasant, from where there is a fort's eye view of the Grenadines, occasionally as far as Grenada. There are just five apartments in the main house, where the open-fronted dining room serves French, Italian and creole fare and looks out onto a pretty garden where peacocks, dogs and donkeys roam; moderate.

Spring on Bequia (© 458 3414, US reservations © 612 823 1202) also has a dramatic setting looking over the palms on Bequia's isolated east coast. Just 10 rooms in a hillside cottage built of local stone with shingle roofs in Martinican style. Freshwater pool and tennis court, moderate to expensive. For a more traditional Caribbean beach hotel you can try the **Friendship Bay Hotel**, PO Box 9 (© 458 3222, fax 458 3840). There are 27 rooms in blocks just above the beach and around the main house on the hillside. Some watersports and a nice bar on the beach, but quite quiet, moderate to expensive. Back in town, in pride of place on the Belmont waterfront is the **Frangipani**, PO Box 1 (© 458 3255, fax 458 3824), an inn which has retained an air of the family house that it once was (it is the house of the Prime Minister, James Mitchell). The 15 rooms are in the old house and in cottages around the gardens, where copper sugar boilers are shaded by mango trees and red and white frangipani; moderate.

If you want to be on the beach, away from the relative bustle of Port Elizabeth, try **Keegan's Guest House** (© 458 3530) in Lower Bay, with nine cheap rooms (includes breakfast and dinner) or **Lower Bay Guest House** (© 458 3675), lost in a tropical garden, where a double room is very cheap. In town, on Back Street just behind the jetty, is **Isola and Julie's** guest house (© 458 3304), with 19 quite simple rooms with private bathrooms, all meals available; cheap.

© (809)– *Eating Out*

There is a surprising variety of dining on offer around Bequia—Italian, French and French creole—as well as international fare, but the best of Bequia is really to be found in a couple of excellent West Indian restaurants. **Dawn's Creole Garden** (© 458 3154) has a charming and intimate setting on the hillside in Lower Bay (follow the signs). There are plenty of varieties of fresh fish in Dawn's creole sauce (clove, ginger and nutmeg), accompanied by breadfruit, sweet potato and plantain. You can have a four-course fixed dinner for EC$51 or a shortened version for EC$42. Another classic is **Daphne Cooks It** (© 458 3271), in a side-street opposite the pier in town. Excellent creole food: local soups, curried and creole dishes served with frittered plantain, christophene and yam followed by exotic fruit sorbets or impossible pie. Ring to reserve a table and a favourite dish, full meal EC$45. **Le Petit Jardin** on Back Street in town serves French cuisine (a Bequian chef trained in France). You sit in a breezy wooden dining room or in the garden. *Poulet aux noix and crevettes* (shrimps) *sauté à l'anisette*, followed by *meli-melo de goyave*.

On the Belmont waterfront, the **Gingerbread House** has an upstairs view of the yachts in harbour through a filigree of gingerbread fretwork. Salads and burgers by day, fancier fare at night, including gingerbread-style curries, spicy or mellow in coconut. Ever popular **Mac's Pizzeria** serves the obvious pizzas as well as other dishes such as salads and Macnuggets (codfish balls) on a wooden veranda above a luxurious tropical garden. The bamboo-fronted **Green Boley** is right on the waterfront too. Very easygoing, with simple local fare and tropical fruit juices to a Caribbean musical accompaniment.

Many of the restaurants double as bars. The Belmont waterfront can be quite lively. Try the Whaleboner at the Frangipani, where there is a steel band on Thursdays in season. The Gingerbread Restaurant has live music, a string band, a couple of times a week; De Reef on Lower Bay is busy on Fridays and on Saturdays the crowd moves on to Lower Bay. The hotels have an occasional jump-up.

Mustique

The island of Mustique takes its name from the French word for mosquito but thankfully has little more to do with them than that. It has a lore all of its own. Its image is one of almost absurd exclusivity, an enclave reserved for the very rich—famous, notorious or anonymous. Names as incongruous as Princess Margaret and Mick Jagger have made this place their retreat.

The island is run as a company, **The Mustique Company**, and over the last thirty years they have turned an undeveloped scrubby outcrop into an exclusive enclave of 20th-century luxury. Shareholders invest in the company by buying a plot of land and building on it—a not inconsiderable investment as the going rate for a plot is about 1 million US dollars. The company takes care of the infrastructure of the island, including health care and the education of the local children. Incredibly neat, Mustique has a sedate air, pricked by the occasional character who washes up at Basil's Bar. It is possible to come across the transient millionaires around the island, if you can spot them among the roving sailing-bums.

Lovell Village is the recognizably West Indian part of the island and it is here that many of the people employed by the Mustique Company live, as well as the fishermen, some of whom were here for generations before the company arrived.

Flights to Mustique come from Barbados and St Vincent. Scheduled flights are by Mustique Airways and Air Martinique. There are no boat services to Mustique.

Some of the most pleasant **beaches** scattered around the island are: **Endeavour Bay** in the north, and windswept **L'Ansecoy Bay**, where the rusted carcass of the *Antilles* cruise liner can be seen. Secluded **Macaroni Bay** is on the east coast, with mounds of bright white sand and one or two umbrella shades. **Gelliceaux Bay** is a pleasant cove with shallow water, secluded in the south of the island.

For sailors there is just one suitable **anchorage** in Mustique, to be found on the west coast in Grand Bay. Even so, the waters can be a little rolly at any time of the year. Basil's Bar is right there, though, and you can take on limited provisions in the small shop.

Diving is arranged through **Dive Mustique** (✆ 456 3486) which works from the beach near the Cotton House Hotel.

Just 3 miles by 1½, the island is small enough to walk around in a couple of hours (look out for the iguanas, which are pretty big, and for the mysterious miniature cattle which leave their prints when they come to drink at the pools by night), but if walking seems too energetic then it is possible to hire a horse and ride round. Mini-mokes and mopeds are also available for hire from the company; enquire at the main office near the airport. If price is a concern do not bother. It is not far to walk anyway.

✆ *(809)–*   ***Where to Stay***

Visitors to Mustique generally take a villa, one of the 30-odd luxurious piles dotted around the island. These vary in style from an Etruscan palace to chi-chi gingerbread cottages, with two rooms and more. All come with maid service, gardeners and cooks, in fact all that isneeded to ensure the ultimate restcure. With names like *Nirvana, Serendipity* and *El Sueño* you get the idea that this might be as near to heaven as the developed world of the late 20th century can manage. Villas are not cheap. Prices for a two-bedroom villa start at US$3500 per week in winter and $2800 in summer; three bedrooms range from $4500 in winter and from $3000 in the summer.

Four-bedroom villas start at $6000 in winter and $4300 in summer, and five bedrooms are $8000 or more in the winter and $5700 in summer. Then you add 7% government tax and 8% administration charge. Contact **Mustique Villa Rentals**, PO Box 349, St Vincent. In Britain they can be contacted at Chartham House, 16a College Avenue, Maidenhead, Berks SL6 6AX (✆ 0628 75544, fax 0628 21033) and in the USA through Wegner Associates (✆ 212 758 8800, fax 212 935 2797).

Mustique has one hotel, the **Cotton House Hotel** (✆ 456 4777, fax 456 5887, UK reservations ✆ 0453 835801, US reservations ✆ 800 223 1108), set in the restored shell of a hilltop plantation warehouse from the 18th century. The 20 rooms and suites are decorated with antiques and are scattered around lawns and tropical verdancy, each with a balcony overlooking nearby islands, or west for the incomparable sunsets. The main house has a candlelit dining area on the veranda and a pool set in restored coral rock walls; luxury. For those who might feel a little extravagant staying at the Cotton House, Mustique has a guest house, **Firefly** (✆ 458 4621). The cry goes that you do not have to be a millionaire to stay on Mustique because you can come here, but if you do, be sure to come with plenty of loot even so. There are just four rooms looking over Britannia Bay and the Grenadines to the south. Bed and breakfast; moderate.

Basil's Bar, also a restaurant, is a popular haunt, on Wednesdays particularly when the yachts bring their passengers ashore and the millionaires venture out from their villas. It is a seaside bar from paradise, bamboo cane with a rush-work roof, jutting out into the water on stilts, from where you can admire the sunset and the views of the Grenadines over the gin palaces that bob in the bay. Entry to the jump-up on Wednesday night costs about US$10 and drinks will set you back about US$5. There is a local bar with a pool table in Lovell Village, the **Piccadilly** pub where cheap(ish) meals and beer can be found.

Canouan

Crescent-shaped Canouan lies 25 miles from St Vincent and measures 3 miles by 1½. It is home to less than 840 people, farmers and fishermen, most of whom live around the only settlement, Charlestown on Grand Bay. This large and protected bay is the place to head for in a yacht. There are a couple of points where you can anchor. On land there are just a few shops in Charlestown where you can get simple food, but the hotels and guest houses will welcome you for a meal. There are day anchorages around the island, including Rameau Bay and the calm waters off the Canouan Beach Hotel in the southwest.

For land-based explorers there are many hidden coves and beaches and the snorkelling is particularly good in Windward Bay and Glossy Bay. Popular walks include Mt Royal and the Careenage. The attractive old stone church in the north of the island was abandoned when the population went south after the hurricane of 1921. There are daily flights from St Vincent and four-times-weekly visits by the mail boat.

Dive Canouan (✆ 458 8648) works out of the Canouan Beach Hotel and offers instruction as well as day sails to other islands.

✆ *(809)–*   ***Where to Stay***

The **Canouan Beach Hotel**, PO Box 530, Kingstown (✆ 458 8888, 458 8875) is near the airstrip, with 43 rooms in cottages among tropical greenery, set on a spit of land with white sand on either side and a fine view of the other islands. Full board, windsurfing, sailing, diving, and daily catamaran excursion; moderate to expensive.

There are two small guest houses on the island: **Villa le Bijou** (✆ 458 8025), with 10 rooms in a converted house above Charlestown, shared baths and spectacular views of the Grenadines from the terrace, and the **Anchor Inn Guest House** (✆ 458 8568), with just four rooms near the beach in Grand Bay; both are cheap, breakfast and dinner included. It is also permitted to camp out in Canouan.

Mayreau

With just 180 inhabitants and no airstrip, this island of 1½ square miles is almost the most secluded of them all (the Tobago Cays nearby win that claim). There are no roads or cars and there is not even a jetty big enough to take the mail boat, so the week's supplies are offloaded into smaller boats. Cows making a journey from Mayreau are winched up on to deck, and if alighting here they are simply herded off into the bay and left to swim for it. The islanders lead a very simple life. Electricity has not really reached Mayreau yet (except in the two hotels), but telephones have recently made an appearance.

There are a couple of excellent **anchorages** for passing yachts in Mayreau, though there is not much other than a couple of restaurants on offer on the island itself. In the north, Salt Whistle Bay is a very attractive half-moon cove and further south you come to the main settlement, where you can anchor out from the jetty.

If you are based on land Mayreau has **beaches**, excellent ones, on all sides. The best known are at **Saline Bay** and **Salt Whistle Bay**. But there are many others; snorkelling is recommended at the northern point and on the windward beaches, where the sand is framed with sea grape bushes. Head windward on the day that the cruise ship puts in and dumps its passengers in Saline Bay, or alternatively take advantage of the island's views from the high ground, north to Canouan, east to the Tobago Cays and south to the majestic peaks of Union Island.

The **Salt Whistle Bay Resort** (boatphone 493 9609, or call on VHF channel 16), contact 1020 Bayridge Drive, Kingston, Ontario, Canada K7P 2S2 (✆ 613 634 1963, fax 613 384 6300, US toll free ✆ 800 263 2780), is set on a stunning ½-mile, crescent-moon bay. It is about as remote as you can get; 27 luxurious rooms with old-time elegance in stone cottages hidden among a sandy garden of palms. Some watersports; very expensive.

Dennis's Hideaway (✆/fax 458 8594) is set on the hillside in the middle of Mayreau's town, three plush rooms in modern West Indian style and a huge balcony. Dennis will also feed you and occasionally play guitar, on the small veranda dining room, which collects a crowd of passing yachtsmen in the evenings; cheap. The **Island Paradise** Bar and Restaurant serves local food on a veranda above Dennis's.

Tobago Cays

The Tobago Cays (pronounced 'keys') are five uninhabited islets set in the circle of Horseshoe Reef, an underwater world as spectacular as the island scenes above the surface. The water is crystal clear all around, out to the limit of the reef, which is marked by a circle of silver breakers. You will cruise in between the reefs and drop anchor in the shallows of a pristine white sand beach.

Devotees of the Tobago Cays talk of them as the closest thing to heaven and somehow it is true. It is among these thirty islands and cays that you will find that well-known bit of real estate, beloved of Bacardi drinkers, the dazzling strip of sand with a single palm tree.

Any yachting cruise in the Grenadines will stop off here on request and you can take a day trip to the Cays from Union Island (day trippers come from as far away as Barbados). You are unlikely to be on the only yacht in the area in high season (December until April). The islands have recently been granted national park status, so there is no building on the cays and no spear-fishing. You are asked not to leave any litter (which has been a problem recently). There are a number of **anchorages** around the islands, some of them a little breezy as the winds race straight in from the open sea, but usually calm because of the protecting reefs. There are anchorages in the lee of all the Tobago Cays.

Union Island

Midway down the Grenadines is spectacular-looking Union Island, its parched yellow slopes draped down from the sharp peaks of the oddly named Mount Parnassus and Mount Olympus, also known as the Pinnacle. Just over three miles square, Union Island has a population of 2000. The island has quite a positive buzz at the moment and the normal listless feel has been replaced by a more businesslike air. The island is clean and money is coming in from a large tourism development (due to include a 150-room hotel, a golf course and a 300-slip marina). Union Island is a sailing centre and yachts crowd in the bay off the main town of Clifton.

Union Island is a gateway in the area because the airport serves as dropping-off point for the other islands nearby: Mayreau, the Tobago Cays, Palm Island and Petit St Vincent. The island is well served by air to the new airport outside Clifton: contact LIAT (© 458 8771), or Air Martinique (© 458 8826). It is also possible to sail from here to Carriacou in the Grenadian Grenadines (twice-weekly ferry) for about EC$10, and of course to St Vincent on the mail boat. There is a small **tourist office** in Clifton (© 458 8350).

The main **anchorage** in the southern Grenadines is at Clifton, in the southeastern corner of the island. A natural gathering point is the Anchorage Yacht Club, where you can take on fuel, fresh water and ice, get a shower and laundry and then retire to the bar. In the town itself you can get the same supplies at the Sunny Grenadines dock and of course there are the local shops for simple victuals. Day sails around Union Island include the secluded Chatham Bay on the leeward shore and of course the many other islands nearby. Union Island is a port of entry to St Vincent and the Grenadines.

Big Sand beach in Belmont Bay has shallow water and fine sand screened by bushes, but perhaps the best place to go for a secluded day at the beach is over the hill at **Chatham Bay** with miles of (as yet) undisturbed strand. There are no facilities in these places, so be sure to take water and a picnic if you will want them. Snorkelling on reefs around the

146   *St Vincent and the Grenadines*

island and **scuba diving** off Union Island and Mayreau (where there is the 1918 wreck of the British gunship *Purina*) can be arranged through **Grenadines Dive** (✆ 458 8138, fax 458 8122). *Single-tank dive US$50, boat trips available.* There are plenty of day yacht trips from Union Island. Try the catamaran *Jet Set* (✆ 458 8647) or *Capt Yannis* (✆ 458 8513), *both about US$60.* If you wish to charter a yacht, contact the Anchorage Yacht Club.

✆ (809)– *Where to Stay and Eat*

The **Anchorage Yacht Club** (✆ 458 8211, fax 458 8365) has 10 air-conditioned rooms in a garden of palms looking out over a passable beach towards Palm Island. There is a constant bustle and turnover, Grenadine-style, of yacht crews and passengers, many of them French-speaking from the islands to the north. Be careful after the usual intake of rum punch, as the sharks kept in the pool at the waterfront seem to loom ever larger as the evening draws on. The restaurant, on an open terrace, serves French food. Rooms and self-catering cabanas; moderate to expensive.

At the other end of Clifton is the **Sunny Grenadines Hotel** (✆ 458 8327, fax 458 8398), with 18 rooms in small units with ceiling fans, set among the palm trees with a sometimes lively bar that gives on to a rickety wooden jetty, perfect for lounging in the evening light; cheap. Local fare in the dining room, including curry conch and steamed snapper. The **Clifton Beach Hotel** (✆/fax 458 8235) and the nearby Guest House provide simple and clean fan-ventilated rooms; cheap, guest house very cheap. **Snagg's** Guest House in Clifton (✆ 458 8255) also has very cheap rooms. You can hire apartments in Union Island; contact the Clifton Beach Hotel.

There are one or two restaurants in Clifton outside hotels. Try **T. & N. Restaurant, Bar, Variety Store and Bike Rentals**, upstairs in Clifton, for local dishes of chicken and fish creole. The **Lambi Supermarket, Bar and Restaurant** is on the waterfront, serving regular Caribbean dishes, including lambi (conch), of which the pink shells are set into the wall.

In the centre of town is **Boll Head** restaurant, a simple spot with tables inside and out. Fish, chicken or a lambi dinner, or a roti takeaway. On the road to the airport, **Sydney's** Bar and Restaurant serves sandwiches and fish and chips. You can get a pea soup and plenty of reggae at **African Roots Culture** in town, and excellent local juices in season. The **Eagle's Nest** is the local club.

Palm Island

Until recently with a population of just two cows, Palm Island, or Prune Island as it used to be known, has been transformed over the last thirty years into an island resort with 24 fan-ventilated rooms in stone houses facing out to sea over the magnificent **Casuarina** beach, that runs the length of the sheltered west coast. There is an easy air of retreat here, with no telephones or televisions in the rooms. Just over 100 acres in size, the island is strewn with palm trees and lies about one mile from Union Island, a short hop in the motor launch. There are two restaurants and watersports including windsurfers, sunfish and scuba. MAP, expensive (✆ 458 4808, fax 458 8804, US reservations ✆ 800 776 PALM).

Petit St Vincent (PSV)

Petit St Vincent, a self-contained island resort (✆/fax 458 8801, US toll free ✆ 800 654 9326), is the most southerly of the St Vincent Grenadines; from here it is possible to see people walking about on Petit Martinique, part of Grenada. But this is about as close to the crowds as you will get on PSV (as habitués know it), because this island resort specializes in seclusion. You get peace at a price at PSV. You can even have room service at your beach hammock. It seems rich and exclusive, but with a good anchorage it also sees passing yachtsmen, who mix in here with customary Caribbean ease.

Exertion is a walk to the beach and, since the island is completely surrounded by them, that will not be too far. The cottages are spread out for maximum seclusion. You communicate to room service by flag, simply by placing an order in the post box, raising the flag and retiring to further inactivity. If you do wish to stretch some muscles, there is a tennis court and watersports are laid on.

If prices concern you, however, then this place might not be for you, as such luxury comes at an undisclosed sum (*about US$700 per couple per night in the winter season and $400 or so in the summer months*).

herding zebus

History	152
Getting There and Around	154
Tourist Information	156

St Lucia

Beaches and Sports	157
Castries	159
North from Castries to the Cap	161
South to Soufrière	162
Where to Stay	166
Eating Out	169

Hold St Lucia, and the rest may perish!

The call to arms on behalf of St Lucia was raised so often that she became known as the Fair Helen of the West Indies. Desire to possess her moved whole armies and led to her changing hands fourteen times. She is a charmed isle, not so much for her strategic value nowadays, but for her people, among the friendliest and most forthcoming in the Caribbean, and for her natural beauty: hidden coves, tropical abundance and the Pitons, twin volcanic pyramids from the south seas. Lying between Martinique and St Vincent, St Lucia (pronounced 'St Loosha') is another island peak in the Windward chain, with slopes that soar from the sea to a central mountain spine crested by Morne Gimie (3117ft), and fall away in forest-clad hills to lush valleys of bananas, tropical overgrowth and beaches mounded with golden sand. Some 27 miles by 14, St Lucia has a volcanic vent, a fumarole called La Soufrière, a bubbling and stinking morass which claims the dubious distinction of being the only drive-in volcano in the world.

The 145,000 St Lucians are mostly descended from Africans who were brought to the island as slaves in the sugar heyday of the 18th century. More than one-third live in the capital, Castries, which shambles over hills above a sheltered harbour in the northwest. St Lucia is the most developed of the Windward Islands and has some industry, including oil refining, furniture and clothing manufacture. There is a positive air about the island at the moment; there is plenty of building and the island is attracting investment from within the Caribbean area. Agriculture is still important, however and many of the islanders live a simple West Indian existence, tied to the land, producing sustenance and a small living from produce sold in the markets. Bananas, grown by St Lucia's two thousand banana farmers, are the biggest crop and they account for about 70 per cent of export earnings.

St Lucia has a tangled and romantic history: she was disputed bitterly by the British and French for over a hundred years, and the island is littered with the ghostly fortresses of forgotten wars, still visible among the encrustation of modern hotel plant. The influence of the French remains in the mornes, mountain-peaks and anses, in the sheltered bays, in the culture—the population is mostly Catholic and there are distinct flashes of French style in the way they act and dress—and in the language. Every visitor will hear the strains of the

Saint Lucia

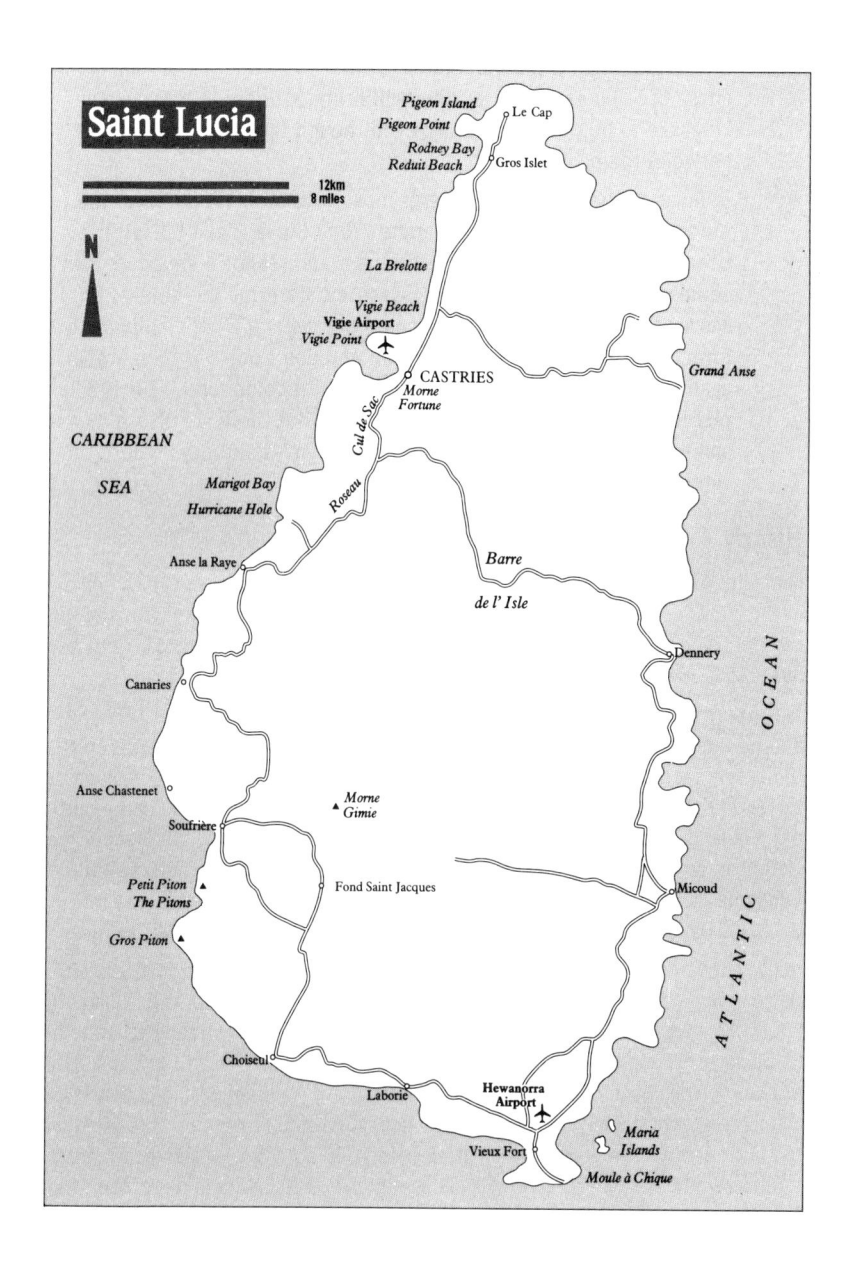

12km
8 miles

N

Pigeon Island
Pigeon Point — Le Cap
Rodney Bay
Reduit Beach — Gros Islet

La Brelotte

Vigie Beach
Vigie Airport
Vigie Point

CASTRIES
Morne Fortune

Grand Anse

CARIBBEAN

SEA

Marigot Bay
Hurricane Hole

Roseau
Cul de Sac

Anse la Raye

Barre
de l' Isle

Dennery

Canaries

Anse Chastenet

Soufrière

Morne
▲ *Gimie*

Petit Piton ▲
The Pitons

Fond Saint Jacques

Micoud

Gros Piton ▲

A T L A N T I C   O C E A N

Choiseul

Laborie

Hewanorra
Airport

Vieux Fort

Maria
Islands

Moule à Chique

151

local *patois* spoken in the streets, tantalizingly like French for a moment and yet impossible to pin down. English is the official language of St Lucia and so parents will bring up their children in the language to help them 'get on', even though they talk in *patois* between themselves.

St Lucia is one of the Caribbean's most popular destinations at the moment—the 18th-century war-cry 'To St Lucia! To St Lucia!' has been raised once again and now the air- and seaborne invaders have come in their droves, swamping Castries, storming the heights of Morne Fortune. The island has opted particularly for the all-inclusive format, in which people pay up front and don't pull out their wallet again, hardly venturing forth from the resort compound. This is a pity because the island is good to explore. But there are also some small and charming spots hidden away in coves and bays where the calm and beauty of Fair Helen still remains.

History

Santa Lucia first appears on a royal *cedula* of 1511 marking out the Spanish domain in the New World, and then on a Vatican globe of 1520. It is not known who discovered it, or why it was named after the virgin-martyr of Syracuse, but the St Lucians celebrate St Lucy's Day, 13 December, as their national day.

Hewanorra, as the Caribs called St Lucia, was a favoured hide-out for the pirates and privateers of the 16th century. They came to scourge the Spaniards in the Indies and men like Frenchman François de Clerc (better known to the Spaniards as *Pie de Palo* because of his wooden leg) would lie up at Pigeon Island in the north of the island, on the look-out for shipping to plunder, just as the admirals of the European navies would 200 years later. In 1553 de Clerc left for a grand tour in which he sacked the major towns in Santo Domingo, Puerto Rico and Cuba.

Attempts to settle St Lucia began at the turn of the 17th century. The first, in 1605, really happened by accident, when the *Olive Blossom* limped to St Lucia after being blown off course on the Atlantic crossing. She was headed for the Guianas in South America, but, short of supplies, 67 of her passengers took their chances in St Lucia and bought huts and food from seemingly friendly Carib Indians. The Caribs soon changed their tune, though, and after five weeks of hostilities just 19 of the settlers were still alive, so they made a final purchase of a canoe and paddled off to South America. Another English attempt in 1639 survived for eighteen months unmolested before the Caribs attacked. The Indians winkled them out of their fort by burning red pepper in the wind, a trick they used to catch sleeping parrots. Almost all the British were killed.

Just as Charles I of England granted St Lucia and other islands officially in the Spanish domain to the Earl of Carlisle in 1627, so Cardinal Richelieu felt free to offer islands 'not possessed by any Christian prince' to the French West India Company in 1642, and soon the French settlements in the West Indies began to appear. The scene was set for the next two hundred years; settlements, battles and treaties, a rivalry that would see St Lucia change hands a ridiculous fourteen times. Once the Caribs were wiped out, the island steadily turned from a rabble of deserters, loggers and turtlers to a prosperous colony, cultivating sugar.

With Louis XVI guillotined in January 1793 in Europe, Britain and the Republic of France were at war again in the Caribbean and the revolutionaries raised the *tricolore* in St Lucia. With its revolutionary sympathies and a guillotine erected in the capital, the island became known as *St Lucie la Fidèle*. The British fought their way back into Castries in 1796, but the *Armée française dans les bois* (a forest-based guerrilla force) held the rest of the islanders to ransom for another year. The subsequent war and treaty left St Lucia in British hands and the planters promptly got back to the business of cultivating sugar. The slaves were emancipated in 1834.

In 1885 Castries became one of the two principal coaling stations in the British West Indies, along with Kingston, Jamaica, filling a thousand steam-ships a year and gaining yet more importance when the Panama Canal was opened in 1914. Women would be seen climbing the gangways with 110lb baskets of coal on their heads, smoking pipes or singing shanties.

After the Second World War, as the West Indian islands moved towards political self-determination, St Lucia became self-governing in 1967 and then took Independence on 22 February 1979. The country is still a member of the British Commonwealth, with an elected Parliament after the Westminster model. At present the island is governed by the United Workers Party under Prime Minister John Compton, holding nine seats to the St Lucia Labour Party's eight.

St Lucia's economy depends mainly on tourism, but bananas also contribute to foreign exchange earnings. Most are shipped out by *Geest* and are sold in Britain as Windward Island Bananas. Despite some fears that the price of Central American 'dollar bananas' would undercut this market when the European Community adopted the single-market agreement in 1993, producers have been allowed to retain preferential quotas for the foreseeable future.

Flora and Fauna

Like all the Windwards St Lucia has exuberant flora: coastal mangrove swamps (near Savannes on the southeast coast) where you can see the mangrove cuckoo and the tropical mockingbird and warblers, and plains flown over by hawks and herons. The white bird that keeps a silent vigil by the grazing cows is the cattle egret, which found its way over from Africa earlier this century. In the higher reaches of rainforest you will find the Antillean crested and the purple-throated hummingbird. The upper rainforest is also home to the endangered St Lucia parrot. On the offshore islands you will come across tropicbirds and magnificent frigatebirds.

There are far fewer mammals, but there are many reptiles, from frogs to iguanas. One you will certainly hear is the tree frog, who peeps rhythmically at night, particularly after a rainstorm. Turtles also come to lay their eggs on St Lucian beaches between March and August. Those with a particular interest in the natural life can contact the Forestry Department (✆ 453 6086, fax 453 6087). They can arrange tours for birders and plant and animal watchers. The National Trust (✆ 452 5008, fax 453 2791) also manages a number of St Lucia's Nature Reserves, which include the Maria and Fregate Islands on the east coast.

✆ (809)– **Getting There**

St Lucia has quite good air links. Flights from outside the Caribbean fly into Hewanorra International Airport near the south coast and 40 miles (over an hour's ride) south of Castries. If you are flying within the Caribbean, it is probably better to aim for Vigie Airport just outside the capital. There is a departure tax of EC$27 and a security charge of EC$10.

Cruise passengers are well looked after at Point Seraphine in Castries, where there is a shopping mall to keep you occupied from the moment you leave the ship.

By Air from the UK: BWIA (✆ 454 6249) and British Airways (✆ 454 6172) both have twice-weekly flights. On days when no direct flights are operating, the best connections are via Barbados. Charter operators also offer seats from UK and Europe.

By Air from the USA: BWIA has a daily direct flight from Miami and New York, and American Airlines fly daily from Miami and weekly from New York. Otherwise you can travel via their hub in Puerto Rico (served from all over the States) from where you can make the link on American Eagle. Air Canada flies weekly from Montreal and Toronto.

By Air from other Caribbean Islands: There are links to most of the major islands nearby. LIAT (✆ 452 3051) flies to Barbados, north to Antigua and south to Trinidad and Caracas. Air Martinique (✆ 452 2463) originates in Martinique and flies south to the Grenadines. American Eagle (℡ 452 1820) has a daily link to San Juan, Puerto Rico. If you wish to charter a plane try Helenair (℡ 809 452 7196) and Eagle Air Services (℡ 452 1900).

Getting Around

Private **minibuses** run all the main routes around the island. Gros Islet and the north are well served and buses continue until as late as 10pm (longer on a Friday), leaving from Darling Road. Buses heading south leave from around Bridge Street, departing on and off until late afternoon. For a day trip to Soufrière you must be quite careful because the last bus back to Castries leaves at midday, after which time you will have to take the longer route via Vieux Fort. Some sample prices are: **Castries** to Gros Islet EC$1.50, to Dennery $2 and to Soufrière or Vieux Fort $5. 75c will get you to the top of Morne Fortune.

Taxis can be arranged easily enough at hotels, in town or at the airport or by **Courtesy Taxi Service** (℡ 452 3555); if you are lucky the driver will give you an impromptu guided tour. By the hour a taxi costs about EC$60, and a day tour in a taxi can be shared by 4 people for about EC$300. Sample one-way fares are: **Castries** to Vigie airport EC$12, and to Hewanorra airport, near Vieux Fort EC$120, to Rodney Bay $35 and the Cap Estate in the north $40.

Car hire gives more independence for exploring the inland byways like the rainforest road out of Soufrière and the route to Grand Anse northeast of Castries. A temporary driving licence is required, costing EC$30 on presentation of a valid home licence to the police at either airport or in Castries. An international licence is valid. Driving is on the left, generally.

Many hire companies have desks at the airports and typically they will require a deposit of US$100. Cars cost from US$40 per day, from **Avis** in Castries (℡ 452 2202 or 452 2700) or **National**, nearer to Gros Islet (℡ 450 8721 or 450 8028). Jeeps are available through **Cool Breeze Jeep Rental** (℡ 459 7729) and you can hire motorbikes through **Wayne's Motorcycle Centre** in Vide Bouteille (℡ 452 2059), motorbikes EC$75 a day and scooters EC$60.

Island tours around St Lucia can be arranged through **Solar Tours** in Choc Bay (℡ 452 5898) and **Barnards Travel** (℡ 452 1615). If you would like to tour the island by helicopter—in half an hour you can fly between the Pitons, hover in rainforested valleys and zoom yachts—contact **St Lucia**

Helicopters (✆ 453 6950) or **Eastern Caribbean Helicopters** (✆ 453 6952), departure from Point Seraphine. North and south island tours are about US$200 for 10 minutes (max three people).

Tourist Information

The St Lucia Tourist Board can be contacted at:

UK: 421a Finchley Road, London N3 6HJ (✆ 071 431 4045, fax 071 431 7920).

USA: 9th Floor, 820 Second Avenue, New York, NY 10017 (✆ 212 867 2950, fax 212 370 7867).

Canada: 4975 Dundas Street West, Suite 457 Etobicoke 'D', Islington, Ontario M9A 4X4 (✆ 416 236 0936, fax 416 236 0937, toll free ✆ 800 456 3984).

Germany: Postfach 2304, D–61293 Bad Homburg 1 (✆ 06172 30 44 31, fax 06172 30 50 72).

France: ANI, 53 rue François 1er, Septième Etage, Paris 75008 (✆ 147 20 39 66, fax 147 23 09 65).

In St Lucia itself write to the main tourism office in the **Point Seraphine Shopping Complex**, across the harbour from downtown Castries, where the cruise ships dock, PO Box 221 (✆ 452 4094, fax 453 1121). There are also helpful tourist information offices in Jeremie Street in Castries, at **Vigie** airport (✆ 452 2595) and at **Hewanorra** airport in the south (✆ 454 6644). The Tourist Board puts out two publications—*Visions of St Lucia*, a glossy magazine with practical details and feature articles and the monthly broadsheet, *The Tropical Traveller*, for a more topical view. *The Voice* newspaper is published in Castries three times a week, on Tues, Thurs and Sat, with local news and events. Two popular Saturday papers are the *Star* and the *Crusader*.

Money

The official currency of St Lucia is the Eastern Caribbean dollar, which is fixed to the US dollar at EC$2.65 = US$1. US dollars are widely accepted in tourist areas, but generally the word 'dollar' usually refers to the Eastern Caribbean dollar. It is worth establishing which currency you are working in. **Banks** are open Mon–Fri, 8am–3pm with an extra stint until 5 on Friday afternoons and they give a better exchange rate than the hotels. **Shops** are open weekdays 8.30–12.30 and 1.30–4, Sat 8–noon. The **IDD code** for St Lucia is **809**, followed by a seven-figure number. On-island you must dial all seven digits.

Beaches

St Lucia's best white-sand beaches lie on the protected leeward coast at the northern end of the island, between Castries and the northern tip. Here you will find the most active beaches, with watersports available. To the south of Castries most beaches have black volcanic sand, often in secluded coves where the mountains fall steeply down to the coast.

The most popular beach on the island is **Reduit Beach** in Rodney Bay, miles of mounded sand so soft that you stumble trying to get through it. It is a 20-minute drive from the capital, and most watersports are on offer. There is a whole array of bars and restaurants to retreat to behind the beach. There are one or two more secluded strips of sand on **Pigeon Island**, across the bay.

On the route back to town, **La Brelotte**, where you will find the Windjammer resort in a steep-sided bay, is worth a couple of hours in the afternoon sun. Just outside Castries is **Vigie Beach**, a 2-mile stretch with hotels at intervals, with sand that slopes gently away into crystalline water. A particularly charming half-moon bay, mounded with golden sand, is at **La Toc** bay just south of Castries. Further south there are a number of secluded coves on the west coast south of Castries that can only be reached by boat.

Anse Chastanet, close to Soufrière on the leeward coast, is an idyllic cove with grey sand that is sheltered between massive headlands. Soufrière itself has a passable beach. Further south, to the windward side of the island, is **Anse des Sables**, a shallow and open bay swept by the Tradewinds that is renowned for windsurfing.

Beach Bars

Some of the best beach bars are connected to the hotels. There are two or three along Reduit Beach, of which the most preferable is **Spinnakers**, set on a deck right on the sand. There are a couple of excellent waterfront bars beneath the palm trees in **Marigot Bay** and if you happen past **Anse Jambette**, just further south, while it is open, that is well worth hoving to for. Close by, **Anse Mamim** is a bar in a charming setting in a tiny cove. Finally, **Anse Chastanet** has a fine tropical bar and a superb view over the grey sand to the sunset.

Sailing

St Lucia is a popular and busy yachting centre and it has good marinas and technical services as well as the many active bars and restaurants easily accessible to yachtsmen. The sailing is good; all down its west coast, St Lucia is indented with coves that make protected harbours for yachts. Charter expeditions can be arranged around the island, or farther afield, perhaps to the Grenadines in the south, in crewed or bare-boats. There are a number of **ports of entry** in St Lucia: Rodney Bay in the north, Castries (though these are difficult and you are really better not to use them), Marigot Bay and Vieux Fort at the southern tip.

There are three main **marinas** on the island. In the north, Rodney Bay marina is the largest and it lies in a lagoon approached by a channel behind Reduit Beach (you can anchor in the lagoon itself and at the southern end of Reduit Beach). There are slips with water and electricity and there are good shoreside facilities including chandlery, supermarkets, showers and shops as well as a number of restaurants within an easy dinghy ride. There are also mechanical workshops, repair yards and a long-stay storage area.

In Castries harbour there is a small marina and boatyard in the calm inlet of Vigie Creek, also a couple of restaurants and shops within walking distance. A few miles south of Castries is the famed Marigot Bay, a wonderfully secluded inlet which features the Moorings. You can take on water, ice and fuel and there are a couple of hotels with restaurants. Although it is situated a little to upwind of the normal heading between the islands, there are anchorages and limited facilities at Vieux Fort at the southern tip of St Lucia. For **day sails** you might head for Anse Cochon, about three miles south of Marigot Bay, or further on down to Soufrière, where there are a number of sheltered places to pause within sight of the magnificent Pitons. There are plenty of restaurants and bars to stop by in.

St Lucia has good marina and shipyard facilities: in Rodney Bay is the Rodney Bay Marina (✆ 452 0324) and a chandlery, Rodney Bay Ship Services (✆ 452 9973); and in Castries Harbour the Castries Yacht Centre (✆ 452 6334) for major repairs and chandlery. Two charter companies work out of Rodney Bay: **Sunsail Stevens** (✆ 452 8648) and **Trade Wind Yacht Charters** (✆ 452 8424). A great place to start a yachting holiday is Marigot Bay, where the **Moorings** (✆ 451 4256) are based with their large fleet of bare-boats.

If you are crossing the Atlantic, in November/December each year is the Atlantic Rally for Cruisers, culminating in St Lucia. Contact **World Cruising Ltd**, PO Box 165, London WC1B 3XA (✆ 071 405 9905, fax 071 831 0161).

Watersports

You can fix most watersports at Reduit Beach, including glass-bottom boat rides, waterskiing (*EC$45 for 20 mins*) and parasailing (*EC$80 a ride*), or a trip on a sunfish or a hobie cat. Contact the operators on the beach. **Windsurfers** are available at the main beaches through hotel watersports shops, but the best winds are in the south of the island, near Hewanorra Airport.

For a day cruise of yo-ho-ho down to the Pitons, you can try the ever-popular catamaran *Endless Summer* (℗ 450 8651) or the trimaran *Surf Queen* (℗ 452 8351). The 140ft square-rigged brigantine *Unicorn* (℗ 452 6811), which was used in the television series *Roots*, also makes the trip, as does the motor yacht *Vigie*.

For **deep-sea fishing**, trailing a line for marlin and sail-fish, contact **Mako Watersports** (℗ 452 0412) or **Captain Mike's Watersports** (℗ 452 7044) in Vigie Cove. *Half-day US$400, full day US$800.* There is a bill-fishing tournament in St Lucia each October.

Diving is excellent, with visibility up to 100ft and colourful coastal marine life. Instruction and equipment (including underwater cameras) are available through the large operators. Most of the diving takes place on the west coast; two popular areas are Anse Cochon and Anse Chastanet near Soufrière, the home of **Scuba St Lucia** (℗ 459 7355, or 450 8009 at the St Lucian Hotel) where the reefs start at 15ft below the surface. Also recommended is **Buddies Scuba** (℗ 452 5288) in Vigie and **Dolphin Divers** (℗ 452 9485), who operate out of Rodney Bay and Marigot Bay. *A single-tank dive costs around US$40.* Most hotels will provide **snorkelling** gear for a minimal fee if you wish to chase after an angelfish or a stretched trumpetfish.

Other Sports

Golfers can play on the 9-hole course in the Cap Estate (℗ 450 8523), near the northern tip of the island *green fee EC$20*. Clubs, carts and caddies are available for hire. **Tennis** is available at all the big hotels and most will let you play on their courts. Hire of horses and riding instruction is available through **Trim's Riding Stables** (℗ 450 8273) on the Cassabar side or **North Point Riding Stables** (℗ 452 8273) in the Cap Estate, *price about US$25 per hour*. Rides will take you for a picnic and a canter along the beach in a secluded cove on the Atlantic coast. Some hotels also offer tours by bicycle.

Castries

If history were replayed as you cruised into Castries harbour, the hills around you would swarm with troops, the air hang heavy with the smell of gunpowder and the ground and the harbour would be stained scarlet with blood. Castries was one of the most bitterly contested places in the whole of the Caribbean.

The town lies on the protected leeward coast of the island, at the head of an irregular, almost landlocked bay, framed by forested hills that rise in folds into the distance. The harbour mouth is guarded by **Vigie Point** (French for look-out), covered in yellow-brick barracks and the graveyards of campaigns past—you get a good view of them as you come in for the final wobbly descent into Vigie airport.

Castries takes its name from the Maréchal de Castries, a French colonial minister, who was governor of the island in 1784. The name stuck, despite being rejected at the time of the French Revolution, when the town was known as Félicité-ville. Set out on a gridiron pattern, the centre of the town is mostly modern, concrete and functional. Near the market on Jeremie Street there is even an area of neo-brutalist housing estate imported from sixties England. But despite Castries's rather unfortunate habit of burning down (1796, 1812, 1927 and 1948), it has a few pockets of old creole architecture, mostly in the southeast corner of the town at the top end of Chaussee Road. Their balconies overhang the pavement on sturdy wooden stilts and the gingerbread patterns on the eaves here are more intricate and prettier than on any island in the eastern Caribbean except for Trinidad.

The centre of the town is **Derek Walcott Square**, recently renamed after he won the Nobel prize for literature (its previous name 'Columbus Square' had long been controversial). On the east side of the square, next to a magnificent saman tree, is the **Roman Catholic Cathedral**, which has an iron-work interior with a patterned roof and colourful murals in which many of the figures are depicted as Africans.

The liveliest area of town however is the **Market**, 5 minutes' walk away on Jeremie Street, a magnificent old red iron market erected at the turn of the century. Recently renovated, it is jumbled full of furniture, straw bags and sweetmeats. Outside, Jeremie Street is alive with the chatter of the market ladies from the country, who sit watching over piles of eddoe, tannia, christophene and yam.

Morne Fortune (pronounced 'Fortunay' and supposedly meaning the Hill of Good Luck) looms above the town, and it is here that the fiercest battles took place in the 18th century. Nowadays the soldiers would be fighting their way through the scarlet and purple blooms of the bougainvillea in the private gardens as the road winds its way back and forth to the summit. The old imposing military hulks, barracks, stables and gun emplacements have been taken over by the modern-day establishment as official buildings. Close to the summit stands the partially restored Fort Charlotte, which dates from the late 18th century.

Nearby is Government House, the official residence of the governor-general, built of red stones with white trimmings in the 1890s. It had something of a habit of killing governors. As Sir Algernon Aspinall relates in his *Pocket Guide to the West Indies*, one inhospitable Governor Farquharson was obliged to entertain a bishop; when it was time to retire he said, 'I suppose your lordship has heard of the insalubrity of this place; every room in the house has already witnessed the death of some Governor, but none of them has had the honour of killing a bishop; so, my Lord, you have only to make your selection.' The bishop departed immediately and Governor Farquharson died of fever in the house two years later.

The Morne dominates the town and from the top you get one of the finest views in the West Indies. To the north it commands Vigie airport and then along the coast to Pigeon Point. On clear days it is quite possible to see Martinique. The view is also spectacular to the south, where the Pitons are visible in the distance.

North from Castries to the Cap

As you head north out of town, a side road leads past the fish market and the Institut Franco-St Lucien, a curious white pyramid, and on to the Point Seraphine cruise ship dock.

Time was, not so long ago, when the cars had to be cleared off the road to allow planes to land at Vigie airport, which handles short-haul island-hopper flights. Now the airstrip runs alongside **Vigie Beach**, so if you want some last minutes of sun and sand before leaving, there are 2 miles of protected bay here. It is the site of many a forgotten invasion and the fortifications that opposed them, 18th-century strongholds that now lie buried under the bastions of the 20th-century Caribbean tourist hotels. The island opposite the Halcyon Beach Club is called **Rat Island**, a former nunnery, now deserted.

From the top end of Choc Bay a side road branches through the hills to the other side of the island where you will find the attractive half-moon bay of Grand Anse on the Atlantic coast. The family of the Empress Josephine had a sugar estate at Paix Bouche on the windward side of the island. Despite Martiniquan insistence to the contrary, the St Lucians claim that Josephine was born in St Lucia. At the **Marquis Estate** (✆ 452 3762) you will see a working plantation producing bananas and *copra* (dried coconut) and hear descriptions of old-time crops such as cocoa and coffee, and of course sugar. After the estate visit you can take a visit down the Marquis River to an Atlantic coast bay for a swim.

The main road north, which is being steadily developed with houses and shopping centres, emerges from the rolling hills on to **Rodney Bay**, named after the British admiral who made St Lucia his headquarters in the late 18th century. This is the location of Reduit beach and many of St Lucia's hotels and restaurants. In the bay the yachts and gin palaces lie at anchor in formation, just as Rodney's warships did two hundred years ago.

Across the marina entrance stands the village of **Gros Islet**, famed for its parties on Friday nights when the few streets of simple, brightly painted clapboard houses seethe with dancers until the early hours. The town was proudly called Révolution when St Lucia was holding out at the time of the French Revolution. The 'islet' (Pigeon Island) from which the town takes its name is in fact no longer an island. It was joined to the mainland in the early seventies by an artificial causeway, part of a vastly expensive tourist development programme that foundered, leaving just a few abandoned foundations and a perfectly protected and stunning bay.

Pigeon Point, Pigeon Island that was, lies 1 mile across the bay, a barren outcrop with two peaks that the British fortified as soon as they took the island from the French in 1778. The stone ramparts and defences are still visible, 18th-century gun batteries and gun slides, 19th-century barracks and cookhouses. Since the earliest visitors came to St Lucia, Pigeon Island has been used as a vantage point to watch over Martinique, visible 20 miles away. Now the area is a National Park and there is a small museum, *adm*, in the recently restored officer's mess. Among the wartime memorabilia is a visual display of the Battle of the Saints in 1782, in which Rodney had his finest hour.

At the northern tip of the island is the **Cap Estate**, an expensive residential area with smart villas and a golf course. Worth a visit in this area is the gallery of the St Lucian-born artist, Llewelyn Xavier, *adm free, paintings from a few hundred dollars*. Go straight ahead at the second roundabout, past the house that looks like a banana and it is a white building up on the left. Art on view includes work by locals Derek Walcott and Roy Lawaetz, Mr Canute Caliste from Carriacou and several Haitians, as well as Xavier himself, but the trip is worthwhile for the view alone, which takes in both the Atlantic coast and the Pitons.

South to Soufrière

The route to Soufrière from Castries follows a tortuous path on the leeward coast of the island, a series of switchbacks struggling up over the headlands and cruising down into the river valleys where fishing villages nestle among the palms. Alternatively, take a yacht and coast down-island for two hours and you will see the road straggle southward against the backdrop of St Lucian mountains, so often shrouded by passing rainstorms. Whichever way you go, the journey culminates in one of the most exciting views in the whole of the Caribbean, the twin peaks of the Pitons that soar from the sea's edge like vast tropical pyramids.

On land the journey starts at the summit of Morne Fortune, and drops into **Cul de Sac**, a wide valley once riffling with sugar cane and now carpeted with banana trees. There is an oil refinery with its huge bunkering silos in the valley. From here the road climbs a ridge and drops into another huge valley, at **Roseau**, also filled with bright green banana leaves that splay gracefully in an arch until their tips reach the ground. As you descend you come to the turning to the hidden **Marigot Bay**, an idyllic hideaway in a steep-sided harbour festooned with palm trees, where yachts sit serenely on the calm of Hurricane Hole, an extremely safe anchorage. In 1778, Admiral Barrington is supposed to have eluded d'Estaing by bringing his fleet into the bay and camouflaging the ships with palm fronds. More recently

Dr Doolittle with Rex Harrison was filmed here. A small boat-taxi links one side to the other. Back on the main road, the best view of the Roseau valley is from the heights just as you leave it to drive farther south.

The two fishing towns of **Anse la Raye** and **Canaries** lie on river mouths at the sea's edge. From here the road cuts deeper into the undergrowth, a profusion of majestic ferns that sprout from the deep brown earth and ancient lianas that hang from high above.

Finally the road clears another summit and emerging from the dank rainforest you see the twin points of the **Pitons** standing out in the glare of the sun. The word 'piton' means 'spike' and they are thought to the sides of an eroded volcanic crater. They have long been a sailor's landmark and are spectacular when viewed from the sea, but the best view is from the leeward coast road because they have an identical shape and move beside one another as you descend into Soufrière.

The town of **Soufrière** itself lies in a valley beneath the Petit Piton (2461ft). It is one of the oldest settlements in St Lucia, a thriving port in the mid-18th century, and takes its name from the volcanic vent nearby that emits sulphurous clouds. For a while in the 1790s it held the honoured republican name of *La Convention*, after the revolutionary tribunal in Paris.

The town is quite tatty and obviously poor, but around the central Elizabeth Square there are some attractive old stone façades and wooden creole homes surviving from French times, their eaves a gingerbread filigree beneath corrugated iron roofs.

the Pitons St Lucia

On Saturday morning there is a market on the seafront and perhaps you will see cocoa beans drying in the sun on the pavement, before they are processed into cocoa sticks. The bay is extremely deep, dropping straight away as steeply as the Pitons rise above the surface. For those brave enough to swim, the water has warm and cold patches, released by the volcano beneath the surface.

Inland from Soufrière, the road comes to the **Diamond Falls and Botanical Gardens**, *adm*, at Diamond, where a path leads through tropical gardens into a cleft with a waterfall gushing into a small rockpool. The water descends 1000ft from the volcano above, where it leaves the ground at 106° Fahrenheit and has discoloured the river bed orange and gold with the volcanic mud. The water has similar properties to the water of Aix-les-Bains in France and is reputed to have considerable curative powers, 'efficacious in cases of rheumatism and kindred ills'. If you are happy to risk carbonate of magnesia and phosphate of lime then you can take the waters (brought down from higher up the mountain). Alternatively you can take a steamy bath in it. The gardens are pleasant to visit and you can expect to see typical Caribbean plants such as lobster claw and ginger lily, but also less usual ones like breadnut (a relative of the breadfruit) and a gri-gri palm with a hairy trunk. From the gardens an aqueduct leads towards the 2000-acre Soufrière Estate, where coconuts, cocoa and bananas are grown and processed.

The road to Diamond continues inland, climbing steadily into the St Lucia rainforest and losing itself in Fonds St-Jacques, now a nature reserve, where in the wild orchids and the montane woodland you might catch a glimpse of the endangered St Lucia parrot among the flitting hummingbirds.

Travelling south from Soufrière, the road climbs for a couple of miles or so to the **Sulphur Springs**, St Lucia's well-behaved *solfatara*. In the collapsed crater is a bubbling and steaming morass, 7 acres in size, devoid of plant-life, with grey mudpools that hiss and smell gently of stink-bomb.

There was a vapour explosion at the Soufrière in 1766, but nothing too violent has happened since then. It is not expected to erupt because it constantly lets off steam. Paths are marked and you are not advised to walk around on it because the mudpools have been known to move suddenly (one person was swallowed to the waist and ended up with 3rd-degree burns on his bottom). You may see a couple of rusty pipes sticking out of the ground, an attempt to tap the heat for power generation.

As the tourist brochures say, the Soufrière is a 'drive-in' volcano. For the tourists who dare venture forth from the protection of their car, there are guides who will ply them with more Soufrière 'lore' for a small fee.

From the mountain heights of the Pitons, the road steadily descends to the southern plains that once blew with sugar-cane, to **Vieux Fort** at the farthest tip of the island. It passes through the fishing villages of **Choiseul**, with its black and white cemetery and **Laborie**. Both are quiet and unaffected West Indian towns, full of clapboard houses on blocks, standing in neat yards in the shadow of breadfruit trees. Perhaps you will arrive on the day when the open-air butcher is at work, boiling up black puddings for passers-by. At Choiseul, the Arts and Crafts Development Centre displays and sells local handiwork including rocking chairs and carvings. There is a small restaurant if you want to stop for lunch.

Vieux Fort

Named after a fortress mentioned by a 17th-century island-hopping monk, Abbé Raynal, windswept Vieux Fort stands on an open bay, looking south towards St Vincent. Vieux Fort is St Lucia's second town. It was here that the sugar industry was first set up in 1765, but now the town is quiet and the few streets seem empty. Hewanorra International Airport nearby was first built by the Americans during the Second World War as a refuelling point on their routes between the United States and Europe; now it receives long-haul flights from both directions.

Sticking out into the rough water between the Atlantic and the Caribbean by Vieux Fort is the **Moule à Chique** peninsula, offering fine views towards St Vincent, a grey-green stain about 25 miles away to the south.

The **Maria Islands** lie off the Atlantic coast just out of Vieux Fort and are kept as a nature reserve. Those interested in discovering the delights of the *kouwès* snake (this is the only place on the globe where this species of grass snake lives), a lizard called *zandoli te* and the wheeling world of frigatebirds and brown noddies should contact the National Trust (✆ 452 5005). There is a small **museum** of natural life by the Hewanorra runway opposite the islands, *open Wed–Sun, 9.30–5, adm.*

Vieux Fort to Castries—North along the Windward Coast

The Windward road winds along the rough Atlantic coast, over the spurs and the valleys thrown off by the central spine of mountains, and passes through the plantations that provide St Lucia's food and export fruit. The centres are the towns of **Micoud** and **Dennery**. Between the two is the Fregate Island Nature Reserve. There is an observation trail where you can hope to see St Lucian orioles and tremblers and where frigatebirds nest on the islands in the summer months. At Dennery is one of the island's largest banana plantations, where you will see the huge bright green leaves unscroll and become steadily shredded by the wind. From here the road cuts inland, over the **Barre de l'Isle** ridge, among the lianas and bushy ferns high up in the rainforest, and then descends into Cul de Sac valley before climbing the back of Morne Fortune and dropping into Castries.

Festivals

The St Lucians celebrate Independence on 22 February with official activities and their national day on 13 December with a round of sailing races, fêtes and jump-ups, but the highlight of the St Lucian cultural calendar is **Carnival**, a pre-Lenten blow-out of costumed street-parades led by bandwagons (artics stacked with speakers). Calypsonians and Kings and Queens of the Bands play to the crowds in the Marchand Stadium before they spill onto the streets, where the beat is so strong that even the buildings seem to rock in time with the dancers (in fact, parts of Castries are built on reclaimed land and they really do move).

There are a number of smaller festivals, many of them centred around music. A **Jazz Festival**, with international musicians, is held in May and on 22 November the patron saint of music, St Cecilia, is remembered by island calypsonians and panmen. During the day musicians from outlying villages ride the roads playing from vans and then in the evening they collect for competitons. The **Rose** and the **Marguerite** (on 30 August and 17 October) are also musical celebrations, set around an imaginary court and its retinue, complete with finery and ceremonial garb and each with its flower cockade (a rose or a marigold). They stage a ball, and they are led by a chanterelle and a band (banjo, quattro, boom boom and drum). Well worth attending if you are on-island. The creole language (spoken by most St Lucians) is remembered on **Jounen Kweyol**, held on the weekend nearest 28 October. Culinary and musical blow-outs are staged.

℡ (809)–

Where to Stay

The majority of St Lucia's hotels are on the beaches of the northern leeward coast, facing the calm Caribbean Sea and the sunset. There are plenty of humming hives of high-pressure luxury in the typical Caribbean beach resort mould, but St Lucia also has some charming smaller hotels offering classic Caribbean seclusion in dramatic settings, tucked away in the island's coves or in view of the Pitons. Many hotels follow an all-inclusive plan, including a number of more luxurious resorts, but there is still a good range of properties for the independent traveller. Hotel bills (unless you are in an all-inclusive resort, of course) are supplemented by a government tax of 8% and most hotels also levy a 10% service charge.

expensive–luxury

The white arches and orange roof tiles of the **Windjammer Landing Villas Beach Resort**, PO Box 1504 (✆ 809 452 0913, fax 452 0907, UK ✆ 0800 373 742, US ✆ 800 743 9609, Canada ✆ 800 267 7600) stand out starkly against the shades of green on Labrelotte Bay north of Castries. There are 114 extremely comfortable and elegant one- to four-bedroom villas, all with maid service and some with their own plunge pool and sunning area. Tennis and watersports by day, and in the evening you can dine by the swimming-pool. Close by is a low-key and extremely comfortable smaller hotel, the **East Winds Inn**, PO Box 193 (✆ 452 8212, fax 452 5434, UK reservations ✆ 071 741 9511, US ✆ 212 5458437). Set in a very attractive lawned garden of bamboo and mango trees, there are stone deluxe rooms with gingerbread pointings, screened windows, bamboo and rattan furniture, stonework showers and large terraces, or breezy octagonal cottages with louvred windows. The 26 rooms give onto a covered sitting and dining area and bamboo beachfront bar above a good stretch of sand. Elegant and quiet; very expensive, all-inclusive plan.

If you prefer a more formal hotel set-up you can try the **Royal St Lucian Hotel**, PO Box 997 (✆ 809 450 9999, fax 450 9639, UK reservations ✆ 081 741 9030, US ✆ 800 255 5859) which stands right on Reduit Beach. It is large and has all the international standard trappings of the 20th century, from air-conditioning, cable television and king-sized beds down to the third telephone in the bathroom. Near the northern tip of the island you will find **Le Sport**, PO Box 437 (✆ 450 8551, fax 450 0368, US ✆ 800 544 2883, UK ✆ 0800 590794), which devotes itself to a scheduled body-holiday for office-weary executives. As the name suggests, there are plenty of sports. And for less energetic rejuvenation you can try the Moorish relaxation palace (algae bubble baths and seaweed wraps, loofah rubs, swiss needle showers and massage). Calorized cuisine or plain old chocolate indulgence. All-inclusive plan; very expensive.

There is a clutch of excellent hotels around Soufrière, set in some of the most dramatic surroundings in the Caribbean. At **Jalousie Plantation**, PO Box 251 (✆ 459 7666, fax 459 7667, UK ✆ 0800 220761, US ✆ 800 392 2007), the Petit Piton towers overhead like a massive pyramid. The 114 rooms are each lost in their own pocket of superb tropical gardens, most invisible from the next. It is very private in the rooms, but the facilities are there for a 20th-century rest-cure—beauty and sports area, horse riding, watersports on the (black sand) beach, Great House and waterfront dining room, shops, beach bar and helipad. Luxury. A smaller but equally private hotel, the **Ladera Resort**, PO Box 255 (✆ 459 7323, fax 459 7954, US ✆ 800 841 4145), stands 1000ft above Jalousie, perched on the shoulder of the Petit Piton. The six three-bedroom villas and 13 one-bedroom suites are open-fronted to take best advantage of the view and they have an delightful intimacy with the tropical night, the breeze and the peep of the tree frogs. Very elegant, old-time Caribbean feel with dark-stained wood and antique furniture, some private pools and room service. Not far away, **Anse Chastanet Beach Hotel**, PO Box 7000 (✆ 459 7000, fax 459 7700, UK ✆ 0800 894 057, US ✆ 800 841 4145) is tucked into its own remote and pretty cove. Some rooms are down by the grey sand beach, where there is a lively beach bar; others, huge and open to the breeze and mountain views are ranged on the rising hillside above the main house; very expensive. Across the harbour of Marigot Bay the Club Mariner **Hurricane Hole Hotel** (booking through the Moorings, ✆ 451 4357, fax 451 4353, US ✆ 800 334 2435) has 16 large and breezy cottages built of stone. Comfortable, with wicker furnishings and terraces that look through coconut and golden palm to the bay.

moderate

A charming hillside retreat, hidden away on the palm-clustered hillsides of Marigot Bay, **Doolittles Resort**, PO Box 101 (✆ 451 4974, fax 451 4973, US reservations ✆ 813 530 5424) has 10 hillside villas and eight studios, each with bright décor, ceiling fans, louvred windows and a screened veranda. Very low-key and quiet, but with a friendly crowd of passing yachtsmen in the bay. **Humming Bird Beach Resort** (✆ 459 7232, fax 459 7033) is a small, intimate hotel set in a profuse tropical garden right on the dark sand beach of Soufrière Bay. 10 comfortable rooms are clustered around the pool, a couple with dark wooden four-poster beds. Atmospheric and sometimes lively bar, stone-built and hung with parrot batiks, sea fans and flags; moderate to expensive. If you would like to be near Reduit beach without spending too much, try the friendly **Candyo Inn**, PO Box 386 (✆ 452 0718, fax 452 0774). It has 12 very neat and pretty studios and apartments with white tiles, wicker furniture and floral fittings. Restaurant and small pool in the garden. Good value. Another option nearby is the **Islander Hotel**, PO Box 907 (✆ 452 0255, fax 420 0958), which has 20 apartments and 40 rooms, all comfortable with kitchenettes and cable television, each one festooned in tropical greenery and set around the pool and grassy garden, close to all the activity of Rodney Bay.

cheap

There are any number of **guest houses** in St Lucia. Some will provide meals, but many are simple, without a pool, and generally they do not accept credit cards. **E's Serenity Lodge** (© 452 1987) is clean and comfortable, set in a modern villa in Sunny Acres just north of Castries. It is friendly and serves breakfast and dinner if you want. Most of the way up the Morne you will find **Bon Appetit** (© 452 2757). Quiet, rarified air, superb view, simple double and single rooms. Not far off, **Mrs Dubois** (© 452 2201) has four rooms above La Toc Bay, restaurant attached. The cheapest deal in town is **Lee's Guest House** (© 452 4285); very cheap. At **Gros Islet** you can get clean and simple rooms at the **Blue Lagoon** (© 450 8453, fax 453 7714), a modern house with a garden and kitchen facilities; very cheap.

In Soufrière there is very simple accommodation at the **Home Hotel** (© 459 7318), share baths and cold water or the **Tropical Palm** (© 459 7487). In Vieux Fort, perhaps as a stop on arrival at Hewanorra or just before leaving, try **Kimitrai** (© 454 6328).

Eating Out

St Lucia's French heritage extends into the food and the West Indian ingredients take on new life here in such creole dishes such as *soupe germou* (pumpkin and garlic soup) and *pouile dudon* (treacle and coconut chicken stew). As in any other of the islands, it is worth getting a spread of the vegetables, cooked in all the different ways—plantain boiled and fried, breadfruit, yam and christophene. Most large or hotel restaurants will accept credit cards; local ones will accept EC (Eastern Caribbean) dollars willingly and US dollars at a pinch. All bills are supplemented with an 8% government tax and most add 10%, or sometimes 15% for service as well.

expensive

Close to the top of the Morne is **Bon Appetit** (© 452 2757), one of the most sympathetic spots on the island. There is a view as far as Martinique from the tiny dining room, which is decorated with murals and menus painted by the hostess. The fare is international—seafood crêpe to start or heart of palm, followed by grilled crayfish with fresh island vegetables. Remember to reserve a table in season. The well-known **San Antoine** (© 452 4660) has a certain old-time ambience, set in a 19th-century stone great house with tall arched windows. You begin with cocktails at the bar looking out through the trees, and then move through to the subdued, candle-lit dining room. The menu is French and international—*fruits de mer en papillote* or *sautéd filet de poisson* in a crust of *fines herbes* and served in an orange sauce. The **Green Parrot** has another commanding view over Castries, orchestrated by the patron and island luminary,

Chef Harry. There is a French and creole menu as well as entertainment some nights. Try soup *A la la* or *doward St Jacques*, served with a volley of St Lucian vegetables; yam frites, coquettes, gombo, *chou à pomme* and *germou*. Four-course dinner available.

Just outside Castries in Vide Bouteille is **D's Restaurant** (✆ 453 7931), which has an excellent deal at lunch and so is always popular with local businessmen. At dinner you dine by candlelight on the veranda, chicken in coconut cream or mint and yoghurt, or lightly grilled fish. Two other restaurants have charming settings on Castries harbour. At **Jimmie's** (✆ 452 5142) you sit on a floral veranda above the activity of the boats. Simple lunches, more elaborate dinners: a seafood crêpe or Madras fish in curry butter sauce. Across the water is the **Coal Pot**, where you dine on an elegant veranda open to the breeze. Flying fish in batter or spicy curry served in a coconut shell.

moderate

A good place for an inexpensive meal in town is at **Paul's**, a local bar and restaurant serving oriental and local food—Malaysian chicken in green papaya or fry fish or chicken. It is best to get a table on the veranda over Bridge Street, but the pub-style interior is fun. **Kimlan's** is another trusty favourite with the locals. Simple St Lucian fare on a balcony above Derek Walcott Square.

The Rodney Bay area also has a number of good restaurants, many of them with the added advantage of a waterfront setting on the lagoon. There is always a lively air about the **Charthouse** (✆ 450 8115), *closed Sun*, which is set on the waterfront in a timber-frame house hung with ferns and palms. You dine on seafood, hickory-smoked ribs and steaks.

Another very popular restaurant, where expatriates and yachties gather, is the **Bistro** (✆ 452 9494), which is set above the water on a trelliswork deck. Wooden tables with red and white decor and a long list of seafood and other dishes, even including shepherd's pie. **Eagles Inn** (✆ 452 0650), *closed Fri and Sat*, has a subdued atmosphere in a forest of pretty greenery with views across the channel to Gros Islet. The menu is French creole—chicken breast Dominic, in a cucumber and mushroom sauce, or curry pot colombo. Always a good red snapper.

If you think you might like an air-conditioned speakeasy with a feeling of mock-gangsterism, then try **Capone's** (✆ 450 0284), where the menu is Italian. Start with a Prohibition Punch, followed by chicken in cream and pineapple. The bill comes in a violin case. If you cannot remember the code-word ('Al sent me'), then there is a pizzeria next door. Ever popular by day for simple fare on its verdant veranda is **The Lime** (© 452 0761). It also serves dinner *nightly except Tues*. Filet of fish *bonne femme* in white wine and mushroom sauce.

cheap

You can eat simple local fare in a pretty wooden house, the **Golden Apple** in Gros Islet, and there are a couple of pizzerias in the area, **Key Largo** and **Peppino's**. Another excellent place for local food is **Laurel's** on the road to the Windjammer Resort.

If you are exploring the **Soufrière** area you can try the hotels: **Dasheene** has a magnificent setting, though you should reserve the best table or arrive early, and there is a nice dining room down on the beach at Anse Chastanet. In the town itself **Humming Bird** has a lively dining room and there is good local food at **Jacquot Restaurant** and **Captain Hooks**. A restaurant with a difference is **Bang between the Pitons**, which as the name suggests sits on the waterfront between St Lucia's twin peaks. The setting is like a West Indian village (something of a departure for the owner, who developed the island of Mustique in the Grenadines) and there are pretty clapboard houses and palm trees set around a yard where the tables sit under shelters. The menu is Caribbean, with sunshine soup (from pumpkin), followed by jerk (from Jamaica) and escoveitched fish. Access easiest by boat. **Marigot Bay** is an another idyllic stopover, where you can linger over a fish in creole sauce or a salad at **Doolittle's** or **Odin's** down in the bay or at **Jay-Jay's** up above.

very cheap

You will find endless snacks and pastries on offer in St Lucia, some of them fried on braziers in front of you. A *float* is a deep-fried dough cake and you will find variations such as codfish or corned beef fritters. Finish off with a coconut pattie or a delicious St Lucian fruit cake. In Castries there are also a number of take-away vans where you can get a juice and a local meal in a polystyrene box in the daytime.

Bars and Nightlife

Most of the big hotels offer some entertainment, so you may see a few thighs singed under the limbo pole and hear Caribbean classics such as 'Yellowbird' and 'Scandal in the Family', but there are some more local entertainments too, in which you will find the locals making the best of Bounty Crystal, a local white rum, or Old

Fort, and the award-winning Piton, La Bière Sent Lisi. Two good haunts in town are **Paul's**, where a lively crowd often gathers, and **Kimlan's**, which stages jazz on Saturdays. **Le Jazz**, right on the road in Marissol, also offers food and jazz.

On the waterfront on Rodney Bay you will find the **A-Pub**, frequented by white St Lucians and semi-permanent yachtsmen; darts, backgammon and the occasional *karaoke*. Close by, the **Lime** is a popular gathering point at the weekends and particularly on Wednesday nights before the crowd moves on to **Splash**, the discotheque at the St Lucian Hotel. On Fridays the crowd gravitates around the **Late Lime Club** for jazz, *adm expensive (women free on Weds)*. **Club Society** is a much more St Lucian affair, in Grand Rivière where you will hear local music and the heavy tones of Jamaican dub and dancehall.

But the best-known party in the island is the weekly jump-up on Friday nights at **Gros Islet**, where four or five clubs spill out on to the street, speakers turned into the road pumping out soca, reggae and the latest zouk from Martinique, visible just a few miles to the north. It has become a bit of a tourist event, but it is still quite fun. You can pick up grilled fish and chicken legs, cooked in braziers on the street and served with hot pepper sauce. A less crowded variation on the theme is outside **Jay-Jays** on the road that leads down into Marigot Bay.

Further Reading

One of the English-speaking Caribbean's most celebrated authors is St Lucian, the poet and playwright Derek Walcott, who won the Nobel Prize for Literature in 1992. His works, which often adapt worldwide themes to a Caribbean setting, include *Omeros*. Another St Lucian author is Garth St Omer, whose works include *The Lights on the Hill*. If you can track down a copy of *St Lucia, Tours and Tales*, by Harriet Durham and Florence Lewisohn, do so, because it gives a well-presented and amusing background to the island. And you might even find a copy of the *St Lucia Diary of Lt J. H. Caddy*, a military man who served time in the West Indies in the 1830s—a revealing description of his life riding out, dining out and occasional military manoeuvres during his stay in St Lucia in 1833–4, published by the St Lucia Archaeological and Historical Society. The Sunshine Bookshop in Gablewoods Mall has a good selection of foreign newspapers and books about the Caribbean.

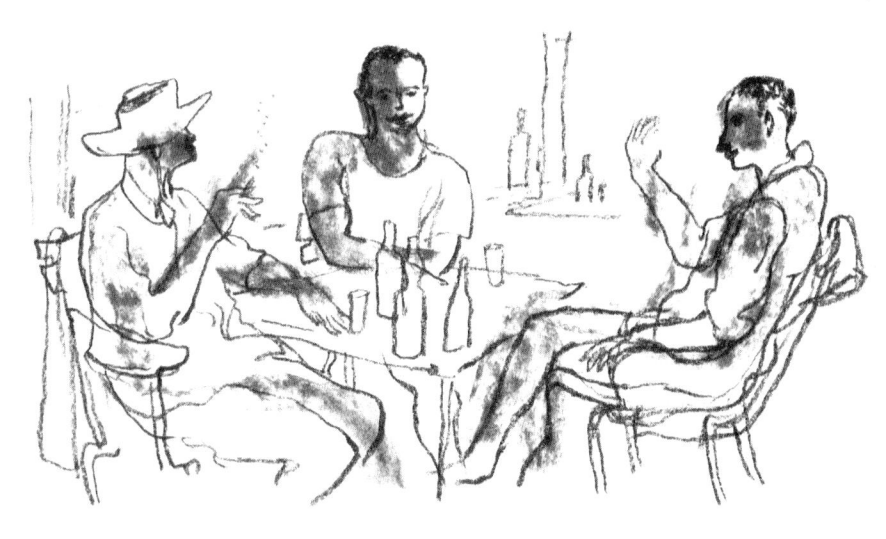

History	176
Getting There and Around	179
Tourist Information	181
Beaches and Sports	182
Fort de France	186
South of Fort de France	188
N2—The Caribbean Coast	191
St Pierre	192
North of St Pierre	194
St Pierre to the Atlantic Coast	194

Martinique

N3—Fort de France and the Pitons du Carbet	196
N1—Fort de France to the Atlantic Coast	196
Where to Stay	198
Eating Out	201

Martinique has traditionally been the flagship of French culture in the Caribbean. It was the richest of the colonies and in the last century its social hub, St Pierre, the Paris of the Lesser Antilles, was renowned all over the Americas. Fashion followed Paris to the letter, and the great plays of the age were staged in the St Pierre Theatre.

Though the spirit of St Pierre died in 1902, when the city was destroyed in a cataclysmic volcanic explosion, Martinique is still that little bit more chic. The island is more developed than its confrères, and with 385,500 citizens, one-third of whom live in the capital Fort de France on the southeast coast, it is the most populous island in the Lesser Antilles after Trinidad.

Martinique is a central link in the eastern Caribbean island chain, lying between the Windward Islands of Dominica and St Lucia. It measures 48 miles by 19 at its widest point (75 by 30km) and with its curious skiing-glove shape it has an area of 416 square miles (1080sq km). It seems larger because it is so highly developed. The north is dominated by the steep volcanic mountain of Mont Pelé (4656ft) and from there the land steadily falls away south to the central sugar plains of Lamentin and Fort de France, before rising again into the mornes (hills) of the southern peninsula. The island is of volcanic origin, except in the south, where age-old coral limestone formations have been pushed up out of the sea.

The French heritage constantly bombards the eyes, from the billboards to *boules* on the town-square. The Martiniquans have a surprisingly faithful attachment to France, stronger than their compatriots in Guadeloupe, whom they consider a little wild and unpredictable. Despite subsidies from France that amount to a total of about 70 per cent of the island's GDP, Martinique receives a lot from tourism, which brings in approximately as much as the rest of Martinique's exports combined, valued in 1989 at about 1 billion francs. The next principal earner is agriculture: one-third of the land is under cultivation and you will see banana plantations everywhere and sugar-cane, which is used for sugar and rum.

Most of the tourism in Martinique is concentrated around a few towns in the south, and you can certainly have a good time there enjoying the best of the island's beaches and the restaurants. But Martinique gives an excellent exposure to French Caribbean life, and it can be a stimulating and satisfying island to explore.

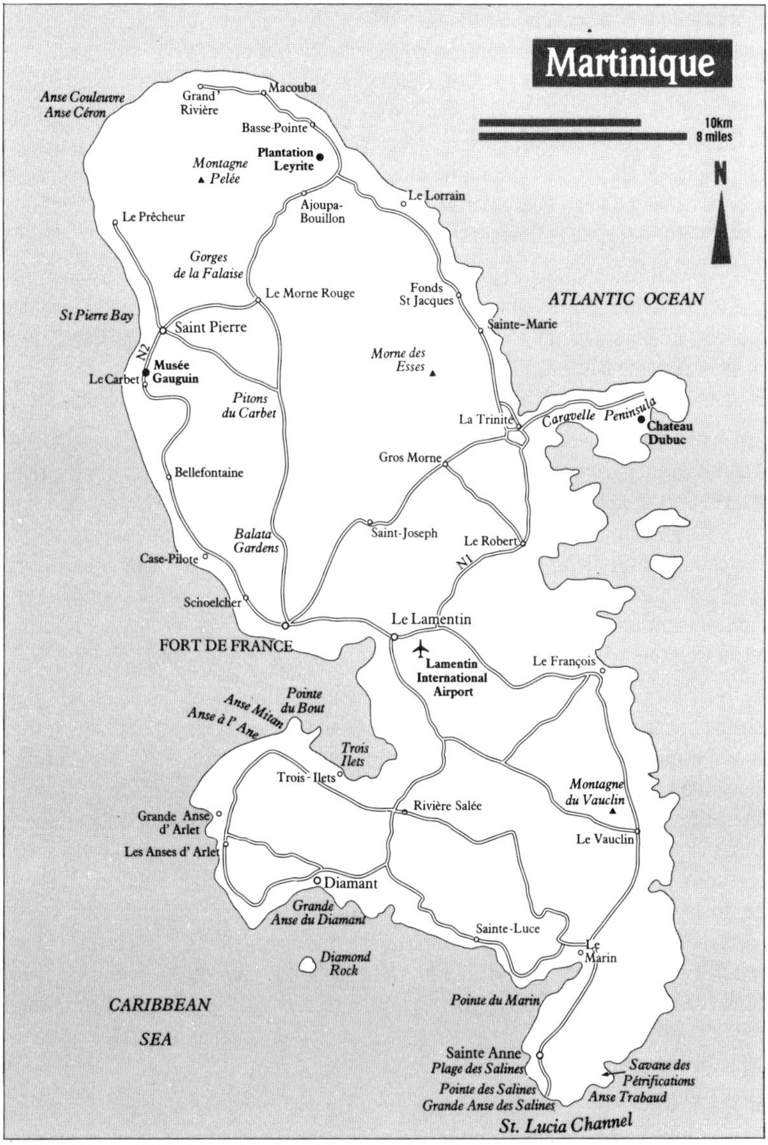
Martinique
10km
8 miles
N
Anse Couleuvre
Anse Céron
Grand' Rivière
Macouba
Basse-Pointe
Plantation Leyrite
Montagne Pelée
Le Lorrain
Ajoupa-Bouillon
Le Prêcheur
Gorges de la Falaise
Le Morne Rouge
Fonds St Jacques
ATLANTIC OCEAN
St Pierre Bay
Saint Pierre
Sainte-Marie
N2
Musée Gauguin
Le Carbet
Morne des Esses
Pitons du Carbet
La Trinité
Caravelle Peninsula
Chateau Dubuc
Gros Morne
Bellefontaine
Saint-Joseph
Balata Gardens
Le Robert
Case-Pilote
N1
Schoelcher
Le Lamentin
FORT DE FRANCE
Lamentin International Airport
Le François
Pointe du Bout
Anse Mitan
Anse à l' Ane
Trois Ilets
Trois-Ilets
Montagne du Vauclin
Rivière Salée
Grande Anse d' Arlet
Le Vauclin
Les Anses d' Arlet
Diamant
Grande Anse du Diamant
Sainte-Luce
Le Marin
Diamond Rock
CARIBBEAN SEA
Pointe du Marin
Sainte Anne
Plage des Salines
Savane des Pétrifications
Pointe des Salines
Grande Anse des Salines
Anse Trabaud
St. Lucia Channel

History

Martinique was discovered at the turn of the 15th century, on Columbus's first, second or fourth voyage, depending whose history you believe (it was actually his first landfall on his fourth voyage). Columbus apparently thought the island was inhabited by a tribe of Amazons because he was greeted only by women shouting '*Madinina*'. The Carib men must have been away raiding another island. Similarly, the origins of the name Martinique have been obscured by zealous historians. It may have been named for St Martin, but most think that the name derives from the Carib word '*Madinina*', thought to mean 'the island of flowers'.

With or without menfolk, the island was left to the Caribs until 1635, when the Breton d'Esnambuc arrived from St Kitts with a hundred colonists and settled on the leeward coast near Le Carbet. They planted a cross and erected a fort, and after years of running battles with the Caribs they came to an arrangement in which the French lived on the Caribbean coastline and the Caribs on the Atlantic side.

Just as Barbados became the leading British island, so Martinique became the leading French colony in the 1650s. The islanders became fantastically rich growing sugar and smuggling it out to Europe, and they had an uneasy relationship with the French Crown. In 1717 the governor tried to enforce the *exclusif* (a law stipulating that trade from Martinique must be made exclusively with France) and promptly found himself taken prisoner with his intendant and simply sent back to France as an unwanted nuisance. A more conciliatory governor was sent out to replace him, one who was prepared to turn a blind eye to the smuggling.

In the 18th century Martinique changed hands a number of times, like all the islands in the area, snatched by roving navies and swapped for other prizes at the end of each successive war. A new storm rose on the horizon as the ideas of the Revolution reverberated in the Caribbean. Martinique was divided along traditional lines; the townspeople, or *patriotes*, adopted the cockade and allied themselves with the revolutionaries, and the planters struck for the Royalists. Initially the *patriotes* took the island, rallied by the Revolutionary Lacrosse from St Lucia. General de Rochambeau and the Revolution came to the island in triumph; Fort Royal became République-ville. But within a year the planters had turned the tables and had contrived to get the British in, restoring the *ancien régime* and their prosperity. Martinique was relatively stable for the next twenty years under British rule and did not see the troubles that occurred in the other colonies of Guadeloupe and Saint Domingue.

In the first half of the 19th century, forces were mobilized against slavery in France, initially by Cyrille Bissette, a Martiniquan, and then by Schoelcher. Slave riots took place in Le Carbet, St Pierre and in Grande Anse. With the coming of the

Second Republic, the abolition of slavery in the French islands was proclaimed on 27 April 1848.

1902 was a momentous date for the colony because of the eruption of Mont Pelé, which completely destroyed St Pierre, then the commercial and cultural centre of the island. Fort de France took its place. In 1946, Martinique became a *département* with the same status and responsibilities as any other in *le métropole* and in 1985 it became a *région*.

Three Crowned Heads

In the 17th century, a Françoise d'Aubigné, the daughter of a colonial functionary, spent her childhood at the northern parish of Le Prêcheur, just as the colony was becoming prosperous. When she returned to Europe, she embarked on a course that would take her to the royal court of France. She became Madame de Maintenon and in 1684 she secretly married Louis XIV.

Martiniquan legend relates a story of two young cousins, Yéyette and Aimée, who were walking one evening when they came across an old woman known in the area as a fortune-teller. They gave their palms to be examined and eventually she made her pronouncement: 'You', she said to the first, 'will be an empress, and you,' talking to Aimée, 'will be more than an empress.' She walked off, refusing to respond to their pleas for more detail.

Aimée Dubuc de Rivery was soon sent to a convent in France to complete her education and the incident was forgotten. But on her return journey to Martinique she was caught in a storm off the European coast and was taken captive by Barbary pirates. The Bey of Algiers sold the passengers of the ship as slaves, but kept Aimée because he was captivated by her beauty. Eventually he made a present of her to the Grand Turk in Constantinople. There, she penetrated the deepest secrets of the seraglio, to become the favourite of the Sultan, lover of his successor and finally the Sultana Validé, adoptive mother of Emperor Mahmoud II.

Her cousin Yéyette was born Marie-Rose Joséphine Tascher de la Pagerie, in Trois-Ilets in 1763. Her family had fallen on hard times, but when offered an advantageous match her parents married her off to the son of a former governor, Alexandre Vicomte de Beauharnais, and she too went to France. At one stage Joséphine was condemned to death as a noble, but she was set free when Robespierre fell and within a few years she married Napoleon Bonaparte, general of the French army in Italy. On 2 December 1804 she became his empress.

Many consider Joséphine a shallow woman, and it is somewhat surprising that the Martiniquans should be so proud of her, particularly as she was behind the reintroduction of slavery in the French islands in 1802. There was a curious incident in 1992, in which a statue of Joséphine on the Savanne in Fort de France was beheaded. Some said it was a simple act of violence, but the head was never found, so it may well have been a political statement.

Two Dominican Monks

Two Dominican monks, **Père Dutertre** and **Père Labat**, visited Martinique in the 17th century and wrote memoirs of their trips. Their stories and observations about life make fascinating reading.

Père Dutertre was a soldier and romantic who turned to the Church late in life and came to the Caribbean in the 1650s. He was fascinated by the novelties of the New World and on his return he wrote his *Histoire Générale des Antilles Habitées par les Français*. The work is full of observations about the natural life of the islands and of the Carib Indians, whom he makes into naturally egalitarian and melancholic dreamers, probably one of Rousseau's sources for his idea of the **noble savage** a hundred years later.

Père Labat spent ten years in the Caribbean until 1705, living mainly in Martinique, but undertaking missions all over the area, which he relates in his *Nouveau Voyage aux Iles de l'Amérique*. In his book you will find him tending souls by spiritual means or defending them with a cannon instead, celebrating Mass for buccaneers and chatting with enemy admirals. He details the system of compensation among the buccaneers for the loss of a limb, he invents a new system for distilling sugar into rum and, being a confirmed gastronome, he sprinkled his writing with descriptions of meals of sumptuous proportions. His interest is inexhaustible, he is unfailingly humorous, earthy, adventurous and an incorrigible busy-body.

Strangely, he is wrongly accused by folk tradition in Martinique of introducing slavery into the island. A hundred years ago, his name was used as a threat against naughty children: *Moin ké fai Pè Labatt vini pouend ou!* (I'll make Père Labat come and take you away) and his ghost would apparently be seen walking the mornes above St Pierre at night because his soul could find no rest. Certainly he was sanguine about the treatment of slaves—he ordered one man to be given three hundred lashes—but it was a cruel age.

He had a number of close shaves too. At one point his ship was captured by Spanish pirates after he had refused to fire the only cannonball because it was needed to crush the garlic. He was about to be put to death, but a moment later he found all his captors on their knees around him. While rootling through his luggage they had found a cross of the Holy Inquisition. Of course it was there completely by chance, he claims, but it was enough to set him free.

There is an abridged English translation of his work, *The Memoirs of Père Labat*, by John Eaden, published in 1931.

Lafcadio Hearn

The traveller **Lafcadio Hearn** lived near St Pierre for two years in the late 1880s and he painted a series of tender pictures of Martiniquans and their lives: the *blanchisseuses* (laundresses) who rise at 4.30am when the local alarm clock, the *cabritt bois* (a cricket), stops chirruping, covering the rocks on the River Roxelane with the washing that they beat and scrub; the *porteuses* who carry supplies weighing up to 120 pounds on their heads, singing as they cross the mountain range in the heat of the day; a man infatuated by the *guiablesse* (a zombie), who leads him to his death when he tries to kiss her. It is all a bit romanticized, but his *Two Years in the West Indies* is a charming book and gives an unforgettable picture of Martinique before St Pierre was destroyed by Mont Pelé.

Flora and Fauna

Martinique has the best of both worlds, the verdant profusion in the mountainous rainforests and the open plains that now blow with sugar-cane and bananas, where cattle once were allowed to run wild in buccaneer-style farming. The rainforest is fantastic and well worth seeing, simply by driving through it. There is an excellent display of tropical plants and trees at the **Balata Gardens** just north of Fort de France.

The island is unfortunate, however, in suffering from a scourge that most of the Windwards lack—the *fer de lance* snake. Called *trigonocephalus* because of its triangular head, it grows up to 6ft long and has a pair of eyes that are supposed to glow orange in the night. It is curious that it came to be here in the first place, as its nearest relatives are somewhere in South America. In the times of fierce competition during the sugar years, snakes were sometimes surreptitiously introduced into the islands to make other planters' jobs more difficult, but the *fer de lance* has been here since before the Europeans arrived. Though the snake is extremely poisonous to humans, it poses little danger to visitors because it steers well clear of any tourist habitations. However, if you are rootling around in the undergrowth or stealing a stem of bananas, then watch it.

✆ *(596)–* *** Getting There***

By Air from Europe: Air France (✆ 55 33 00) has daily flights from Paris and weekly connections from other French cities including Lyon, Toulouse, Bordeaux and Nantes. These are supplemented by charters operated by Nouvelles Frontières (✆ 70 59 70) and Air Liberté (✆ 59 81 81) from Paris. There are no direct flights from other European countries; travellers can connect in Paris, or fly via Barbados, St Lucia or possibly Antigua.

By Air from the USA: American Airlines (✆ 51 12 29) has regular services through San Juan, Puerto Rico, and Air France flies from Miami.

By Air from other Caribbean Islands: The island's carrier, Air Martinique, has hopper flights to Union Island, Mustique, St Vincent, Barbados and St Lucia, and Air Guadeloupe flies north along the island chain, via Dominica and Antigua to St Martin. Air France flies to San Juan and Port au Prince in Haiti. LIAT (✆ 51 10 00) also serves islands to the north and south of Martinique, originating in Antigua and Trinidad. An airport security tax of Fr35 is payable by all passengers leaving Martinique.

By Boat: There are two ferries which run hydrofoils between Martinique and Guadeloupe, touching Dominica *en route*: **Caribbean Express** at Terminal Inter Iles in Fort de France (✆ 63 12 11, fax 63 34 47), daily except Tues; and **Madikera** (✆ 91 60 87).

Getting Around

If you wish to get a bus from the airport into Fort de France (no buses run the route directly), you must cross the main road, beyond the car park in front of the terminal, and flag down a *taxi collectif* on the other side.

Public **buses** are a cheap way of travelling around the island and they depart from **le Parking**, on the waterfront at Fort de France, or from the main square in other towns. You will find both public buses, which follow a vague time schedule, and *taxis collectifs* (TCs), share-taxis (can be a minibus or a car) that run a fixed route and do not depart until they are full. At the terminus, ask around and you will be directed to the first one headed in your direction.

Public buses are only allowed to stop at official stops, but you might be able to flag down a TC on the roadside if you are lucky. *Arrêt!* shouted loud enough to be heard above the noise of the stereo system, is the word used to indicate that you want to get off. The buses run from 5am until about 7pm and the TCs a little longer. On Sundays and on public holidays the public transport system packs up in mid-afternoon and you can quite easily be left isolated. Some prices are: **Fort de France** to airport Fr10; Trois Ilets Fr20; St Pierre Fr17; to St Anne Fr30.

The tourist areas on the other side of Fort de France bay (Pointe du Bout, Anse Mitan, Anse à l'Ane) are best served by **ferry** (*vedette*). These leave from the waterfront next to the Savane, close to Fort St Louis, and keep up a regular schedule to Pointe du Bout from 6am until about midnight; 20-minute crossing, return fare Fr25.

Taxis are also readily available at the **Parking** downtown or the airport and can be ordered at any hotel. Taxi companies include **Taxis Savane** (✆ 60 62 73) and **Radio Telephone Taxi** (✆ 63 63 62). Some examples of fares are: from **Lamentin airport** to: city-centre Fr80, Pointe du Bout Fr160, St Anne Fr270. Taxi-drivers are willing to take day tours (many of them speak English). If divided between four people, the price for a day's drive is reasonable value, but be sure to fix the price beforehand.

For maximum mobility, plenty of **hire cars** are available. In comparison with other islands nearby, Martinique's roads are good, though the islanders tend to drive with an abandon both French and Caribbean. Driving is on the right and your own licence is valid for the first 20 days, after which time an international driving licence is required. Maps are usually handed out by the hire companies. Found at the airport, in Fort de France and in the tourist centres, the hire companies offer cars from about US$35–40 per day. Major credit cards are accepted as deposit, otherwise expect to put down about US$350. Companies include: **Avis** (✆ 51 26 86), **Europcar** in Fort de France (✆ 73 33 13), and **Hertz** (✆ 60 64 64). A slightly cheaper option is **Parking** (✆ 60 10 93). Many companies have outlets at the airport. You can rent scooters through **Funny Rent Motorcycles** (general ✆ 63 33 05), with outlets all over the island.

Island tours are easy to organize in full-day and half-day tours (usually taking in a meal as well). Three tour operators are: **Caribtours**, Pointe du Bout, Trois-Ilets (✆ 66 02 56), **STT Voyages** at 23 rue Blénac, Fort de France (✆ 71 68 12) and **Madinina Tours**, 89 rue Blénac (✆ 70 65 25).

Tourist Information

In **France** there is a Tourist Information Office at 2 rue des Moulins, 75001 Paris (✆ 44 77 86 22, fax 49 26 03 63), and in **Sweden** at POB 717 Frettvägen 14, S 1818 07 Lidingo Suede (✆ 468 765 58 65, fax 765 93 60). In the **US**, the French West Indies Tourist Board is at 610 Fifth Avenue, New York, NY 10020 (✆ 212 757 02 18, fax 212 247 64 68), and in **Canada** at 1981 Avenue MacGill College, Suite 480, Montreal PQH 3A 2W9 (✆ 514 844 85 66, fax 514 844 89 01).

The main tourist office on the island is on the waterfront in Fort de France, at 26 rue Ernest Deproge, BP 520, 97206 Fort de France Cedex (✆ 596 63 79 60, fax 73 66 93), and is open weekdays 7.30–12.30 and 2.30–5.30, and Sat 8–noon. There is also one in the airport at Lamentin (✆ 51 28 55).

With its suitably sexy slogan, *Une Histoire d'Amour entre Ciel et Mer* (a love story between sky and sea), the Martinique Tourist Board puts out several publications, including *Choubouloute*, providing useful information like taxi prices and ferry times, and the restaurant guide *Ti Gourmet*, to help you get to grips with the all-important dining experience.

The American Consulate in Martinique is at 14 rue Blénac, Fort de France (✆ 63 13 03).

In the case of a medical **emergency**, contact the Hôpital Zobda Quitman (✆ 55 20 00) and if you need to contact the police, call 17. The **IDD code** for Martinique is **596**, followed by a six-digit local number.

Money

The currency of Martinique is the French franc (US$1 = Fr5.5 approx). US dollars are accepted in the larger hotels, but it is more convenient to carry francs for shops and restaurants. Major credit cards are also accepted in tourist areas and in Fort de France. Traveller's cheques in dollars or francs are accepted in many shops in town. Sometimes payment by credit card or by traveller's cheque will mean a discount on prices. Service is included (*compris*) in restaurant bills on the island. **Banks** are open for exchange on weekdays, 7.30–12 noon and 2.30–4. There is a bank in all the main towns. **Shops** are open 8.30–6, with a long break for lunch in the heat of the day (usually 12–2.30).

Beaches

Martinique has beaches to suit every taste—busy strips with hotels and watersports or the more isolated palm-fringed coves with fishing villages. Most lie on the protected Caribbean coast, but there are one or two hidden in the nooks and crannies of the Atlantic shore. The sand is better in the south; in the north it tends to be dark and volcanic. Beaches are public in Martinique (*though you may have to pay in some cases for access over private land*) and most hotels do not mind outsiders, though one or two discourage them for the benefit of their guests. *Most charge for the use of their beach-chairs.*

The best beach on the island is right at the southern tip, the **Grande Anse des Salines**, which gets crowded at the weekends, but can be fairly free during the week. There are some small snack bars and a restaurant, le Point de Vue at the far end of the sand, where you can retreat and soak up the scene over a creole platter. Just beyond here is the more secluded **Grande Terre** beach. It is a long drive through the back-country to **Anse Trabaud** and the **Baie des Anglais** (*fee Fr15*), where there is an excellent strip of sand, and to **Cap Chevalier** which is very busy at the weekend and popular with windsurfers because of the good winds. The sea is protected from the full force of the Atlantic by offshore reefs and there are plenty of snack stalls for a meal. A quieter, remoter, but charming cove is the steeply shelving beach at **Pointe Macré**. On the Caribbean side, around St Anne, the **Pointe du Marin** is a very popular beach which attracts the body-beautiful and nut-brown beach poseurs. All watersports are available here and there is a line of little cafés and restaurants above the beach where you can linger over an Orangina and a lobster salad. Just south of the town is the more secluded **Anse Caritan**, *adm free*.

Between St Luce and Diamant there are a number of passable spots, including the **Plage Corps du Garde**, where there are facilities and 2 miles (3km) of strand that is constantly washed with breakers, though parts are marked as dangerous for swimming. And around the western tip you will find a string of cracking dark sand coves in the **Anses d'Arlet**. Look out for **Bar Chez Edouard** in Petite Anse d'Arlet, a hip spot with a hip owner. **Ti Sable**, a more formal beach bar, is on the Grande Anse d'Arlet. A cove with a beach bar, a popular day out, is **Anse Noire**.

The area south of Fort de France is very popular and many of the hotels are located on the beaches here (easily reached by ferry from the city): **Anse Mitan**, a fine strip of white sand with a host of hotels and bars to retire to if the sun becomes too hot; **Pointe du Bout**, man-made beaches crowded with high-pressure vacationers, and **Anse à l'Ane**, a 500-yard strip of brown sand between two huge headlands. You can find watersports equipment at all three and they can be quite crowded.

If you are in the north of the island, your nearest beaches are in the lee of the Caravelle Peninsula, but only go on a calm and sunny day because otherwise the sea will be rough. However, you might go to Le Carbet, where there is a deep stretch of sand and north to Le Prêcheur, where **Anse Céron** and **Anse Couleuvre** are secluded coves with black sand and coconut palms. Take a picnic.

Sailing

Martinique is a popular starting point for yachting vacations, many of which head down the island chain towards the Grenadines. The principal **anchorages** are in the southern area of the island, between the capital Fort de France and the southern tip. Fort de France Bay has a number of anchorages and marinas with extensive facilities. The principal centre for yachts is in the Baie des Flammands, right off Le Parking in downtown Fort de France. **Customs** is onshore and all the bars and shops you could ever want from a Caribbean island are a short walk away (also taxis and local buses). All facilities available. If you are in need of repairs, there are a couple of **boatyards** around the point, of Fort St Louis, in the Baie du Carenage. There is also a **marina** on the southern shore of the bay, at

Pointe du Bout, where you can take on all fuel and water you need. There are plenty of restaurants and bars in the area and also calm anchorages in the recesses of the coastline.

To the south of Fort de France, the Cul de Sac Marin is another huge and calm bight almost enclosed by land. In the town of Le Marin itself you can put in at the Club Nautique (© 74 92 48) who will let you take on fuel and water. You can also anchor off the town of St Anne, where there are more restaurants and shops, but no specialist sailing services. An excellent daytime stop, if you are sailing between the two principal marinas, is in the coves of Les Anses d'Arlets, where there are bars and restaurants. They are also calm enough to stop for the night.

In the north of the island, St Pierre is usually a comfortable anchorage, where you can drop anchor in the south of the town or around the pier. There are no facilities, but of course there are excellent shops for provisioning. There are ports of entry in Fort de France, Trinité, Le Marin in the south and St Pierre in the north.

A number of the big charter firms work from here offering skippered or bare boats. Contact **Moorings Antilles Françaises** (© 74 75 39, fax 74 76 44) and **Star Voyage**, Port de Plaisance (© 74 70 92, fax 74 70 93), both in Le Marin, and **Ship Shop** in Fort de France (© 71 43 40), which offers crewed yachts for hire. **Marinas, chandleries and boatyards** include Ship Shop, and Avimer in Anse Mitan (© 66 05 45).

Watersports

Windsurfing (*planche à voile*) is a popular sport on Martinique and you can hire equipment on all the major beaches (*about US$20 per hour*). Advanced sailors should head for the Atlantic coast, around Vauclin for waves and Tartane on the Caravelle Peninsula for surf. You can hire boards at Cap Chevalier, **Sun Alizé** (© 74 71 56) on the busy Anse Michel beach and any number of operators at Pointe Faula outside Le François: try **Le Club Nautique du Vauclin** (© 74 50 83) and the **Sail Club** in Anse Spourtoune (© 58 2432). **Waterskiing** and **jetskiing** can be arranged at the large resort areas on the Caribbean side.

Coasting the Caribbean shore of Martinique in a yacht is a fun day out from Fort de France and St Anne and a number of operators offer day trips around the island or across to St Lucia for a weekend. Try the catamaran *Nosy-bé* (© 76 76 65) and the yachts *Yassou* (© 76 87 41) or *Bambou Yachting* (© 47 17 71). And there are semi-submersible boats for a dry view of the corals: **Aquascope Seadom Explorer** at Pointe du Bout marina (© 68 36 09) and **Aquascope Zemis** in St Anne (© 74 87 41), reserve in advance.

Diving (*la plongée*) is popular and well-organized and is available in all the resorts. The best dive-sites for corals are around the southern edge of the island, off St Anne, around Diamond Rock and on the southwest coast around Les Anses d'Arlets (excellent for **snorkelling**), where you will find forests of seafans and sponges. There are many other reefs along the Caribbean coast, as well as some wrecks off St Pierre, sent to the bottom in 1902.

Many of the big hotels have diving and teaching facilities (a medical certificate and insurance is necessary). *A single tank dive coasts around Fr200.* **Planète Bleue** (℗ 66 08 79) works from the Pointe du Bout marina, **Sub Diamond Rock** is on the south coast at the Novotel Diamant (℗ 76 42 42) and **Histoire d'Eau** in St Anne (℗ 76 92 98). In St Pierre contact **Carib Scuba Club** (℗ 55 59 84).

Other Sports

There is one golf course on Martinique, the **Golf de l'Impératrice Joséphine** (℗ 68 33 49), just south of Trois-Ilets, an 18-hole Robert Trent Jones course. It gets booked up, but it is worth a try, *green fee Fr250.*

If you would like to see the rolling mornes or the beaches of southern Martinique on **horseback**, then there are several stables on the island. Try **Ranch Jack** above Anse à l'Ane (℗ 68 37 69), or **La Cavale** in the Diamant area (℗ 76 22 94) and in St Anne, **Ranch Val d'Or** (℗ 66 03 46).

For **walkers**, organized trips into the rainforest are arranged by **La Maison du Tourisme Vert**, BP 437, 9 boulevard Général de Gaulle (℗ 73 19 30) in Fort de France. They arrange walks every other Sunday and can arrange individual guides. Also try **Une Journée Verte** in St Luce (℗ 62 54 23).

If you would like to explore the island by **mountain bike**, contact **V. T. Tilt** at Pointe du Bout 97229, Trois Ilets (℗ 66 01 01) and **Basalt** in Bellefontaine (℗ 55 05 46). As well as the northern rainforest, they run tours through Les Anses d'Arlets and the beaches of the southern coast.

Cockfights

Cockfighting can be seen in many islands in the French- and Spanish-speaking Caribbean. It is quite a spectacle and may well appear cruel to a visitor, but it is a sport followed avidly by the Martiniquans. The *pitt* is a circular ring banked steeply with seats, which on Sunday becomes a mêlée of gamesmen with fistfuls of notes, shouting to place their bets. All goes silent when the cocks are brought in by their owners, carefully prepared for months with alcohol to make their skin hard and groomed especially for the fight. The owners posture in the ring for a while, showing off their beasts to the crowd, testing the sharpness of the knives attached to their claws. Eventually the two cocks are released in the ring and all hell breaks loose: in the fury of the pit where the cocks lunge and lash, and in the stands, where men are standing and yelling, brandishing their fists. There are cockpits in Morne Rouge, Ducos, Lamentin and Rivière Pilote.

The Mongoose (Mangouste) Versus the Snake

The mongoose was originally introduced to Martinique to reduce the snake population. Ironically, the animals promptly struck up a mutually beneficial arrangement in which the mongoose would avoid the snake by sleeping during the night and have a free run at the chickens (and other birds, some of which have become extinct as a result) in the daytime. As if in revenge, the islanders now wheel the two out against one another for sport.

Fort de France

The capital of Martinique is set on a huge bay on the leeward side of the island, looking out on to the Caribbean Sea. Framed with hills of dark green rainforest, it was chosen, like all Caribbean capitals, for its harbour and strategic value. Now, transatlantic yachts lie in the bay, attracted more to the waterfront cafés than the protective walls of Fort St Louis.

Though it has been the administrative centre of Martinique since 1681, Fort de France was a dozy and unhealthy backwater until the beginning of this century, when the eruption of Mont Pelé destroyed the illustrious town of St Pierre farther north. From just 10,000 inhabitants living in the gridiron streets between the Rivière Madame and the Rivière Monsieur, it has exploded to a city of over 100,000 people, spilling into suburbs along the coast and creeping steadily farther up into the surrounding hills. The people of Fort de France are known as the *Foyalais*, from a corruption of the town's 17th-century name, Fort Royal.

The original settlement grew up around the looming battlements of **Fort St Louis** on the promontory, first established in 1639. The fort is still in the hands of the army and though it is quiet now, it has been assaulted any number of times. In 1674, 160 men were faced by the Dutch Admiral de Ruyter, who arrived at the head of 48 ships and 3000 men. The French evacuated the fort pretty quickly and so the Dutchmen, lulled into a false sense of security, paused over some kegs of rum, only to find themselves harried by sober and determined Frenchmen. The Admiral cut his losses when a thousand of his men were killed and let the town be. Access to the fort is restricted. If you wish to visit, you must write to the officer in charge, who will arrange a visit to the network of caverns, dungeons and ramparts. The fort juts into the sea, enclosing on one side the old *carenage*, where ships would be 'careened'. Weights were tied to their masts and they were tipped up so that their hulls could be cleaned. Adjacent is the Baie des Flamands (flamingos), where hundreds of yachts ride at anchor.

Bordering Fort St Louis, the **Savane** is the large central park of Fort de France, towered over by a line of vast royal palms. Their solid grey trunks are like marble columns, soaring to 100ft before they burst into curved fronds. Beneath such a regal canopy stands the statue of Joséphine, the Martiniquan who became an empress. Before she was 'beheaded', her face was turned towards her home in Trois Ilets, across Fort de France bay to the south. Two other memorials are dedicated to the war dead and to Belain d'Esnambuc, the explorer and founder of the colony, who stands scouring the horizon for land. The Savane, where the Martiniquans come in the evenings to 'promenade', is bordered by cafés and by the boulevard Alfassa waterfront, the site of all major events such as carnival and military parades.

Facing the Savane on the Rue de la Liberté is the **Musée Départemental** (℗ 71 57 05), *open weekdays 9–1 and 2–5, Sat until noon, adm*, which deals with the history of the island. The life of the Arawaks and Caribs, from their first arrival at the time of Christ to 1500, when the Spaniards appeared, is portrayed in a rich display of pottery and pictures.

At the northwestern corner of the Savane is the **Bibliothèque Schoelcher**, a baroque iron agglomeration of arches, domes, fretwork and rivets, touched with russet and turquoise. The building was constructed by Henri Picq for the Exhibition of 1889 in Paris, at which the Eiffel Tower was the centrepiece, and then was dismantled and shipped out here to accommodate the library of Victor Schoelcher.

The streets of Fort de France are narrower and the buildings taller than in most Caribbean towns. The pavements are cluttered with small Peugeots and the shop windows decked out with chic-looking mannequins. In true French form, the street names commemorate many of France's political and literary heroes.

The classical building opposite the Bibliothèque is the **Préfecture**, the seat of the administrator, appointed by the Interior Minister in Paris. Other attractive buildings in the town include the Palais de Justice, which overlooks a small square with a statue of Schoelcher, and the old hôtel de ville, now a theatre. On the place du Père Labat is the **Cathédrale St-Louis**, the sixth to be built on the site. This one dates from 1878, its predecessors having been destroyed by fire, hurricane and earthquake. It has beautiful stained-glass windows, an impressive organ and metalwork balustrades.

On the banks of the Rivière Madame is the **Parc Floral**, a former exhibition ground with trees and modern sculptures (now unfortunately used as a car-park as well). There are artists' galleries and cafés in the former military barracks at the rear, where there is a museum devoted to island geology, *open Tues–Fri 9–12.30, 2–5.30*. Outside is a series of markets dotted among the streets, with ranges of tables sheltering under huge gaudy parasols, selling anything from locks of straight black hair (to be plaited into tight African curls) to avocados. Worth a visit is the fish market on the western bank of the Rivière Madame, where women sell the fish caught and landed by the fishermen, from dawn until about 5pm.

The hills surrounding the capital are covered with high-rise blocks and the '*instituts*' of a developed French *département*. As in the other islands, the *bons bourgeois* build their homes high on the hills for the fresher air and the commanding view. Across the Rivière Madame, the suburbs clamber up into the hills both inland and west along the coast, to Schoelcher. If you would like Fort de France's secrets to be revealed in a guided tour, contact **Azimut** (© 60 16 59), who offer historical, shopping and night-time tours.

South of Fort de France

The many coves and white-sand beaches make Martinique's southwest coastline the magnet for the tourists. They centre around two areas, **Pointe du Bout**, near **Trois-Ilets**, within sight of Fort de France across the bay, and at **St Anne** at the southern tip of the island.

If you do not cross Fort de France bay by ferry, the main road skirts the bay, past the airport, and the D7 turns right at Rivière Salée. **La Maison de la Canne**, (© 68 32 04), *open daily 9–5, except Mon, adm*, is devoted to the history of sugar and is set in a restored rum distillery. It displays impressive models and sugar hardware.

Just before the town of Trois-Ilets another central piece of Martiniquan history is on view in **Le Musée de la Pagerie**, (© 68 34 55), *open daily 9–5, except Mon, adm*, the childhood home of the Empress Joséphine. Some of the sugar estate buildings have been restored and filled with the empress's belongings, including portraits and some letters written to her by Napoleon. The setting, in a small valley of typical Martiniquan profusion, is idyllic. Close by is the **Domaine de la Pagerie**, *open Mon–Fri, 9–5*, a working horticultural garden where you will see Caribbean flora in all its extreme fertility.

Trois-Ilets is a small town set around a square above the sea which takes its name from the three small islands in the bay. It was in the 18th-century church that the future empress was christened Marie-Rose Joséphine Tascher de la Pagerie in July 1763. Her mother, Rose-Claire du Verger de Sannois, is buried in the church. Just north of here is the tourist resort of **Pointe du Bout**, a conglomeration of hotels, cafés and boutiques and a marina which has grown up on the point and on the white-sand beach of Anse Mitan.

The coastal road rises into cliffs as it turns south and the land becomes drier and more windswept, where the shoreline is pitted with tiny coves with a profusion of coconut palms and small strips of sand. Some are used by fishermen, whose orange and green boats are slung with blue nets set out to dry. The road winds up over the cliffs and down into **Grande Anse d'Arlet**. It is a charming bay, less known than the beaches at Pointe du Bout, but popular with yachtsmen. Farther on by 2 miles is another cove with the picturesque village of **Les Anses d'Arlet** between the headlands and then a third cove called the Petite Anse d'Arlet.

The best route to take from here follows the vagaries of the coastline and descends from the heights of Morne Larcher to the town of Le Diamant, which is set on the magnificent sweep of the Grande Anse du Diamant and its 2-mile beach with brown sand and crashing breakers.

Diamond Rock

Off the Point, 1 mile from the shore, is the **Rocher du Diamant**, a pitted outcrop that rises sheer from the water to over 500ft. This rock, sometimes referred to as HMS *Diamond Rock*, witnessed one of the most curious of all episodes in the eternal struggles for empire between the French and British at the turn of the 18th century. The two nations were facing each other across the St Lucia Channel. From his look-out at Pigeon Island on St Lucia, Commodore Hood was stuck. All he could do was watch as the French ships dodged behind the Rock within the cover of their own guns, and sailed away unharmed. Hood decided to fortify the Rock.

For eighteen months it stood as a British enclave within cannon-range of Martinique, denying the channel to French shipping. It was garrisoned by 120 men, who hoisted five cannon up on a rope from a ship, the HMS *Centaur*, 'like mice, hauling a little sausage' and built fortifications and outhouses. It became quite a community, with goats and rabbits and the Captain's dog and cat. Rope ladders were fixed to get from the upper battery to the shore and the mail and food were delivered in a communication bucket from the supply ship.

In May 1805 the French military descended on the Rock in force. The two sides slugged it out for three days and two nights, until the British capitulated. When he eventually got back to Barbados the commander,

Diamond Rock

Captain Maurice, was court-martialled for surrender, but then congratulated by Nelson for putting up such a good show. Ruins remain dating from the time the French sacked the Rock, but they are rarely visited and the crossing is often rough.

Heading further east, you will come to the **Trois Rivières Rum Distillery**, *open Mon–Fri, 9–noon, 2.30–5*, a working sugar and rum factory, where between February and July you can see the cane fed into the machines, cut to length, moved along a conveyor through three-stage crushers and the juice run down into a collecting vat while the bagasse is returned to fire the hundred-year-old steam-engine. Hot and noisy, but interesting, and then you test the vintages—1982, 1979 and the mellowest of all, 1969. There is another distillery at Rivière Pilote, **La Mauny**, with guided tours five times a day (*10am, 11, 12.30, 2, 3.30*).

On the dry **St Anne** peninsula, where the beaches are excellent, stand the towns of Le Marin, where there is an attractive coral-rock church, and St Anne, a small town primarily concerned with tourism. Farther on by 5 miles (8km) you come to the **Pointe des Salines**, where the land is covered in cactus scrub. From the point St Lucia is clearly visible on a fine day, beyond the lighthouse on the Ilet Cabrits. Beyond the salt flats (or salt ponds depending on the season) is the **Savane des Pétrifications**, a moonscape of petrified wood where nothing grows. Sadly, many of the pieces have been removed over the years, but it still looks pretty ghostly.

From Le Marin the road leads across to the Atlantic coast, on a leisurely return to Fort de France. **Le Vauclin** is the first town, with an active fish-market. Inland is the **Montagne du Vauclin**, at 1640ft the highest in the south of Martinique. From the top, the panorama is fantastic, stretching as far as the Caravelle Peninsula in the north and to the southern tip of the island.

North of Vauclin is **Le François**, where the attractive old wooden houses are steadily being swamped by the new concrete suburbs. There is a classic French West Indian cemetery, with mausolea covered in black and white tiles, but the church looks as though it might be about to undergo a space-age transfiguration.

Habitation Clément, *open daily, 9–5.30, adm*, is one of the finest colonial plantation houses in the whole Caribbean. On a hilltop sheltered by huge and ancient trees stands a house with a wooden interior and a tiled and louvred gallery, furnished with superb colonial antiques. There is a display of the process of rum, with exhibitions and films of coopering and the distillery which worked until 1978. Ageing and bottling still continue here, so the sweet smell of rum still hangs in the exquisite gardens.

The road back to Fort de France passes through the Lamentin plains, the agricultural heartland of the island, blowing in green waves of bananas and sugar-cane.

N2—The Caribbean Coast, Fort de France to St Pierre

The road (N2) from today's capital to its spiritual ancestor, the once-august city of St-Pierre, runs along the Caribbean coast, clinging to the headlands that cast out into the sea and sweeping down into the bays. The land is steep and rugged, with a covering of scrub that makes it look a bit like Corsica. North of Case-Pilote the dry cliffs at sea level give way to tropical rainforest in the foothills of the Pitons du Carbet, Martinique's second-highest peak.

Schoelcher, 3 miles (5km) from the centre of Fort de France, was a fishing village by the name of Case-Navire until 1899, when it was renamed in honour of the abolitionist shortly after his death. Now the *commune* of Schoelcher, creeping ever higher into the hills, takes the overspill from Fort de France. It has one of the colleges of the University of the French Antilles.

A number of small towns, each laid out in typical French Antillean style, with a town hall and church facing one another across the square, lie in the mouths of the valleys. Fishermen work from the black-sand beaches and you will see their blue nets spread out to be repaired. Their boats are painted bright colours to make them visible at sea and given lyrical evocative names such as *Regret de mon père* and *On revient toujours*.

Case-Pilote is named after a Carib chief who lived in this area and who welcomed the French when they settled, allowing Père du Tertre and the other Dominican missionaries to work among his people. Towards the end of his life he moved to Rivière-Pilote in the south of Martinique. **Le Carbet** takes its name from the rectangular thatched houses in which the Caribs lived. The town, which has a number of pretty wooden houses, fronts on to a coconut-lined beach on which Columbus is supposed to have landed during his visit. Not far inland is the **Plantation Lajus**, home of Rhum J. Bally, *open Mon–Fri, 8–4, Sat 8–2.3, adm*. The rum is not distilled here, but you will see it aged in vats and oak barrels, turning the fiery white 'rhum agricole' into a mellow gold. The old creole house, built 1776, and the garden can also be visited.

In the hills above Anse Turin, signposted from the main road, is the **Musée Gauguin** (© 77 22 66), *open daily 9.30–5.30, adm*, commemorating the French artist, who lived on Martinique in 1887 before moving on to Tahiti in the Pacific. There is a permanent exhibition of his letters and sketches, and some paintings (in reproduction). Other traditional Martiniquan topics are covered as well, including a description of the checked *madras* head-dress and its intricacies by Lafcadio Hearn. Work by local artists is also on show. There is a butterfly farm and museum off the road to St Pierre.

St Pierre

Until 1902, St Pierre was the cultural and commercial heart of Martinique and one of the prettiest towns in the Caribbean, considered the Paris of the Lesser Antilles. The red-roofed warehouses were stacked in lines on the hillside, overlooking the magnificent bay, where 30 ships might sit, delivering luxuries to the *Pierrotins* and loading the sugar loaves and rum puncheons that were the town's stock-in-trade. The oldest town on the island, it grew up around the fine harbour, protected from the Atlantic trade winds by Mont Pelé. Although the administrative centre soon moved to Fort Royal because of its superior strategic setting, the town thrived immediately from its beginnings in the 17th century.

The cobbled streets and the seafront promenade of 'Little Paris' were walked by the smartest Antillean ladies of the day, creole beauties with brown skin dressed in voluminous and brightly coloured skirts, parasols over their shoulders to keep off the sun. Cafés and cabarets did a grand trade on Saturdays as did the cathedral on Sunday. In 1902, the illustrious town of 26,000 inhabitants was the most modern in the area, with electricity and telephones, and connected from one end to the other by tram. But for all the human endeavour, St Pierre was living beneath one of the Caribbean's most violent volcanos, the **Montagne Pelée** (the bald mountain). It had stayed silent for the first two hundred years of the town's existence, until 1851 when it grumbled, blanketing the town with volcanic ash and creating a lake in its crater.

Towards the end of April 1902 the rumblings started again, this time accompanied by plumes of smoke that flashed with lightning. Four people from St Pierre climbed to the lip of the crater and found that the lake had disappeared and that it was now a cauldron of boiling mud, with an icing of ash racing over the surface in the wind. The rivers fed by it were poisoned by sulphur emissions and ran with dead fish.

On 5 May, the crater split open and an avalanche of mud and lava slid down the the mountain, engulfing a factory and killing 25 workers. Despite the ever-increasing plumes of smoke, still lit by lightning, the Governor came from Fort de France to urge the Pierrotins not to leave. News came that the Soufrière volcano on the island of St Vincent had blown and it was thought that this would relieve the pressure on Mont Pelé. Though about 1000 did choose to leave for Fort de France at dawn the next morning, the majority stayed put.

At a couple of minutes before eight the next morning the mountainside itself split and gaped open as the eruption began. A vast cloud of flames, molten lava and poisonous gases spewed up through the crater, thrown to a height of 300ft before sweeping down the mountainside at 250 miles an hour and engulfing the town. With a temperature of 400°C, the cloud vapourized the town and then poured on down to the sea, turning it into a seething cauldron and setting the ships ablaze or capsizing them with a tidal wave.

Within two minutes 30,000 people were killed. They were knocked to the ground by the force of the *nuée ardente* and carbonized where they lay. Grasses wilted and pots and pans drooped in the heat. The city passed into complete darkness, pierced only by the light of burning houses. There was one survivor in the city itself. Auguste Cybaris had been thrown into a police cell the night before for being drunk. No doubt he woke with a start at eight the next morning, but the thick stone walls of his cell protected him from the heat and the grilled window kept out the fumes. He lived out his days until his death in 1955 with the Barnum Circus, performing in a replica of his cell.

One ship also survived, the HMS *Roddam*, which was cut from its mooring by the tidal wave. Several of the crew were burned alive on deck by showers of molten lava and others died jumping overboard. The ghostly shell, heaped with grey volcanic ash, crawled into the harbour at Castries, St Lucia, later that day, its captain severely burned but still at the wheel.

The volcano continued to spit fire and lava over the next few months, but gradually calmed. At the same time, there arose one of the most curious phenomena in the whole history of the Caribbean. In November of 1902, a glowing needle of solidified lava began to protrude from the crater. The plug steadily pushed upwards, until it reached a height of 800ft. After nine months it eventually collapsed.

After so many stories about the cataclysm at St Pierre and the talk of the ruins, it comes as a bit of a surprise to discover that people actually still live there. It is a busy country town. No doubt the inhabitants have faith in the team of boffins who live on the slopes of the mountain listening out for future rumbles. The cobbles of the old town can be seen protruding through the tarmac and the blackened walls and stairways still run down to the palm-lined promenade on the waterfront. The skeleton of the old theatre and the stone shells of the 18th-century warehouses have a slightly foreboding air, but the market and shops bustle happily around them. However, they still stand in the shadow of Mont Pelé, a monstrous and brooding colossus.

The **theatre**, with its double staircase, is a copy of the one in Bordeaux. Just nearby is the cell in which Cybaris spent the night after his drinking spree. Across the Roxelane River is the Quartier du Fort, the site of the first settlement on Martinique. The ruined fort near the seafront was erected by d'Esnambuc in 1635 when he arrived, planted a cross and claimed the island for France.

The **Musée Volcanique**, *open daily 9–5, adm*, established in 1932 by the American vulcanologist Franck Perret, has an explanation of the volcanic eruption and exhibits including clocks that stopped at 8am precisely and nails fused together in the heat of the *nuée ardente*. Guided tours do a circuit and release you to admire the view of the bay from the balcony. **Le Musée Historique de St Pierre**, (✆ 79 74 32), *open daily 9.30–5, Sun 9.30–12.30, adm*, on the rue Victor Hugo, contains pictorial exhibits of life in St Pierre before the disaster in 1902.

A commanding view of St Pierre Bay can also be had from the road that climbs past the cemetery. From here it continues into the rainforest in the foothills of the Morne des Cadets in Pitons du Carbet and to Fonds St Denis, an agricultural village perched on the mountainside over hairpin bends. This road was the original approach from Fort de France to St Pierre; called *La Trace*, it was cut out of the hills by the Jesuits in the 17th century.

North of St Pierre

As the road follows the coast north, skirting the slopes of Mont Pelé, you come to a less developed side of Martinique. **Le Prêcheur**, one of the first areas to be settled in the 17th century, was the childhood home of Françoise d'Aubigné, who would later become the Marquise de Maintenon. There are hot volcanic springs on the route up Mont Pelé. Farther north, along a difficult road is **Habitation Céron**, *adm*, a classic Martiniquan estate house engulfed in rainforest. As well as the normal sugar estate buildings there is a '*gragerie*', or cassava mill, and a walk through the gardens where the plants are named.

Anse Ceron itself is a black-sand beach of unmanicured beauty. The coastal road does not run all around the island, but stops just beyond here. However, it is possible to walk from here through the forest to the village of Grand' Rivière. The 12-mile (20km) walk over the cliffs of St Martin takes about six hours, though you should allow longer in the rainy season when the going is harder.

St Pierre to the Atlantic Coast

The route to the Atlantic coast leaves St Pierre from the Quartier du Fort and cuts uphill into the botanical turmoil of the rainforest, climbing to **Morne Rouge** in the col between the Pitons du Carbet and Mont Pelé. A hundred years ago this route was walked by the *porteuses*, with huge trays on their heads, laden with anything that needed to be carried to the Atlantic coast. It is a route steep enough to make a car strain, but these young women would carry up to 100lb for 15 hours a day with nothing but a drop of rum and some cake to keep them going. Just beyond Morne Rouge is the dropping-off point for hikes headed to the summit of Mont Pelé. If you attempt this, it is advisable to take a guide. Also, as there are often clouds parked on the summit, take a waterproof jacket to keep off the wind and wet. There has been only one rumble from Mont Pelé since 1902, but if it starts to rain pumice stones, clear out quick. Alternatively, the route passes over to the Atlantic coast, through the forest, where the road is overhung by vast sprouts of bamboo and 10ft tree ferns. **Ajoupa-Bouillon** is a pretty town laid out either side of the main road, which is lined with flowers and a red plant called '*roseau*'.

From here, two natural sites are worth visiting: the **Saut Babin**, a 40ft waterfall half an hour's walk southeast of the town, and the **Gorges de la Falaise,** *adm*. For the latter, you cut in from the road just above the town, going north on a path into the forest (about half an hour's walk, essential to ask for directions) and you will come to the river, which has carved a narrow bed for itself out of the volcanic rock. Take a swimming costume; can be crowded. At **Les Ombrages** Botanical Gardens, *open 8–4*, there is a botanic path through the rainforest, shaded by 100ft bamboo trees. The plants are marked—*calathea ornata* (called musical paper) and *culotte du diable* (devil's trousers).

As the mountainside descends and turns into plains, so the rainforest gives way to cultivation: pineapples, bananas and fields of sugar-cane. In the 18th century, this area was covered with plantations, cane as far as the eye could see, broken periodically by a cluster of buildings: the estate house, outbuildings and a windmill.

Basse Pointe, on the coast, is the birthplace of the mayor of Fort de France, Aimé Césaire, and has had a strong East Indian influence since the Indians came to Martinique in the last century as indentured labourers. There is a Hindu temple just outside the town. Inland is the **Plantation Leyritz**, (© 78 53 92) *open 8–6, adm*, an old plantation house which has been restored as a hotel (with rooms in the slave quarters) and gardens. Machinery is scattered around the grounds and the old outhouses are fitted out as a restaurant. It was here that Presidents Gerald Ford and Giscard d'Estaing met in 1976. There is also a funny exhibition of intricate dolls made from dried flowers.

The village of **Macouba**, named after the Carib word for fish, stands on cliffs at the northern tip of the island, looking out over the channel to Dominica. It was a prosperous settlement in the 17th century, when it derived its wealth from the cultivation of tobacco.

The final stretch of road continues through wild country to **Grand' Rivière**, an isolated fishing village.

N3—Fort de France and the Pitons du Carbet

In the 17th century, the Jesuits cut a road through the mountainous interior of Martinique, linking the new administrative centre of Fort de France with the social and commercial hub at St Pierre. *La Trace* was initially just a track cut into the rainforest, used by horses and pedestrians, but in the 19th century it was enlarged by the army and then in the 20th century it was made into a major road. Today it makes a spectacular drive through some of the island's best scenery.

Across the Madame River, La Trace climbs through the prosperous suburb of Didier, favoured by the creole ascendancy for its commanding panorama, where spectacular villas perch above Fort de France in gardens of tropical flowers. As the town thins, the road winds into primeval rainforest, clinging to the hillside.

Suddenly a mirage arises before you, the **Sacré Cœur** from Montmartre, transported to Martinique... It is an almost exact replica, but here its dome and spires stand brilliant white against the sparkling green of tropical rainforest. It was erected in 1923 to give thanks for the lives of those who died in the First World War.

Soon La Trace becomes buried in the rainforest and the mountains loom either side. Above the capital by 5 miles (8km), at the **Jardin de Balata**, (© 64 48 73), *open daily 9–5, adm*, the botanical pandemonium is momentarily set into order. Hundreds of species have been brought from tropical regions all over the world and cultivated in the garden, numbered so that you can put names to them: bananas, bamboos, orchids and endless palms. As you walk the paths you will see ferns like velvet, shrubs with flowers like little plastic animals or shaped like a fisherman's hat, and all around a plethora of palm trees. After a tropical shower the whole garden glints in the sunlight and the view opens out again as far as St Lucia. The gardens, an enjoyable tour even for uncommitted gardeners, give an idea of the absurd abundance of the Caribbean islands. The N3 then moves into the peaks and valleys of the Pitons du Carbet, running a contorted route as far as Deux Chous, where the old road descends into St Pierre and on to Morne Rouge.

N1—Fort de France to the Atlantic Coast

The N1 road heads east from Fort de France, past the airport at Lamentin, and into the central fertile plains, where much of Martinique's agriculture and industry is located. It emerges on the Atlantic coast at Le Robert, a fishing town on a wide bay.

La Trinité is the second-largest town on the island and an administrative centre for the northern Atlantic coast. The town is set on a sheltered bay and has an esplanade that teems with activity when the day's catch is brought in. In the hills above, the town of Morne des Esses is known for its weaving, techniques supposedly developed from their Carib heritage. The **Basket Weaving Workshop**, *open Mon–Sat, 8.30–5, adm free*, is devoted to the art.

The town lies in the lee of the **Caravelle Peninsula**, a windswept outcrop that juts 7 miles (11km) into the Atlantic Ocean. The peninsula is mountainous, with a shoreline of cliffs and small coves, and a network of paths for walkers who wish to see the varied flora. Near the point are the ruins of the **Château Dubuc**, *open Mon–Fri, 8.30–midday, adm to the museum*, the remaining walls of a 17th-century castle with a magnificent view. There is a small museum and an assortment of sugar-coppers, from which the estate derived some of its wealth—the rest in smuggling. . The N4 leads from Trinité back to Fort de France, cutting through the hills via Gros Morne, the seat of government during the patriots' rebellion in 1790.

Continuing north along the coast, the N1 comes to **Sainte Marie**, with an attractive church built in Jesuit style. Just beyond the town is the working **Rhum St James** distillery and museum, (© 75 30 02), *open weekdays 9–1, 2–4.30, weekends 9–noon*. The old creole plantation house and the modern factory stand near one another, looking on to a garden full of sugar relics of all ages—crushing gear and steam engines. Inside the creole estate house is more sugar paraphernalia: rum barrels and boiling coppers, alongside a history of the sugar industry in Martinique. The informative tour is free and it culminates in a tasting-room, stacked to the ceiling with bottles of rum, which are available for purchase.

L'Habitation Fonds St Jacques was once a thriving Dominican community and sugar plantation. It was run by Père Labat, who resided here in the 1690s, taking over a run-down plantation and turning it into the most prosperous on the island within two years. Some buildings have been restored and there is a small museum on the subject of sugar in the 18th century. The coastal road continues to wind through the plantations and along the shoreline to the town of Lorrain.

Festivals

Bastille Day, 14 July, is celebrated in the Antilles as in France, but the major festival in the year is **Carnival**, which starts on the day after New Year's day and continues until the beginning of Lent, when there are five solid days of dancing and street parades. On Lundi Gras they stage 'burlesque weddings', Mardi Gras is the day of the red devils and Ash Wednesday sees black and white costumes and culminates in the burning of *Momo*, the Carnival spirit.

Many towns also celebrate their saint's day, in the **fête patronale**, with a round of races, competitions, outdoor dances and barbecued chicken legs. They take place mostly between July and January, and it is well worth checking the newspaper or with the tourist board. Towns also hold cultural festivals, with shows, parades and sailing races: Le Robert (April), Saint Pierre (May), Le Marin and Sainte Marie (both August).

In April, the **Martinique Food Show** brings together the island's best cooks and their dishes in competition with one another, and in July Fort de France stages a series of concerts and theatrical events at its **Cultural Festival**. November sees the annual sailing race to bring over the first case of Beaujolais Nouveau from the *métropole* and in December Martinique clubs and venues come alive with an International Jazz Festival or the World Crossroads of the Guitar, held in alternate years.

the yoles rondes

The *yoles rondes* are distinctive Martiniquan yawls with square sails and it has become popular to race them. They have huge square sails on a bamboo mast and are sailed by a crew of 11 or 12 men who clamber about on poles a good 6ft out above the water to make the best of the winds. They are often raced at the traditional Martiniquan *fêtes patronales*, but there is also a special eight-day regatta held around the island each July.

✆ *(596)–* **Where to Stay**

There are just a couple of enclaves of quiet and luxury in Martinique and the difference in prices with other Caribbean islands reflects this. Martinique is really best in the mid range of accommodation, and you will find the full range of settings, from the modern Caribbean dream on the beach to tiny *auberges* set in old gingerbread houses, hidden in the rainforest. Many of the best hotels are quite isolated, particularly from Fort de France, and so it is a good idea to have a car to get around. It is worth doing a bit of exploring and moving from place to place. Rates quoted here are for a double room, though breakfast will usually be included.

expensive–very expensive

By far the most original and most elegant hotel in Martinique is **Habitation Lagrange**, 97225 Le Marigot (✆ 53 60 60, fax 53 50 58), which is set in a beautifully restored sugar plantation house, turreted and wrapped around with a cast iron balcony, dating from the end of the 17th century. You approach on a rickety riverside track and through the wild greenery you appear in a calm creole enclave. Just 16 rooms in all, brightly decorated and furnished with creole antiques, wickerback and rocking chairs and murals and curious sculptures. Very personable style and service, the only four-star hotel with French Caribbean chic. If the beach is the most important feature, you can find international standards of comfort and service at the **Méridien** (℡ 66 00 00, fax 66 00 74) and the renovated **Bakoua** (℡ 66 02 02, fax 66 00 41), which stand like factories on man-made beaches of Trois Ilets.

moderate

There are plenty of friendly and comfortable small hotels scattered around the island: on the south coast you will find a charming retreat, the **Relais Caraibes**, La Cherry, 97233 Le Diamant (℡ 76 44 65, fax 76 21 20), where 15 rooms (air-conditioning, no fans) are set in neat and pretty cottages in a sparse garden. Creole and Far Eastern furniture adorn a charming, covered dining room in the main house, which stands on a hill overlooking the pool and then on to the Rocher du Diamant and St Lucia. It is quite isolated, but you can hire a car there and guests can use the facilities of the Novotel Diamant on the beach down below; moderate to expensive. The **Frégate Bleue**, 97240 Le François (℡ 54 54 66, fax 54 78 48) also has an easy French Caribbean charm, with seven rooms in a private house. A good feel with modern comforts (air-conditioning, television and telephones, kitchenette and pool) but antique furniture and Persian carpets; moderate to expensive. The **Hotel Leyritz Plantation**, 97218 Basse-Pointe (℡ 78 53 92, fax 78 92 44), also has an isolated setting, in handsome gardens on cane- and banana-covered hillside in the northeast. The 18th-century plantation house has been rebuilt as a hotel and the slave quarters turned into the 50 hotel rooms (considerably improved since 200 years ago). The hotel can get a bit busy during the day, as a lot of visitors come by for lunch, but the early evening restores the plantation idyll.

Not far off you will find one of the island's most attractive creole houses, the pink **St Aubin Hotel**, 97220 Trinité (℡ 69 34 77, fax 69 41 14). The 18th-century house stands out on a hillside of tropical greens, with balconies running all the way around the outside; 15 rooms. The **Squash Hotel**, 97200 Fort de France (℡ 63 00 01, fax 63 00 74) is on boulevard de la Marne just out of the city heading north; comfortable with business facilities, even a squash court for the sports-minded executive. Beware, the bar has a ringside view of the squash courts.

For a more typical Caribbean hotel you can try **Les Amandiers**, 97228 Sainte Luce (℡ 62 32 32, fax 62 33 40) on the south coast. The hotel has very comfortable rooms and suites in blocks in a pretty garden just up from a passable beach; entertainment over dinner. The **Impératrice Village**, 97229 Trois Ilets (℡ 66 08 09, fax 66 07 10) has 59 self-catering rooms, dressed up in old Caribbean style, with louvred windows and sloping, tiled roofs and modern comforts, television, air-conditioning and telephones. It has kitchenettes so that you can look after youself, but also a restaurant. Not quite on the beach, but close to the action of Anse Mitan.

cheap

Over the hill you will find an excellent place to stay at the **Auberge de l'Anse Mitan** (✆ 66 03 19, fax 66 01 05), a retiring enclave of faded elegance hidden at the far end of Anse Mitan beach, overlooking the bay and the mornes one way and constantly under threat from the tropical jungle behind it. Built in the 1930s, it has 20 rooms and six studios furnished with dark wicker and hung with old prints; cheap to moderate. Another option in the middle of Anse Mitan is the friendly **Bonne Auberge**, 97229 Trois Ilets (✆ 66 01 55, fax 66 04 50) and its restaurant Chez André, both festooned in greenery, with 32 comfortable and simple air-conditioned rooms in blocks. No pool, but the sea is a minute's walk away.

An excellent hotel with an easy Caribbean feel, on the beach at Diamant, is the **Hotel Diamant les Bains** (✆ 76 40 14, 76 27 00), with rooms in the hotel building and cabins scattered around the garden of palms and ginger-lily. The rooms are pretty with white décor and bright colours (television, air-conditioning, fridge and telephone). The hotel is friendly and serves good local food on the terrace above the garden. Miles of brown sand beach to walk. Another off-beat and enjoyable spot is **La Petite Auberge**, 97228 St Luce (✆ 62 59 70, fax 62 42 99), which was built as a large, luxurious family home in the seventies and is now a small hotel. There are 12 quite simple rooms overlooking a pool, and the downstairs floor is given over entirely to the restaurant and bar. Difficult to get a room sometimes, but worth the effort. **The Last Resort**, 21 rue Osman Duquesnay (✆ 74 83 88), is a friendly haunt buried in the back-streets of Le Marin (if that seems possible in so small a town). A yachting crowd filters through the simple rooms and central sitting area and dining room with tropical birds and statues. Some rooms share baths; cheap to very cheap.

On the grey sands of Grand Anse d'Arlet, a double room, simple but comfortable enough with air-conditioning, is available in the **Hotel Tamarind** (✆ 68 67 88). On the Atlantic coast you will find some good retreats. **Le Madras**, 97220 Tartane (✆ 58 33 95, fax 58 33 63) is on the northern side of the Caravelle Peninsula. It has 14 neat, modern rooms and a dining room with a view of the bay. The **Abri Auberge Verte**, 97216 Ajoupa Bouillon, (✆ 53 33 94, fax 53 32 12), is a good stopover in the northeast of the island. There are 12 rooms in hillside cottages with louvres and terraces; a pool and an overlarge dining room with creole food. The friendly management arranges anything from hikes to cock-fighting evenings. In St Pierre you can stay at **La Nouvelle Vague**, 97290 St Pierre (✆ 74 83 88) with a waterfront restaurant on the terrace. Perhaps the most congenial setting in this area is **Le Grain d'Or**, between St Pierre and Le Carbet, on Anse Turin. The attractive old wooden house has a pool and a terraced restaurant (*myriade d'accras, lambi citron*), and 8 rooms. There are some other cheap places to stay in town; try **Taverne La Malmaison** (✆ 63 90 85), right on la Savane in central Fort de France, and a cheaper option nearby, the **Hotel Tortuga** (✆ 71 53 23), with simple rooms.

very cheap

There are not many very cheap places to stay on the island, but Martinique is linked to the **Association des Gîtes Ruraux** and their office is at 9 boulevard Général de Gaulle in Fort de France (✆ 73 67 92, fax 63 55 92) or by post at BP 1122, 97248 Fort de France Cedex. They have some 240 gîtes around the island, including flats and houses for rent by the week and by the month.

Another cheap alternative is **camping**. **Courbaril Camping** (✆ 68 32 30) has spaces in Anse à l'Ane, opposite Fort de France, for around US$5 per night, with chalets too. In St Anne, the **Camping Municipal** (✆ 76 72 79) has spaces and facilities just off the beach.

✆ *(596)–* *Eating Out*

Martiniquan Fare

Martiniquan food has a traditional French flair and is considered by many to be the best in the Caribbean. Here, you can make your holiday almost entirely gastronomic, as there are cafés and open-air restaurants to linger in at every turn. You will find traditional *cuisine gastronomique*, but also its Caribbean or creole equivalent. Lovingly prepared, the dishes are often spiced and of course, it is all in the sauces.

Some creole dishes, many of them slightly more luxurious versions of usual Caribbean dishes, are: *crabe farci*, a very spicy stuffing of crabmeat in a crab-shell, traditionally served on Easter Monday; the avocado *féroce*, with a spicy fish filling; *blaff*, a way of cooking fish (the name is supposed to imitate the noise it makes when thrown into the water) with thyme, peppers, clove, parsley and onion; *accra*, seasoned cod or greens fried in batter; *écrevisses, soudons, oursins* and even *chatrous*, shrimps, clams, sea urchins and octopus; *colombo* is the delicate French Caribbean version of curry goat or chicken and *z'habitants* is a local preparation of crayfish. *Touffé* is a method of cooking in a casserole, as is *fricassé*, another popular dish. *Boudins* are local spiced sausages. *Blanc manger* is a traditional pudding, a sort of coconut custard, made with milk, coconut, cinnamon, vanilla and nutmeg.

Many of the hotels have fine kitchens, but it would be a pity to miss out on one of the island's best-loved pastimes by dining only there. Fort de France has its share of restaurants, some in the heart of town, others overlooking the mêlée from verandas on high. France's other colonial interests are also represented in Martinique in Vietnamese and African restaurants. There are small restaurants to be found all over the island, so if you wish to join the Martiniquans in an afternoon's gastronomy, ask them when you come to a new town. Despite the local association with rum, which is drunk often as a liqueur, there is certainly something of the traditional French homage for wine, imported in large quantities. A recent addition is pizzerias, which have appeared in all the main tourist towns.

The booklet *Ti Gourmet* lists many of Martinique's restaurants, with translations of the menus into English, recipes and useful facts about which are open on Sundays. Prices are for a main course at dinner time (excluding shrimp and lobster), divided as follows: *expensive*—above Fr100; *moderate*—Fr50–100; *cheap*—less than Fr50. Lunch is usually a little less expensive, but not much. Service, however, is *compris*.

In and Around Fort de France

expensive

There are a number of excellent restaurants in and around Fort de France. **La Mouïna** (© 79 34 57), *lunch and dinner, reserve, closed Sat and Sun*, high up on the Route de la Redoute, has the lovely setting of a Martiniquan villa, where the dining room is set on the balcony above the garden. Smart and subdued, dinner is candle-lit and the menu is French and creole. A house speciality is the *assiette créole*, with stuffed crab, crayfish and boudin with local vegetables, followed by *l'île flottante* (meringues in *crême anglaise*). **La Grand' Voile** (© 70 29 29), on Pointe Simon, overlooks the yachts in harbour from an upstairs dining room decorated with beams and lanyards. *Nouvelle cuisine créole*, neatly presented local fare— *saumon au coco amer et ses pâtes fraîches* and *cassolette de soudons marinières* (local clams in onion and garlic). Follow up with a *nougat glacé*. **La Fontane** (© 64 28 70) *closed Sun and Mon*, on the route de

Balata is highly thought of. Set in a charming colonial house with antique furniture, the menu is French and creole, with some novel combinations such as lamb in a mango sauce, and the service very much French.

moderate–cheap

Le Mareyeur (℡ 61 74 70), *music on Fridays, closed Sat lunch and Sun*, is a seafood restaurant off the main road to Schoelcher, heading north out of town. Quite a simple dining room with red and white chequered tablecloths, but the fish are exotic—*beignets de requin* (shark fritters), *palourdes farcies* (stuffed clams) and fish fricasséed, blaffed and paellaed. A welcoming place. A lively restaurant on the rue Voltaire, dressed up in an old-time French Caribbean country setting with straw and hanging plants, is **Espace Créole** (℡ 70 05 95). Hearty creole reception and fare— boudins, colombos and fish in coconut milk, followed by home-made ice-creams. Another excellent creole restaurant can be found on rue Victor Hugo, at **Marie Sainte** (℡ 70 00 30) *lunch only, closed Sun*. *Accras*, *écrevisses* and *beignets* in a simple dining room.

There is a vegetarian restaurant in the centre of town, near the Cathedral, **Le Second Souffle** (℡ 63 44 11). Try *filet de concombre* (cucumber filet) followed by *salade de fruits saison au miel*.

A fun and **cheap** way to eat is to go to the caravans parked between the Savane and Fort St Louis. Communal tables are set out under large awnings, where you will sit among Martiniquan families on an evening out, everyone shouting above the sound of *zouk* music and the roar of rebellious gas stoves. It stays open late, and you can get a brochette or a platter loaded with tropical meat and veg.

Anse Mitan and Pointe du Bout

moderate

The **Villa Créole** in Anse Mitan (℡ 66 05 53), *closed Sun and Mon lunch*, has a candle-lit gingerbread veranda looking on to a profuse garden. Creative creole and French cuisine is accompanied by the serenading of the patron and others and then dancing. Try the *filet de St Pierre meunière à la crême antillaise* or *filet de poisson sauce capresse*; moderate to expensive.

There is another friendly restaurant close by, **Chez André**, under the awnings at the Bonne Auberge Hotel. It boasts a veranda setting draped in flowers for *velouté de lambi* (cream of conch soup) and *accras de crevettes* (shrimp fritters). On the road to Pointe du Bout there is a very nice dining room with a bamboo ceiling and plenty of greenery at **Au Poisson d'Or**

(✆ 66 01 80), *closed Mon*. Créole fare—*soupe z'habitants* followed by *chatrou sauce creole* with *christophenes au gratin*—or simple veal chop with *frites*. You can dine on a veranda with a view at **L'Amphore** (✆ 66 03 09), a French and creole restaurant: *marengo de coq créole* followed by *nougat glacé au coulis de goyave* and a myriad different coffees; moderate to expensive. Not far off, along the waterfront by the ferry jetty, **Le Langouste** has a fixed menu or *z'habitants* and *colombo de poulet* à la carte. There are pizzerias in the area where you can pick up a simple meal.

Over the headland in **Anse à l'Ane**, try **Pignon sur Mer**, *closed Sun evening and Mon*, where there is a pretty yard fenced off from the beach. Creole fare—*daube de lambis* (conch) *à la crème de champignons*, or *filet de bœuf au ti-vieux*; moderate. Close by is **Chez Jojo** (✆ 68 37 43), which has a simple beach setting and serves local food—*boudin de lambi* and *ananas* (pineapple) *flambé*.

There are a string of waterfront watering holes, part bar, part restaurant, in the Anses d'Arlet. **L'Anse Noire**, on the black sand beach of the same name, has a lovely setting under palm trees and behind bamboo fences. Local food—fish, chicken, lobster and salads. In the Grande Anse d'Arlet you will find a clutch of good places to retreat from the overhead sun. **Les Délices des Anses** is good for fricassees and colombos and **L'Amandier**, all wickerwork on the waterfront; both moderate to cheap. Perhaps the nicest of all is **Le Flamboyant des Iles** (✆ 68 67 75), *closed Sun evening and Tues*, at the southern end of the bay, on another pretty veranda. *Nouvelle cuisine* creole—*touffé de requin* (shark casserole) or *accras de crevettes à la farine de manioc* (shrimp fritters in cassava), followed by *beignets de grand-mère* (granny fritters); moderate, . In Diamant town, the brightly painted **Le Diams** is a pleasant stop on the square, at lunch or dinner—huge *salades gourmandes*, some more sophisticated fare—*mérou* (grouper) cooked in vanilla, followed by *blanc manger* and coconut.

Farther along the coast in St Luce you can get a nice meal on the main square at **Kaï Armande**. Friendly and simple, serving local and seafood, as well as some African specialities. Try a *yassa* or a *mafe* (with a nut base) or the *bisque d'écrevisses*; moderate. For such a large marina town, Le Marin is surprisingly short of restaurants. There is a café down in the marina. Otherwise you could try the small hotel, **the Last Resort** (✆ 74 83 88).

In **St Anne** there is a charming dining room at **Poï et Virginie** (✆ 76 76 86), *closed Mon*. You dine on the waterfront (best seats right above the sea), set with wicker furniture, the walls lined with bamboo and hung with Haitian paintings. You might try the *plateau de fruits de mer* for two (*araignées, tourteaux, cigales, gambas, soudons, huîtres, langoustes* and *palourdes*). Phone 24 hours in advance for this. Otherwise lobster-tail with mayonnaise; moderate to expensive. Another smaller restaurant, just along the seafront, is **La Dunette** (℃ 76 73 90), where you will find chicken *pipiri* (grilled and served with rice cooked in cinnamon and coconut). You might also try **Les Tamariniers** for novel creole cuisine.

On Saint Anne beach there are plenty of places where you can be waylaid when the idea of tanning palls: **Les Filets Bleus** has a palm garden with statues looking down onto the beach. Fine local fare—*court bouillon* or *civet de chatrou*; moderate to expensive. At **Le Touloulou** you can have snacks and meals, or perhaps just an Orangina and an *ananas flambé*. There are many crêperies and snackette wagons both on the beach and in the town. At the southern point of the island, at the end of Grande Anse des Salines, you will find **Aux Délices de la Mer** (℃ 76 73 71), which has a fantastic view of the bay and the hills beyond from its terrace. *Oursins frits* and *colombo de crevettes*. There are also snackwagons on the bay.

On the Atlantic coast you will find two attractive restaurants with good creole food in Trinité. The better is probably **Le Don de la Mer**, with fresh fish followed by *banane flambée*; alternatively, try **L'Oasis** for fricasseed lobster and *christophene au gratin*. One of the most renowned kitchens on the island, for its local cuisine, is at **Le Colibri** (℃ 61 91 95), in Morne des Esses. Clothilde Paladino has won prizes forher original variations on local recipes, including *tourte aux lambis* (conch pie), *écrevisses buisson* and *bisque*, *soufflé de christophene* and *flan au coco*. Family-run with a West Indian welcome; good value too.

In **St Pierre** there is another waterfront view from the terrace at **La Vague de St Pierre** (℃ 78 14 34). Here you will be served with traditional French creole fare—fricassee and colombo and blaff, on a deck above the sea. There is another fine view over the whole town and bay from **Le Fromager**. Pickled flying fish and *canard à l'ananas*—but watch out for bus tours. You get excellent value at the **Grain d'Or** in Anse Turin just south of the town. Traditional Martiniquan fare; cheap to moderate.

Bars and Nightlife

The traditional Martiniquan apéritif is *ti punch*, which is prepared with the same ceremony as the local food. The sugar (or cane juice) is heaped in the glass and the lime is squeezed quickly and dropped in before the white rum is poured and stirred vigorously. In times past only the cane juice would have to be paid for in bars because the rum was so plentiful. There is an infinity of local bistros, rum shops and supermarkets in Martinique.

There are plenty of bars in Fort de France and the busiest area is the Parking on the waterfront. The hip **Le Terminal** overlooks it from a balcony, where a mix of local executives and visitors loiter over absinthe cocktails or one of about fifty beers until 2am. The **Monte Carlo Club** on the boulevard Allègre has a cocktail bar with live jazz sometimes. **Cocoloco** on rue Ernest Déproge stages a local band nightly and **Papagayo** has Latin music in the video bar. **L'Electra**, just off the Parking, is a louder affair, with music, pool and pictures of motorbikes all over the walls. Close by are **Dernière Scéance** and **Le Pub**, two private drinking clubs with music that will probably let you in. The boulevard Allègre has a number of billiard halls, bars and slot machine arcades among the crêperies. The many nightclubs and discotheques include the **New Hippo** on boulevard Allègre, for variétés, and **Club Bitaco**, with two bars and two dance-floors, high in the hills of Ravine Vilaine (you have to follow the Route de Redoute off the bypass behind the downtown area). Any town staging a *fête patronale* will have public dances where you will be welcome to join in. For more local discotheques, of which there are many out in the sticks, you can ask around.

Some of the hotels have discos and they also stage folklore shows. Classical cultural events are staged in the Hopital Civil on the road up towards Didier. You might also check CMAC (Centre Martiniquais d'Actions Culturelles), ✆ 61 76 76, and SERMAC (✆ 60 48 77) in the Parc Floral.

There are two **casinos** on the island, open from 9pm until 3am, one in the Méridien and the other in Schoelcher at La Batalière Hotel, *adm.*

History	210
Getting There and Around	215
Tourist Information	216
Beaches and Sports	217
Roseau	218
South and North from Roseau	221

Dominica

The Transinsular Road	224
Carib Territory	225
Where to Stay	226
Eating Out	229

Dominica is practically all mountains and rainforest, a jumble of peaks and spurs so rugged and dramatic that the island has its own microclimate. Of all the islands that Columbus is supposed to have described to Ferdinand and Isabella of Spain by crumpling a piece of parchment and throwing it on to the table with a 'like this, your Majesties', Dominica is the one he would be most likely to recognize today. Wags claim that it has hardly changed since he was here five hundred years ago.

In its 29 miles by 16, Dominica has mountains over 4500ft, higher than anything on the British Isles. The water-laden winds of the Atlantic Ocean clamber up its slopes and then stack in huge clouds on the mountaintops, poised immobile before they ditch their load. The rainfall here is measured in tens of feet and romantics will tell you there is always a rainbow somewhere in the mist-veiled peaks of the island. The vegetation is explosive—a garden untended for ten years will be 5ft under with trees as thick as your leg—and the natural life is unparalleled. Dominica is overwhelmingly green.

Dominica (pronounced 'Domineeker') is the least developed of the Windward Islands and for all the fertility, it is hard to make a living. Many parts of the island are very poor and you will see more subsistence farmers working small plots cut out of the hillside than on the other islands. For years it was difficult enough to get to the island and relatively recently new roads have opened up parts that before could only be reached on horseback. Vans travel between the villages selling anything from tinned milk to Sunday dresses.

Apart from its wildlife, Dominica's most remarkable heritage is that it is home to the last surviving traces of the Carib race. To the Caribs, the island was Waitukubuli or 'tall is her body' and the wild terrain meant that it was the last island to be settled by Europeans. Once proud and warlike, the Caribs were left in peace on Dominica for a while, but ultimately they could not defend their homeland from the newcomers. There are no native Carib-speakers left, but their descendants are easily recognized in Dominica by their Amerindian features.

A quarter of the island's 75,000 or so population live in the capital Roseau, on the protected Caribbean coast. The island lies between two French islands, Guadeloupe to the north and Martinique to the south. The island was settled by the French—the official language

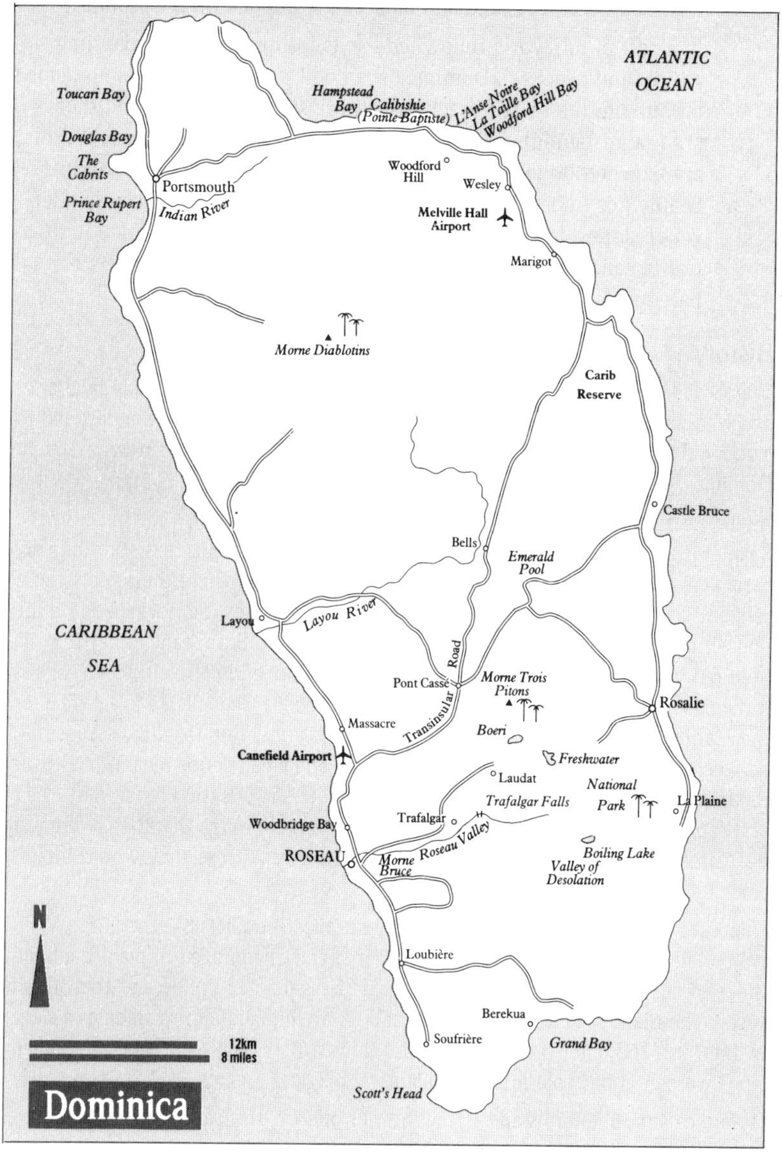
ATLANTIC OCEAN
CARIBBEAN SEA
Toucari Bay
Douglas Bay
The Cabrits
Portsmouth
Prince Rupert Bay
Indian River
Hampstead Bay
Calibishie (Pointe Baptiste)
L'Anse Noire
La Taille Bay
Woodford Hill Bay
Woodford Hill
Wesley
Melville Hall Airport
Marigot
Morne Diablotins
Carib Reserve
Castle Bruce
Bells
Emerald Pool
Layou
Layou River
Transinsular Road
Pont Cassé
Morne Trois Pitons
Rosalie
Massacre
Boeri
Canefield Airport
Freshwater
Laudat
National Park
Trafalgar Falls
La Plaine
Trafalgar
Woodbridge Bay
ROSEAU
Morne Bruce
Roseau Valley
Boiling Lake
Valley of Desolation
N
Loubière
Berekua
Soufrière
Grand Bay
12km
8 miles
Scott's Head
Dominica

has been English for the last 180 years, but French patois can be heard all over the island and most of the population is Catholic.

In a part of the world renowned for its 'palm-fringed and dazzling white-sand beaches', Dominica is an odd man out. There is not a lot of tourism; the scarce beach resorts are set on dark sand and there are few restaurants and bars in the typical Caribbean mould. Visitors are expected to join in local life. Dominica is unpretentious and its beauty lies rather in its spectacular interior and its coral-clad, underwater slopes. It rightfully calls itself the Nature Island of the Caribbean. Even five hundred years after Columbus crumpled his parchment, patches of Dominica are still 'unexplored jungle'.

History

Waitukubuli was christened on 3 November 1493, as Columbus made land after five weeks at sea on his second voyage to the New World. It was a Sunday, and to give thanks for the safe passage of his fleet the explorer called his new discovery Dominica.

As the heartland of the 'Cannibal Isles', Dominica was given a wide berth by the Spaniards, and only pirates, fishermen and foresters braved its coasts. In the very early years, the Spaniards considered making a harbour where their ships could refit and take on water after the Atlantic crossing, but they did not reckon on the opposition of the resident Indians. The Caribs kept the Europeans at bay for two hundred years. Dominica was officially neutral as late as 1748, left 'to the undisturbed possession of the native Indians' (Treaty of Aix-la-Chapelle), and a retreat for the Caribs squeezed out of the neighbouring islands. But Dominica's position between the two French colonies of Martinique and Guadeloupe meant that it was too important to be disregarded for long, and in the 1750s the French moved in. The campaign against the Caribs was so ruthless and thorough that there were just 400 survivors, who retreated to the windward coast where they would be left alone.

Dominica was caught in the crossfire of the European conflicts like the other Windwards, blockaded each time war was declared and encouraged to plant madly in times of peace. Traditionally, the French settlers planted coffee and the British sugar. The island was also a **free port** and for a while did a brisk trade as a slave market. In 1763, after the Treaty of Paris granted the island to Britain, the French lands were promptly sold to English planters.

Dominica's mountainous and fertile interior offered easy sanctuary for runaway plantation slaves, or *maroons*, who hid out in small communities in the hills. Initially they were happy with just their freedom, but, rallied by leaders with names such as Congo Ray, Jacko, Zomble and Jupiter, they soon began to steal cattle and torch estate buildings, encouraging other slaves to join them. The island militia was first sent out against them in 1785, flushing them out in the network of tracks in the hinterland.

As the French Revolution took its effect in the Caribbean, French Royalists fled to Dominica from Martinique and Guadeloupe. Republican revolutionaries followed them and offered freedom to the island slaves if they rose up against the planters (slaves on the French islands had been freed in 1794). They sent in arms to the maroons and there was an invasion from Guadeloupe in June 1795, but the hills were cleaned out again and it was repulsed.

With the French in the ascendancy again in Europe in the early 19th century, Dominica was threatened once more, along with the other British Caribbean islands. In 1805, armed ships appeared in Roseau Bay, flying the Union Jack. At the last moment they tore it down and ran up the *tricolore* instead. Admiral La Grange was besieging the island for France and he blockaded Roseau. After chasing up and down the island, La Grange ransomed the town for £12,000, took all the slaves he could lay his hands on and sailed off to St Kitts.

Maroons were still hiding out in the hills and they rose up again in a guerrilla war between 1812 and 1815. Eventually crushed by the Rangers, the leaders were hanged, but their memory remains in the peak near the town of Belles, Morne Nègres Marrons.

With Emancipation in 1834, Dominica became a refuge for French slaves from the neighbouring islands, where slavery had been reintroduced in 1802. Until 1848, when the French banned it once again, the slaves would make the perilous journey on homemade rafts at night in their bid for freedom. Dominica's own freed slaves moved away from the plantations, preferring to cut a plot of land out of the fertile interior, growing the produce they needed and selling the surplus at market. The new Dominicans were self-reliant and independent, with a spirit that would erupt into violence at times—there were riots when the government demanded taxes for roads or even called a census.

Dominica is large and fertile, but the island was particularly poor. Some industries flourished, however, the most notable being Rose's, now part of the Cadbury Schweppes group, which provided lime juice for British ships. The drink became popular beyond the requirements for naval rations and in 1875 a factory was set up in Roseau to extract lime juice from the thousands of acres that were planted with the fruit. For a while, Dominica was by far the world's largest producer of limes and the fruit brought in about half of the country's export earnings. Since the Second World War this has declined and bananas have taken their place.

Despite spending most of its colonial life in the Leeward Isles, in federation with Antigua and Montserrat and islands further north, Dominica is much more similar to the Windward Islands and it became one of them in 1939. In 1951 the vote was given to all Dominicans over the age of 21 and the island became self-governing in 1967. In the ground-swell of the new political freedom, the Dominica Labour Party, led by Edward Le Blanc, rallied the new voters and was thrust to power. The seventies saw social unrest as demonstrations, racist attacks and strikes held the island to ransom and a state of emergency was declared more than once. The *Dreads*, called so because they wore their hair in dreadlocks, took to the hills, hiding out as the maroons had done two hundred years before.

On 3 November 1978, 485 years to the day after the island was discovered by Columbus, Dominica took its independence from Britain. Then a few months later Hurricane David arrived—Roseau was literally flattened, there were 37 deaths and 80 per cent of the population was left homeless. The political unrest continued; an emergency government had to be installed and then there were two coup attempts and an invasion party was arrested before it left the States.

Today Dominica has steadied politically after more than a decade of rule by the Dominica Freedom Party, headed by Eugenia Charles, first elected in 1980 as the Caribbean's first woman Prime Minister, and most recently in 1990, when she was returned to the 21-seat Parliament with a majority of one. Elections are due before the end of 1995.

Writers and Artists

The writer Jean Rhys (1890–1979) came from Dominica. Her family owned an estate in Grand Bay and she was born in Roseau, but left the island when she was 16, moving to Europe. Many of her books include nostalgic memories of the Dominica of her childhood. Fame came with *Wide Sargasso Sea* (1966), some of which is set in the oppressive atmosphere of colonial Dominican society at the turn of the 19th century. Another Dominican authoress and politician, Phyllis Shand Allfrey, wrote the novel *The Orchid House*, also set on the island and recently screened by the BBC. The story of a private soldier's life is recorded in *Redcoats in the Caribbean* by James Aytoun, published by Blackburn Recreation Services Dept for the Cambridgeshire Regiment.

Dominica was very fortunate in the visit of the Italian painter, Agostino Brunias, who stayed on the island for many years in the late 18th century, recording the Dominican way of life and events. His paintings are extremely lively, giving a fascinating view of the lives of the free creoles, the plantations, vendors' stalls, dances and women washing clothes in the streams, much of which activity can still be seen in its different form today.

Flora and Fauna

Much of Dominica is 100ft deep in tropical rainforest, undergrowth, overgrowth and canopy so thick that it is dark at midday. Trees vie with each other to grow tallest, stretching up to reach the sunlight, while lianas and creeping vines take an easier route, grappling the tree-trunks and using them to climb. In the branches sit orchids and ferns that explode in graceful curves. The forest gushes with water, it squawks and chirrups and is truly a botanist's utopia. With so many species in such good condition, it has been called a living museum.

There are many marked **walking trails** in the parks and guides are readily available. On paths the best footwear is a light pair of walking boots, but if you are walking up rivers you might opt for the local red, gold and green plastic sandals, nicknamed *toyotas* (because they hold the road well). Also remember a waterproof coat, a picnic and if you are out for a long day, take a jersey too. As with anywhere, you are advised to take little money and jewellery with you when you go off the beaten track in Dominica.

The **Morne Trois Pitons National Park**, a 17,000-acre reserve of rainforest in the centre of the island, is the Caribbean's oldest nature reserve and it contains many of the island's natural attractions. Perhaps the best dropping-off point is **Laudat** in the upper Roseau Valley (the Trafalgar Falls are just outside the park); from here it is possible to reach the **Titou Gorge** and the **Freshwater** and **Boeri Lakes**. A very long day's walk will take you to the smelly and steaming **Valley of Desolation** and the **boiling lake**, high in the mountains. (*See* 'The Roseau Valley', p.220, for more detail about the sights.) Off the transinsular road are the **Middleham Trails**, leading to lost waterfalls and just outside the park is the **Emerald Pool**, a tame but popular cascade falling into a rockpool. Other visits to falls in the south include a walk up the **Sari-sari River** from La Plaine and the **Victoria Falls** above Delices. The **Northern Forest Reserve** is far larger and contains the island's highest peak, Morne Diablotin and the parrot habitat, where you are most likely to see the island's two endangered parrots.

More information and help with guides can be found at the **Division of Tourism** (✆ 448 2351) or the **Division of Forestry** office (✆ 448 2401, ext 3417), situated in the Botanical Gardens in Roseau. Tours and guides can be arranged through **Dominica Tours** (✆ 448 2638) and **Ken's Hinterland Adventure Tours** (✆ 448 4850). Also **Antours**, PO Box 428, Roseau (✆ 448 6460, fax 448 6780). Tour operators have a wide range of suggestions to add.

Some 135 species of bird live in Dominica or migrate here with the tourists for the better weather during the winter season. Among the common bananaquits and bullfinches, the exotic flycatchers and fluorescent hummingbirds, Dominica has two endemic parrots. Both are endangered, and the sisserou is portrayed on the national flag. The sisserou, or imperial parrot, is one of the largest parrots in the world and has a purple breast and green wings. The smaller red-necked amazon or jacko is a little less scarce and might be seen racing by in a flash of scarlet. To have a hope of seeing the parrots (a trip can be arranged through one of the operators above) you may have to get up extremely early and hike into the hills to a special hide. Another bird almost unique to Dominica is the siffleur montagne which whistles its single melancholy note every few minutes in the rainforest.

As all over the Caribbean, fauna is much more limited. Agouti and a rare 3ft iguana scurry around the heights and in the constant susurration of island insects you may see cockroaches wiggle antennae four inches long. Out at night you may come across luminous flickering points that are fireflies and hear the blacksmith beetle, so large and monstrous that it clanks.

There are five species of snake, none of them poisonous. One of the rarest but most surprising is the shy boa constrictor, known as *tête chien* because of the shape of its head. Outside the Amazon basin it is found only in Dominica. It has been known to grow to 20ft long and as thick as a man's leg. There is an early story of a Dominican who was resting under a tree and woke up to find his leg inside one of these snakes up to the thigh. Friends helped him extricate himself, putting wedges on the snake's teeth and chopping it up into pieces to release him.

It might be possible (depending on the season) to arrange to catch crayfish and frogs, later served as mountain chicken. Frog-hunting happens at night, with the aid of burning torches that have a fatal attraction for the animals.

Whale watching is possible from Dominica in the season (May to October), when the whales come from up north to mate and calve in the calm, deep waters on the leeward coast of Dominica. Humpbacks, pilot whales, dolphins and particularly sperm whales, accompanied by their 20ft calves, have been known in the area. Tours can be arranged through the Anchorage Dive Centre (✆ 448 2638).

✆ (809)–

Getting There

By Air: there are no direct flights to Dominica from outside the Caribbean and so you have to change, usually in Antigua, St Lucia, Barbados or Sint Maarten. LIAT (✆ 449 1421) has about 10 flights a day, originating in Antigua or Barbados; Winair flies from St Maarten and Air Guadeloupe (both ✆ 449 1060) flies from its home and on to Martinique. You can charter a flight through Caribbean Air Services (✆ 449 2771). There are two airports on Dominica: Melville Hall (code DOM) and Canefield (DCF). Melville Hall is inconveniently located on the eastern side of the island, 35 miles northeast of Roseau, so it is probably best to aim for Canefield, on the west coast just north of the capital. There is a departure tax of EC$20 and a $5 airport security tax.

By Boat: a couple of ferries touch Dominica on their way from Martinique to Guadeloupe. Caribbean Express (✆ 448 2181) and Madikera Car Ferry (✆ 448 6977) pass four times a week, docking at Woodbridge Bay. Reserve a seat in season and during school holidays.

Getting Around

Public transport is mostly by Japanese van, with teenage minders leaning out of them to shout for passengers, and by unwieldy government bus. The major routes are all served, but only infrequently after noon and hardly at all on Sundays (it is possible to get stranded in outlying areas, because the buses tend to go to Roseau in the morning and return in the early afternoon). However, **hitching** works quite well (you may be lucky enough to get a ride in one of the old Bedfords with the colourful wooden cages on the back). Though most would probably not take it, drivers might appreciate being offered a couple of dollars for the ride.

Buses travelling **south** go from the bottom end of King George V Street near the Old Market Square; for the **Roseau Valley** from the top end opposite the Police Headquarters. If you are heading **north**, buses leave from near the new Market building, next to the West Bridge. Sample bus prices, all set by the government, are: **Roseau** to Laudat EC$3, Soufrière $3, Canefield Airport $1.50, Castle Bruce $7, Portsmouth $8.

Taxis also have fixed rates. **Roseau** to Canefield airport EC$20, the southern hotels EC$15, Papillote EC$20 and **Canefield** to southern hotels EC$35, Castaways EC$40 and Portsmouth area EC$110. The trip to

Melville Hall airport is charged by the car, at EC$140, for a maximum of four people. For a tour, taxis can be hired for about EC$45 per hour.

Hire cars are available in Roseau from **Avis** (✆ 448 2481) at 4 High Street in town, **Valley Rent a Car** on Goodwill Road (✆ 448 3233), **Wide Range Car**, 81 Bath Road (✆ 448 2198) and **STL Car Rental** (✆ 448 2340). Hire costs around US$45 per day, jeeps US$55. You will need a local driver's licence, which can be obtained from the Traffic Department in Roseau or at the airport, price EC$20.

Tourist Information

UK: you can contact the Dominica Tourist Office at 1 Collingham Gardens, London SW5 0HW (✆ 071 835 1937, fax 071 373 8743) or the Caribbean Tourism Organization, 120 Wilton Road, London SW1V 1JZ (✆ 071 233 8382, fax 071 873 8551).

USA: contact the Dominica Consulate Office, Suite 900, 820 Second Avenue, New York, NY 10017 (✆ 212 599 8478, fax 212 808 4975) or the Caribbean Tourism Association, 20 East 46th Street, New York, NY 10017 (✆ 212 682 0435, fax 212 697 4258).

On the island itself, the **Dominica Tourist Board** is reached at Box 73, Roseau, Dominica (✆ 448 2351, fax 448 5840). For tourist **information** there is a kiosk at the Old Market Place on the waterfront and one at each of the airports. The tourist board publications include the small magazine *Discover Dominica* and the quarterly tourist paper *The Tropical Traveller*. The local newspaper is the *New Chronicle*, which is published on Fridays.

The main hospital in Roseau is the **Princess Margaret Hospital** (✆ 44 82231). For emergency services, dial 999. The **IDD code** for Dominica is **809** and this is followed by a seven-digit island number. When you are on-island, dial the full seven digits. It is best to address letters to the Commonwealth of Dominica, because otherwise they often end up in the Dominican Republic. You are advised to be careful about personal security when in Dominica, particularly on isolated beaches and remote roads. Do not leave valuables unattended on the beach at any time.

Money

The currency of Dominica is the EC$ (US$1 = EC$2.65). Prices are often published in both dollar currencies, so it is worth knowing which currency you are dealing in. **Banks** open daily 8–3, staying open until 5 on Fridays. **Shopping hours** are 8–4 in the week, often with a stop for lunch, and Saturdays 8–1pm.

Beaches

Dominica has no white coral-sand beaches in the typical Caribbean mould and most beaches tend to be dark volcanic grey or jet black. Beach-bound tourists tend to head for the north of the island, where there are some golden-sand beaches in the coves on the northeastern coastline.

Hampstead Bay, **Calibishie** (Point Baptiste) and **Woodford Hill Bay** are quite remote, but are dramatic and overhung by cliffs. Take a good map and all you need in the way of food and drink, though you will find a good beach bar, the **Almond Beach Bar**, at Calibishie. Around Portsmouth the sand is black, but you will find good stretches of beach with hotel bars to retreat to. **Douglas Bay**, north of the Cabrits, has nice sand and **Prince Rupert Bay** has a broad sweep of sand down from Portsmouth. Further south, **Castaways** is a good bar on a pleasant, sunset-facing strip of sand. Around Roseau, the waterfront is made up of fist-sized rocks that clatter as they race and recede with the waves.

River-bathing

Perhaps preferable to sea-bathing is swimming in Dominica's **rivers**. There is plenty of flowing water on the island. So much, in fact, that they sell it to drier islands such as Antigua and Sint Maarten to the north. Waterfalls are also a good bet, because there is usually a pool beneath them. Some good places to swim are at the Trafalgar and Middleham Falls (*an hour's walk*), the Rosalie river on the east coast and the White River in La Plaine, whose source is the boiling lake. Otherwise, ask around. For a full day's outing you can float and clamber down the **Layou River**, starting at Belles in the rainforest on the transinsular road and working your way down through the Layou flats towards the west coast.

Sailing

Dominica is really a stopover between the two more developed French islands of Martinique and Guadeloupe and there is not much to detain you, unless you wish to explore the natural life of the island, which is extraordinary. But there is a passable **anchorage** in the north, Prince Rupert Bay, which lies off the town of Portsmouth. Here you can anchor beneath the Cabrits in the north or off the Coconut Beach Hotel a couple of miles to the south. There are the hotel dining rooms and a few bars but not much else around the town. In the south you should anchor off the clutch of hotels around the Anchorage. Roseau is a short ride off and you will even find a Chinese laundry there. The **ports of entry** to Dominica are in Portsmouth and in Woodbridge Bay just north of Roseau. You are advised to be careful with regard to the security of your yacht in Dominica.

Watersports

Watersports are not that developed in Dominica and if you wish to go **windsurfing** or to take out a small sailing boat you will have to contact one of the hotels (try the Anchorage or Castaways). A day's sail is also possible. A general watersports operator is **Dominica Tours** (© 448 2638) at the Anchorage Hotel. **Nature Island Dive** (© 449 8181, fax 449 8182) offer kayaking and snorkelling around the southern area as well as hiking and mountain-biking in the mountainous interior.

Dominica has a recently established reputation for **scuba diving**. Dives take place on the reefs along the leeward coast, mainly in the south near Scott's Head in Soufrière bay, where there is a new Marine Park, and also in the Marine Park in Douglas Bay just north of the Cabrits. Brain corals, black corals and sponges are all on view on the walls and boulder-strewn drop-offs; also excellent fish-life with larger schools and a greater variety than elsewhere. Dominican oddities include hot and coldwater springs under the surface (at Champagne in Soufrière Bay you will see and and feel the warm bubbling water, discoloured with sulphur and iron) and clear water beneath cloudy river outflows. Wrecks also occasionally turn up too.

Dives (*about US$45 per tank*), equipment hire and instruction can be arranged through **Dive Dominica Ltd** at the Castle Comfort Guest House (© 448 2188, fax 448 6088) just south of Roseau, who have dive packages on offer, **Dive Castaways** in Mero (© 449 6244, fax 449 6246) and the **Anchorage Dive Centre** (© 448 2638, fax 448 5680) with three locations in the north and south. Also **Nature Island Dive** above.

Snorkelling is good off the north coast, for instance at Hodge's Bay and Douglas Bay and particularly in Soufrière Bay. Equipment can be hired at the watersports shops or at the hotels.

Roseau

Roseau, Dominica's capital, has 20,000 inhabitants, about a quarter of the population, and is the only sizeable town on the island. Towered over by the mountainous hinterland of Dominica, it stands at the mouth of the Roseau river, taking its name from the French word for the reeds that grew here, which the Caribs used to poison their arrow-tips. Lacking a proper harbour, it was never intended to be the island's capital, but the intended site of Portsmouth was found to be unhealthy and so the administrators moved here in the late 18th century.

Roseau is a traditional West Indian waterfront town. It was extensively rebuilt after Hurricane David in 1979, but it has not been redeveloped in concrete; many of the old creole houses have been rebuilt as they were. Only the occasional satellite dish stands out among the shanties and the streets of traditional warehouses near the waterfront. With strong stone foundations and shuttered doorways that let through the breeze, the old storehouses and shops are topped with wooden upper storeys and steep roofs, many of them embellished with gingerbread fretwork. Some have balconies over the pavement, supported by sturdy wooden columns and giving welcome shelter in Roseau's regular tropical rainstorms. Although the town looks a little neglected, its roofs rusted and the buildings a bit run down, these attractive houses give Roseau a charming atmosphere.

Wherever you go in Dominica people seem to greet you, usually in French patois, but the liveliest spot in Roseau is the market, which can be found next to the rivermouth. There is a large covered area of tables, but the Dominicans mostly prefer to spread out their produce—guava, grapefruit, golden apple and ground provisions—on the ground in the open, with golf umbrellas to protect them from the sun and plastic sheeting at the ready for when it rains.

At the other end of the **Bayfront**, as the newly restored Roseau waterfront is known, is **Dawbiney Market Plaza**, a cobbled square with a fountain, formerly the site of Roseau's slave trading and public executions. There is a small tourist information desk on the square.

Walking northwest on Castle Street and Virgin Lane, you come to the Roman Catholic **Cathedral of the Assumption**, built in dark stone with Romanesque arches and completed in 1841. Even though the majority of Dominica's population was Catholic, the official Anglican government would grant no money for the building of the Cathedral. Summoned by a bell, the faithful would come out at night and carry stones from the Roseau river to the site. **Fort Young** is now a hotel, but once was Roseau's main defence. It was erected in 1775 and visitors to the hotel will still see a few slim cannons hanging around the foyer and courtyard.

Behind the town, at the foot of Morne Bruce, are the **Botanical Gardens**, which date from 1891. Landscaped with open lawns, it must be the only place of its kind that appears less fertile than the country surrounding it. There are 150 species, including traditional Caribbean plants such as allamanda and bougainvillea and some less known: pompon rouge, or powder puff. Trees include cannonball, teak and pink poui, and a giant baobab tree that came down in 1979, when Hurricane David uprooted over half the garden's species, still lying on top of the yellow school bus that it crushed. It has even begun to flower again. A couple of Dominica's endangered parrots can be seen in an aviary in the gardens.

Roseau

A path climbs **Morne Bruce** from the gardens, 500ft up through the creaking bamboo, to the crown-like Catholic memorial. The Morne takes its name from the 18th-century engineer who fortified it and it gives an excellent view across the town, covering the bay. Most of the buildings have fallen down now. Earlier this century the Morne was thought to be haunted: troops would be heard marching and a bugle sounded on dark nights.

The Roseau Valley

The extension of King George V Street leads out of the town and across a clattering wooden suspension bridge into the Roseau river valley, straight into the Dominican heartland. The bridge may seem high, but the Roseau river has been known to rise 20ft in as many hours. Some of Roseau's more prosperous citizens have retreated into the cooler heights of the valley, side by side with farmers who manage to terrace and cultivate the absurdly steep valley walls.

At the head of the valley, 5 miles up-river from Roseau, just beyond the village of Trafalgar, are the **Trafalgar Falls**, two spectacular cascades that tumble 90ft from the lip of a gorge, the water whipped into a maelstrom by upward winds, splattering down among titanic black boulders and orange iron-discoloured rocks. The prodigious vegetation provides pockets of quiet as you climb, before you emerge into the blanket of fine spray and white noise that fills the gorge, a deafening hiss and roar that drops into the pools of hot and cold water. The falls are considerably smaller now that some of the water has been harnessed for hydro-electricity.

The Trafalgar Falls are easy to reach on a short outing from town and you can drive to within ten minutes of them. Take a swimming costume and gymshoes if you like clambering over rocks and consider getting a guide (*for perhaps EC$10*). You might need a jersey for your return because it can also get a bit cold and wet in the wind.

Twin pipes lead down from the falls, carrying water to a hydroelectric generating station, passing **Papillote Wilderness Retreat**, where a small hotel is set in a

tropical paradise

charming 12-acre garden of truly Dominican profusion and rushing water spewed out by ornamental iguanas. Paths lead among forests of white-leafed hibiscus, bromeliads and aroids, and orchids like butterflies, all sheltered by vast sprays of bamboo overhead. There is also a naturally heated mineral bath, for which the water comes from the springs higher up the mountain. This is a good place to stop for lunch on the veranda (© 448 2287).

Morne Trois Pitons National Park

At the head of a side valley is the village of Laudat, the best dropping-off point for the 17,000-acre reserve. You can reach the **Freshwater Lake** by vehicle, a couple of miles beyond Laudat. The lake is at 2500ft and was haunted variously by a vindictive mermaid who would lure travellers to drown them and according to Oldmixon in 1708 by 'a vast monstrous Serpent, that had its Abode in the beforementioned Bottom [an inaccessible Bottom in the high mountains]. They affirm'd, there was in the Head of it a very sparkling Stone, like a Carbuncle of inestimable Price; that the Monster commonly veil'd that rich jewel with a thin moving skin, like that of a Man's Eyelid, and when it went to drink or sported itself in the deep Bottom, it fully discovered it, and the Rocks all about receiv'd a wonderful Lustre from the Fire issuing out of that precious Gem.'

A 45-minute walk beyond the Freshwater Lake, towards the Morne Trois Pitons, the island's second-highest peak, is the **Boeri Lake**, in the crater of an extinct volcano. The vegetation thins at this height and the rainforest gives way to montane and elfin growth, giving good views, on days when the rainclouds are not obscuring them.

But Dominica's volcanic heartland is the **Valley of Desolation**, appropriately named because nothing can grow there—even Dominican vegetation is killed off by sulphur emissions. This foetid area, among the jumble of (almost) extinct volcanoes, four hours' walk away and over two mountains, is laid with titanic boulders and sulphurous cesspools of diabolic colours. The volcano beneath it all erupted last in 1880, showering Roseau with volcanic ash.

At its centre is the **Boiling Lake**, a seething and bubbling morass like an angry jacuzzi, constantly steaming at between 180 and 200°F, and fed by (occasionally poisonous) gases from underneath that make the whole lake rise by several feet. It has been known to measure about 70 yards across, but it is smaller at the moment. It has also been known to disappear down the plug-hole, re-emerging with a geyser spout and monumental rumbling.

South from Roseau

The road south from Roseau leads along the coast through the suburbs of Charlotteville and Castle Comfort, past a clutch of the island's hotels. In the 18th century a string of forts and batteries ran along the coast to the southern tip at Scotts Head. From Loubière, an impossibly steep road branches inland, climbing to the oddly named Snug Corner and over the summit, descending beneath the cliffs to the citrus orchards and banana plantations at **Bereuka** on Grand Bay, where fort ruins stand beneath the vast cliffs of the windward coast.

Eventually you come to the valley of **Soufrière**, one of the earliest areas of the island to be settled by the French. The town takes its name from the sulphur outlets farther up the valley, which flow into the river and provide heated water for bathing or washing clothes. It is a pleasant walk up the river among the 60ft bamboo trees that creak constantly and over to Grand Bay on the Atlantic side of the island, but if you feel like refreshing yourself with a drink, be careful, because you might scald your hand.

The southern point of the island is dominated by Scotts Head, a spit of land jutting into the Caribbean Sea. There is little left of Fort Cacharou that once dominated it, but it was attacked many times in the past. On one occasion Dominicans sympathetic to the French got the British soldiers drunk and spiked their guns with sand, enabling the French to overrun the fort. The view from Scotts Head to Martinique, 20 miles south, and back along the leeward coast of Dominica, is stunning.

North from Roseau to the Leeward Coast

Despite being proposed in the 18th century, the road link from Roseau to Portsmouth, Dominica's second town in the north of the island, was one of the last to be completed, with some cuttings into the cliff-face up to 50ft deep. The journey had to be made via the other side of the Island or by boat until well into this century. The leeward coast is supposedly in the 'rain-shadow' of Dominica's central mountain range, meaning that it is dry (by Dominican standards). However, it can still drench you without a moment's notice.

The road follows the coast, passing Woodbridge Bay, the cruise-ship dock and the deepwater port, where goods for the capital are unloaded. Just before the airport at Canefield is the **Old Mill Cultural Centre**, in the grounds of an old plantation estate. The gardens contain an aqueduct and water-wheel as well as less ancient steam-driven cane-crushing gear. In the museum, **Lavi Dominik**, are displays of Dominica's pre-Columbian history, with exhibits of Carib lifestyle and weaving, representations of the colonial age in the work of Agosto Brunias and the Porters, as well as an exhibit of the old Parliamentary mace, presented to the House of Assembly in 1770 and used for the 208 years before Independence in 1978, when another mace of local wood was adopted in Parliament.

Just beyond Canefield is the settlement of **Massacre** (pronounced more as in French than as in English), the site of a sad episode that took place between two half-brothers, one half-Carib, the other European, in the early 1600s. Indian Warner was born in St Kitts, son of Governor Warner by a Carib woman, but had to flee when his father died and so he went to Dominica, becoming a Carib chief. The massacre took place when his brother Phillip was sent by the Governor of the Leeward Islands on a campaign to 'put down' the Caribs in 1674. Phillip and his troops are supposed to have feasted with the Caribs and he initiated the massacre by stabbing his brother.

Soon the leeward road passes beneath Dominica's highest peak, **Morne Diablotin** (4747ft), which takes its name from the black-capped petrel, a diabolically ugly bird that once lived on its slopes, prized by hunters in the 18th century. With webbed feet and black and white plumage, the diablotin was about the size of a duck and nested in the ground, flying down to the sea to fish at night. The view from Morne Diablotin is superb, but more often than not it is obscured by the clouds that hang on Dominica's mountains.

The road continues to Dominica's second town of **Portsmouth**, crossing the **Indian River** just before the town. It is possible to arrange canoe trips up the river, where the banks are tangled with mangrove roots and the canopy is festooned with flying tropical overgrowth.

Portsmouth, another tired-looking town of 3000 inhabitants with dilapidated wooden buildings, stands at the head of Prince Rupert's Bay, sheltered in the north by the promontory of the Cabrits. The bay itself takes its name from the royalist prince who arrived in the West Indies in 1652 to find that Barbados and the

Leeward Islands were in the hands of the Commonwealth. Two centuries ago the bay would see as many as 400 navy ships at anchor if a campaign was brewing.

On the northern side of the bay is the promontory of the **Cabrits National Park**, two forested hills scattered with the fortifications of Fort Shirley. The Fort, dating from the 1770s, has been restored to its fearsome brimstone glory after more than a hundred years of decay since it was abandoned in 1854 by the British. The restoration received an award from American Express. The word *cabrits* derives from the Spanish word for goat—animals left here as fresh meat for future arrivals low on stocks after the Atlantic crossing. Marked trails cover the promontory and there is a small museum, *adm free*.

From Portsmouth a side road leads north past the anchorages at Douglas Bay and Toucari Bay. It was from an estate just north of Toucari that John Mair and friends watched the Battle of the Saints in April 1782. They were breakfasting in the portico as the battle began (*see* **Guadeloupe**, p.263).

The main road around the island leads inland from Portsmouth, winding into the hills, violent Dominican fertility alternately soaked and shone upon at half-hourly intervals, and rejoining the north coast after 5 miles. In this area Dominica's best beaches can be found in the coves that look out on to the islands of Marie Galante and the Saints. Beneath bright orange and muddy cliffs are beaches of large-grained golden sand, flecked with jet black magnetic particles (*see* 'Beaches', p.217).

The road continues to the villages of Wesley and Marigot, where unlike most Dominican villages they speak English and not French creole as their first tongue. They were settled by Antiguans and other Leeward Islanders who came as construction labourers and stayed when their work was finished.

The Transinsular Road to the East Coast

The grandly named Transinsular Road, formerly known by the even grander name of the Imperial Road, winds its laborious way into the Dominican highlands from Canefield airport. For years, journeys to the Atlantic coast had to be made by boat or on horseback along paths throttled by vegetation, but the Imperial Road commenced its journey to windward in 1909, setting off into the jungle and only emerging on the Atlantic coast in the late fifties.

It always seems to be raining somewhere up in Dominica's hinterland and you will certainly see a few rainbows among the peaks. The road also provides an excellent way to see some of Dominica's extraordinary fertility (you cut through the northern part of the Morne Trois Pitons National Park). There are whole slopes covered with elephant ears and creeping vines, fluorescent green ferns so large that they might fly away and waterfalls that descend from heights invisible from below in the spray.

The **Middleham Trails** lead off the main road and cross over the hills to the Roseau Valley at Laudat, via the Middleham Falls, a stunning waterfall 500ft in height. At Pont Casse the road splits three ways, left to the Layou Valley and back down to the Leeward Coast and right to Castle Bruce and the southeast corner of the island. The transinsular road continues straight to the Atlantic coast just short of Marigot and Melville Hall airport. At **Belles** it is possible to join the higher reaches of the Layou River for a day-long hike and swim through flats and gulleys that emerge on the Layou road a couple of miles short of the west coast. Take a pair of gym-shoes and a swimsuit and arrange for someone to meet you at the bottom.

Back on the Castle Bruce road, a tamer walk through the jungle can be made at the **Emerald Pool**. Walkways are carefully marked out and lead down to the small pool, where a tiny cascade races into the warm and dank recess and roots like knotted fingers grapple rocks furred with moss. However, do not expect it to be isolated enough to go skinny-dipping.

The road passes beneath Dominica's second peak, **Morne Trois Pitons**, and then throws off another branch that leads to **Rosalie** and to **La Plaine**. Atlantic breakers pound the windward shore, where there are cliffs hundreds of feet high. Before the road was built, stores had to be winched up from the bays below. In Dominican creole, the Atlantic coast is known as *au vent*, literally 'in the wind', a reference to the trade winds.

Carib Territory

The Caribs retreated to the Atlantic coast of Dominica in the 18th century when Europeans took over the island. In the one hundred years to 1750 their numbers had reduced from about 5000 to 400 and they knew their struggle was lost, so they took up a peaceful life as far as possible from the invaders.

The Carib Territory itself (which was then called the Carib Reserve) was not created until 1903, when the Governor Hesketh Bell allotted some 3700 acres to the few hundred remaining Caribs. A hereditary chief was presented with a mace and an official sash and was referred to as 'King'. However, he was implicated in a smuggling racket in the thirties and the position went into abeyance until 1952, when the 'Chief' was reintroduced as an elected post, still within the local government system.

The Caribs have adopted a West Indian lifestyle, living in clapboard houses on stilts rather than their original *carbets* (pointed thatch huts) and they make a living in a similar way to other Dominicans. They do maintain some Carib traditions, such as building canoes, dug out from trees that they fell high up in the forest, and their skilful weaving of rushes and reeds. They sell woven baskets, mats and ornaments.

One curious object is known as the *wife-leader*. It is a mesh of interwoven reeds that tightens when you put it over your finger and pull it, trapping you.

There are said to be no pure-bred Caribs left in the Territory, but the Carib features, which are like those of South American Indians, are immediately recognizable. Carib hair, dark and sleek and once the pride of their ancestors, is still much admired by Dominicans today (many of whom have tight African curls).

Festivals

Dominica maintains a traditional **Carnival** in the days before Lent (still called Masquerade from the French celebrations) with feasting and revelling in the streets and bands of players dressed in fantastic costumes. Other celebrations include **Independence Day** (3 November), which is strong on folk arts, including music and dance as well as the traditional Caribbean jump-up. In 'conte', or story-telling, raconteurs compete with one another in telling humorous anecdotes of everyday life. **Domfesta** is an annual festival of local arts, crafts and performing arts held in July and August. **Jounen Kweyol**, a celebration of the creole language and customs, with cooking, radio and national costume, is celebrated on the last Friday in October. Like many Catholic Caribbean countries, some villages in Dominica celebrate their Saint's days with a Mass and then a party.

✆ (809)–

Where to Stay

Dominica's hotels are mainly small, family-run affairs, many of them in the old-time buildings around the coast or hidden among the island's overbearing foliage (as you sit on the veranda you can practically see it grow). Except in the most popular hotels in season, there is usually no difficulty in finding a room. If you wish to hire a villa, contact the tourist board, but two excellent ones are mentioned below. The government levies a tax of 5% and most hotels charge service of another 10%.

moderate

The **Fort Young Hotel**, PO Box 519 (✆ 448 5000, fax 448 5006), on the waterfront in Roseau, is the island's most elegant and comfortable. It is set in the old battlements of the fort that guarded the town approaches for a couple of centuries. The attractive courtyard is still laid with flagstones and the pool and bar are lost in foliage. There are 27 comfortable rooms and suites on the battlements, most with a sea view. The newest comer is the **Garraway Hotel** (✆ 449 8800, fax 449 8807), a modern building which stands tall on the Bayfront. It is modern and plush to international standards of comfort, with air-conditioning, deep carpets, king-sized beds and cable television. It has 31 rooms and suites; moderate to expensive. The **Reigate Hall Hotel** (℃ 448 4031, fax 448 4034) has a superb view from its commanding position above the Roseau Valley. Old-time Dominican comfort prevails in the original stone of the old house and the heavy furniture of the central area. It has 17 air-conditioned rooms and suites.

There is a small cluster of friendly and comfortable hotels on the coast a mile south of Roseau, all with a fine view west to the sea horizon. There is no beach here really, but smooth fist-size rocks that clatter and jangle as the waves move over them. The **Evergreen Hotel**, PO Box 309 (℃ 448 3288, fax 448 6800) is very low-key with small blocks of rooms around a seafront garden. The new rooms are very comfortable, but the original house has charm too. Pool and terrace above the sea, where there is a chic modern dining room. Just 16 rooms. The **Anchorage**, PO Box 34 (℃ 448 2638, fax 448 5680) has a slightly busier feel, with 33 rooms overlooking the sea (go for the ones upstairs which have a bit more charm) and a lively terrace dining room. If you are a diver the best place to head for in this area is the **Castle Comfort Diving Lodge** (℃ 448 2188, fax 448 6088), which offers good packages. If you want to stay right on the sand, **Castaways**, PO Box 5 (℃ 449 6244, fax 449 6246, US toll free ℃ 800 626 0581), is Dominica's best beach hotel, set on black sand at Mero, a few miles north of Roseau. There is a large and attractive terrace with the bar and the Almond Tree restaurant, from which the wings run on either side, containing 27 rooms in all. Also, a dive shop, though no pool. One of Dominica's most charming spots can be found on the beach south of Portsmouth, at the **Picard Beach Cottage Resort**, PO Box 34 (℃ 445 5131, fax 445 5599), a collection of eight wooden, old Caribbean-style cottages set in a pleasant tropical garden right on the beach. Each one has a small veranda, perfect for lounging and taking in the sunset. Very quiet and low-key. Just south of here is the **Coconut Beach Hotel**, PO Box 37 (℃ 445 5393, fax 445 5693), which has a slightly busier feel as it is popular with yachtsmen washed in on the tide. It has 32 units, with air-conditioning or a fan, some self-contained. Very nice waterfront bar and restaurant above the grey sand.

If you would like stay in a classic, old-time West Indian villa, **Pointe Baptiste**, c/o Mrs G. Edwards, Calibishie (℃ 445 7369, fax 445 8343), has one of the loveliest settings in the Caribbean. It is set on the clifftops of the north coast, and the main house has a huge balcony, where you can settle and take in the islands of Marie Galante and Guadeloupe. There is a golden sand beach just below and an old-fashioned aura so rarely found anywhere nowadays. Housekeeper service, villa rates about US$1000 per week (for six people) in season. Close by, taking advantage of the beach, are **Red Rock Haven Homes**, PO Box 71 (✆ 448 2181, fax 448 5787), Point Baptiste's modern counterpart. Very comfortable. There are just three wooden cottages, each with a full kitchen and a fine view of the valley from the huge balconies. Housekeeper service for cooking if you want, about US$700 per week (one bedroom), US$1400 (two bedrooms). A pretty and comfortable villa in the Laudat Valley houses the two **D'Auchamps Apartments**, PO Box 1889 (✆ 448 3346), about US$300 a week for two bedrooms.

cheap

A cheap option if you want to be on the sand is **Mamie's on the Beach** (✆ 445 5997, fax 445 4295), with just eight rooms in a modern house to the north of Portsmouth. Dominica has some extremely fine **rainforest retreats**, very unlike your typical Caribbean hotel. The rooms are often quite basic, though most will have hot and cold water, but the settings are supreme. In the heights of the Roseau Valley, near the village of Trafalgar, is the **Papillote Wilderness Retreat**, PO Box 67 (✆ 448 2287, fax 448 2285), which is practically throttled by its 12 acres of tropical garden. Eight rooms and suites, overlooking the falls. The restaurant is on the garden terrace and serves local food. Not far off is **Ophelia's** (✆ 448 3438, fax 448 3433), set around an old wooden creole house painted brightly in red and white. Easy life and home cooking. The **Layou Valley Inn**, PO Box 192 (✆ 449 6203, fax 448 5212), is hidden in the hills of the Dominican heartland and has superb views over the multiple greens of the rainforest of the upper Layou valley. Just six rooms and good home cooking. Farther afield, on the edge of the Carib Territory, you will find a warm welcome at **Floral Gardens** (✆/fax 445 7636). Quite rustic, but an excellent riverside escape in a pretty tropical garden, good creole food.

In Roseau there are a number of small hotels and guest houses, including **Vena's** on Cork Street (✆ 448 3286), the birth-place of the Dominican novelist Jean Rhys, which offers simple, cheap, rooms. A friendly and dependable haunt where chat and cheap rooms are available is the **Kent Anthony Guest House** in the middle of town on Marlborough Street (✆ 448 2730). Not far off, **Bon Marché**, 11 Old Street (✆ 448 2083 or 448 4194) also has cheap rooms. For accommodation in **Portsmouth**, go to **Douglas's Guest House** (✆ 445 5253), very simple; very cheap.

✆ (809)– **Eating Out**

Dominica is quiet and you will not find that many places to eat out at night outside the hotels. You will find good traditional Caribbean food, however: callaloo or pumpkin soup followed by fish or a curry goat sitting among prodigious quantities of local vegetables such as plantain, green fig and breadfruit. Dominica also has one or two specialities, such as *mountain chicken* or *cwapaud* (in fact breaded bullfrog legs), crab-backs stuffed with land-crab meat and tiny fish in cakes called *tee-tee-ree*, fish-fry which are caught at the river-mouth in a sheet. There is a government tax of 5% and most restaurants add a service charge of 10%.

For an evening out of subdued old-Roseau ambience try **La Robe Creole** on Fort Street (✆ 448 2896), set in a stone town-house with arched windows and doors. The waitresses wear the traditional *madras* costume from which the restaurant takes its name. Steamed shrimp with creole sauce and mountain chicken in beer batter and coconut flakes, followed by banana flambéed at your table. Mainly a creole menu. Two lively and less formal spots on King George V Street are the **Orchard** Restaurant, set in a pretty town house with simple table settings and **Callaloo** (✆ 448 3386). Both offer regular Dominican fare, lambi or goat, chicken or fish, with ground provisions and guava pie. There are not that many restaurants open at night, so it is worth considering the hotel dining rooms: Fort Young in Roseau and Evergreen and the Anchorage in the Castle Comfort area, all with good waterfront settings. You can also try **River Side** Restaurant in Loubière, which has a coconut-sheltered patio lined with bamboo right on the waterfront. Fish broth followed by shrimp on ginger cabbage and oil dung. You will get the best in local fare at the **World of Food** at Vena's, where the open dining room gives on to a paved garden with a a mango tree (you dine to a constant thud and bump, bump, bump in season); chicken and fish and a volley of local vegetables. **Kent Anthony's** offers trusty local fare, as does the **Cartwheel Café** down on the Bayfront. If you want a Chinese meal (with Dominican adaptions), try **Paiho** on Church Street: shark fin soup on an old Dominica balcony above the street.

There is a little more variety at lunch. **Guiyave** (✆ 448 2930) has a very attractive setting with a green and white balcony upstairs overlooking Cork Street. Baked chicken with glazed spinach followed by local ice-cream. **Mangé Dominique** has a covered veranda setting on Cork Street, and good local fare. Roseau also has plenty of *snackettes*, usually teeming with schoolkids on their lunchtime break, where you can get a lunchtime pattie and a fruit juice—sorrel, soursop, lime and tamarind according to the season—followed by a coconut cake. Finally, don't forget **Al's**; 12 different flavours of ice-cream, *open until 10pm*.

Around Portsmouth you can try the hotel dining rooms and the **Purple Turtle Beach Club** and if you are on an island tour there is the **Almond Beach Bar** in Calaibishie where you can find classic island fare and juices.

Bars and Nightlife

Some of the hotels have happy hours, barbecues and a band in season—the Anchorage has an occasional steel band—but otherwise you will rely on Dominican entertainment—rum shops, discos and local fêtes, which are at their liveliest at the weekend. There are limitless rum shops on the island, where you will be welcome to try out a few of the Dominican rums: Red Cap, Soca rum, D Special and if you can find it some Mountain Dew. *Bois Bandé* (pronounced 'bawbandy'), a local concoction made from tree bark, has an interesting story which you might enjoy investigating.

Wykie's bar on Old Street is a favourite with island-execs and passers-through, a cosy creole bamboo-lined town house, and the **Piña Colada Bar** on Bath Road attracts a lively crowd sometimes. Just north of the town is the **Good Times** bar—part bar and part restaurant, for chicken or fish with salad—from where people stumble across to the **Warehouse** discotheque (*Wed–Sun*). Other discotheques include **Night Box** in Pottersville near the bridge in town. There is a mix of music: Jamaican reggae, soca from down south and French Caribbean zouk.

Rum Shop

the travellers tree

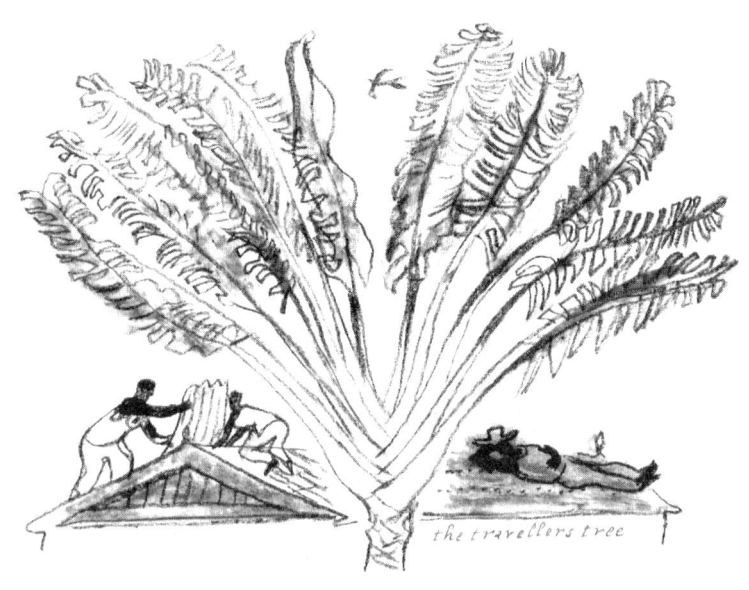

History	234
Getting There and Around	236
Tourist Information	238
Beaches and Sports	239
Grande-Terre	243
Basse-Terre	246
Where to Stay	251
Eating Out	255
La Désirade	260
Marie Galante	261
The Saints	263

Guadeloupe

The *région* of Guadeloupe is made up of a number of islands scattered over 150 miles (240km) of the Lesser Antilles. Altogether they have an area of 658 square miles (1705sq km) and a population of around 410,000. Of the smaller islands, the Saints, La Désirade and Marie Galante lie close to Guadeloupe itself; St Martin (which shares an island with the Dutch Crown colony of Sint Maarten) and St Barts (St Barthélémy) lie to the north, amongst the Leeward Islands. Guadeloupe is by far the largest of the group and is shaped like a huge butterfly.

Guadeloupe is in fact two islands, pushed together by geological movement, and each wing shows a different side of the Caribbean: in the west, Basse-Terre is mountainous and has the explosive luxuriance of the volcanic islands, its slopes covered with banana plantations and rainforest; the softer contours of Grande-Terre to the east have the coral reefs and white-sand beaches. Besides the exotic combination of French and West Indian elements, the large size of the island and the variety of countryside make Guadeloupe one of the most rewarding islands to visit.

The small town of Basse-Terre on the west coast of the island is the capital of Guadeloupe, but Pointe-à-Pitre on Grande-Terre has long been the commercial centre. Grande-Terre is more populous and industrialized, and its gently sloping mornes are covered in 12ft curtains of sugar-cane. The island's economy has always been agricultural. Coffee gave way to sugar (and rum) and most recently to tropical fruits such as bananas. But as with so many Caribbean islands, tourism has grown here and become the primary industry most recently. Unemployment runs at around 30 per cent, but the standard of living is kept at a roughly similar level to that of mainland France and so Guadeloupe appears far more prosperous than other islands nearby.

There is an old saying of the French Caribbean which refers to '*les Grands Seigneurs de la Martinique et les Bons Gens de la Guadeloupe*'. From the start Martinique was the senior, more prosperous island and its business interests in Guadaloupe continue today. But the Guadeloupeans have an independent cast of mind and they have always gone their own way. For the Guadeloupeans, the Martiniquans have too slavish an attachment to France. It is one thing to be 'Black Frenchmen', but if it has the effect of burying their own culture, then they will rebel against it.

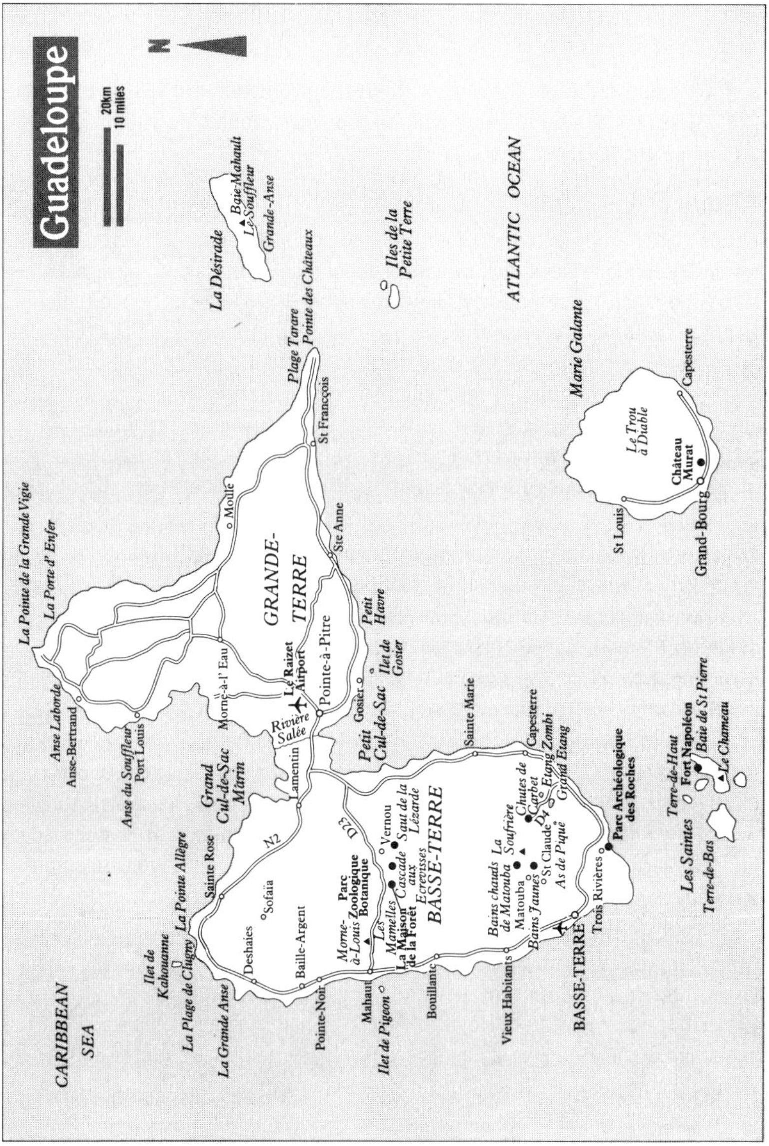

Guadeloupe
20km
10 miles
N
CARIBBEAN SEA
ATLANTIC OCEAN
La Pointe de la Grande Vigie
La Porte d' Enfer
Anse Laborde
Anse-Bertrand
Anse du Souffleur
Port Louis
Grand Cul-de-Sac Marin
Morne-à-l' Eau
Moule
GRANDE-TERRE
Le Raizet Airport
Pointe-à-Pitre
Rivière Salée
Gosier
Petit Cul-de-Sac
Ilet de Gosier
Petit Havre
Ste Anne
St François
Plage Tarare
Pointe des Châteaux
La Désirade
Baie-Mahault
Le Souffleur
Grande-Anse
Iles de la Petite Terre
Marie Galante
Capesterre
Le Trou à Diable
Château Murat
St Louis
Grand-Bourg
Ilet de Kahouanne
La Pointe Allègre
La Plage de Clugny
La Grande Anse
Sainte Rose
Sofaïa
Deshaies
Baille-Argent
Pointe-Noir
Mahaut
Ilet de Pigeon
Morne-à-Louis
Parc Zoologique Botanique
Les Mamelles
La Maison de la Forêt
Cascade aux Ecrevisses
Vernou
Saut de la Lézarde
D23
N2
Lamentin
BASSE-TERRE
Bouillante
Vieux Habitants
Bains chauds de Matouba
Matouba
Bains Jaunes
La Soufrière
St Claude
As de Pique
Chutes de Carbet
Etang Zombi
Grand Etang
D4
Sainte Marie
Capesterre
Parc Archéologique des Roches
Trois Rivières
BASSE-TERRE
Les Saintes
Terre-de-Haut
Terre-de-Bas
Fort Napoléon
Baie de St Pierre
Le Chameau

Politically Guadeloupe has benefited from more autonomy in recent years, but it has also become more answerable for budget expenditure. France grants a huge amount of cash each year and the material benefits are clear to see, but there are some Guadeloupeans who would rather go it alone, without the protection of the republic. The issue is an emotive one which erupts occasionally in violent campaigns, as it did in the late 1970s.

History

To the Caribs Guadeloupe was *Karukera*, thought to mean 'the island of beautiful waters'. Columbus was struck by the beauty of the waterfalls on the heights when he passed by on his second voyage in November 1493. He christened the island *Santa Maria de Guadalupe de Extremadura* but soon moved on. The 'Cannibal Isles' were dangerous country and, apart from one attempt by the Spaniards in 1525 to settle Guadeloupe so that their ships could take on water and refit here after the Atlantic crossing, the island was left alone. It was another hundred years before the next Europeans arrived in force. Led by de l'Olive and Duplessis, six hundred French settlers disembarked in June 1635. They attacked the Caribs, driving them off the island within a few years to refuges in Dominica and St Vincent.

Guadeloupe was administered from Martinique. Not only did the Martiniquan governor general have the ultimate say on affairs in Guadeloupe, but Martinique maintained a commercial hold. Trade to France had to be conducted through St Pierre, where the merchants would inevitably give a low price for Guadeloupean sugar, even after the extra costs of transportation. Revenge was sweet when four years under British rule (1759–63) turned out to be very prosperous ones for Guadeloupe because vast markets opened up to them in Britain and America.

During the French Revolution the Guadeloupean *patriotes* gained the upper hand, ousting the planters. They welcomed the revolutionary Victor Hugues and the new regime was installed. A guillotine was erected and three hundred were beheaded. From Guadeloupe, Victor Hugues rallied the slaves and liberal Frenchmen on all the Windward Islands with the promise of freedom, but within two years the rebellions were crushed and Hugues' position in Guadeloupe was unsure.

A momentous event took place on 16 Pluviôse of Year 2 (4 February 1794). Following the declaration of the Revolutionary Convention in Paris, the slaves in Guadeloupe were set free. However, a reactionary regime was installed at the beginning of the 19th century and slavery was re-established in July 1802. There were bloody riots, and many Africans preferred to commit suicide rather than submit to slavery once again. Finally in 1848 the slaves were freed once more, largely due to the efforts of Victor Schoelcher, who was subsequently elected deputy for Guadeloupe.

Guadeloupe was blockaded in the Second World War because it sided with the Vichy Government, but soon after the war Guadeloupe, like Martinique and French Guyana on the South American coast, became a French overseas *département*, with the same status as the mainland *départements*.

Flora and Fauna

Guadeloupe is a geographical oddity because the butterfly's two wings are islands of completely different geological origin, separated by a small stretch of sea, the Rivière Salée. It is the meeting point of the two island chains that make up the Lesser Antilles—an inner chain of tall volcanic peaks that runs from Grenada up to Saba and the outer ring of coral islands from Marie Galante through Grande-Terre to St Martin and Anguilla.

Still odder are the names of the two islands: Basse-Terre and Grande-Terre. You might think that Grande-Terre would be the taller mountainous island, smothered in tropical rainforest, and that Basse-Terre would be lower. It is the other way around. There is a logical explanation, originating in now obscure sailing terminology. Basse-Terre is simply the 'lower ground' with regard to the prevailing wind. The pattern is repeated in the islands of the Saints, where Terre-de-Bas is downwind of Terre-de-Haut.

Guadeloupe can offer the best of Caribbean flora in its two halves. Grande-Terre's coast is lined with mangrove bushes and the white coral beaches for which the Caribbean is famous. And in Basse-Terre there is the spectacular beauty of the rainforest as well as the attraction of the Soufrière volcano.

The **Parc National** covers some 12,000 acres of the Basse-Terre mountains and they are as fertile as any in the Windwards. In the upper branches of the rainforest is another forest of hanging plants and explosive greenery—orchids and cycads, lianas grappling upwards to reach the sunlight and dropping aerial roots. Here you will see Guadeloupe's three hummingbirds and the woodpecker, a *tapeur* in French, and maybe the Hercules beetle, a 6-inch monster that makes a metallic clanking noise. The stunted elfin woodland in the windswept heights of the mountains has a whole new flora of dwarf palms and creepers.

Racing among the jumbled mountains are endless waterfalls that tumble into rockpools; ideal spots for a dip. There are lakes, hot springs, and in the south, the curiosity of the volcanic peak itself, where the ground steams constantly. The mountains are also crossed by a series of tracks, many of which make a good day's walk. Some leave from and return to **La Maison de la Forêt** on road D23, others are more adventurous and cross from one side of the island to the other (see 'Basse-Terre'). Guided tours can be arranged through the **Organisation des Guides de Montagne de la Caraïbe** (© 80 05 79) and the

Office National des Forêts, Jardin Botanique, 97100 Basse-Terre (✆ 80 24 25, fax 80 05 46).

There is little wildlife on Guadeloupe, but what there is can be seen in the zoo on **La Route de la Traversée** (D23) that cuts across the middle of the park. In the hills you might be lucky enough to see the *raton laveur*, the racoon, or an *agouti*, a little mammal like a guinea pig introduced by man into many of the islands. On the lower land of Grande-Terre the flora and fauna are completely different and you will see egrets and endless doves on the rolling mornes, and sandpipers, snipe and yellowlegs (greater and lesser) around the mangrove swamps. On the coast there are pelicans and tropicbirds. You can find these, alongside a host of crabs and other crustaceans in the **Réserve Naturelle de Grand Cul de Sac Marin,** 650 acres of mangrove and swamp and 850 acres of marine park.

Getting There

✆ (590)–

Like Martinique, the main airline of Guadeloupe is Air France (✆ 82 60 00). Air Guadeloupe (✆ 82 47 00) runs inter-island services from the airport at Le Raizet, a couple of miles from Pointe-à-Pitre.

By Air from Europe: There are daily flights on Air France from Paris and a weekly service from Marseille and Lyon. There are also charter flights on AOM (✆ 83 12 12), Air Liberté (✆ 93 08 58) and Corsair (✆ 90 36 36) from Paris and other French cities.

By Air from North America: Air France serves Guadeloupe from Miami and connections from the USA can also be made via San Juan in Puerto Rico which is linked to Guadeloupe by American Eagle. From Canada there are flights from Montreal on Air Canada.

By Air from other Caribbean Islands: Air France has many daily flights to Martinique. There are also services on LIAT (✆ 82 12 26), Air Guadeloupe, Air France, Air St Barthélémy (✆ 91 44 76) and Winair to San Juan, Antigua, Sint Maarten (both airports), St Barts, Dominica.

By Boat: Two companies run ferries between Guadeloupe and Martinique, touching Dominica *en route*: **Caribbean Express** (✆ 83 12 45, fax 91 11 05) at Quai Gatine in Pointe-à-Pitre and **Madikera** (✆ 91 60 87, fax 82 15 62), at La Darse in central Pointe-à-Pitre.

Getting Around

The public **bus** system is a good way to get around Guadeloupe and it reaches all major towns, eventually. The buses can usually be heard before they are seen, as they are all equipped with extensive stereo systems. If you want to get on one, simply wave it down and if there is space the driver will stop. You will get to know the music of Guadeloupe, and your fellow passengers, well. There are bus-stops, but it is not necessary to use them unless you want to escape from the sun; to get off, you must either yell *Arrêt!*, or press the buzzer, which usually sounds like an air-raid siren. Buses leave when they have enough passengers and run from dawn until about 6pm. On Sundays and on public holidays the public transport system packs up in mid-afternoon and you can quite easily be stranded.

If you are catching a bus from Pointe-à-Pitre, your departure point will depend on the destination. The route along the south coast of Grande-Terre (Gosier Fr8, St Anne Fr10, St François Fr15) is served from near the **Place de la Victoire**, on the eastern edge of La Darse, next to the ferries. To the northern part of Grande-Terre, buses depart from the **Mortenol Station**, across the dual carriageway from the Centre des Arts. Buses to the airport leave from the town centre, on rue Peynier, cost Fr9.

If you are headed for Basse-Terre (island), all buses leave from the Bergeverin Station on **boulevard Chanzy**. Ask around for the correct bus; some go just to Lamentin or around the northern coast to Deshaies, others turn south and run down the eastern coast and on to Basse-Terre, the island capital. The trip to Basse-Terre takes around two hours and costs Fr30 (Fr25 to Trois-Rivières). The last bus in both directions between the two major towns departs at around 6pm. Miss it and you are stranded.

Guadeloupean **taxis** work on a fixed-rate and can be picked up in Pointe-à-Pitre (place de la Victoire, boulevard Chanzy and others), at the airport and at all major hotels. Some taxi drivers speak some English and will give an impromptu tour. They are happy to take a party out for the day at around Fr500 for a half-day and Fr800 for a full day (four people). Some taxi numbers are: **Radio-taxis CDL** (✆ 20 74 74) and **SOS Taxis** (✆ 83 63 94).

Sightseeing trips, taking in the principal sights on one or other island and usually with a lazy lunch-stop scheduled, can be arranged through the travel agents in town, or through any hotel lobby. Try **Petrelluzzi Travel**, rue Gambetta (✆ 90 37 77), **Jet Tours** (✆ 82 26 44) and **Georges Marie Gabrielle Voyages** (✆ 82 05 38). **Héli-Inter Caraïbes** (✆ 91 45 00) offers sight-seeing by helicopter, zooming the Chutes de Carbet and the Pointe des Chateaux.

Car hire: Guadeloupe is a large island and to get the best of its great variety, you really need a car for at least some of the time. With the benefits of the EEC, the roads in Guadeloupe are (usually) quite good, and

Guadeloupean drivers push them to the limit. A foreign driving licence is valid for 20 days (a year's driving experience is necessary) and after that an international driving licence is needed. Avoid driving in central Pointe-à-Pitre if humanly possible. Deposit is around US$300, unless you pay by credit card. Rates start at about US$35 per day. Some firms with offices at the airport are: **Avis** (✆ 82 43 37), **Europcar** (✆ 82 50 51), **Carpentier** (✆ 82 35 11) and **Karukera Car** (✆ 83 78 79). Motorbike rental is possible through **Moto Guadeloupe** (✆ 82 17 50) and **Vespa Sun** (91 30 36) in the city or **Easy Rent** (✆ 88 76 27) in St François.

Tourist Information

Tourist information offices abroad are at these addresses: **France**: 1 place Paul Verlaine, 92100 Boulogne (✆ 46 04 00 88, fax 46 04 74 03); **US**: 610 Fifth Ave, New York, NY 10020 (✆ 315 0726); **Canada**: 1 Durdan St, West, Suite 2405, Ontario NS123 (✆ 593 6327); **Germany**: Pettsmannstraße 58, 6000 Frankfurt am Main 1 (✆ 28 33 15, fax 28 75 44).

On island, there are Tourist Information Offices in: **Pointe-à-Pitre**, Office Départementale, 5 square de la Banque, 97110 Pointe-à-Pitre (✆ 590 82 09 30, fax 83 89 22) just off the place de la Victoire opposite la Darse; **Basse-Terre**, in the Maison du Port (✆ 81 24 83); and **St François**, on the avenue de l'Europe (✆ 88 48 74). Office hours are 8–5 weekdays and 8–noon Sat. There is also a small information desk at **Le Raizet** airport, which is very helpful. The Tourist Board produces a booklet called *Bonjour Guadeloupe*, full of useful facts like where to get your hair cut as well as advice on beaches and nightclubs. If you're on a gastronomic steeplechase, the pocket-sized *Ti Gourmet* has restaurant information and *Sentiers Gourmands* lists the finest creole restaurants on the archipelago.

To **dial** directly to Guadeloupe, the **IDD code** is **590**, followed by six digits. On the island, the six digits suffice.

In a medical **emergency**, there is a casualty room at the main Pointe-à-Pitre **Hospital** at Abymes, emergency number ✆ 89 11 20. The **police** can be reached on ✆ 82 13 17 in Pointe-à-Pitre.

Guadeloupe is generally lower-key than Martinique, but you may find that the Guadeloupeans are quite private. This is not to be confused with unfriendliness, because if you ask for assistance, even in faltering French, they will usually go out of their way to help you. A refreshing fact, in comparison to other islands, is an almost complete absence of hustlers, who can be trying elsewhere. Here, the state guarantees a certain standard of living and so there are very few of them.

Money

The **banks** open 8–noon and 2–4 on weekdays. Some banks open on Saturdays; try Crédit Agricole and Banque Nationale de Paris. Credit cards will be accepted anywhere that is accustomed to tourists. However, if you go off the beaten track be sure to take francs, the legal currency of Guadeloupe (US$1 = Fr5.5 approx). Hotels will change money, at a slightly inferior rate to the banks. In restaurants service is *compris*. **Shops** keep similar hours to the banks in the morning and take a similar two-hour lunch, but usually stay open until 6pm.

Beaches

For soft white sand brushed by palm trees and susurrating waves, go to the southern side of Grande-Terre. Some beaches become quite crowded because the area is fairly built-up with hotels, but you can find seclusion at the eastern end towards Pointe des Chateaux and in the north of Grande-Terre. Take a picnic with you because there are fewer cafés there. Alternatively, there are the less typical beaches on the northwestern coast of Basse-Terre, where the sand is golden brown and comes in large granules. This area is much less populous, but has some excellent beaches which have a wilder charm about them.

Bathing topless is quite normal in Guadeloupe (though the West Indians themselves do not usually do it) and bathing nude is permitted in some places. All beaches are public and most hotels will allow you to use their facilities.

On the south coast of Grande-Terre, Gosier, with its strip of hotels, is best avoided unless you wish to hire windsurfing equipment or go waterskiing. Opposite the town, a few hundred yards out to sea is a small island, the **Ilet de Gosier** (where people generally bathe nude). Trips to the island can be arranged from the waterfront or in the hotels in the area.

Petit Havre and the other coves close to it are less populous and worth investigating. Heaped with blinding white sand, **Caravelle Beach** is crowded and popular. At one end is Guadeloupe's Club Med, a factory of entertainment, patrolled by peak-capped security monitors—just don't overstep the line of the high-tide mark. The main beach at St Anne is very popular, though you may have to pay for parking. Some of the island's best beaches are beyond **St François**, on both sides of the tapering spit of land towards Pointe des Chateaux. Try **Anse à la Gourde** and the 1¼ miles (2km) of **la Plage des Salines**. There is a nudist beach at **Plage Tarare**.

The eastern coast of Grande-Terre is not usually good for swimming because of the force of the Atlantic; however there is a reef-protected beach at **Le Moule**, with bars and plenty of crowds. There is a secluded strip towards the northern point, **La Porte d'Enfer** and two fine beaches on the northwestern coast, **Anse du Souffleur** at Port-Louis and the **Anse Laborde** just out of Anse-Bertrand.

The spurs and shoulders thrown off the mountains of Basse-Terre produce small protected coves between steep headlands and in the northwest you will find a string of excellent beaches: **La Plage de Cluny**, near La Pointe Allègre, **Tillette**, **La Perle** and finally **La Grande Anse**, a huge bay backed with tall palms and stacked with golden sand, one of the most attractive beaches on the island.

The beach at **Malendure**, opposite Pigeon Island, is very busy even though the sand is dark. There is diving over on Pigeon Island and of course you can always bargain for an African carving.

Beach Bars

In Grande-Terre you will find bars and bistros along the popular beachfronts, to retreat to when the sun is at its height. St Anne and St François have a string of waterfront cafés where you can cast a critical eye at the windsurfers' technique over a beer. You can have a good day out at the **Plage de l'Autre Bord** outside Le Moule, where there are a number of beach bars and small huts for a local meal.

In easy-going Basse-Terre you will find beach bars spread out in the isolated bays. On the **Plage de Malendure** there are snackwagons and a pretty bar above the sand called **Chez Toulouse**, and on the mile-long strip of **Grand Anse** near Deshaies there is a crêperie under the palms. But the best of all is **Chez Françine** on the Plage de Cluny at the northwestern tip of the island. Françine has a wooden house and a covered terrace swallowed in banana and bougainvillea underneath the palms. There are deck chairs on the sand and soursop or coconut milk to accompany *accras* (codfish batterballs). Well worth stopping for.

Sailing

Guadeloupe is a great place in which to base yourself for a sailing holiday. All the facilities of the developed French Caribbean island are there (from the many different sorts of cheeses on sale in the supermarkets to the chandleries and boatyards), but there are also the smaller island to explore. The main centres are in the flatter easterly island of Grande Terre, but if you are travelling up or down the island chain there are facilities in Basse Terre too. There are ports of entry in Pointe-à-Pitre (in the Bas du Fort marina), in Basse Terre, Deshaies and Marie Galante.

Close to Pointe-à-Pitre is the Bas du Fort marina, where there are hundreds of slips, with easy availability of fuel and water; nearby are a supermarket and other shops and a string of waterfront bars and restaurants; and in the east there is a full service marina at St François. Day sails along the southern coast of Grande Terre include the Ilet du Gosier and St Anne.

On the west coast of Basse Terre you will find a marina a couple of miles south of the town of Basse Terre, where you can take on water, fuel and ice. There are supermarkets and shops in town and repair facilities in the marina. Near the northwestern tip of the island is a protected anchorage between two large hills, the bay of Deshaies, an ideal starting point for the journey north. There are no specialist yachting facilities, but there are supermarkets and a bakery where you can stock up with French food. A popular stopover (either daytime or overnight) in between the two major anchorages is at Pigeon.

Yachts can be chartered, bareboat or crewed, for a day, a week or more (for sailing trips to Marie Galante, the Saints and Dominica), from the companies in the Port de Plaisance marina in Bas-du-Fort, just outside Pointe-à-Pitre: **Moorings Antilles Françaises** (✆ 90 81 81, fax 90 84 87), **Star Voyages Antilles** (✆ 90 86 26, fax 90 85 73), **Cap Sud** (✆ 90 76 70, fax 90 76 77), and **ATM Yacht**, with crewed and bare-boats, based in Point–à–Pitre (✆ 90 92 02). There are boatyards and chandleries at the Bas du Fort Marina (✆ 90 84 85) and at the Rivière Sens marina near Basse-Terre.

Watersports

Windsurfing (*planche-à-voile*) is very popular and equipment can be hired all along the southern coast of Grande-Terre. The best winds for advanced sailors are in St François, on the Plage du Lagon, where you will see the sailboards beating back and forth on the sideshore winds; board hire through **Jumbo Fun Board** (✆ 88 60 60). Over on the north side in Le Moule, an offshore reef causes waves; hire through **Emeraudes et Diamants** (✆ 23 52 67), about Fr60 per hour. It is sometimes possible to **surf** in this area. **Waterskiing** can be arranged on the calmer beaches (there is a club, AGSN, in the Baie Mahault, ✆ 26 17 47) and hotel watersports shops also have smaller sailing dinghies like sunfish for hire to non-guests. **Kayaks** are often available.

If you are the sort for a more leisurely tour, rum punch in hand on a glass-bottomed boat, *Paoka* runs visits to the islands in the Cul de Sac Marin (℃ 25 74 78) from Baie Mahault and **Nautilus** (℃ 98 89 08) takes day cruises to the Ilet Pigeon from the Plage de Malendure. **King Papyrus** (℃ 90 92 98) leaves from the dock at Bas-du-Fort on daytime jaunts of tee-ree-ree and walking the plank and night-time sails where the mountains of Basse-Terre loom like Titans in the moonlight.

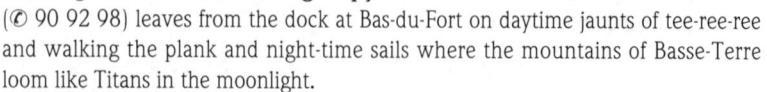

Deep-sea fishing can also be arranged, day and half-day tours in search of tuna and kingfish in the Caribbean Sea. This is particularly big on the west coast, where you can go out with **Le Rocher de Malendure** (℃ 98 70 84, fax 98 89 92) in Malendure. In Grande-Terre you can contact **Caraïbe Pêche** (℃ 90 97 51) in the Bas du Fort marina.

Diving (*plongée sous-marine*) is also at its best on the west coast of Basse-Terre off Bouillante, where there is a marine reserve established by Jacques Cousteau around the Ilet de Pigeon. Contact **Les Heures Saines** (℃ 98 86 63, fax 98 77 76), who dive under PADI and NAUI as well as CMAS, the French system, in Malendure, or **Aux Aquanautes Antillais** (℃ 98 87 30, fax 90 11 85). *Single-tank dives cost around Fr200 or US$35.*

Other Sports

On land, exploration of the National Park is best done on foot and there are two main drop-off points: **La Traversée**, the D23 road across the middle of the island and the foothillsof **La Soufrière**. Guided walking trips can be arranged through the **Organisation des Guides de Montagne de la Caraïbe**, whose offices are at the Maison Forestière in Matouba (℃ 80 05 79). Other adventurous tours—canoeing and river-hiking—can be arranged through **Espace Loisirs**, 97118 St François (℃ 88 71 93, fax 88 44 01), **Parfum d'Aventure**, 97180 St Anne (℃ 88 47 62, fax 88 47 91) and for personal treatment, **Emeraude Guadeloupe**, 97120 St Claude (℃ 80 16 09, fax 81 21 17). These companies also arrange tours by **mountain bike**, called VTT in French.

On Grande-Terre a number of other options are available, including **riding**, on the beaches or for a day's picnic, possible through **La Ferme de Campêche** (℃ 82 11 54) and **Le Relais du Moulin** (℃ 88 13 78), on the road between St Anne and

St François. On the edge of St François there is an 18-hole Robert Trent Jones **golf** course (© 88 41 87).

Grande-Terre—Pointe-à-Pitre

The town of Pointe-à-Pitre, the commercial capital of the island and major port, lies on the southern side of Grande-Terre, in the Petit Cul-de-Sac, the inlet formed as the two parts of the island have pushed together. It has a population of 26,000 concentrated in the centre of the town, but 100,000 altogether including the suburbs along the coastline. The town first began to grow in the 1760s, during the British occupation of Guadeloupe, and supposedly takes its name from a Dutchman named Pieter, who had lived on the point near La Darse a century earlier.

Pointe-à-Pitre is hardly an attractive town, though some two-storey wooden buildings do give an inkling of its former mercantile pride. It has developed haphazardly, upset by earthquakes (1843), fires and hurricanes, the latest of which, Hurricane Hugo, cut through in 1989. In the centre, the old Pointe-à-Pitre has a similar charm to that of a French provincial town, with buildings with louvred windows and balconies close on one another and the smells of coffee and pâtisseries exuding on to the street below. Beyond the Boulevard Chanzy, the newest *quartiers* have sprung up in a crop of ferro-concrete monstrosities from the fifties, proof against earthquake perhaps, but incredibly ugly. They have forced the traditional West Indian shacks farther out along the coast.

La Darse (meaning harbour) is still the heart of town-life. Markets appear on the wharves at dawn, as the ferries and the buses come and go, dropping people off for the day's work. Just above la Darse is the main square, **place de la Victoire**, whose name commemorates victory over the British by Victor Hugues and the revolutionary army in 1794. In his reign of terror, Victor Hugues erected the guillotine here, but now the square (partly given over to a car park, unfortunately) is more peaceful. It is planted with royal palms and *flamboyant* trees (some sadly torn out by Hurricane Hugo), and is lined with cafés, where the *Pointus* (the inhabitants of Pointe-à-Pitre) like to take the evening air. Behind the square, on the rue Alexandre Isaac, is the **Cathedral of St Peter and St Paul**, constructed in Empire style in 1807 and newly repaired after Hurricane Hugo.

The main street, **rue Frébault**, lined with shops full of goods from mainland France, leads through the commercial heart of the town, down to **Marché de St Antoine**, an iron market with a red corrugated-iron roof. Guadeloupe may be one of the most developed islands in the area, but this is a truly Caribbean institution. It pulses from early morning, with the smell of fruits and spices, and offers anything from avocados to earrings for sale. Even for French speakers, the joking and haggling in creole is impossible to keep up with.

The **Musée Schoelcher**, *open weekdays 9–11.30 and 2–5.30, and Sat mornings until noon; adm*, is set in an impressive townhouse with a double staircase on the rue Peynier and contains some of the personal collections of the abolitionist, assembled in his fifteen-year struggle to outlaw slavery in the French colonies. General exhibits include a 'magnetic purifying filter' that provided clean drinkable water in the 19th century. Another leading light in Guadeloupe is celebrated in the **Musée St-John Perse**, *open weekdays 8.30–12.30 and 2.30–5.30 and on Sat mornings, adm*, set in an elaborate late 19th-century creole house on the rue Nozières. The poet and diplomat, Alexis Saint-Léger was born on the island of a long-standing family and was awarded the Nobel Prize for Literature in 1960.

The Southern Coast of Grande-Terre

Protected from the Atlantic, the southern coast has the mildest climate on the island and has become the centre for the tourist industry. The action of the waves on the limestone coral shores has pushed up white-sand beaches, and on them the hotels have mushroomed. The main areas are Bas du Fort, just out of Pointe-à-Pitre to the south, and the towns of Gosier, St Anne and St François.

Leaving Pointe-à-Pitre on the road to Gosier (N4), you pass the buildings of the University and come to Bas du Fort, where there are a number of tourist apartment blocks around a marina. Round the point is the Guadeloupe **Aquarium**, which exhibits tropical fish from all over the world in the twenty or so tanks. You will see lion fish with fancy-dress tail and fins, fish that shine as though lit by ultra violet in a discotheque and a trapezoidal character called *lactophrys triqueter*, who will spit poison at you. It culminates in the walk-through shark tunnel. *Open 9–7, adm expensive*. Commanding la Grande Baie, a little farther round and covering the approaches to Pointe-à-Pitre, is the **Fort Fleur d'Epée**, *open daily 9–6, adm free*. These coral-rock ramparts cut into the hillside were stormed and gallantly defended in the days of Empire but are now visited mainly by picnickers and lovers.

The town of **Gosier**, a centre of tourism on the island, spreads along the shore for several miles and the hotels have encrusted around the old town, cluttering the hillside down to the beaches and bringing with them a plethora of restaurants, bars and discotheques. The name Gosier derives from the *grand gosier*, or pelican, which can be seen all over the Lesser Antilles and which occasionally fishes off the Ilet de Gosier, a couple of hundred yards off-shore.

St Anne and **St François** are two other towns whose incomes have switched from fishing to sport fishing, though among the motorboats with huge fishing-rods sticking into the air, you will still see *gommiers*, the brightly painted local fishing boats. Both towns still have a promenade, where fishermen's houses and restaurants mingle, looking across the sea towards Dominica.

pelicans

In the early years of the 18th century, when the *Grands Fonds* inland from here were carpeted with 10ft of sugar-cane, St Anne was a commercial centre, but by the end of the century it was already in decline, its prosperity destroyed by Guadeloupe's internal turmoil. On the dock at St François, where the yachts are moored, you will see local West Indian life as the ferry from the island of La Désirade puts in. Its inhabitants are mainly farmers and they bring their sheep, stuffed into sacks with just their heads sticking out, to sell in Guadeloupe.

Beyond St François, Grande-Terre tapers to a spike pointing out into the Atlantic Ocean and culminates in the cliffs of **Pointe des Châteaux**. The wind is strong off the ocean here and the waves have carved eerie shapes out of the rocks, including a blowhole that answers moments after a wave has disappeared under the lip of the rock. The landscape looks a little like Brittany, as though Guadeloupe had simply broken off the west coast of France and been transported 4000 miles west. From the cross on the point, high above the waves, it is possible to see La Désirade, a table-mountain emerging from the sea 6 miles (10km) away, and the uninhabited islands of Petite Terre. On the northern side of the peninsula is the **Plage de Tarare**, a nudist beach.

The N5 leads north from St François through the canefields to **Le Moule**, on the Atlantic coast, where the waves come barrelling in relentlessly—suffering continuously from the Atlantic winds, the houses were built with no doors facing east. The town knew some prosperity as the principal port on Guadeloupe's eastern coast in the sugar years, when ships would edge in on the waves to the anchor ports still visible, but now it is poor and broken down. Le Moule was wasted by Hurricane Hugo in 1989 and many of the buildings were destroyed. The **Musée Edgar Clerc**, *open 9–12.30 and 2–5.30, closed Wed afternoon, adm*, is devoted to pre-Columbian history with Arawak archaeological remains on view.

A number of roads lead back to Pointe-à-Pitre among the limestone hillocks and through the rolling forested countryside, the **Grands Fonds**, where some white families have lived since they fled there in the turmoil of the Revolution.

The Southern Coast of Grande-Terre

Northern Grande-Terre

Alternatively, you can continue into the northern area of Grande-Terre, where the land lies lower and in places is covered with mangrove swamp. It is fertile land, and everywhere you will see the cone-shaped shells of abandoned windmills, some still with their crushing gear discarded inside. In **Morne-à-l'Eau** is one of the best examples of the French West Indian chequerboard cemetery, with acres of black and white tiles on the mausolea. On the Festival of All Saints there is a ceremony in which the whole graveyard is lit with candles. At **Port Louis**, there is a view over the Grand Cul-de-Sac Marin enclosed between the two halves of the island. Basse-Terre rises spectacularly, grey-green in the distance, topped with vast clouds.

On the northwestern coast of the island is **Anse Bertrand**, another town that was most prosperous in the sugar heyday of the 18th century. The most northerly point on the island is **La Pointe de la Grande Vigie**, where the cliffs stand 250ft above sea level. On a clear day Antigua, 35 miles (56km) north, is visible from the point. Close by is **La Porte d'Enfer** (Hell's Gate), a massive fissure in the cliffs.

Basse-Terre (the Island)

A coastal road circles Guadeloupe's mountainous volcanic wing and, through the middle of the island, La Traversée cuts a path up and over the rainforest to the Caribbean coast. Leaving Pointe-à-Pitre, the N1 crosses to Basse-Terre over the **Rivière Salée**. Before the two parts of Guadeloupe were linked by bridge in 1906, the crossing was made by ferry. Once, a party of Guadeloupeans were making for a ball in Pointe-à-Pitre when they were swept out to sea. Garbed in evening dress, they drifted for five days before washing up on St Thomas in the Virgin Islands.

The main road (N1) to the town of **Basse-Terre** takes a left turn and travels down the eastern coast, beneath the towering mountainsides, before crossing over to the Caribbean coast near the southern tip. **Sainte-Marie** is thought to be the place where Columbus landed on his second voyage in 1493, meeting his first Caribs.

Capesterre takes its name from its position (*Capesterre* means windward in French, and the village is upwind of *Basse-Terre*). In the town is one of the last *manioqueries*, where cassava flour is grated from manioc tubers. The Indians once used fan coral as a grater, before straining out the poisonous juices in the wet mix.

The **Plantation Grand Café**, a working banana plantation, *open Wed–Fri, 9–12, adm*, is worth a visit. The tour includes an explanation of the process of cultivation, gathering and washing, sorting and boxing, a visit of the plantation house and, not to be missed, an alley with about 20 different species of banana and plantain from all over the world.

As you leave the town of Capesterre you pass along the **Allée du Manoir**, a tunnel of magnificent royal palms. They stand like living grey columns (the telegraph wires were once simply nailed into them), soaring to 100ft, bursting with spiked fronds and tapering in a single 10ft spine.

Inland and uphill from St Sauveur, at the end of the **D4** road that winds up through the banana plantations into the rainforest, are the three **Chutes de Carbet**. Two of the falls cascade into rockpools from over 300ft. The middle one falls 350ft and can be reached on a well-marked path, and the lowest tumbles 65ft into a pool where you can take a dip after the short walk. From here the path leads on up into the rainforest, towards the summit of the Soufrière, a three-hour walk. It is these falls that Columbus mentions in his diary when he talks of 'a waterfall of considerable breadth, which fell from so high that it seemed to come from the sky'. Back down the hill, there are several lakes just off the road: the **Etang Zombi** and the **Grand Etang**. The **As de Pique**, a lake in the shape of an ace of spades, is beyond the serene Grand Etang.

The N1 coastal road continues to the village of **Trois-Rivières**. Down the hill and close to the harbour (where boats leave for the Islands of the Saints) is the **Parc Archéologique des Roches Gravées,** *open 9–5, adm*, where the main exhibit is a series of maniacal squiggles and outlandish faces on a rockface. They were carved by Arawak Indians before the Caribs bludgeoned their way on to the island in about AD 1000. The rock is set in a small botanical garden, in which plants are marked, including those used by the Arawaks. Another few miles brings you through a ravine to the Caribbean coast and down into Basse-Terre.

Basse-Terre (the Town)

The town of Basse-Terre (14,000 inhabitants), the administrative capital of Guadeloupe, lies on the coast in the shadow of towering volcanic mountains. It is just 20 miles (33km) from Pointe-à-Pitre as the crow flies, but the journey takes about two hours by road because it twists so laboriously over its 44-mile (70km) length. Some of the route is impossibly steep and windy, but take heart; lines painted on the road show that the Guadeloupeans actually compete in cycling races along here.

Founded by Houël in 1643, Basse-Terre is built on a hill and is much more attractive than the commercial city of Pointe-à-Pitre. It retains an antique feel that the other town has lost. Just above the port, stone houses with upper storeys of shingle-wood tiles and clapboard crowd over the narrow streets. The imposing official buildingsand town houses with wrought-iron balconies give it a gentrified air.

Behind the activity of the main streets, on the few areas of flat ground, there are two main squares: the **jardin Pichon** and the **place du Champ d'Arbaud**, surrounded by the old buildings of Basse-Terre. Covering the harbour from the southern edge of town, **Fort Delgrès**, *open daily 9–5, adm free*, is another lumbering colossus of a fortress with huge embrasures that now stand unemployed. It expanded steadily from its beginnings in about 1650, when Houël erected the first battlements and has also seen plenty of action. There are acres of ramparts and it is easy to imagine the roar of the cannon and the smell of cordite. There is a small museum in the fort, giving a good run-down of its history and of Basse-Terre.

Like any prosperous Caribbean port, the town has spread up the hill where the wealthier inhabitants take a cooler and loftier view of the proceedings in the city centre. The district of **St Claude**, strung out over the bends of a sinuous mountain road, contains some the most attractive houses on the island. A side road leads to the town of **Matouba**, which has a large East Indian population (who came here as indentured labourers in the last century). From the village, the **Trace Victor Hugues** leads up into the rainforested mountains and on to La Maison de la Forêt or down to Petit Bourg. *It is a demanding 8-hour, 19-mile (30km) walk.*

High in the rainforest is the **Maison du Volcan**, a museum, *open 10–6, adm free*. It is set in a garden in a beautiful creole villa, and tells of vulcanism in general and La Soufrière, which lurks just above it, in particular. Also close by are the **Bains Jaunes**, hot water springs, and the **Chutes du Galion**, more waterfalls. The road leads farther up on to the slopes of the volcano itself, an extremely steep path, wide enough for one car, that stops 1000ft below the craters, at **Savane à Mulets**.

La Soufrière lives up to its name, as the summit is a morass of sulphurous fumaroles and solidified lava flows where plants are poisoned before they take root. It is still quite active, constantly letting off steam and occasionally rumbling and showering the neighbourhood with flakes of volcanic dust. It erupted in 1695 and in 1797. In 1837 the whole of Basse-Terre quaked but

tropical paradise

this was followed by 120 years of silence until 1956 and then considerable activity in the 1970s. There were dust and gas explosions, geysers appeared from lakes, the rivers turned into mud and lava flows and at the height there were a thousand tremors a day. At one point 70,000 people were evacuated from the southern end of Basse-Terre.

From Savane à Mulets you can make the summit in under three hours, on a path that passes between boulders tossed out by the eruptions. At 4813ft (1467m), La Soufrière is the highest point in the eastern Caribbean. When the clouds are not in attendance (though they makes the whole climb that much more eerie), the view from the top is a cracker.

D23—La Traversée, Basse-Terre

La Traversée (D23) cuts across the middle of the island of Basse-Terre, climbing to the twin pyramids of the Mamelles (at 2500ft) and emerging on the Caribbean coast at Mahaut. The road gives an excellent view of the rainforest in all its luxuriance, with occasional panoramic flashes between the trees.

At Vernou, a retreat where the wealthy have built their villas and set them in tropical gardens, is the **Saut de la Lézarde** (the lizard's leap), a small waterfall and rockpool. Higher in the rainforest, where it becomes dark because the canopy is so thick and grotesque mosses creep on the floor, is the **Cascade des Ecrevisses**, a tame fall where the Guadeloupeans like to go for a day out at the weekend.

La Maison de la Forêt, *open daily, 10–5, adm free*, is a museum that describes Guadeloupe's natural life, from the *pâte calcaire* of Grande-Terre and early volcanic rumblings 15 million years ago to the flying cycads and bromeliads of today's tropical rainforest. It is well set out and explains the forest ecosystem. There are a number of marked walks through the forest that start and finish at the museum.

The Traversée reaches its summit at the Mamelles, from where there is a spectacular view, and then descends in hairpins to the coast. From the heights a number of paths lead off into the forest, some of them the old *traces* that were walked by the *porteuses* with huge loads on their heads. The **trace des crêtes** leads down to the Caribbean coast near Marigot and the **route Forestière de Grosse Montagne** leads back towards Pointe-à-Pitre. **Morne-à-Louis**, unfortunately scarred by its television transmitter, offers more views over the cumulus of peaks in mountainous Basse-Terre. Just down the hill from here is the **Parc Zoologique et Botanique**, where a lacklustre series of cages among the creeping vines exhibit Guadeloupe's limited fauna and unlimited flora. La Traversée joins the N2 on the Côte-sous-le-Vent (the rain-shadow), the Caribbean coast, at Mahaut.

N2—Around the Northern Tip of Basse-Terre

From the Rivière Salée the **N2** runs to the northern tip of the island and then down the length of the western coast. To begin with the land is blanketed with sugarcane, but this changes as the road passes into the shadow of the mountains.

The **Domaine de Valombreuse**, *open 9–5, adm*, is a working garden laid out over 10 acres where you can see an overwhelming variety of tropical flora: spice gardens, orchids, exotic shrubs and flowering trees and a humid river ravine with tall trees and creepers. At the **Domaine de Séverin** you will see a working sugarcane crusher, with a conveyor about 2ft wide driven by a water-wheel (it gives an idea of the labour intensity of this old industry). There is a small museum and shop next door, where you can buy the eventual product, rum. The **Musée du Rhum**, *open daily 9–5*, close by in Bellevue above Sainte Rose, continues the story. It gives a history of cane—sweet bamboo—from Persian times to its use in Europe in the sweet drinks of the 17th century and of course in rum. Plenty of rum paraphernalia—machetes, carts and copper boilers. Rum is on sale.

Pointe-Allègre is the northernmost tip of Basse-Terre and it was the spot chosen by the first settlers of Guadeloupe in June 1635. It was a shaky start, as they were constantly battling the Caribs. Eventually they decamped and headed for the southwestern coast at Basse-Terre.

Deshaies is an attractive fishing village that lies in a small bay, from which the road winds up and over to **Pointe-Noire**, a town dating from the 17th century. The **Maison du Bois**, *open 9–5, adm*, is a small museum just south of the town, with exhibits of traditional machinery, tools and furniture from the French Antilles, all in tropical woods. The secrets of boat-building, straining the poisonous juice from manioc to make cassava meal, and the styles of gingerbread woodwork on the eaves of Caribbean houses are displayed. It is worth a visit.

The **trace des contrabandiers** (smugglers' route) leads across the mountain range in the centre of the island from the Maison du Bois. A three-hour walk through the forest passes beneath Morne Jeanneton and will bring you into the hills above Lamentin. At **Mahaut**, La Traversée (D23) cuts across the island on the quickest route back to Pointe-à-Pitre. Alternatively, the N2 continues down the coast to Malendure, the popular beach and dropping-off point for the Pigeon marine reserve. Founded in 1636, **Vieux Habitants** was supposedly named by its early inhabitants, who moved here after serving out their indenture (a three-year contract in exchange for their passage to the island), to avoid confusion with those who still had time to serve. From here the road continues to Basse-Terre.

Festivals

Carnival gets going at the very beginning of the year and there are parades and competitions all over the island each weekend as Lent approaches. It all culminates in a three-day street party on *Lundi Gras*, *Mardi Gras* and *Mercredi des Cendres* (Ash Wednesday), when the spirit of *vaval* is burned for another year. The whole thing is taken very seriously and it is fun to follow on with the streams of dancers as they parade around the towns, dressed as imps and buccaneers, shuffling and dancing to the relentless beat of drum-driven French Caribbean music.

Other celebrations include Bastille Day (14 July) and musical Saint Cecilia's day (22 Nov) and each individual town's saint's day, the *fête patronale*. One of the Caribbean's most enjoyable spectacles is the **Fête des Cuisinières**, the Cook's festival, which takes place in August in Pointe-à-Pitre, in which island delicacies are dedicated and gastronomic parades take place before the customary over-indulgence in eating and dancing.

© *(590)–*

Where to Stay

Guadeloupe caters for most tastes, with a few havens of discerning grandeur at the top of the range through the big beach hotels to smaller haunts that attract a crowd of independent travellers exploring the island. If you are hopping around, two very useful lists are the *relais créoles*, or inns, and the slightly cheaper *gîtes*—both c/o Office du Tourisme, 5 square de la Banque, 97110 Pointe-à-Pitre (© 82 09 30, fax 83 89 22). Some of the nicer ones are mentioned in this section, but the list is not complete.

Bas du Fort and Gosier on Grande-Terre are the island's principal resort areas and they have lines of hotels muscling in on beach space. Elsewhere on the southern coast, St Anne has a few beach resorts and St François has lately put in a challenge with several new hotels. After a week on the beach you might like to move to easy-going Basse-Terre, which has some fun *relais* and *gîtes* dotted around the countryside. In larger hotels they will probably speak English, but you will need some French if you step beyond the main tourist areas. Breakfast is usually included in the room rate. A service charge of 10% or 15% will be added to your hotel bill.

Grande-Terre

very expensive

Le Hamak, 97118 St François (© 590 88 59 99, fax 88 41 92) is the most elegant hotel on the island, an enclave of rarefied luxury tucked away on its own just out of the town. The 56 rooms are hidden in magnificent gardens of bougainvillea behind the sand and palms of a man-made beach. It is stately and quiet and lives up to its name—the veranda of every room is slung with a hammock. Flights are possible straight from Antigua to St François airport. If you like a more active beach club in equivalent luxury you can try the nearby annexe of the Méridien hotel, **La Cocoteraie**, PO Box 37, 97118 (© 88 79 81, fax 88 78 33). The 52 suites are in blocks ranged tightly around a huge pool, with dining room and pool bar on islands in the middle. Rooms are brightly decorated in pink, blue and green, or a sort of symphony in pastel. Watersports available. The **Auberge de la Vieille Tour**, Montauban (© 84 23 23 fax 84 33 43), sits on a headland above the sea in Gosier and has recently expanded to 160 rooms, which makes it large, but the setting is still good overlooking attractive grounds that slope towards the hotel's own beach. It retains something of an old colonial air, in the plantation house and the subdued atmosphere of the two restaurants and bar, spiked only by the windsurfers down below and the boutique in the old windmill.

expensive

La Toubana, PO Box 63, 97180 St Anne (© 88 25 78, fax 88 25 57), is one of the most sympathetic hotels on the island. It stands high above a sandy cove and has a very attractive hilltop dining-room terrace looking over the pool and to the islands and on to Dominica (or Club Med the other way). Some entertainment in the evenings. The 32 rooms are scattered in bungalows on the descending hillside, very comfortable with kitchenettes and surrounded by gardens. Some bungalows for four people, tennis court. For a more formal beach hotel surrounded by all the activity of Bas de Fort, try **Hotel Fort Fleur d'Epée**, 97190 Gosier (© 90 40 00, fax 90 99 07). Restaurant above the waves, beauty salon, *pétanque*, all the watersports and evening entertainment. Rooms and suites with all modern comforts: air-conditioning, television.

moderate

The **Relais du Moulin**, Chateaubrun, 97180 St Anne (© 88 23 96, fax 88 03 92), is also set around an old windmill. The 40 rooms, some with kitchenettes, are in bungalows and apartments scattered around charming tropical gardens, and although they are 600 yards from the beach, there is a pool. The inn has a family atmosphere, with tennis, riding and bicycle touring on offer. Moderate to expensive. Another pleasantly unassuming *relais créole* is the **Cap Sud Caraïbes**, route de la Plage, 97190 Gosier (© 85 96 02, fax 85 80 39), on the hill at Petit Havre, halfway between

Gosier and St Anne. A simply designed block stands above a pool on the hillside a few minutes' walk from the Petit Havre beach. Private and friendly. There are two simple but pleasant hotels right on the beach in St Anne. The oddly named but stylish and friendly hotel **Mini Beach** (© 88 21 13, fax 88 26 87) has an elegant colonial foyer with high-backed wicker chairs and a piano. There are six comfortable rooms and three bungalows, all watersports close by. Another nice retreat close by is the **Auberge Le Grand Large** (© 88 20 06, fax 88 16 69), where there are simple rooms in the main house and in colourful bungalows set in a profuse tropical garden (some kitchenettes). **Village Caraïbes Carmelita's**, 97190 Gosier (© 84 28 28, fax 84 58 12), is another trusty option close to the beach in St Felix, with 14 air-conditioned bungalows, some with kitchenettes, in a lawned garden with a pool.

cheap

A charming small hotel on the hill outside Gosier is **Les Flamboyants**, 97190 Gosier (© 84 14 11, fax 84 53 56), with a pool and open gardens out front, which overlook the Ilet de Gosier and Basse-Terre beyond—a moment of calm in the holiday hustle of the tourist town. The main house is an old villa, with trophies, sharks and turtles on the wall. It has 15 rooms, quite simple, with breakfast only, though some have kitchenettes. Also in Gosier, **Serge Hélène Guest House** (© 84 10 25, fax 84 39 49) is an amusing option, where the very simple studios are in a block overlooking a garden of Guadeloupean profusion.

If you need to be in Pointe-à-Pitre, you might try the space-age **Hotel Saint John**, 97110 (© 82 51 57, fax 82 52 61), in which the 41 rooms lurk in a profusion of arches and overhanging eaves. There are two places to stay on the Place de la Victoire: **La Maison de Marie Galante** (© 90 10 41, fax 90 22 75) and the **Hotel Normandie** (© 83 37 15), the latter slightly cheaper. At the **Relais des Antilles**, 38 rue Denfert, 97110 Pointe-à-Pitre (© 83 43 62) there are 10 simple rooms.

Basse-Terre

Here the hotels are a little bit more spread out—this half of Guadeloupe does not have so many of the picture-postcard beaches, but some of the hotels and inns have excellent settings above the water or hidden in the rainforest. Some hotels will have a car ready at the airport if you request it.

moderate

Just off la Traversée (D23) you will find a charming hotel at **L'Auberge de la Distillerie**, 97170 Petit Bourg (© 94 25 91, fax 94 11 91, US reservations ℃ 800 373 6246), which is set on a hillside looking back towards Grande-Terre. Next to the main house stands a large covered terrace with the dining room, pool and occasional discotheque. It is friendly and low-key—the sort of place where you can entertain the other guests on the piano. Named after tropical flowers, the 14 rooms are quite simple, but comfortable, and they have an air of old-time Guadeloupe, each with a balcony and a hammock giving onto a profuse garden. The same family have another stylish hotel nearby, the **Creol' Inn** (℃ 94 22 56, fax 94 07 54). The theme is old-time Caribbean, so each (quite small) wooden 'case' (cottage), has a veranda, louvres and gingerbread and a gently sloping green tin roof. No restaurant, but small snack bar and shop with food, well-equipped kitchenette, telephones, televisions and fans.

At the southern tip of the island, in **Trois-Rivières**, you will find the **Grand' Anse Hotel** (℃ 92 92 21, fax 92 93 69), set on the hillside a few hundred yards up above the sea. The 16 air-conditioned bungalows stand around the central pool and restaurant, which serves creole food. Good views from the balconies.

cheap

Alternatively you might try **Bel Ô Plage**, 97130 Bananier (℃ 86 91 01, fax 86 70 14), which is not on the beach at all, but right on the road. The hotel is friendly though, and there are 10 comfortable, air-conditioned rooms with private bathrooms and good views of the Saints. In Basse-Terre itself is the **Gîte Le Houëlment**, 34 rue de la République (℃ 81 44 72), right at the foot of town. And there are simple rooms outside the town at **La Casa du Père Labat** (℃ 81 98 79). Three very simple rooms, air-conditioning or fan, with a fine creole dining room; cheap to very cheap.

Equally charming and quiet is the **Gîte de Vanibel**, 97119 Vieux Habitants (℃ 98 40 79), which is set among the restored remains of a plantation high up in the hills. Self-catering apartments, made modern but retaining the stained wood, the louvres and the verandas of times past. Classic Caribbean gardens and some of the coffee plantation machinery still on view. Farther north you will find some waterfront hotels with a theme of sportfishing and diving.

Le Rocher de Malendure, 97125 Bouillante (℃ 98 70 84, fax 98 89 92) has nine bungalows of which three sit on the *rocher* itself. Also in this area, **Iguana's Hotel**, 97125 Bouillante (℃ 98 91 91, fax 98 91 76) offers 10 rooms in a modern hotel at the roadside and there are very simple rooms at **La Case sous le Vent** (℃ 98 84 92) in Pigeon just down from

Malendure Beach. *En route* for Grande-Terre you will find an excellent stopover at **Le Duc'Ery**, 97170, Petit-Bourg (✆ 95 73 95, fax 94 36 03), a modern house with old creole overtones which stands high above an agricultural valley. Friendly reception, assistance with tours in the area, and good prices.

There are two **camp-grounds** on Basse-Terre—**Les Sables d'Or** (✆ 28 44 60) in Deshaies and slightly further south, **La Traversée** (✆ 98 21 23) in Pointe Noire.

✆ *(590)–* **Eating Out**

With its French roots, Guadeloupean cooking is excellent and the island will not disappoint those who wish to take part in a gastronomic steeplechase or just take some time out from the rigours of sitting on a beach. And many of the the settings are heavenly too, small cafés on the waterfront (St Anne and St François each have a string of them) and verandas on a hillside grappled by allamanda and slender fingers of bougainvillea, with the tremulous thunder of the rain on an iron roof.

The Guadeloupeans cook a full range of French food, but the island is famed for its creole food: fish and island meats like goat, spiced sauces, tropical vegetables and fruits. There are Guadeloupean versions of many dishes you will find in Martinique (their point of origin is usually contested) and they will be stamped with the island flavour. Snapper, *lambi* (conch) and *langouste* (lobster) are favourites, in a *blaff* (a way of boiling fish), or goat in a *colombo* (a French West Indian curry), served with flavoured rice 'n' peas or local vegetables such as plantain or christophene and spiked with creole sauces. French wine is often drunk with a meal but, like their confrères in Martinique, the Guadeloupeans are slaves to the *petit punch*, a rum-based apéritif that is small only in name.

There are literally hundreds of restaurants and cafés in Guadeloupe (at the last official count about 700), so the choice is limitless. There are Vietnamese and even Lebanese restaurants here. Part of the fun is stopping when you see one you like the look of. Most are fairly relaxed, but in the smarter ones men are sometimes required to wear a jacket. Eating out is not exactly cheap, but service is *compris*. Categories are based on the price of a main course: *expensive*—Fr100 and above; *moderate*—Fr50–Fr100; and *cheap*—less than Fr50.

Grande-Terre

expensive

La Canne à Sucre (✆ 82 10 19), *closed Sun*, has an ocean-liner-like setting right on the dockside in Pointe-à-Pitre, and you can sometimes look out on to cruise-ship hulls on both sides. The impression is really made in the dining room itself, where you dine on reproduction antiques beneath gathered pink curtains, a menu of *nouvelle cuisine antillaise—papillotte de dorade en feuille de banane sauce chien* (dorado served in a banana leaf in *sauce chien*). Downstairs is an open-air bistro, *plat du jour* Fr50, an afternoon stop, which gets very full when the cruise ships are in port.

An excellent French restaurant in a comfortable setting is **Côté Jardin** (✆ 90 91 28), *closed Sun*, in the Bas du Fort marina. You sit at elegant white-laid tables in wicker chairs, some with huge peacock backs, with all the activity of the kitchen in view. *Gambas flambés du planteur passion* or *cuisse de canard confite* served with *pommes sautés paysanne*. Popular with business and political people for lunch, cool and elegant for dinner.

Close by is **La Plantation** (✆ 90 84 83), *closed Sun*, which has a slightly more subdued air in a setting of mock-antiquity, overlooking the activity of marina. Only the clink of cutlery breaks the gentle murmur of conversation here, as you dine on classical French and creole cuisine—*friandise de langouste à la mandarine impériale*, dishes served under *cloches*, which when removed reveal immaculate presentation on huge plates. Finish off with the colourful *arlequin glacé de coco et framboises au jus de kiwi*.

Chez Deux Gros (✆ 84 16 20) is well worth finding for a meal. 'Restaurant et Brocante' (restaurant and antique dealership), it is right on the main road heading east from Pointe-à-Pître, about a kilometre beyond the second turning to Gosier. You approach it through an overgrown tropical garden and go into a house filled with weird and wonderful bric-à-brac—Art Deco lamps, clocks and bronze statuettes—and music from the forties, fifties and sixties. Very genial atmosphere, with tables inside among the antiques or outside under tropical bowers. Innovative local cuisine; *papaya lambi* followed by snapper in passion fruit and to finish with, *le collier de la reine*, a ring of exotic desserts on the plate. The main course is expensive, but the antiques you can bargain for. Remember to reserve a table.

High on the coast road between St François and St Anne (well signposted) is a charming gastronomic retreat, **Les Oiseaux** (✆ 88 56 92), a *restaurant frantillais* (i.e. the best local ingredients cooked in French style). The restaurant's breezy veranda setting looks onto a pleasant tropical garden: *brochette de vivaneau au miel pays* or *requin au coco* (shark in coconut).

On the outskirts of **St François** is **Le Vieux Carré** (✆ 88 58 64), set in an old colonial house, where you take your cocktail to fifties' jazz music before dinner, and then move out on to the veranda with a view of the well-tended garden. Menu à la blackboard and food intentionally simple, most of it grilled—*filet de canard grillé* or *agneau au thym*, followed by local ice-cream.

A sedate day out, lingering over a long lunchtime, can be enjoyed at **Le Château de Feuilles** (✆ 22 30 30), *closed Mon, otherwise open daily for lunch, dinner Fri, Sat, ring to reserve*, which is set in a charming creole villa and garden miles from anywhere in the north of Grande-Terre, near Campêche (well sign-posted). French and creole fare—*choucroute de poisson de papaye verte*, *charlotte au corossol* (mousse and cream) and a between-course swim if you feel like it, just beside the tables, followed up with one of 20 different varieties of fruit-flavoured rums.

moderate

There is a string of bistros on the waterfront in St Anne and particularly in St François. At the 'old port', **Kotésit** (✆ 88 40 84) has a pretty setting with blue and white awnings on a wooden deck. French and creole fare: *panaché de poisson poêlés* with a wicked chocolate cake. Also **Le Zagaya**, *ouassous flambés* or *à la provençale*, followed by a *clafoutis aux fruits*.

Two other popular spots, with a view of the windsurfers, are **Les Pieds dans l'Eau** and **Le Mareyeur**. In the marina area, the nicest place to eat is **La Chaloupe**. In **St Anne** you will get an excellent creole meal at the small and friendly **Mini Beach** (✆ 88 21 13). In an open dining room to an occasional piano accompaniment, *poisson grillé*, *sauce antillaise* or lobster (live from the vivier), followed by *fondant de chocolat*.

Just out of town **Le Flibustier** (✆ 82 23 36), *closed Mon, Sun evening*, has a certain style—set on a hill like a pirate's look-out and decorated inside with the beams of a galleon. Quite rumbustious, wine by the pitcher, chef with tied-back hair, who barbecues your meal and then presents it to you on a huge wooden platter. Naval battles and portraits of pirates on the walls.

In **Gosier** you will find a good creole meal at **Mérou d'Or**, down at the waterfront opposite the Ilet de Gosier. Fresh fish—*blaffs* and *poissons en papillotte* in a typical French West Indian dining room with madras tablecloths. There are plenty of waterfront bistros in the **Bas du Fort marina**, where you can wander between video bars while you decide where to eat.

La Sirène does a good crêpe. There are many cafés around the place de la Victoire in Pointe-à-Pitre.

cheap

Recently a number of roadside pizzerias and *roulottes* (snackwagons) have put in an appearance all over Guadeloupe. An excellent place for a simple plate of chicken and chips is **Express Grill** on the main road outside Gosier. Open daily until 1 or 2am. If you are feeling peckish late at night in **Pointe-à-Pitre**, there are snackwagons on the place de la Victoire. Afterwards you might like to grab an ice-cream from the vendors with wooden buckets (they will explain how they work too).

Basse-Terre

Basse-Terre also has a number of good places to eat around the whole island, but particularly on the free and easy west coast around Malendure.

In **St Rose** you will find superb creole fare at **Chez Clara** (© 28 72 99), *closed Wed, Sun evening*, on the waterfront road. Very comfortable deck with wicker chairs, presided over by Clara herself—fish landed on the pier right across the road, or *lambi ragout* with *gratinde fruit à pain*. Popular with the locals; moderate.

The **Domaine de Séverin** (© 28 34 54), *lunch daily except Mon, dinner Thurs–Sat*, is in an old plantation house on the northern slopes of the island on a sugar plantation. *Ecrevisses* (crayfish, from the pond on the estate) *en civet au vin rouge* or *feuilletté de lambi*; expensive.

If you are on **Grand Anse**, you can catch a good lunch on the tropical terrace at **Le Karacoli** (though you may find yourself dodging the tour buses). Creole food—*assiette belle négresse*, with all the seafood you might want to try. And across the main road you will find an easy stopover at **Le Fruit à Pain**. In nearby Deshaies there are a number of bars and restaurants strung along the waterfront. The coolest is **Au Coin des Pêcheurs**. Local and French fare: *poulet panga* or *fricassé de lambi*. **Le Mouillage—Les Pieds dans l'Eau** is popular for creole cuisine; *blaff de poisson et légumes* followed by *banane flambée*. **Le Madras** (© 28 40 87), *lunch and dinner, closed Wed*, offers creole fare inside a small, dark dining room set with madras tablecloths. *Boudin lambi* and stuffed crab backs.

Further south you come to **Le Rocher de Malendure** (© 98 70 84), overlooking Pigeon Island, which has an excellent, split-level dining room lost in tropical greenery, where you can retreat after a morning's diving. Fish restaurant—*escalope de marlin pané* or *ouassous en sauce*, some meat dishes.

La Touna (℃ 98 70 10), in the town of Bouillante, also serves fish on the waterfront, landed right on the deck outside. The cuisine is creole and French, seafood and fish, on a neat and pretty veranda: *darne de daurade* in six sauces, some bar-trade with deep-sea fishermen. **Caprice des Iles** (℃ 81 74 97) offers good French and creole cuisine just before Basse-Terre, right next to the road but with a terrace on the sea. Accras, boudin and shark in a saffron sauce; moderate.

In Matouba, high above the town of Basse-Terre, there is a nice lunch-time stopover at **Chez Paul** (℃ 80 29 20). Accras followed by *féroce* with hot pepper or a fricassee with a spicy sauce and of course a volley of local vegetables; moderate. In the town itself you can get local fare at **Le Houëlment**.

Bars and Nightlife

Zouk is the current musical beat of the French Caribbean, another bustling rhythm with a double beat, often with echoes of West Africa. It can be heard on the buses and in the clubs, each as crowded as the other, along with just about all the other Caribbean beats. You get to know the songs as they are played over and over again: hear them again when you get home and you will start to twitch. Most clubs have a door charge of around US$10, which usually includes the price of a drink.

Outside the hundreds of bistros and bars you will find a few spots where the hip chicks and lover-boys gather for an early evening drink. They are centred around the tourist areas. Among the many waterfront eateries at the Bas du Fort marina is **Le Jardin Brésilien**, a video bar with a list of cocktails as long as your arm. Perhaps try an Anaconda or a Karma, according to your mood. Live music and even fashion shows occasionally in season. From here you can move on to II3.14.

In Bas du Fort itself you can catch a cocktail in the piano bar at **Rive Droite**, before moving on, just next door, to the **Madison Square** disco, **Le Cleudo** or the **Victoria**.

In Gosier you might start at **L'Endroit** in Montauban before going on for a dance at **La Cascade** (Tues–Sat) or **New Land** (weekends only). A good place to enjoy a hilltop view and a cocktail is **La Toubana Hotel** outside St Anne. And in St François there are plenty of bars around the marina and there are good local discos at **L'Acapulco** (open at the weekends) and **Juliana's**. There are casinos at **Caraïbe Club** in Gosier and in St François.

La Désirade

'Quand bleuira sur l'horizon la Désirade.'

Apollinaire

La Désirade takes its romantic name from the Spanish *deseata* (the desired one). In the 16th century the standard Atlantic crossing arrived at Guadeloupe and after four or five weeks at sea the sailors would be longing for land. La Désirade was often the island they saw first. It lies about 6 miles (10km) off the Pointe des Châteaux, the easternmost tip of Grande-Terre. It is a table mountain, 8 miles by 1 (13 by 1½km), rising 900ft above sea-level, windswept and covered in cactus scrub. The northern coast is a line of rugged cliff-faces, cut into strange shapes. The south of the island is protected from the wind and it is here that the 1600 inhabitants have chosen to live, spread along the coast from the main settlement of Grande-Anse.

La Désirade is dry and was settled only by a few poor white settlers. For many years it was a leper colony. Without the plantations there were no slaves and so the population of La Désirade remains predominantly white (also true on Terre de Haut in the Saints, but not so in Marie Galante). Today life is extremely simple and the economy of the island is mainly agricultural or connected with the sea (fishing and boatbuilding). It is one of the least developed islands of the Caribbean—a reliable water supply was only introduced in 1991, by pipe from Guadeloupe. If you would like an utterly secluded escape, you can find it in La Désirade.

✆ *(590)–* *Practical Information*

You can reach La Désirade by air from Le Raizet on scheduled flights (twice daily, reservations ✆ 82 47 00) or by ferry, leaving daily from the marina at St François (✆ 88 48 63). Yachts also cruise over there for the day from the marina and you might get a ride. When on the island, you can reach a taxi on ✆ 20 00 62 and hire a car or a bicycle through Loca 2000 (✆ 20 02 78), who will also take you on an island tour. Alternatively you could walk the length of the island in a single day. Look out for the ruined buildings of the leper colony near Baie Mahault and iguanas and agoutis. Reef-protected, golden-sand beaches are at Grande-Anse, Le Souffleur and at Baie-Mahault. Island tours and scuba diving can be arranged through Tony Dinane (✆ 20 02 93).

There are just a few places to stay on the island; **L'Oasis du Désert** (✆ 20 02 12), with 10 rooms, and **Le Touareg** (✆ 20 01 78), both in the Quartier du Désert, both quite simple and cheap. Camping is possible at

Baie Mahault and people let out rooms in their houses. Restaurants include **Chez Marianne** in Quartier du Bourg and the fish and creole restaurant **La Payotte** (℃ 20 01 94).

Marie Galante

In contrast to La Désirade, Marie Galante has a more typical history for the Caribbean. The land was fertile enough to bear sugar and so in the 18th century it was covered with it down to the last square inch. Sweeps of cane blew in the breezes and every few hundred yards were the cone and sails of a sugar-mill. The cane still grows, but Marie Galante's hundred mills, which once stood proudly at nearly two for every square mile, are run down and are steadily being devoured by tropical undergrowth.

Shaped like a football, Marie Galante is a flat 59 square miles (153sq km) and looks similar to Grande-Terre, just 20 miles (32km) to the north.

The 16,000 inhabitants live on the protected areas of the coast, around the main settlement of Grand-Bourg. Sugar is still important to the economy (there are three remaining distilleries and Marie Galante rum is renowned) and there is some agriculture. The rum is the principal ingredient in the celebrations on Marie Galante, which are so popular with the people from Dominica that on public holidays they come streaming over in small boats to join the *fête*.

The island takes its name from Columbus's flagship, the caravelle *Santa Maria de Galante*, in which he led his second expedition to the New World in 1493. After coasting Dominica and failing to find a harbour, he saw Marie Galante and cruised north. For a while the island became a refuge for the Caribs fleeing the larger islands but in the age of empire it quickly became a strategic base, the first stop on an invasion attempt on Guadeloupe. The Dutch stripped the island systematically in 1676 and the British occupied it a number of times before it finally settled to France in 1815.

There are some calm **anchorages** in the northwest, near the town of St Louis, where you can buy ice and food, or stop off in the local restaurants. Further south, the main town of Grand Bourg has shops for provisioning as well as a customs and immigration office.

There are some very attractive **beaches** on the western coast of the island, to which the Guadeloupeans come for the weekend. The best are the palm-backed strand at **Vieux Fort** in the northwest and the calm **Petite Anse** near Capesterre in the southeast and, close by, **Plage de le Feuillère**, where you will find the beach restaurant **Le Békéké** and the **Fun Evasion** Mistral windsurfing school (✆ 97 35 21). Scuba diving is available through **Maison Poullet** (✆ 97 75 24).

Inland there are canefields and sugar-mills (*moulins*) on view—the **Moulin de Basse** and one at the **Château Murat**. In the Château, which has been restored to its 18th-century splendour, is the **Eco-Musée de Marie Galante**, *open 7.30–12.30 and 2.30–5.30, mornings only at the weekend, adm free*, dedicated to island traditions and of course the history of sugar. There are a number of sugar factories and rum distilleries: **Distillerie Poisson** in the west and **Distillerie Bielle**, inland at Rabi. North of here is a cave that goes by the name of **Le Trou à Diable** (the Devil's Hole), which goes quite deep underground. You should take a torch and the right footwear if you venture down it.

✆ (590)– *Practical Information*

There are regular flights (usually three a day) from Le Raizet (✆ 82 47 00) to Basses airport (✆ 97 82 21) in the south of the island. Ferries link Marie Galante to Pointe-à-Pitre several times a day, an hour's sail from La Darse in Place de la Victoire, and the journey brings you to Grand-Bourg. A tour to the island can be arranged from Pointe-à-Pitre; yachts occasionally make the crossing from St François. Taxis can be contacted on ✆ 97 81 97 and there are cars for hire (best booked in advance) through Socagam (✆ 97 80 38) or Eurodollar (✆ 97 06 02). It is quite possible to make a tour of the island in a day.

There are only a few places to stay on Marie Galante and all of them are family-run and fairly simple, all cheap. The **Auberge de Soledad** (✆ 97 75 45) is in Grand-Bourg, with 18 rooms and **Le Salut** is in the northwestern town of St Louis (✆ 97 10 26), with rooms. **Chez Hajo** (✆ 97 32 76) has just six rooms in the town of Capesterre. **Au Village de Ménard** (✆ 97 77 02, fax 97 76 89) has five simple bungalows, set around a pool on a clifftop near St Louis, for those who are happy to look after themselves. There are about 15 *gîtes* on the island (*see* **Guadeloupe**, 'Where to Stay', p.251).

Each of the hotels has a dining room, but you can find good French and creole food at **Le Touloulou** (✆ 97 32 63), which is set on a simple veranda on the sand of Petite Anse de Capesterre—conch in puff pastry, or *oursins* (sea urchins), with a generous helping of local vegetables. Also in Capesterre is **l'Auberge de la Roche d'Or** (✆ 97 37 42), a family-run creole restaurant with a pretty dining room. In Grand Bourg try **Le Neptune** (✆ 97 96 90) in a very attractive palm and tropical garden setting on the waterfront; creole food and seafood—*palourdes* (clams) and grilled crayfish. In St Louis try **L'Arc en Ciel** (✆ 87 21 66). It's worth phoning in advance to see if they're cooking.

The Saints

The Saints are a collection of small islands that lie 7 miles (11km) south of Basse-Terre. They are volcanic, and rise sharply out of the water to nearly 1000ft, but they look tiny between the colossi of Basse-Terre and Dominica, the next Windward Island down the line. Stand on Le Chameau, the highest point on Terre-de-Haut, and you will feel as though you are on the lip of a swamped volcano crater; the islands make an almost perfectly round bowl.

Two of the islands are inhabited (3000 people in all) and their populations are curiously different. Terre-de-Bas was a plantation island and the people are mostly descended from the Africans taken there as slaves. Terre-de-Haut, on the other hand, was never planted and so there were never many slaves. Instead the islanders were descended mostly from white Frenchmen, originating from Brittany and Normandy—you can still see their blond hair and blue eyes. Their skin does not tan in the sun and it is clear that many of them are in-bred.

They are renowned fishermen, though, and before the age of baseball caps they would wear strange looking *salako* hats to protect themselves from the sun—white material stretched over a bamboo frame that sits close on the head like a small parasol. These 'coolie hats' are thought to have been brought by a Chinaman in the last century.

The Saints were supposedly named by Columbus in honour of All Saints' Day. They were settled and fortified in 1648 in order to defend the island of Guadeloupe. The ramparts can still be seen on the heights.

The Battle of the Saints

To British historians, the Saints' most famous moment came in 1782, when the islands had a ringside view of the most decisive naval battle of the period, one which established British dominance in the Caribbean for the next thirty years.

The Battle of the Saints (La Bataille de la Dominique to the French) was fought on 12 April 1782. The British were beleaguered at the time, having recently lost the American War of Independence. De Grasse had successfully cut the British supply lines, and now he was turning to the British Caribbean colonies. His target was Jamaica, the richest British colony, and he was on his way to join the Spanish navy at Santo Domingo to attack it.

Leaving Martinique, de Grasse headed north. He was sighted by Rodney and the chase was on. For three days Rodney shadowed de Grasse without being able to commit him to a fight. Eventually they met off the Saints and the two lines, each of 30 ships, bore down on each other in slow motion in parallel and opposite directions, the French coming from the north. At eight in the morning the first broadside was fired. The fleets filed past one another, cannonading, until eleven o'clock when Sir Charles Douglas, with Rodney on the bridge of the *Formidable*, saw a gap in the French line, just a few ships behind de Grasse's flagship, the *Ville de Paris*. He steered for it and broke through the French line. The ships to his rear followed him through and in the manoeuvre they separated the French flagship from the bulk of the fleet. The French ships, so close together they made 'one object to fire at', were decimated. De Grasse stayed on his flagship, with 110 guns and 1300 sailors, throughout the conflict and when finally she was taken, he was one of only three men left uninjured.

The whole scene had been clearly visible from Dominica and the Saints, and as darkness fell ships were seen burning into the night. Five of the French ships were taken and one sunk and the rest of the tattered fleet headed for Cap Français under Admiral Bougainville and for Curaçao off the coast of South America. When the two Admirals met, de Grasse is supposed to have said, 'You have fought me handsomely', and Rodney to have replied, 'I was glad of the opportunity'.

In the Second World War the islands saw no action. Fort Napoléon was used as a prison for those Guadeloupeans who disagreed with the decision to side with the Vichy Regime.

The Islands

There is one main settlement on Terre-de-Haut, called Bourg, which is set on a superb harbour. It is very attractive and has a silent, magical air. There are just four or five very attractive streets of creole houses, almost all of them with red tin roofs. Between the cafés on the waterfront you will see the fishermen who sit and chat over a game of dominoes all afternoon. Terre-de-Haut is pretty touristy (it sees quite a lot of day-trippers from the mainland), but it handles it well and the island has a charming feel.

The main **anchorages** are centred on Terre d'en Haut, where there are calm spots off the main town of Bourg des Saintes (with supermarkets and bakeries, but no major yachting facilities), and the small island in the bay, the Ilet à Cabrit. There are no **customs and immigration** offices in the Saints, though this is not usually a problem. If your yacht is in need of **repairs**, you are advised to go to Guadeloupe.

The best **beach** is in Baie de Pont Pierre, but there is also good sand at Marigot Bay. On the south coast you will find seclusion at Anse du Figuier, named for the tree rather than the leaf, though even fig leafs are discarded at Anse Crawen. Windsurfing can be fixed up through Centre UCPA (© 99 54 94), which also arranges catamaran excursions, and Guy Maisonneuve (© 99 53 13). For scuba, contact Guy Maisonneuve or Diving Nautique des Saintes (© 99 54 25).

On land, all the 'sights' are within walking distance (eventually). The lumbering fortress on the hilltop, **Fort Napoléon**, is the island's principal sight, *open 9–noon, adm.* It commands the bay and has a magnificent view to Guadeloupe and down to Dominica. The fort has exhibitions of modern art and a museum of local history (including pictures of the Battle of the Saints) set in the vast, cool stone ramparts. Outside, among the cannon runners in the grass on the once formidable battlements, there is a cactus garden. You can visit **Ilet à Cabri** (Goat Island) where there is another fort, called Fort Joséphine. Another peak worth climbing is La Bosse du Chameau (camel's hump) at the other end of the island, where the *tour modèle* dwarfs Fort Napoléon and gives a fine view from nearly 1000ft over the whole area. **Grand Ilet** is a protected sea-bird reserve and can be *visited by prior arrangement.*

© *(590)–*   *Practical Information*

The Saints are linked by many ferries from Pointe-à-Pitre (1 hour's sail) and from Trois-Rivières (20 minutes) on the southern coast of Basse-Terre. Terre-de-Haut has a magnificent harbour and it is a pleasure to see the peaks glide by as you arrive. There are also two daily flights from Pointe-à-Pitre to Terre-de-Haut, but if you do not like flying, beware, because the landing can be a bit hair-raising. There are several daily sailings from Bourg to Terre-de-Bas, often touching Bois-Joli. Terre-de-Bas has an airstrip suspended on a spit of land 100ft above the sea. There are no cars for rent, but on Terre de Haut you can hire a scooter through ARS (© 99 52 63) or X-Becane Lognos (© 99 54 08).

© *(590)–*   **Where to Stay**

Only Terre-de-Haut has places in which to stay and the most charming of these is the **Auberge des Petits Saints aux Anacardiers** (© 99 50 99, fax 99 54 51) on the hills above town, one of the red-roofed houses, with a terraced dining room and pool looking out over cracking views over the bay and on to the clouded Soufrière on Basse-Terre. It has 10 double rooms;

moderate. The **Bois Joli Hotel** (✆ 99 50 38, fax 99 55 05, US reservations ✆ 800 373 6246) is tucked away in its own garden at the other end of the island at Anse à Cointre. There are 21 rooms and eight bungalows scattered around a central house where there is a pool and pleasant deck above the sea; moderate. Back in Terre-de-Haut's beautiful main bay, beneath Fort Napoléon and beyond the house built like a boat that juts out into the water from a cliff, are two other small hotels, the **Kanaoa** (✆ 99 51 94, fax 99 55 04), which is set in attractive creole style buildings with a waterfront dining terrace; moderate, and **Le Village Créole**, with 22 duplexes in a garden of croton and bougainvillea; moderate. There are also a number of small guest houses and rooms for rent at good prices (✆ 91 64 33, US reservations ✆ 800 373 6246). There are just a few villas available in Terre-de-Bas.

The hotels have some good dining rooms, but there is also a clutch of bistros and salad bars set on the waterfront in Bourg. There are two good restaurants right on the waterfront: **Le Café de la Marine** for French fare and the **Centre Nautique des Saintes**. In town, try **Coconuts** for fruit cocktails and a simple meal. Some restaurants have a bar trade, and there is a nightclub, **Le Cha Cha**, open at weekends.

St Jacques

The least known of all the Saints is the island of Saint Jacques. Christened *Santiago de los Vientos Alicios*, it was jokingly known as 'Jack of all Trades' to the English filibusters who plied their trade of 'cruize and plunder' from its shores. The only historian to mention it is a certain Father Jerome Zancarol, who wrote that the food was good, girls were beautiful and that the islanders' morals were the worst he had come across anywhere in the world, a veritable Gehenna.

Apparently, sailors have heard the sound of violins on the 61st meridian, but the only record of the island's illustrious story is in *The Violins of St Jacques*, by Patrick Leigh Fermor.

Note: page numbers in *italics* indicate maps. **Bold** entries indicate main references.

air travel 2–4, 8–10
see also under individual islands (getting around; getting there)
Allfrey, Phyllis Shand 212
Antigua, sailing 41
apartments 33
Arawak Indians 44–5
bananas **49–50**
Barbados 54–84, *55*
  Accra Beach 64
  Andromeda Gardens 74
  Animal Flower Cave 71
  Bajan food and drink 79–80
  Banks Brewery 72
  Barbados Wildlife Reserve 59
  bars and nightlife 64–5, 82–4
  Bathsheba 73
  Bay Street 68
  beaches 54, 63–4
  bookshops 84
  Bottom Bay 64
  Bridgetown 67–9
  Brighton Beach 64
  Broad Street 68
  Bussa's rebellion 58
  Careenage **67**, 68
  Cherry Tree Hill 71
  Codrington College 73
  Cotton Tower 73
  Crane Beach 64
  cricket and the constitution 59
  eating out 79–82
  economy 58
  emergencies 63
  Farley Hill 71
  festivals 75–6
  flora and fauna 59–60
  Flower Forest 74
  Folkestone 64
  Foul Bay 64
  Francia Plantation House 72
  further reading 84
  gardens 60, 74
  Garrison Savannah 69
  Gay's Cove 64
  getting around 61–2
  getting there 60
  Grenade Hall Forest and Signal Station 71
  Gun Hill Signal Station 72
  Hackleton's Cliff 54, **71**, 73
  Harrismith Beach 64
  Harrison's Cave 70
  Heywood's Beach 64
  history 56–8
  Holetown 70
  House of Assembly 68
  Lord Nelson's statue 67
  Maycock's Bay 64
  money 63
  Morgan Lewis Mill 72
  Mount Gay Visitor's Centre 69
  Mount Hillaby 72
  Mullins Bay 64
  museum 69
  National Trust in Barbados 67
  newspapers 63
  Oistins 74
  Paradise Beach 64
  Pelican Village 68
  politics 56, 58, 59
  population 54
  Public Buildings 68
  Ragged Point 64, 75
  Rasta Mall 68
  River Bay 64
  Rockley Beach 64
  rum 79–80
  sailing 65
  St James's church 70
  St John's Parish Church 73
  St Michael's Cathedral 68
  St Nicholas Abbey 71
  Sam Lord's Castle 74–5
  Savannah Club 69
  Scotland and St Lucy in the North 70–2
  shopping 84
  Silver Sands Beach 64
  Six Men's Bay 64
  social services 54
  Speightstown 70
  sports 66–7
  Suburbs and the South Coast 74–5
  Sugar Heartland— Bridgetown to the Atlantic Coast 72–4
  Sunbury Plantation House and Museum 75
  Synagogue 68
  tourist information 62–3
  Trafalgar Square 68
  Treasure Beach 64
  Turner's Hall Wood 72
  University of the West Indies 70
  Villa Nova 72–3

Index

(Barbados *cont'd*)
  watersports 65–6
  Welchman Hall Gulley 70
  West Coast—North to Scotland and St Lucy 69–70
  West India Rum Refinery 69
  where to stay 76–9
  Willoughby Fort 57
  Worthing Beach 64
Battle of the Saints 263–4
beaches 12
  see also under individual islands
beer 19
Bequia *135*, **137–41**
  beaches 138
  eating out 140–1
  watersports 139
  where to stay 139–40
Black Caribs 118, 119
boats 4–5, 10
  see also under individual islands (getting around; getting there)
Bonaparte, Napoleon 177
bookshops 12
Brigands' War 118
brokers, yacht 37
Brunias, Agostino 212–13
Bussa's Rebellion 58
Byron, Admiral Foulweather Jack 89
calendar of events 12–15
calypso 51
camping 34
Canouan *135*, **143–4**
Carib Indians 44–5, 225–6
  wars with 118–19
carnivals **12–13**, 51
  see also under individual islands (festivals)
Carriacou 109–14
  beaches 112

Belair 111
  eating out 113–14
  festivals 111
  getting to 109–10
  Hillsborough 111
  history 110–11
  Mr Canute Caliste 111
  sailing 112
  watersports 112–13
  where to stay 113
centipedes 21
charter companies, boats 37
charter flights 2, 3, 4
children 15
cholera 20
climate 15–16
  winds and weather 36, **42**
cockfighting 185–6
cocktails 18–19
coconuts 20
Columbus, Christopher 45–6
compas 51
Concorde 2
condominiums 33
Continental Plan (CP) 32
Courteen, Sir William 56
créole language 48
cruise ships 4
culture
  English speaking Caribbean 46–7
  French Caribbean 47–9
currency *see* money
customs and immigration 5, 41
dancehall music 51
departure taxes 5
diving 26–8
Dominica 208–30, *209*
  Almond Beach Bar 217
  bars and nightlife 230
  Bayfront 219
  beaches 217, 224
  Belles 225

Bereuka 222
Boeri Lake 213, **221**
Boiling Lake 213, **221**
Botanical Gardens 219
Cabrits National Park 224
Calibishie (Point Baptiste) 217
Carib territory 225–6
Castaways 217
Cathedral of the Assumption 219
Dawbiney Market Plaza 219
Douglas Bay 217
eating out 229–30
economy 211
Emerald Pool 213, **225**
emergencies 216
festivals 226
flora and fauna 213–15
Fort Cacharou 222
Fort Young 219
Freshwater Lake 213, **221**
getting around 215–16
getting there 215
Hampstead Bay 217
history 210–12
Indian River 223
La Plaine 225
Laudat 213
Lavi Dominik 223
Layou river 217
market 219
Massacre 223
Middleham Trails 213, **225**
money 216
Morne Bruce 219, **220**
Morne Diablotin 223
Morne Trois Pitons National Park 213, **221**, 225
North from Roseau 222–4
Northern Forest Reserve 213

Old Mill Cultural Centre 223
Papillote Wilderness Retreat 220–1
politics 212
population 208, 218
Portsmouth 223
Prince Rupert's Bay 217, **223–4**
river bathing 217
Rosalie 225
Roseau 218–20
Roseau Valley 220–1
sailing 217
Sari-sari river 213
Scotts Head 222
shopping 216
snakes 214
Soufrière 222
South from Roseau 221–2
Titou Gorge 213
Toucari Bay 224
tourist information 216
Trafalgar Falls 213, **220**
Transinsular Road to the East Coast 224–5
Valley of Desolation 213, **221**
Victoria Falls 213
walking trails 213
watersports 218
whale-watching 214–15
where to stay 226–8
Woodbridge Bay 223
Woodford Hill Bay 217
writers and artists 212–13
drinks 18–20
 beer 19
 cocktails 18–19
 fruit punches 20
 rum 19, 79–80
 soft drinks 19–20
 water 22
 see also under individual places (eating out)

drugs 5
Dutertre, Père 178
electricity 16–17
European Plan (EP) 32
FAP (Full American Plan) 32
Fédon's Rebellion 89
ferries 10
fishing 28
food 17–20
 see also under individual islands (eating out)
France, political approach to the Caribbean 49
freighters 10
fruit punches 20
fruits 18
Full American Plan (FAP) 32
golf 29
Grenada 86–114, *87*
 Annandale Falls 103
 Bacolet Bay 96
 bars and nightlife 96, 109
 Bathway Beach 96
 Bay Gardens 101
 beaches 95–6
 Black Bay 101
 Botanical Gardens 100
 Calvigny Point 102
 Carenage 99
 Carriacou 109–14
 Concord Falls 101
 Dougaldston Estate 101
 Dr Groom Beach 95
 eating out 107–8
 economy 89
 emergencies 95
 Esplanade 99–100
 Fédon's Rebellion 89–90
 festivals 104
 flora and fauna 93
 Fort George 100
 getting around 94
 getting there 93–4
 Glover Island 102
 Gouyave 101–2

 Government House 100
 Grand Anse 95, 102
 Grand Etang to the East Coast 103–4
 Grand Mal Bay 96
 Green Flash 114
 Green Hole 99
 Grenville 104
 history 88–9
 invasion by United States 90–1
 Kick 'em Jenny volcano 109
 La Sagesse beach 96
 La Sagesse national park 93
 L'Anse aux Epines 95
 Les Tantes 109
 Levera Bay 102
 Levera Beach 96
 Levera National Park 104
 London Bridge island 109
 Magazine Beach 95
 markets 100
 Marquis 102
 Marryshow House 100
 Minor Spices Society 100
 money 95
 Morne Fédon (Mt Qua Qua) 103
 Morne Fendue 104
 Morne Rouge Bay 95
 museum 99
 National Park 93, 104
 Nutmeg Cooperative Association 102
 Palmiste Bay 96
 Petit Martinique 109, **114**
 politics 90
 population 86
 Queen's Park 101
 revolution and invasion 90–1
 Richmond Hill 100
 River Antoine Distillery 104

DOM–GRE 269

Roman Catholic Cathedral 99
sailing 96–7
St George's 86, 89, **98–101**
St George's Parish Anglican Church 99
Sauteurs 102
Scot's Kirk church 99
shopping 95
the Sisters 109
South Coast 102–3
spices 86, **91–2**
sports 98
Telescope Beach 96
tourist information 94–5
watersports 97–8
West Coast 101–2
Westerhall Point 96
Westerhall Rum Distillery 102
where to stay 105–7
Yellow Poui Art Gallery 100
York House 99
Grenadines 134–48, *135*
Bequia *135*, **137–41**
Canouan *135*, **143–4**
getting around 137
Mayreau *135*, **144–5**
Mustique *135*, **141–3**
Palm Island *135*, **147–8**
Petit St Vincent (PSV) *135*, **148**
sailing 41, **136**
Tobago Cays *135*, **145**
Union Island *135*, **146–7**
Guadeloupe 232–66, *233*
Allée du Manoir 247
Anse à la Gourde 240
Anse Bertrand 246
Anse du Soufleur 240
Anse Laborde 240
Aquarium 244
As de Pique 247

Baines Jaunes 248
bars and nightlife **240, 259**
Basse-Terre (the island) 246–7
Basse-Terre (the town) 246, **247–9**
beaches 239–40
Capesterre 246
Caravelle Beach 239
Cascades des Ecrevisses 249
Cathedral of St Peter and St Paul 243
Chutes de Carbet 247
Chutes du Galion 248
Deshaies 250
Domaine de Séverin 250
Domaine de Valombreuse 250
eating out 255–9
  Basse-Terre 258–9
  Grande-Terre 256–8
economy 232
emergencies 238
Etang Zombi 247
festivals 251
flora and fauna 235–6
Fort Delgrès 248
Fort Fleur d'Epée 244
getting around 236–8
getting there 236
Gosier 244
Grand Etang 247
Grand-Terre 243–4
Grands Fonds 245
history 234–5
Ilet de Gosier 239
jardin Pichon 248
La Darse (harbour) 243
La Désirade 232, **260–1**
La Grande Anse 240
La Maison de la Forêt 235, **249**
La Perle 240

La Plage de Cluny 240
La Plage des Salines 240
La Pointe de la Grand Vigie 246
La Porte d'Enfer (Hell's Gate) 240, 246
La Soufrière 248–9
La Traversée, Basse-Terre 249
Le Marché de St Antoine 243
Le Moule 240, 245
Mahaut 250
Maison du Bois 250
Maison du Volcan 248
Malendure **240**, 250
Marie Galante 232, **261–3**
markets 243
Matouba 248
money 239
Morne-à-l'Eau 246
Morne-à-Louis 249
Musée du Rhum 250
Musée Edgar Clerc 245
Musée Schoelcher 244
Musée St-John Perse 244
Northern Grande-Terre 246
Northern tip of Basse-Terre 250
Parc Archéologique des Roches Gravées 247
Parc National 235
Parc Zoologique et Botanique 249
Petit Havre 239
place de Champ d'Arbaud 248
place de la Victoire 243
Plage Tarare 240
Plantation Grand Café 246
Pointe des Châteax 245
Pointe-à-Pitre 243–4

Pointe-Allègre 250
Pointe-Noire 250
politics 234
population 232, 243
Port Louis 246
Reserve Naturelle de Grand Cul de Sac Marin 236
Riviére Salée 246
rue Frébault 243
sailing 41, **240–1**
St Anne 244–5
St Claude 248
St François 244–5
  beach 240
Sainte Marie 246
the Saints (islands) 232, **263–6**
Saut de la Lézarde 249
Savane à Mulets 248, 249
shopping 239
Southern coast of Grande-Terre 244–5
sports 242–3
Tillette 240
tourist information 238
trace des contrabandiers 250
trace des crêtes 249
Trace Victor Hugues 248
Trois-Rivières 247
Vieux Habitants 250
watersports 241–2
where to stay 251–5
  Basse-Terre 253–5
  Grande-Terre 251–3
guest houses 34
health 20–2
Hearn, Lafcadio 179
hepatitis 20
HIV 21
honeymoon holidays 6
hotels 33
Hugues, Victor 89, 118, 234
hurricanes 16

hustling 24
immigration 5, 41
inns 33
insurance 6, 22
Jeffreys, Judge 57
Joséphine, Empress 177–8
La Désirade 232, **260–1**
Labat, Père 178
language **22–3**, 46, 47, 48
living in the Caribbean 23
manchineel trees 21
MAP (Modified American Plan) 32
maps 23–4
Marie Galante 232, **261–3**
  beaches 261–2
  practical information 262–3
  sailing 261
maroons 210–11
Martinique 174–206, *175*
  Ajoupa-Bouillon 195
  Anse à l'Ane 183
  Anse Caritan 183
  Anse Céron 183
  Anse Couleuvre 183
  Anse d'Arlet 183
  Anse Mitan 183
  Anse Trabaud 182
  Azimut 188
  Baie des Anglais 182
  Balata Gardens 179, **196**
  bars and nightlife 183, 205–6
  Basket Weaving Workshop 197
  Basse Pointe 195
  beaches 182–3
  Bibliothèque Schoelcher 187
  Cap Chevalier 182
  Caravelle Peninsula 197
  Caribbean coast 191
  Case-Pilote 191
  casinos 206

  Cathédrale St-Louis 187
  Château Dubuc 197
  cockfights 185–6
  Diamond Rock 189–90
  Domaine de la Pagerie 188
  Dominican monks 178
  eating out 201–5
  economy 174
  emergencies 182
  festivals 197–8
  flora and fauna 179
  Fort de France 186–8
  Fort de France and the Pitons du Carbet 196
  Fort de France to the Atlantic coast 196–7
  Fort de France to St Pierre 191
  Fort St Louis 186–7
  getting around 180–1
  getting there 179–80
  Gorges de la Falaise 195
  Grand Anse d'Arlet 189
  Grand' Rivière 195
  Grand Terre beach 182
  Grande Anse des Salines 182
  Habitation Céron 194
  Habitation Clément 190
  history 176–7
  Jardin de Balata 179, **196**
  La Maison de la Canne 188
  La Mauny 190
  La Trinité 196
  Lafcadio Hearn 179
  Le Carbet 191
  Le François 190
  Le Prêcheur 194
  Le Vauclin 190
  Les Anse d'Arlet 189
  Les Ombrages Botanical Gardens 195
  L'Habitation Fonds St Jacques 197

(Martinique *cont'd*)
  Macouba 195
  markets **187**, 190
  money 182
  mongoose versus the snake 186
  Montagne du Vauclin 190
  Montagne Pelée volcano 174, 177, **192–3**, 194–5
  Morne Rouge 194
  Musée de la Pagerie 188
  Musée Départmental 187
  Musée Gauguin 191
  Musée Historique de St Pierre 194
  Musée Volcanique 193–4
  North of St Pierre 194
  Palais de Justice 187
  Parc Floral 187–8
  Père Dutertre 178
  Père Labat 178
  Plage Corps du Garde 183
  Plantation Lajus 191
  Plantation Layritz 195
  Pointe des Salines 190
  Pointe du Bout 183, 188
  Pointe du Marin 183
  Pointe Macré 183
  population 174, 186
  Préfecture 187
  Rhum J. Bally 191
  Rhum St James 197
  Sacré-Coeur 196
  sailing 41, **183–4**
  St Anne peninsula 188, **190**
  St Pierre 192–4
  St Pierre to the Atlantic coast 194–5
  Sainte Marie 197
  Saut Babin 195
  Savane 187
  Savane des Pétrifications 190
  Schoelcher village 191
  shopping 182
  snakes **179**, 186
  South of Fort de France 188–90
  sports 185
  theatre 193
  Three Crowned Heads 177–8
  tourist information 181–2
  Trois Rivières Rum Distillery 190
  Trois-Ilets 188
  watersports 184–5
  where to stay 198–201
  yoles rondes 198
Mayreau *135*, **144–5**
merengue 51
Modified American Plan (MAP) 32
money 24–5
  see also under individual islands
Monmouth Rebellion 57
mosquitoes 21
music 50–1
Mustique *135*, **141–3**
newspapers 23–4
packing 25
Palm Island *135*, **147–8**
Petit Martinique 109, **114**
Petit St Vincent (PSV) *135*, **148**
photography 25–6
pirates 152
post offices 26
Practical A–Z 12–34
  beaches 12
    see also under individual islands
  bookshops 12
  calendar of events 12–15
  children 15
  climate 15–16
  electricity 16–17
  food and drink 17–20
    see also under individual islands (eating out)
  health 20–2
  insurance 6, 22
  language 22–3
  living and working in the Caribbean 23
  maps and publications 23–4
  money 24–5
    see also under individual islands
  packing 25
  photography 25–6
  post offices 26
  shopping 26
  sports 26–30
    see also under individual islands
  telephones 30, 42
  time zones 30
  tourist information 31
  where to stay 31–4
    see also under individual islands
  women 34
publications 23–4
reggae 51
Rhys, Jean 212
riding 29
rum 19, 79–80
Sailing Guide 36–42
  anchorages 40–1
  arrival 38–9
  bare-boats 37
  crewed yachts 37–8
  immigration and customs 5, 41
  life on board 39–40
  marinas and chandleries 41
  planning your trip 36–8
  provisioning and rubbish 41–2

sailing A–Z 40–2
security 42
telephones 30, 42
winds and weather 36, **42**
see also under individual islands
Saint Martin, sailing 40
Saints, The 232, **263–6**
  beaches 265
  Fort Napoléon 264, **265**
  Grand Ilet 265
  history 263–4
  Ilet à Cabri 265
  practical information 265
  sailing 264
  St Jacques 266
  where to stay 265–6
salsa 51
sand-flies 21
Schoelcher, Victor 234
sharks 21
shopping 26
Sint Maarten, sailing 40
snakes 21, 179, 186
snorkelling 27–8
soca 51
soft drinks 19–20
special-interest holidays 6–7, 8
spices 86, 91–2
sports 26–30
  diving 26–8
  fishing 28
  golf 29
  riding 29
  sailing 36–42
  snorkelling 27–8
  swimming 12, 21
  tennis 29
  walking 29–30
  watersports 29
  windsurfing 28
  see also under individual islands

St Lucia 150–72, *151*
  Anse Chastanet 157
  Anse des Sables 157
  Anse la Raye 163
  Barre de l'Isle 165
  bars and nightlife 157, 171–2
  beaches 157
  Botanical Gardens 164
  Canaries 163
  Cap Estate 162
  Castries 159–61
  Choiseul 165
  Cul de Sac 162
  Dennery 165
  Derek Walcott Square 160
  Diamond Falls 164
  eating out 169–71
  economy 150, 153
  festivals 166
  flora and fauna 153–4
  Fregate Island 154
  further reading 172
  getting around 155–6
  getting there 154–5
  Government House 160
  Gros Islet 161–2
  history 152–3
  La Brelotte 157
  La Toc 157
  Laborie 165
  Maria Islands 154, **165**
  Marigot Bay 162–3
  markets 160, 164
  Marquis Estate 161
  Micoud 165
  money 156
  Morne Fortune 160–1
  Morne Gimie 150
  Moule à Chique 165
  museum 165
  nature reserves 154
  newspapers 156
  North from Castries to the Cap 161–2
  Pigeon Point (Island) 157, **161–2**
  Pitons 163
  politics 153
  population 151
  Rat Island 161
  Reduit Beach 157
  Rodney Bay 161
  Roman Catholic Cathedral 160
  Roseau 162
  sailing 41, 157–8
  Savannes 153
  shopping 156
  Soufrière town 163–4
  Soufrière volcano 150, **164**
  South to Soufrière 162–5
  sports 159
  Sulphur Springs 164
  tourist information 156
  Vieux Fort 164–5
  Vieux Fort to Castries 165
  Vigie Beach 157, **161**
  Vigie Point 159
  watersports 158–9
  where to stay 166–9
St Vincent 116–34, *117*
  Barrouaille 130
  bars and nightlife 122, 134
  beaches 122
  Botanical Gardens 125–6
  Buccament Bay 122
  Buccament (Peniston) Valley **119–20**, 130
  Calliaqua 129
  carnival (Vincy Mas) 131
  eating out 133–4
  economy 116
  emergencies 121
  Falls of Baleine 131
  Fancy 129

(St Vincent *cont'd*)
  festivals 131
  flora and fauna 119–20
  Fort Charlotte 127
  Fort Duvernette 128–9
  Georgetown 129
  getting around 120–1
  getting there 120
  history 118–19
  Indian Bay 122
  Kearton's Bay 122
  Kingstown 124–7
  Law Courts 124
  Layou 130
  Leeward Highway to
    Chateaubelair 130–1
  markets 124
  Mesopotamia (Marriaqua)
    Valley 127–8
  money 122
  Montreal Gardens 128
  museum 126
  Old Woman's Point 127
  Owia 129
  Peter's Hope Bay 122
  politics 119
  population 116
  Rabacca Dry River 129
  Richmond 122, 130
  rock carvings 129
  Roman Catholic Church
    125
  sailing 122–3
  St George's Anglican
    Cathedral 124–5
  Sandy Bay 129
  shopping 122
  Soufrière volcano 129–30
  South Coast 127–9
  tourist information 121
  Vermont Nature Trails 120
  Vigie 128
  Villa 122
  Villa Point 128
  walking 123–4
  Wallilabou 130
  watersports 123
  where to stay 131–3
  Windward Highway to
    Georgetown 129–30
  Young Island 128
sunburn 21
swimming 12, 21
taxes 5
telephones 30, 42
tennis 29
time zones 30
Tobago Cays *135*, **145**
Topics 44–52
  Caribbean Indians 44–5,
    118–19, 225–6
  Christopher Columbus
    45–6
  the English speaking
    Caribbean and its culture
    46–7
  French Caribbean culture
    47–9
  music 50–1
  'the Muse of Wise Men'
    (bananas) 49–50
  volcanic origins of the
    islands 51–2
tour operators 5–8
tourist information 31
trade winds 42
Travel 2–10
  entry requirements and
    customs 5, 41
  getting around 8–10
  getting there 2–5
  tour operators 5–8
  see also under individual
    islands (getting around;
    getting there)
Trinidad carnival 51
Union Island *135*, **146–7**
United States, invasion of
  Grenada 90–1
villas 33
Virgin Islands, sailing 40
volcanos 51–2, 192–3
walking 29–30
water, drinking 22
watersports 29
  see also under individual
    islands
where to stay 31–4
  see also under individual
    places
windsurfing 28
women 34
working in the Caribbean 23
yachts 4–5, 10
  brokers for 37
  see also **Sailing Guide**
Yellow Caribs 118
Young Island 128, 131
zouk 51

The Cadogan Guides Series

'Most literary critics seem to agree that the guides are divine.'
The Independent

'The characteristic of all these guides is a heady mix of the eminently practical, a stimulating description of the potentially already familiar, and an astonishing quantity of things we'd never thought of, let alone seen.'
The Art Quarterly

'The very best guide [Cadogan *Prague*] that I have come across in a lifetime's addiction to the genre.'
Hilary Rubinstein [editor of The Good Hotel Guide*], The Observer*

'Cadogan Guides are entertaining... They go a little deeper than most guides, and the balance of infectious enthusiasm and solid practicality should appeal to first-timers and experienced travellers alike.'
Michael Palin

'Standouts these days are the Cadogan Guides...sophisticated, beautifully written books.'
American Bookseller

'Once again the Cadogan Guide is the pick of the bunch...the perfect marriage of cultural and practical information...description and humour.'
Sunday Telegraph

'Cadogan Guides have a reputation as the outstanding series for the independent traveller who doesn't want to follow the crowd.'
Daily Telegraph

The Cadogan Guides Series: Other Titles

Country Guides

THE CARIBBEAN
CENTRAL AMERICA
CENTRAL ASIA
ECUADOR, THE GALÁPAGOS & COLOMBIA
EGYPT
FRANCE: THE SOUTH OF FRANCE
FRANCE: SOUTHWEST FRANCE
Dordogne, Lot & Bordeaux
GERMANY
GERMANY: BAVARIA
GUATEMALA & BELIZE
INDIA
IRELAND
ITALY
ITALY: NORTHWEST ITALY
ITALY: SOUTH ITALY
ITALY: THE BAY OF NAPLES & THE AMALFI COAST
ITALY: LOMBARDY
Milan & the Italian Lakes
ITALY: TUSCANY, UMBRIA & THE MARCHES
JAPAN
MEXICO
MOROCCO
PORTUGAL
SCOTLAND
SCOTLAND'S HIGHLANDS & ISLANDS
SOUTH AFRICA
SPAIN
SPAIN: SOUTHERN SPAIN
TUNISIA
TURKEY
TURKEY: WESTERN TURKEY

City Guides

AMSTERDAM
BERLIN
BRUSSELS, BRUGES, GHENT & ANTWERP
FLORENCE, SIENA, PISA & LUCCA
MOSCOW & ST PETERSBURG
NEW YORK
PARIS
PRAGUE
ROME
VENICE & THE VENETO

Island Guides

BALI
CARIBBEAN: N.E. CARIBBEAN
The Leeward Islands
CARIBBEAN: S.E. CARIBBEAN
The Windward Islands
CYPRUS
GREEK ISLANDS
GREECE: THE CYCLADES
GREECE: THE DODECANESE
GREECE: THE IONIAN ISLANDS
MALTA, GOZO & COMINO
SICILY